A SOCIAL SCI | :S | 1
MODERN | S

EXCURSUS IN HISTORY

ESSAYS ON SOME IDEAS OF IRFAN HABIB

A SOCIAL SCIENTIST – TULIKA BOOKS SERIES
MODERN INDIAN THINKERS 1

EXCURSUS
IN HISTORY

ESSAYS
ON SOME IDEAS
OF IRFAN HABIB

EDITED BY **PRABHAT PATNAIK**

 Tulika Books

Published by
Tulika Books
35 A/1 (ground floor), Shahpur Jat
New Delhi 110 049, India

First published in India in 2011

© Social Scientist and Tulika Books

ISBN (Hardback): 978-81-89487-71-3

ISBN (Paperback): 978-81-89487-72-0

Typeset in Sabon and Frutiger
at Tulika Print Communication Services, New Delhi;
printed at Chaman Offset, Delhi

Contents

Modern Indian Thinkers:
Series Introduction

The Indian society has witnessed an unprecedented transformation over the last century. A society characterized for millennia by caste oppression, which included even such inhuman institutions as 'untouchability' and 'unseeability', has now adopted juridical equality, one-person-one-vote, a set of fundamental rights for every citizen and a secular Constitution. This change is so far-reaching that it is nothing short of a veritable social revolution.

The ground for this revolution – which itself was the outcome of a popular upsurge arising in the context of the anti-colonial struggle but of a much broader character – was made possible by a remarkable efflorescence of thought in nineteenth- and twentieth-century India, which expressed itself both on social issues (Periyar, Phule, Ambedkar), and on colonialism and nationalism (Naoroji, Gandhi, Tagore). Its specificity, which accounted both for its intellectual vigour and its social effectiveness, arose *inter alia* from the fact that it dared to go beyond what was routine and conventional, or what was handed down as wisdom either by traditional Indian society or by hegemonic intellectual positions in the west. Not surprisingly, the depth and subtlety of this thought has gone largely unnoticed in the west, which tends invariably to be insular in its intellectual appreciation. But its appreciation even in contemporary India is on the decline. This is partly because the passion for ideas is suffering a recession anyway, and partly because we are tending increasingly to focus exclusively upon western thought and to neglect our own thinkers; both are products of globalization.

This, however, is worrisome because the social revolution of which that intellectual upsurge was the progenitor would languish, even retreat, in the absence of further intellectual nourishment. Even now it is at a cross-roads, confronted with two contending perspectives, the debate between which also is somewhat muted as a result of the general air of intellectual lassitude.

One perspective asserts that the march of India's social revolution, or, put differently, India's transition to modernity, requires essentially a high rate of

economic growth. For this what is needed is the pursuit of economic policies favourable to private capital within a regime of 'globalization', even if
such pursuit leads to an increase in economic inequalities; and successful
social 'negotiations' that seek to maintain peace, preserve a conducive
'investment climate' and thereby make such growth possible.

Such 'negotiations' entail the absence of a project of pursuing any specifically transformative social agenda. All that they require is deft social management, which, by making timely and judicious concessions to this or that
social group which happens to be exerting pressure at any given moment, or
by settling contentious inter-group issues by taking cognizance of the relative strengths of the contending social groups, buys peace for the pursuit of
economic growth. In this process bourgeois class interests get consolidated
of course, but that, it is argued, is precisely how modernity arrived in the
west; far from being a cause of concern, it is precisely the path to be followed. A consolidation of the capitalist order, in short, is seen as being integral
to the carrying forward of India's social revolution.

Against this, the second perspective asserts that the capitalist development that is taking place within a regime of globalization is producing a
deep hiatus within Indian society, where significant material advance on the
part of a small segment of the population is accompanied by absolute immiserization of a vast segment. This immiserization does not consist only in a
reduction in real incomes; it goes together with dispossession, displacement
and expropriation of numerous petty producers, i.e. with a process of 'primitive accumulation of capital' directed against them. And, notwithstanding
the rapid economic growth that is taking place, the employment growth
generated by it is so minuscule that those dispossessed face bleak prospects
of ever being absorbed into the ranks of the gainfully employed. What awaits
them is recruitment into the ranks of the reserve army of labour, as opposed
to the active army. Such a denouement is not only abhorrent in itself, but is
also far from being conducive to the march of India's social revolution,
since it constitutes fertile ground for the growth of destructive tendencies
like communal fascism, fundamentalism, terrorism, regional chauvinism and
the like, which impede such a march.

Besides, the march of the social revolution requires going beyond social
negotiations. Social negotiations can at best achieve adjustments within the
existing society; they can never bring about a transcendence of the existing
society. All the achievements listed above, such as one-person-one-vote, secularism and the institutionalization of fundamental rights, came about not
through a process of social negotiations but as an act of transcendence of
the existing social order, under pressure from a popular upsurge from below.
Social negotiations, in short, compromise the transformational agenda;
resorting to them represents a slide-back from the transcendence perspective

underlying the march of the social revolution and hence a counter-revolution of the sort that *khap panchayats* represent. And since integration into a global order with financial volatility forces the country to eschew any transformational agenda lest it produce conflicts that vitiate the 'investment climate', such a counter-revolution is inherent to the current process of consolidation of capitalism. The proposition that follows is that the carrying forward of the social revolution requires going beyond the pursuit of capitalist development as practised now, which is reminiscent of Lenin's argument in the context of Russia long ago.

Around this basic difference, a number of other differences emerge. One is on the question of nationalism. If integration with global capitalism is to be eschewed, it follows that the economy has to be delinked from its current global integument – which means a revival of the project of 'national' economic development such as had underlain Nehruvian *dirigisme*, though not necessarily in its old form. Any 'nationalism', however, even the inclusive 'nationalism' conceived during the anti-colonial struggle, runs the risk of being a closed universe unto itself, and hence of producing ossification and even an entrenchment of pre-modernity. Gandhi's solution of keeping one's windows open to the breeze from outside may or may not work; but clearly, he was aware of the problem. Modernity, it would follow from the second position, will necessarily require 'delinking' and hence will arrive in an altogether different manner from what the pursuit of 'globalization' (which can only produce a distorted 'dualism') promises; it will have to be a *sui generis* quest (which is not the same as emphasizing some 'Indian exceptionalism').

A second difference also follows from all this. If consolidation of capitalism in the present epoch is associated with a process of destruction of petty production without any concomitant increase in the size of the active army of labour, then, the alternative route to modernity must entail support and protection to the petty producers, and an attempt at a non-destructive transcendence of petty production. But since petty producers constitute the most potent carriers of pre-modern values and attitudes, and defenders of pre-modern institutions, their protection may amount to a preservation of such attitudes and institutions. Here again, it appears that a viable agenda for social transformation will have to negotiate an extremely complex task: of preserving and yet transcending petty production and the social conservatism it typically stands for.

The debate between alternative perspectives on India's way forward must be made explicit and vibrant. Otherwise there will be a lapsing into mere routinized intellectual activity, which will entail a victory by default for the first perspective; opting for a consolidation of capitalism, after all, hardly requires any originality of thought. Besides, some of the issues in this discussion have already figured in earlier debates, such as the debate between Gandhi and Tagore, so that recovering those can help the current discussion. To facilitate this recovery and invigorate the current debate, *Social Scientist* and Tulika Books are bringing out a series of volumes on 'Modern Indian Thinkers'. Each volume will discuss the ideas of one specific author through a series of articles by different scholars.

These articles will necessarily be a mix, whose exact nature cannot, and should not, be rigidly fixed beforehand; but the mix will be partly survey, partly criticism, partly location within a deeper problematic and the unveiling of such a problematic, and partly a carrying forward of the thought. The nature of the contents will itself evolve as we bring out more and more volumes, and learn from our mistakes.

This series is not about 'eminent Indians' or even about 'makers of modern India'. It is not even about Indians who have made outstanding contributions in different fields of thought *per se*. It is about thinkers belonging to different spheres of activity whose ideas bear upon the issue of India's social revolution. This does not mean that they should all belong to the social sciences, whether professionally or otherwise. On the contrary, the series will include scientists, artists from different disciplines, political activists, academicians from varied fields and intellectuals outside of the academia; but the choice of thinkers from this large field will be influenced by the degree to which their work provides a perspective on the carrying forward of India's social revolution.

The varied backgrounds of the thinkers covered may be a cause for some surprise. A series that treats a lesser known academic on a par with an outstanding political leader like Gandhi or a poet like Tagore may even cause disquiet in a milieu where we set up icons and place people within hierarchies. But since the series is concerned with India's social revolution, breaking down such hierarchies and considering thinkers solely as thinkers, i.e. in the context of their ideas alone, is only apposite to its intellectual purpose.

Introduction to *Excursus in History*

Prabhat Patnaik

This is the first in the series of volumes on 'Modern Indian Thinkers' which are being brought out by *Social Scientist* and Tulika Books. It is not a *festschrift* for Professor Irfan Habib; that came out from Tulika almost a decade ago. This is an examination of his work in different areas and an attempt to capture the totality of his thought. The 'Modern Indian Thinkers' this series seeks to celebrate are those who have blazed new trails and produced new ideas outside the beaten track which serve to carry forward India's social revolution. It is only appropriate that Professor Irfan Habib should be among the first to be celebrated as such a thinker.

The fact that he is a 'public intellectual' who has fought steadfastly for democracy and secularism makes him worthy of our respect, but does not *per se* entitle him for inclusion in this group. Nor does the fact that he is a Marxist intellectual, indeed the leading Marxist intellectual of the country, do so. True, Marxism is a revolutionary doctrine, and a Marxist intellectual is *ipso facto* concerned with carrying forward the social revolution, so that everything such a person writes and does is supposed to have this particular objective. But what is of specific relevance in the present context is the quality of the person's contribution. Professor Habib is being celebrated not for being a Marxist intellectual *per se* but for the quality of his contribution as a Marxist intellectual to our understanding of Indian society.

While the core of Professor Habib's research is on Mughal India, he has written extensively on Indian history as a whole. Indeed few other historians, in India or elsewhere, have had the range that Professor Habib displays in his writings on history. To say this is not to suggest that had he not made those remarkable forays into prehistory, and into the history of ancient and modern India, he would not have been reckoned as enriching our insights into Indian society, i.e. that his solid research on Mughal India in itself is of no great significance for an understanding of Indian society. On the contrary, his research into Mughal India, enshrined in his monumental work, *The Agrarian System of Mughal India*, is invaluable for our understanding of contemporary Indian society, even leaving aside his other writings.

This is so not only for the obvious and oft-cited reason that the roots of the present lie in our past, but also for a more subtle reason, namely that past and present are often indistinguishable. When Christopher Hill, the renowned British Marxist historian, used to be asked about his views on Stalin or on the nature of the Soviet Union (as he often was by left-wing students during the heyday of student radicalism, in the late 1960s and early 70s), he would answer with a smile: 'Read my book on the Puritan Revolution in England.' What Hill was referring to is the fact of parallel conjunctures in historical time. If such conjunctures can arise across countries, then they are all the more likely to arise within a country where the past and the present are often inextricably linked, where the past often intrudes into the present.

An obvious example is the absence in India of widespread peasant rebellions, unlike in China where such rebellions were responsible for bringing down several dynasties in the past. Professor Habib, more than anyone else, has drawn attention to peasant revolts in Indian history in the form of the Sikh, Satnami and Jat rebellions, and has talked about the agrarian causes of the downfall of the Mughal empire. But even he, as Shireen Moosvi says in her paper in the current volume, has been acutely aware of the fact that these are not classical peasant rebellions in the Chinese mould, displaying peasant class consciousness in a clear form. When we recall the fact that 2 lakh peasants have committed suicide in the recent years as a consequence of globalization-generated distress, rather than rising in revolt against the regime of globalization, the absence of a tradition of widespread peasant uprisings in India becomes particularly striking. It is as if the present and the past are tied together in this matter of the limits to peasant class consciousness.

True, the totality of Professor Habib's thought emerges only when we look at his work on Mughal India in the context of his other writings; and on the conceptual characterizations that constitute the building blocks of this totality, his position has evolved over time – such as on the question of the Asiatic mode of production or of feudalism in India. But his research on Mughal India is clearly at the core of this totality. And the light that this totality throws on our current predicament itself, not just on some arcane issues relating to what had happened four centuries ago, is immense, as the reader of this volume will realize.

Some salient features of this totality, if one dares to summarize them, are as follows. Unlike in England where the petty mode of production had been loosened from its feudal integument early, permitting pervasive commodity production as a prelude to capitalism, in India, the very immensity of the burden of rent-tax extraction from petty producers by the state, even though such extraction was in money, restricted the scope of commodity production and hence the potentiality of capitalist development. The village community was marked by a hiatus, with caste-based restrictions on labour mobility, and with the village elite together with the zamindars being constituents and local agents of the surplus-appropriating classes. Colonialism, far from being a continuation of this structure, dealt a heavy blow to it: while it was relentless in its expropriation of surplus, the 'draining away' of this surplus brought in its train 'deindustrialization' and mass impoverishment. But the resistance to colonialism by a coalition of forces articulating different class interests, within which the Left was very much represented, also created something new: the formation of a nation on the basis of a programme, first enunciated at the Karachi Congress and subsequently incorporated into the Constitution, which marked a radical break with the past. The Left has to remain committed to the carrying forward of this programme, a process that is beset with severe challenges.

Many of these ideas have been so much with us, precisely because of Professor Habib's labour, that we are in danger of forgetting the arduousness of that labour, exerted against a host of new trends among historians: from the Subaltern school to the Cambridge school to post-modernism, and even against strands of the traditional Left understanding. Like Moliere's Monsieur Jourdain who spoke prose without knowing it, many of us hold Professor Habib's views without knowing their source. Celebrating this Modern Indian Thinker whose views are ingrained in the minds of many is therefore long overdue.

As anticipated in the General Introduction to the series, the essays in this volume are quite heterogeneous: some are in the nature of surveys of particular areas of Professor Habib's work, some critically examine his positions, some elaborate upon his ideas and some carry his ideas forward. To familiarize the reader with Professor Habib's overall intellectual project, there is an exhaustive interview with him, in which he dwells upon a whole range of themes: from Mughal India to the freedom struggle to the problems of the Communist movement. And to give brief introductions to his seminal works, there are not only articles by particular authors, but also some book reviews that were published at the time his books came out.

The fact remains, however, that the essays put together in the present volume only unlock this or that gate to the field of Professor Habib's writings, and the reader will have to make his or her own way through this field. But it is a journey we would like to invite the reader to undertake.

Contributors

SHIREEN MOOSVI, Professor of History, Aligarh Muslim University, Aligarh.

IQTIDAR ALAM KHAN, former Professor of History, Aligarh Muslim University, Aligarh.

KRISHNA MOHAN SHRIMALI, Professor of History, University of Delhi, Delhi.

SABYASACHI BHATTACHARYA, Chairman, Indian Council of Historical Research, New Delhi; former Professor of History, Jawaharlal Nehru University, New Delhi.

VISHWA MOHAN JHA, Reader in History, Atma Ram Sanatan Dharma College, University of Delhi, Delhi.

JAYA MENON, Associate Professor of History, Aligarh Muslim University, Aligarh.

SATISH CHANDRA, former Chairman, University Grants Commission; former Professor of History, Jawaharlal Nehru University, New Delhi.

J.S. GREWAL, former Vice-Chancellor and Professor of History, Guru Nanak Dev University, Amritsar; former Chairman, Indian Institute of Advanced Study, Shimla.

INDU BANGA, Professor of History, Panjab University, Chandigarh.

NAJAF HAIDER, Associate Professor of History, Jawaharlal Nehru University, New Delhi.

AMAR FAROOQUI, Professor of History, University of Delhi, Delhi.

ISHRAT ALAM, Associate Professor of History, Aligarh Muslim University, Aligarh; Member Secretary, Indian Council of Historical Research, New Delhi.

SYED ALI NADEEM REZAVI, Associate Professor of History, Aligarh Muslim University, Aligarh.

AMIYA KUMAR BAGCHI, economist and economic historian; Director, Institute of Development Studies, Kolkata.

UTSA PATNAIK, former Professor of Economics, Jawaharlal Nehru University, New Delhi.

AKEEL BILGRAMI, Johnsonian Professor of Philosophy, Columbia University, USA.

PRABHAT PATNAIK, former Professor of Economics, Jawaharlal Nehru University, New Delhi; Vice Chairman, State Planning Board, Government of Kerala.

C.P. CHANDRASEKHAR, Professor of Economics, Jawaharlal Nehru University, New Delhi.

PARVATHI MENON, historian and journalist; Chief of Bureau, *The Hindu*, Bangalore.

Indian History and Historiography

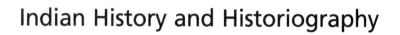

Marxist Theory and the Historian's Practice

Shireen Moosvi

'Constant enquiry, self-examination, and the refining and extension of Marxist positions' are for Irfan Habib, in his own words,[1] the basic tenets of history-writing. Obviously, then, his work in history of over fifty-five years cannot be separated from his Marxist convictions without necessarily bringing into question its academic merit, which has earned recognition even from his critics. An unceasing quest for historical data that are relevant for further refinement and deepening of Marxist perceptions is perhaps the most striking feature of Habib's work. One wonders if the genesis of this trait can be traced partly to a discomfort felt by him, very early in his academic career, with Marx's understanding of pre-colonial Indian society as an unchanging, moribund society with fixed class structures, a view summed up in his oft-quoted statement (1853): 'Indian society has no history at all, at least no known history . . .'.[2]

It almost appears that Irfan Habib's *Agrarian System of Mughal India*, based on his D.Phil. dissertation completed in 1958 and published, after revision and enlargement, in 1963,[3] was undertaken to counter this view of pre-colonial India by a study that was itself set within a framework of Marxist analysis. The massive corpus of factual data here, much of it not known or noticed before, drawn from all possible sources, texts, documents, manuals and dictionaries, and set forth in a duly critical form, is a formidable achievement in itself. This immense mass of description is so arranged as to lead the reader step by step to large-scale generalizations about the classes and forms of class struggle in Mughal India, generalizations that have not been seriously challenged to date.

---

[1] Irfan Habib, 'Problems of Marxist Historiography', *Social Scientist*, Vol. 16, No. 12, December 1988; reprinted in his *Essays in Indian History: Towards a Marxist Perception*, New Delhi: Tulika Books, 1995, p. 4.

[2] From an article published in the *New York Daily Tribune*; cited in Iqbal Husain (ed.), *Karl Marx on India*, New Delhi: Tulika Books, 2006, p. 46.

[3] Irfan Habib, *The Agrarian System of Mughal India (1556–1707)*, first edition, Bombay: Asia Publishing House, 1963.

In the *Agrarian System*, his involvement in discovering and dissecting classes and class struggles seems to over-ride any other interest Irfan Habib may have had in the more theoretical issues debated within the Marxist academe, such as 'modes of production' and the unilinear chain of 'slavery–feudalism–capitalism'. There is indeed a footnote in it[4] doubting the degree of influence of irrigation on agriculture that Marx attributed to the Asiatic mode of production, but Habib's most explicit rejection of that concept was in a sharp criticism of Wittfogel, published even before *Agrarian System* had come off the press.[5] Nor, seemingly, does Habib accept the depiction 'feudal'; the word is never used in the *Agrarian System* to characterize any relationship or institution, not even when he describes the zamindars at length.

However, these questions could not be avoided when, in the 1960s, the theoretical divide in Marxism extended to history, and Irfan Habib sided with those who rejected what they termed 'reformism' and who laid particular stress on class struggle today as well as in the past. This position is expressed in his seminal essay, 'Problems of Marxist Historical Analysis'.[6] Here, his disagreement with the fixed succession of modes of production is made explicit, but, at the same time, he sees the new western Marxist interest in the Asiatic mode as a reflection of the view that 'the class struggles and historical changes emerging from them be regarded only as a European phenomenon and by no means universal', the acceptance of which would 'make the vast majority of mankind an exception to the materialistic conception of history'.[7] Invoking the later silence maintained on it by Marx and Engels, Habib argues that the concept of the Asiatic mode had been put aside by the founding fathers themselves.

He admits, however, that the task of defining the medieval Indian social formation or the prevailing mode of production in pre-colonial India continues to remain a desideratum, since 'one cannot study class struggle without discerning classes'.[8] He feels no hesitation in accepting a multiplicity of contemporary pre-capitalist social formations in different territories, for, had not the *Communist Manifesto* itself treated capitalism as the first uni-

[4] Ibid., p. 256 n. 44.

[5] Irfan Habib, 'An Examination of Wittfogel's Theory of "Oriental Despotism"', *Studies in Asian History*, Bombay, 1961, pp. 378–92. As for the mention of Marx's views on irrigation, see Habib, *Agrarian System*, 1963 edition, p. 256.

[6] Irfan Habib, 'Problems of Marxist Historical Analysis', *Enquiry*, New Series, Vol. III, No. 2, 1969, pp. 52–67. This essay was excluded from Habib's selection of interpretative essays on India, *Essays in Indian History: Towards a Marxist Perception*. Was this due to pure chance or to a deliberate distancing from the opinions expressed in it?

[7] Habib, 'Problems of Marxist Historical Analysis', p. 56.

[8] Habib, 'Problems of Marxist Historiography', p. 5.

versal mode of production and spoken of complex class structures in the social orders preceding capitalism? Habib in effect leaves it an open question as to whether any of the categories of modes of production that Marx had mentioned in his famous *Preface to the Critique of Political Economy* are partly or fully applicable to medieval India. This implies that one has to examine for the purpose, the evidence for specific forms of the labour process and the system of exploitation (and so the process of accumulation) before one can define or describe the mode of production prevailing in India in pre-colonial times.

Irfan Habib's own continuously evolving or changing views of the medieval mode in India are, however, formed (and re-formed?) not simply on the basis of his further exploration of the available evidence, but also from his extended studies of Marx's perception of how capitalism functions and, especially, of how in its development it reacts upon other modes of production, of which colonialism is but one, though very important, aspect. An occasion where he could consider matters on a large canvas came when he was invited to write on the 'Potentialities of Capitalistic Development in Mughal India'.[9] This led him to a further stage of development in his ideas, in a subsequent essay on the 'Processes of Accumulation in Pre-Colonial and Colonial India',[10] where the effort to base his interpretation on what may be termed Marxian political economy is particularly visible. It is patently perceptible that his great personal esteem for Professor R.S. Sharma does not still lead him to accept the latter's approach in the depiction of 'feudalism', in which the western historians' concept of it as a system of fiefs and Pirenne's view of it as a system where commerce is at a low ebb are given equal status with the classical Marxist equation of feudalism with serfdom.[11]

Habib is firm in insisting that the form of labour alone can determine a mode of production (so serfdom → feudalism), while other features may vary. Such a position tends towards exclusiveness, theoretical rigour and austerity – and, critics may say, towards unreality as well, for unmixed forms of labour would be hard to find just as, on the contrary, it would be rare to discover the presence of *all* the features of European feudalism in non-European societies.

When, in the late 1970s, Irfan Habib undertook a detailed scrutiny of Marx's writings on India, leading to his essay, 'Marx's Perception of India'

---

[9] Irfan Habib, 'Potentialities of Capitalistic Development in Mughal India', *Journal of Economic History*, 29, 1, March 1969; reprinted in *Enquiry*, New Series, Vol. III, No. 3, 1971, pp. 1–56.

[10] Irfan Habib, 'Processes of Accumulation in Pre-Colonial and Colonial India', *Indian Historical Review*, Vol. XI, Nos 1–2, 1985/1988, pp. 65–90.

[11] R.S. Sharma, *Indian Feudalism, c. 300–1200*, Calcutta: University of Calcutta, 1965.

(written on the occasion of Marx's death centenary in 1983),[12] we got the first hints of a new approach to Marx's concept of the Asiatic mode. If the form of labour under what Marx, in *Capital*, Vol. I, called 'the petty mode of production' (where peasants and self-employed artisans produced for the market), prevailed alongside the constraints on labour present in the village community and the rent–tax equivalence as the basis of the 'despotic' state (all within the terminology used by Marx), then one can perhaps accept the Asiatic mode for pre-colonial India. Habib, from very early in his studies, insisted on the presence of advanced elements of banking and insurance, and so the pervading role of commodity production, in Mughal India.[13] While, citing Marx, he denied to it any pivotal role in economic development, the presence of merchant capital in such a developed form seemed to constitute his main argument against the theory of the Asiatic mode at that time. But he now argues that Marx himself allowed for the conversion of agricultural surplus into commodities in pre-colonial India,[14] so that commodity relationships cannot be held to be excluded from Marx's concept of the Asiatic mode. The information available now about the form of labour process and about accumulation suggests, he argues, a fairly reasonable approximation to the twin pillars of Marx's Asiatic mode, namely, the village community and the tax–rent equivalence. Marx's 'medieval mode',[15] therefore, given allowance for commodity relationships, can perhaps fairly be called 'modified Asiatic mode' or the commodity phase of the 'Asiatic mode'. Habib, on the other hand, consistently rejects Samir Amin's theory of the 'tributary mode' as being not a mode of production at all, since it takes into account only the tax–rent equivalence and excludes the form of labour process which, in India at least, was heavily influenced not only by the market but also by caste and village community. The tributary mode, being divested of all relationship with the form of the labour process, appears to him to be inconsistent with Marxian methods of analysis.[16]

Reconsideration of the Asiatic mode, and a partial or qualified acceptance of it, seemingly led to two further developments in Irfan Habib's studies. It ignited a new interest in the village community, which he now no more sees as a survival of an earlier social form, kept alive only as a cog in

[12] Irfan Habib, 'Marx's Perception of India', in *Marx on India and Indonesia*, Trier: Karl-Marx-Haus, 1983; reprinted in Habib, *Essays in Indian History*, pp. 14–58.

[13] See his essay, 'Banking in Mughal India', in Tapan Raychaudhuri (ed.), *Contributions to Indian Economic History*, Vol. I, Calcutta, 1960.

[14] Habib, 'Marx's Perception of India', p. 33.

[15] Irfan Habib, 'Classifying Pre-Colonial India', *Journal of Peasant Studies*, Vol. 12, Nos 2–3, 1985, pp. 44–53.

[16] Irfan Habib, 'Mode of Production in Medieval India', in D.N. Gupta (ed.), *Changing Modes of Production in India*, Delhi: Hindu College, 1995, pp. 49–61.

the Mughal revenue administration with its common 'financial pool', a mere collection point for streams of individual tax payments.[17] He now begins to see it, further, as an institution of local control of superior caste elements over the landless labourers and the lower peasantry (with caste restraints and 'demiurgic' labour, to use Max Weber's terminology), and thus forming a system of 'sub-exploitation' by the dominant rural classes.[18]

It is interesting to note, then, that in the revised, 1999 edition of *Agrarian System*,[19] where the entire text was revised but the original arrangement retained, the only chapter that was greatly enlarged and entirely rewritten is the one devoted to the village community. Part of the reason certainly lies in the fact that by now Irfan Habib had collected very rich documentary material on the subject, which was not available to him in 1963, especially Persian and Braj documents from Vrindavan. But partly, too, the larger space devoted to it stemmed from his new understanding of the village community as an instrument of class exploitation. Indeed he speaks now of the 'village aristocracy' in conditions of joining the zamindars as additional junior allies of the ruling class.

Secondly, the concept of the commodity phase of the Asiatic mode of production naturally leads Habib to underline the differences between the immediately preceding pre-capitalist mode in Western Europe (Marx's 'petty mode') and the system of commodity production prevailing in India under 'Asiatic' auspices. The latter, according to him, had too many constraints preventing development into capitalist commodity production, whereas the former had liberated itself from such constraints, which, in its specific case, were those of feudalism.

Implicit in this judgement is an orthodox, yet untraditional restatement of Marx's perception of the conditions in Western Europe, in the period 1500–1750. Whereas Maurice Dobb[20] would assign Western Europe during the period to feudalism as still the prevailing mode despite the disappearance of serfdom, and Paul Sweezy, in a critique of this view,[21] would see a long transitional phase (to capitalism) here, Habib reads so much substantive meaning into Marx's 'petty mode' (as invoked in the last but one chapter of *Capital*, Vol. I) as to make it define the mode of production

[17] Habib, *Agrarian System of Mughal India*, 1963 edition, pp. 118–29.
[18] In Tapan Raychaudhuri and Irfan Habib (eds), *Cambridge Economic History of India*, Vol. 1, Cambridge: Cambridge University Press, 1981, p. 250.
[19] Irfan Habib, *The Agrarian System of Mughal India (1526–1707)*, second revised edition, Delhi: Oxford University Press, 1999.
[20] Maurice Dobb, *Studies in the Development of Capitalism*, London: Routledge and Kegan Paul, 1946.
[21] In Paul Sweezy, Maurice Dobb, Kohachiro Takahashi and Rodney Hilton, *The Transition from Feudalism to Capitalism*, Indian edition, New Delhi: Aakar Books, 2006, pp. 33–56.

during the pre-industrial period in Western Europe. He uses it essentially to distinguish the commodity production under landlordism of this period from 'the natural', serf-based economy of feudalism proper. The immediately pre-bourgeois state in England and France was thus not a feudal (Dobb) or class-independent (Sweezy) state, but a land owners' state in a system of petty production. It was out of this social and economic order, and not out of feudalism, that capitalism really developed.[22] This ties up with Habib's continuing denial of the presence of feudalism in late medieval India, which he has often seen as the result of a desire to locate capitalist potentialities within India just because feudalism is supposed to be the harbinger of capitalism. To him, by its very essence, feudalism could not generate capitalism.

Irfan Habib's position on the Asiatic state as a power instrument of exploitation is totally contrary to the recent (now 'post-modern') tendency to deny the existence of a unified, surplus-extracting state in pre-colonial India. This denial began with Burton Stein's application of the 'segmentary' state thesis to south India[23] and attained semi-mystical dimensions in Andre Wink.[24] The Subalterns' 'autonomy' fixation tends in the same direction. Confronted with these, Habib's approach seems to be stubbornly conventional, based on source and record rather than on *a priori* hypotheses.[25]

In a sense, this made the second, 1999 edition of *Agrarian System* a still more cohesive work. But did it lend his *magnum opus* the ideal completeness that one might rather unreasonably demand of it? It still does not answer, I venture to suggest, or adequately grapple with the question of peasant consciousness, and the limitations of peasant resistance in India as compared to China and Western Europe.

In answering this question one must remember a characteristic feature of Irfan Habib's method of work, viz., his hesitation to take up questions where information is inadequate. He insists that Marxist historians must create their own 'database' and work on related areas without depending on others to do so. Thus his researches have included the creation of a large base of reference material: for example, *An Atlas of the Mughal Empire* (1981) and the forthcoming *Atlas of Ancient Indian History*; numerous studies of individual documents or collections of documents; studies in the history of technology and environment, as well as in gender history and

---

[22] Irfan Habib, 'Capitalism in History', *Social Scientist*, Vol. 23, Nos 7–9, 1995, pp. 16–17.

[23] Burton Stein, *Peasant State and Society in Medieval India*, Delhi: Oxford University Press, 1980, p. 23.

[24] Andre Wink, *Land and Sovereignty in India: Agrarian Society and Politics under the Eighteenth Century Maratha Swarajya*, Cambridge: Cambridge University Press, 1986, pp. 1–8, 34.

[25] In this and the previous paragraph, I draw on Irfan Habib's 'Comments', in Gupta (ed.), *Changing Modes of Production in India*, pp. 64–65.

ideological development; and, finally, the history of the colonial exploitation of India and the national movement.

Since Habib maintained for the second edition of his *Agrarian System* the framework fashioned for the first edition, we can discern the theoretical influence of his later and wider research work only here and there in the revised edition. The handling of the technology of agriculture and crafts is doubtless much surer; geographical details are further improved; and the remarks on the succeeding colonial regime are further sharpened. However, one feels rather disappointed to see that though the discussion of peasant consciousness has been promoted from a footnote in the first edition to the main text in the second,[26] and somewhat refined, the insightful analysis of his 'Forms of Class Struggle in Mughal India'[27] has not been incorporated.

In that essay Habib discusses the barriers to the emergence and growth of peasant class consciousness in late Mughal India, analysing in great detail the effects of caste affinities, the amalgamation of zamindars' grievances with those of the peasants against over-taxation (as in the Jat uprising), as well as the intervention of religious preaching of a particular kind (as in the case of the Satnami and Sikh revolts) that enlarged the scale but weakened the class nature of the revolts.

Habib is sceptical even of the plausibility of the assertion that peasant class consciousness was present but not known to us only because 'the slogans raised by the illiterate peasants were totally lost, [being] left unrecorded by the hostile scribes of the ruling class'. To him it seems 'that the limitation is real, not only apparent. The slogan we hope to find might never have been raised.'[28] One wonders whether he felt the last conclusion to be too pessimistic (or tactically inconvenient from the viewpoint of today's peasant movement) to give it a place in the *Agrarian System*.

There is another issue that one would have expected Irfan Habib, with his growing appreciation of Marx's thesis of primitive accumulation as a major engine of the genesis of capitalism, to consider: the possibility of such accumulation in Mughal India. This possibility is not at all considered in his essay on 'Potentialities of Capitalistic Development in Mughal India'. This was perhaps because at that time, he had not accorded to the phenomenon the importance he gave it later on.[29] It is therefore time now also to

---

[26] Habib, *Agrarian System of Mughal India,* 1963 edition, p. 351 n. 69; and 1999 edition, pp. 404–05.

[27] Habib, *Essays in Indian History*, pp. 233–58; originally published as *Peasant and Artisan Resistance in Mughal India*, McGill Studies in International Development, No. 34, Montreal: McGill University, 1984.

[28] Ibid., p. 257.

[29] Notably, in his contribution to *A World to Win*, edited by Prakash Karat, New Delhi: Leftword Books, 1998.

discuss whether internal expropriation in Mughal India could have led to the creation of capital (merchant capital, at any rate), and, if so, what were or could have been its consequences. If the expropriation (such as of produce and land from peasants) did not lead to such growth of capital, it would be interesting to investigate why. It may lead us to look closely from a new angle at the relationship between the Mughal state and the mercantile classes.

I am sure that the reader will not take such suggestions as being critical of Irfan Habib's existing views and work. The questions themselves have largely arisen out of that work, and out of his own continuous search for linking theory with factual evidence. That, I am sure, is achievement enough.

Reconstructing a
People's History of India

Iqtidar Alam Khan

The foremost thought that comes to one's mind regarding Irfan Habib's contribution to Indian history relates to his being a committed Marxist throughout his long academic career. His commitment to Marxism appears to have become even more unswerving since the fall of the Soviet Union.

Disagreeing from the very beginning with the dominant trend in Soviet Indology of the Stalinist era (at one time greatly admired by many left-leaning students of history, including the present author), Irfan Habib rejects the model of the West European transition to capitalism as not applicable to India. He also disagrees with the concept of the 'Asiatic mode of production' put forth by Marx in 1853. Tracing Marx's reflections on the nature of Indian society from 1853 onwards, Habib establishes that by 1875, he had come to perceive class contradictions within Indian society.[1] Arguing against Karl Wittfogel's thesis of 'hydraulic empires' as early as 1957, Habib did not hesitate to sharply disagree with Marx's formulations about 'Asiatic despotism'. According to him, 'the substantiation offered for this thesis always remained rather slender'.[2]

In the 1980s, Irfan Habib worked out a new theoretical construct of social change for pre-modern India, which he prefers to call 'the medieval social formation'. This model is based on the definition of 'oriental despotism' in Marx's analysis as 'essentially rent-receiving sovereignty', which stands divested of features such as 'arbitrary and absolute monarchy' assigned to it

---

[1] Irfan Habib, 'Marx's Perception of India', in Iqbal Husain (ed.), *Karl Marx on India*, New Delhi: Tulika Books, 2006, p. xx and n. 4. According to Prabhat Patnaik (in K.N. Panikkar, Terence J. Byres and Utsa Patnaik, eds, *The Making of History: Essays Presented to Irfan Habib*, New Delhi: Tulika Books, 2000, pp. 4–5), 'Irfan Habib's first major work, *The Agrarian System of Mughal India* (1963), was an implicit critique of the idea of the so-called "unchanging village community".'

[2] Irfan Habib, 'An Examination of Wittfogel's Theory of Oriental Despotism', *Enquiry*, No. 6, 1961, pp. 54–73.

in the European liberal thought. Citing Marx's fleeting suggestion in a letter of 14 June 1853 that the institution of 'no property in land', i.e. state property, might have been established by 'the Muslims', Habib proceeds to argue that from the very beginning, Marx himself had been prepared to concede that history could well have had a part to play in shaping the basic forms of the structure of Indian society.[3] In the Delhi Sultanate, according to him, tax-rent (set at half the value of the produce) came to be first rigorously imposed in a very large tract under 'Alauddin Khalji (1296–1316).[4] Subsequently, the tendency to maximize surplus extraction persisted in most of the Indian states down to the beginning of the eighteenth century, contributing to monetization of a much larger part of the social surplus than was discernible under European feudalism. This situation facilitated the growth of handicrafts and urban expansion. But unlike in the European case, an essential prelude to capitalism, namely the accumulation of capital, was absent. As illustrated by the West European example, such accumulation would not be possible in the absence of loot and plunder of the colonies and the subjugated peoples of the less civilized parts of the globe. The firm view Irfan Habib has formed on this question within the Marxist framework is borne out by his not refraining from expressing mild disapproval against Marx using the term 'feudal' loosely to characterize the land-holders of Awadh.[5]

In 'the medieval social formation' of Habib's theoretical construct, Indian society of the pre-colonial period is a class society where institutions like caste and village community facilitated the maximization of surplus extraction, which was so very necessary for sustaining a centralized state operating through culturally fragmented ruling elites having competing economic interests. In his discourse on the role of highly centralized medieval Indian states extracting and distributing social surplus among ruling elites, his focus has always been on the class antagonisms and conflicts that were generated in this process. His pioneering work, *The Agrarian System of Mughal India* (1963), an exhaustive study of agrarian relations during 1556–1707, ends with a memorable essay on the 'crisis' of the Mughal empire. Here, the focus is on local insurgencies resulting from increasing ruination of the peasantry and disaffection of the zamindars by the working of the *jagir* system in the second half of the seventeenth century. This thesis, presented with astonishing clarity and richness of documentation, rendered pointless the traditional explanations of the 'fall of the Mughal empire' with reference to 'Hindu reaction' against Aurangzeb or 'incompetence' of

[3] Habib, 'Marx's Perception of India', in Husain (ed.), *Karl Marx on India*, p. xxviii.
[4] Irfan Habib, 'Economic History of the Delhi Sultanate: An Essay in Interpretation', *The Indian Historical Review*, Vol. IV, No. 2, January 1978, p. 296.
[5] Habib, 'Marx's Perception of India', in Husain (ed.), *Karl Marx on India*, p. xxvii.

the later Mughals. In this essay, as well as in other writings, Habib is firmly dismissive of any attempt to characterize income from Mughal *jagir*s or from zamindari rights as 'feudal'. Not being conversant with the intricacies of the debate on 'modes of production', I was tempted to do so in the first version of my essay, 'Middle Classes in the Mughal Empire' (1975), which earned me well-deserved censure.[6]

Dealing deftly with the period 600–1200 in his recent monograph, *Medieval India: The Study of a Civilization* (2007), Irfan Habib shows that his theoretical construct of 'the medieval social formation' does not clash with the idea of 'Indian feudalism' put forth by D.D. Kosambi and R.S. Sharma to characterize the rise of local magnates in several Hindu principalities resulting from the practice of secular, hereditary grants. According to him, the replacement of charioteers by lance-wielding horsemen, made possible by the introduction of the concave saddle and the use of a primitive wooden stirrup, was an additional factor for the fragmentation and decentralization of political authority within the existing state systems. The emergence of *rauta*s (*rawat*s), or Rajput cavalrymen, is seen by him as an addition of a new layer of superior right-holders who survived in the Delhi Sultanate as *khot*s and *muqaddam*s of Ziya' Barani's description.[7]

Irfan Habib combines unrelenting adherence to Marxist tools of analysis with an attitude of reading the available evidence, textual as well as material, with a critical diligence and exactitude reminiscent of the orientalists of past generations. At the same time, while noticing a generalization smacking of cultural chauvinism by any scholar (including an iconic figure like Lynn White Jr.), he can be very harsh and dismissive. This may be illustrated by the following random examples.

(1) A correction suggested in a footnote indicating that in the edited text of *Ma'asir-i 'Alamgiri* of Saqi Mustaid Khan, the term '*barzgar*', meaning 'cultivator', is rendered as '*zargar*', meaning 'goldsmith'. This removes a long-persisting confusion about the social category to which the Satnami rebels belonged.[8]

(2) A comment on the use of the Prakrit term *pasanda* (the same as the Sanskrit *pakhanda*) in one of the Ashokan edicts. The fact that all the religious sects, including Buddhists, are being referred to with a term having a

---

[6] See Irfan Habib, 'Problems of Marxist Historiography', in *Essays in Indian History: Towards a Marxist Perception*, New Delhi: Tulika Books, 1995, p. 6.

[7] Irfan Habib, *Medieval India: The Study of a Civilization*, New Delhi: National Book Trust, 2007, pp. 4–8.

[8] Irfan Habib, *The Agrarian System of Mughal India (1556–1707)*, first edition, Bombay: Asia Publishing House, 1963, p. 344 n. 31.

negative connotation prods one to speculate about Ashoka's *dhamma*, as well as about the tradition of rational dissent in Indian history. One is reminded of Abu'l Fazl's reference to 'cosmetic religiosity (*ghaza-i dindari*)', leading to bloodshed and strife among Indians.[9] The discerning reader's attention is also directed to the spirit of rational scepticism present in Indian culture from the very beginning. Irfan Habib's locating a hymn in the *Rigveda* where sceptics say of Indra, 'where he is',[10] seems to connect the tradition of philosophical scepticism reflected in Ashoka's edict and Abu'l Fazl's remark with the speculative thought of the Vedic age.

(3) While noticing the evidence suggesting the presence of horizontal wind-mills in Sistan during the eighth century, Habib observes: 'some rumour of these might have inspired efforts in Western Europe that led to the erection of vertical windmills there from the thirteenth century onwards'.[11] The possibility of this important technology travelling from eastern Iran to Western Europe prior to the thirteenth century, which was missed by Lynn White Jr., is thus hinted by him in passing.

(4) While commenting on Joseph Needham's suggestion that fundamental inventions like animal domestication and weaving 'can be supposed to have been made at [only] one centre' (in Asia), Habib points to the Amerindian communities, totally cut off from Asia, on their own 'learning to cultivate plants and till with hoes; furthermore, they domesticated the cameloid, raised species of cotton, and also spun and wove both wool and cotton'. These achievements of the Amerindians defy, according to Habib, Needham's suggestion.[12] This idea, that early human groups were able to create similar technologies and patterns of agriculture even when they were totally cut off from each other, one might add, is mind-boggling.

(5) While agreeing that Europe's search for labour-saving devices contributed to progress towards industrialization, Habib sharply differs with Lynn White Jr. attributing it to the 'Christian urge' to lighten labour. 'One may legitimately cite', he writes, 'the virtual genocide of Amerindian peoples by Spain in the Americas, and the trans-Atlantic slave trade carried on so relentlessly by practically all the West European nations where even a rudimentary sense of Christian compassion was forgotten in the drive for economic gain'.[13]

---

[9] Abu'l Fazl, *A'in-i Akbari*, Vol. III, translated by H.S. Jarret and annotated by Jadunath Sarkar, Calcutta: Nawal Kishore Press, 1948, p. 4.

[10] Irfan Habib and Vijay Kumar Thakur, *The Vedic Age, A People's History of India 3*, New Delhi: Tulika Books, in association with Aligarh Historians Society, 2003, p. 25.

[11] Irfan Habib, *Technology in Medieval India: c. 650–1750, A People's History of India 20*, New Delhi: Tulika Books, in association with Aligarh Historians Society, 2008, p. 118.

[12] Ibid.

[13] Ibid., p. 128.

(6) One may end with a reference to Irfan Habib's proverbial command over medieval Persian and his ability to decipher texts written in *shikasta* (broken) hand. The following instances illustrate the textual authenticity of the information relied upon by him in his historical discourse.

(a) His correct reading of the names of *mahals* (revenue circles) of the Mughal empire is an interesting example. Many of these names copied by Abu'l Fazl in *A'in-i Akbari* from documents written in *shakista* are mis-spelt even in the best of manuscripts. In his *Atlas of the Mughal Empire* (1982), Irfan Habib has painstakingly worked out the correct spellings of many of these place-names. For example, he reads 'Nekshab' of Abu'l Fazl's text as 'Bangashat'. Similarly, 'Larwala', 'Khark-kakan' and 'Bandar Sola' of Abu'l Fazl's text are shown to be corruptions of 'Karwala', 'Ladh kakan'and 'Bandar Gogha'.[14]

(b) Another example of the care with which Habib reads a text is reflected in his interpretation of Babur's passage describing the methods of irrigation practised in northwestern India. That this much-quoted passage refers to *pur* and the Persian wheel is well known. On re-reading the passage, Habib added to the text a line indicating the use of 'pot-garland wheel without the ox-driven gearing apparatus', missed by both the translators (A.S. Beveridge and W.M. Thackston) of this famous text. The significance of the addition lies in its testifying to the fact that the old mechanism known as *araghatta* was also in vogue.[15]

(c) There are available in the library of the Centre of Advanced Study in History (Aligarh Muslim University), a number of microfilms and rotographs of manuscripts preserved in different collections, as well as original documents and manuscripts, procured after being identified by Irfan Habib in the course of his researches as carrying significant information on one or the other aspect of medieval Indian history. One may mention, as an instance, the first draft of the *Akbarnama* containing many documents as well as piecemeal information deleted from the final version.

The volumes of the *People's History of India* series that have been already published, as also Irfan Habib's other recent writings including *Medieval India: The Study of a Civilization* (2007), highlight some of his intellectual concerns that impact the underlying theoretical orientation of his historical

---

[14] Irfan Habib, *An Atlas of the Mughal Empire*, Delhi: Oxford University Press, 1982, Introduction, p. XIII.
[15] Habib, *Technology in Medieval India*, p. 28.

narrative in an interesting manner. In these, while not shifting his focus from themes central to 'medieval social formation', he has paid particular attention to the development of arts and literature, and to changes in religious beliefs and social attitudes having a bearing on the position of weaker sections like outcastes, women and children. The sketch of a young Muslim girl taking lessons at the *maktab* reproduced from a fifteenth-century illustration, for instance, speaks of the care with which surviving evidence on these aspects has been retrieved and projected.[16]

Following in the footsteps of his illustrious father and other nationalist historians of the twentieth century, Irfan Habib conveys a perception of India as the home of many faiths which propagated conflicting beliefs and values, and yet, on the whole, survived side by side for centuries. The disappearance of Buddhism is seen more as a consequence of the gradual revitalization of the brahmanical religion than due to any large-scale conflict or suppression.

Notably, Irfan Habib points out that unlike in other parts of the world, for example Iran, Anatolia and Egypt, the Islamic conquest of India did not result in wholesale conversion of the local population. Throughout the period of Islamic domination, an overwhelming majority of India's inhabitants remained non-Muslims. The surviving evidence, which tends to be extensive and varied with the coming of the Muslims, shows that side by side with religious conflict and persecution, a process of cultural adjustment involving political elites as well as the common people was never totally absent. Habib illustrates the point by inviting attention to the Raja of Vijayanagara (supposed to be a protector of Hinduism) assuming the title 'Sultan among Hindu Kings', and to Maharana Kumbha inscribing the word 'Allah' prominently on the tower built at Chitor to commemorate a victory over the Sultan of Malwa.[17]

In his discussion of the religious and cultural interaction between Hindus and Muslims, Habib often reproduces passages from well-known texts revealing information that has not yet been noticed. For example, Sikandar Lodi's famous minister, Miyan Bhuwah, is reported as having justified Ayurveda in his preface to the *Tib-i Sikandari*, by pointing out that 'the Greek medicine did not suit the climate of India and medicinal plants mentioned in that system were either unidentifiable or unobtainable in India'. Similarly, after examining most of the passages in the early Persian texts where the word '*Hindvi*' occurs, Habib explodes the widely held view that it refer-

---

[16] Cf. Habib, *Medieval India*, pp. 63 and 247–59, where stories are reproduced from sixteenth- and seventeenth-century sources with reflections on the lives of ordinary folks, including a 'peasant romance'.
[17] Ibid., pp. 59, 85.

red to a particular language spoken in northwest India that later came to be known as Hindi/Urdu.[18]

Irfan Habib seems to assign an important, sometimes even decisive, role to the centralized states managed by literate elites in promoting the idea of India as a distinct cultural, political and geographical entity. He is, for example, inclined to the view that the 'institutional uniformity' imposed by an urban elite having administrative skills rooted in their knowledge of sciences like geometry and hydraulics, contributed to a large part of northwestern India coming under the rule of a unified Harappan state. But the unification thus achieved was undone with the removal of this elite by invaders.[19] The rise of the Mauryan empire, again, is seen as coinciding with the introduction of a script (Kharoshti), and with the induction of northwestern elements of Greek and Iranian origins into the ruling elite. Practically the whole of the subcontinent coming under one authority, giving rise to the idea of 'Jambudeep', may thus be attributed to the enlightenment of Ashoka and the cosmopolitan elite serving him.[20] Similarly, Habib seems inclined to attribute the territorial expansion and centralization achieved in the Delhi Sultanate and Mughal empire to new ideas of administrative and financial management brought by the Islamic invaders, as well as those evolved in these states by their increasingly composite ruling elites. He places particular emphasis on the contribution of rational minds and men of administrative insight promoted by Akbar.[21] He is in sympathy with Tara Chand crediting the Mughals for steamrolling 'the old plurality of political units', creating 'near unity of an empire directly administered from the centre'.

The idea of India, Habib seems to suggest, acquired a 'nationalistic' flavour with the growth of popular sentiment against colonial rule during the nineteenth century, manifested clearly, for example, in the declarations of the leaders of the 1857 rebellion. Again, it was the enlightened ideas imbibed from Europe that contributed to converting this sentiment into a nationalist awakening, giving rise to India's freedom movement. That this movement eventually absorbed some of the socialistic ideals is borne out by the Karachi Congress Resolution on Fundamental Rights (1931), representing 'the common vision' for a free India 'shared by all sections of the

---

[18] Ibid., pp. 76, 82.

[19] Irfan Habib, *The Indus Civilization, A People's History of India 2*, New Delhi: Tulika Books, in association with Aligarh Historians Society, 2002, pp. 60–67.

[20] Irfan Habib and Vivekanand Jha, *Mauryan India, A People's History of India 4* (later renumbered 5), New Delhi: Tulika Books, in association with Aligarh Historians Society, 2004, pp. 20-51.

[21] Cf. Habib, *Medieval India*, pp. 57–60, 114–17.

National Movement, from the Gandhians to Communists'.[22] In this vision, 'secularism' is perceived a strong pillar of Indian nationhood, which, Habib points out, is now threatened by the forces of Hindutva.

In building an argument on any historical theme, Irfan Habib's foremost concern is always a critical assessment of the available textual and material evidence. In any study he undertakes, the theoretical framework rooted in his world view, though never forgotten, will not overshadow the critical scrutiny of historical evidence. In this respect, his approach is very different from the ordinary run of Marxist history-writing of the Stalinist brand, where evidence is often selected keeping in mind an approved thesis. Habib always refers with respect to historians, from one or the other perspective, whose work is based on critical scrutiny of available information. His attitude towards Moreland is perhaps the most conspicuous example of this attitude. Similar deference is shown by him to the work of 'liberal' historians among his contemporaries as well as of past generations, known for their access to sources and capacity to examine them critically. That the general approach of some of them tends towards 'communal' or 'pro-imperialist' interpretations, thoroughly detested by Habib, does not come in the way of his appreciating their contribution. For example, much that he has written on medieval India is in refutation of R.C. Majumdar's communal interpretation, yet he goes out of his way to hail Majumdar's refusal to endorse P.N. Oak's fantasies about the Taj Mahal being a 'Hindu' monument.

But, when it comes to defending objective history against deliberate distortions, particularly when these are designed to defame and run down a figure like Akbar, Irfan Habib can be very harsh even towards a senior historian with considerable research to his credit. This is illustrated by his biting comments on Ishtiaq Husain Qureshi's suggestion that 'Akbar raised revenue demand from one-fourth to a third of the produce'. Habib first mentions Moreland having 'shown in a comprehensive discussion of the subject, there is the strongest presumption that proportion of one-third revenue demand was inherited by Akbar from Sher Shah's administration'. Then he comments: 'But the temptation to run down that "heretic" is perhaps too great for some, and Dr I.H. Qureshi has made the discovery that "Akbar raised the revenue from one-fourth to a third of the produce in some (some only!) of his dominions." A hereditary trait, in fact.' He then proceeds to illustrate the flimsy nature of the evidence cited by Qureshi.[23]

---

[22] Cf. Irfan Habib, 'An Introductory Essay', in Irfan Habib (ed.), *India: Studies in the History of an Idea*, New Delhi: Munshiram Manoharlal, 2004, p. 14.

[23] Habib, *Agrarian System of Mughal India*, 1963 edition, p. 191 n. 7.

Habib makes a similar harsh comment on K.S. Lal's 'fantastic data' in support of his claim that the population of the Indian subcontinent declined by over a third (37.5 per cent) in the course of the three centuries of the Sultanate (1200–1500), implying 'muder and massacre' on a grand scale during this period of 'Mohammadan conquest'. Lal's estimate of the population for the year AD 1000 is shown to fictitious. The pages of the *Tarikh-i Firishta* cited by Jatindra Mohan Dutta and, on his authority, by K.S. Lal in support of this estimate, Habib points out, do not carry any such information. 'It would seem, then', he writes, 'that the figure of 200 million (for the year AD 1000) is really and truly a figment of the imagination of one scholar resting on nothing more tangible than the imagination of another, Professor Lal on Mr Dutta'.[24]

Irfan Habib has always endeavoured to promote historical research along scientific lines, which, it goes without saying, involves critical assessment of evidence, and its analysis in a rational and broadly humane perspective. He never imposes his own Marxist viewpoint on anyone, but remains most uncompromising when it comes to defending the scientific method in history. For him, history-writing on scientific lines and its dissemination is a part of the continuing struggle against divisive trends.

At the Indian History Congress, the scientific method in history has been sought to be promoted during the last fifty years by circulating, at each of its annual sessions, a volume of papers edited by Irfan Habib. Many of these papers have proved to be trend-setters in the ongoing research on Indian history. Over the last few years, the Aligarh Historians Society has also organized a panel of discussion at the Indian History Congress on a selected theme, which is then published in book form. The second volume in this series, *India: Studies in the History of an Idea* (2004), edited by Irfan Habib, deals with the growth of Indian nationhood.

At Aligarh, Irfan Habib has been promoting the cause of the scientific method in history for the last fifty years, in a variety of ways. Apart from classroom lectures and interventions at seminars, he regularly interacts with scholars, suggesting suitable themes of research as well as helping them to locate source material. With those scholars who impress him as serious researchers, he often shares his own notes. To ensure that information available in textual or documentary form becomes accessible to a wider circle, Habib always encourages scholars at Aligarh to arrange it in the form of calendars, manuals or dictionaries written in English. His *Atlas of the Mughal Empire,*

---

[24] Irfan Habib, Appendix to 'Economic History of the Delhi Sultanate: An Essay in Interpretation', *The Indian Historical Review*, Vol. IV, No. 2, January 1978, pp. 298–303.

published in 1982, is one such research tool that makes it possible for scholars not familiar with the Persian language to access information on the economic and political geography of medieval India. It was again on Habib's suggestion that the late Athar Ali prepared his celebrated dictionary of *mansab*s, under the title *Apparatus of the Empire* (1984). S.P. Verma's *Mughal Painters and their Work* (1994) is another book of the same nature published from Aligarh.

For scholars collaborating with Irfan Habib in producing the volume of *Aligarh Papers* for circulation at the Indian History Congress, it has always been an enormous learning experience. He personally checks each and every paper, suggesting improvements in presentation as well as the basic argument. This has helped many of us improve our communication skills, as also our capacity to analyse available evidence in a given perspective.

For Irfan Habib, academic integrity is always more important than personal equations or ideological affinities. While judging the scholarship of a person as a reviewer, commentator, or member of an assessment or selection committee, he has the Gandhian trait of speaking his mind truthfully, irrespective of his personal equation or ideological affinity with the individual concerned. This has been interpreted in one case even as a manifestation of his 'feudal' culture. Without going into too many details, one may point out that this trait of Irfan Habib not only makes him what he is, but also enables him to help many scholars to improve their performance.

Appendix

Thank you for asking me to read this essay. I will be happy to reply to any further questions that you or the author might have. I am returning the paper under separate cover.

I have read and thought about the essay titled 'Coming of Gunpowder and the Response of Indian Polity' by Iqtidar Alam Khan which you asked me to review for possible publication. I would not recommend that you publish this in its present form. First, because it seems to me that the material in the first part of the essay is redundant. The author has already presented much of this material in his articles published in *JESHO* and the *Indian Historical Review*. I also do not feel that the material on European and Chinese developments is necessary. (It could probably be covered in a paragraph with an explanatory footnote.) Second, the arguments which the author advances for the new uses of weaponry and the response of the Indian polity are both interesting and important. However, he does not do them justice and should be asked to develop these arguments in much greater depth to justify publication.

If I may illustrate: on pp. 23–24 the point about 'possession of heavy mortars cast in bronze' as 'an indication of the degree of authority wielded by a ruler within his realm' is certainly an interesting insight and may well be true. I am not at all certain that Prof. Iqtidar Alam Khan supports this statement by his discussion of Babur. For example, it is not at all certain that Babur increased his revenues in order to buy more weaponry, unless I am mistaken. The entire question of the deployment of musketeers and their cost and their effectiveness needs to be discussed separately and sorted out from the discussion of the mortars – whether this was a development under the Surs or under Akbar is not clear. The position of the Hindu rulers in opposition to Babur and/or the Surs needs to be clarified as well. Is there a cultural difference in the unwillingness to use firearms found among the Rajputs (similar to that suggested for the Mamluks by Ayalon)?

Mapping Early Indian History

Krishna Mohan Shrimali

Having been a student of both history and geography during my Higher Secondary school education (classes IX–XI), I was initiated into and made to realize the significance of cartographic delineations of a variety of human activities. Subsequently, while doing my undergraduate studies in the early 1960s, I got especially fascinated by histories of Great Britain and Europe – largely because I was exposed to a wonderful series of *Sketch-Map Histories* of these regions, prepared under the general editorship of George Taylor.[1] It also gave me an opportunity to reflect upon and lament the woeful absence of a historical atlas on Indian history that could be used by school and college students. Charles Joppen's *Historical Atlas of India* (1907) was but a pathetic consolation. Subsequent works such as the *Oxford Pictorial Atlas of Indian History* by K. Srinivas Kini and U. Bhavani Shanker Rao (1932), as well as the renowned C. Colin Davies' *An Historical Atlas of the Indian Peninsula* (1949), also remained confined to a mere mapping of the boundaries of empires with a distinct focus on the various stages of growth of the British empire. The mapping of pre-modern India was extremely peripheral in these ventures. Invoking my constant curiosity and, of course, occasional irritation, I strove to persuade colleagues in the History Department of the University of Delhi to introduce mapping as part of the under-

---

[1] These *Sketch-Map Histories* owed their inspiration and accomplishment to the happy relations that existed between the history and geography departments of Latmayer's School, Edmonton, London. The series includes: J.L. Gayler, Irene Richards and J.A. Morris, *A Sketch-Map Economic History of Britain*, London–Toronto–Wellington–Sydney: George G. Harrap & Co., 1957: 64 maps and 34 diagrams; Irene Richards, George Taylor and J.A. Morris, *A Sketch-Map History of Britain, 1688–1914*, London–Toronto–Wellington–Sydney: George G. Harrap & Co., 1940/1960: 52 maps; Irene Richards, J.B. Goodson and J.A. Morris, *A Sketch-Map History of the Great War and After, 1914–1939*, London–Toronto–Wellington–Sydney: George G. Harrap & Co., 1938/1953: 52 maps; Irene Richards and J.A. Morris, *A Sketch-Map History of Britain and Europe to 1485*, London–Toronto–Wellington–Sydney: George G. Harrap & Co., 1946: 84 maps; George Taylor and J.A. Morris, *A Sketch-Map History of Britain and Europe, 1485–1783*, London–Toronto–Wellington–Sydney: George G. Harrap & Co., 1939/1961: 55 maps.

graduate curriculum, hoping that it might provide a base and an incentive for a decent, multifaceted atlas of Indian history in the not-too-distant future. Unfortunately, however, it has remained a pious hope, though provision for it has been in force for more than two decades.

In 1961, at the time of the celebrations of the centenary of the Archaeological Survey of India, the authorities of that great institution had announced that it would soon bring out an atlas of Indian archaeology. But it is yet to see the light of day even after the lapse of almost half a century! Similarly, in the late 1960s, the Jawaharlal Nehru University in Delhi had a project on cartographic delineation of the 'Historical Archaeology of the Ganga–Yamuna Doab', which too is yet to be completed. However, Roshan Dalal, who worked on this project between 1974 and 1977, went on to complete her doctoral thesis entitled 'Historical Geography of the Ganga–Yamuna Doab up to AD 300' (in two volumes), which was submitted to the university in 1983. The thesis contains thirty-two maps which are not part of the above-mentioned project.[2] Prior to this, but at another micro-level, Y. Subbarayalu had taken a pioneering step in producing *The Political Geography of the Chola Country* (1972), which mapped the Kaveri Delta and its surroundings between the eighth and the thirteenth centuries.

When, in 1978, Joseph E. Schwartzberg brought out *A Historical Atlas of South Asia*[3] (hereafter, *Atlas*), spanning several millennia (from the prehistoric to the modern times), it became an instant hit. Similarly, Irfan Habib's *A Historical Atlas of the Mughal Empire*, published in 1982, substantially extended the frontiers of Indian historical geography and cartography.

Between 1986 and 2002, during the annual sessions of the Indian History Congress, Habib made fourteen presentations (with maps done by Faiz Habib; hereafter, *Presentations*) on cartographic delineations of early Indian history (up to the thirteenth century). In his well-known modest manner, he designated these as the efforts of 'two laymen'. Of these, the one entitled 'Imagining River Sarasvati' was not a part of the unified series. Complementing these *Presentations* were four similar (in terms of methodology and execution) ventures by his colleague, Zahoor Ali Khan. Here, I would like to analyse the importance of these distinctive attempts to map early Indian history.[4]

---

[2] I thank Roshan Dalal for providing me this information.

[3] This was first published in 1978 by the University of Chicago Press. The second edition, with additional material, was published by Oxford University Press in 1992. We have used only this edition.

[4] These *Presentations* are listed below with specific numbers, which are referred to accordingly. (1) Irfan Habib, 'The Economic Map of India, AD 1–300', presented at the 47th session of the Indian History Congress (IHC), Srinagar, 1986, *Proceedings of the Indian History Congress (PIHC)*, Vol. I, 1987, pp. 141–58. (2) Irfan Habib and Faiz Habib, 'The Geography and Economy of the Indus Civilization', presented at the 48th session of the IHC, Goa, 1987,

The *Atlas* and the *Presentations*:
Methodological Concerns and Contrasts

Number of Maps and Thematic Focus

Although it is tempting to undertake a comparative analysis of the ventures of Schwartzberg and Habib – notwithstanding the obvious differences in the scale and magnitude of the work involved – I shall generally refrain from such an analysis. I do not intend to dissect the maps *per se* as far as the *Atlas* is concerned. However, substantive differences in the methodologies of the two undertakings, wherever necessary, shall be looked into. One of the most obvious of these differences lies in the number of maps relevant for the common period covered in the two attempts, i.e. from prehistoric times to the thirteenth century. While Schwartzberg's *Atlas* has as many as 70 maps (excluding insets, diagrammatic expositions and histograms showing dynastic chronologies), Irfan Habib's *Presentations*, published in the concerned *Proceedings of the Indian History Congress (PIHC)*, include only 28 maps (*PIHC* published only the text and not the maps of the first four

---

PIHC, 1988, pp. 57–65. (3) Irfan Habib and Faiz Habib, 'Mapping Archaeological Cultures, *circa* 1800–800 BC', presented at the 49th session of the IHC, Dharwad, 1988, *PIHC*, 1989, pp. 103–08. (4)Irfan Habib and Faiz Habib, 'Mapping the Mauryan Empire', presented at the 50th session of the IHC, Gorakhpur, 1989, *PIHC*, 1990, pp. 57–79. (5) Irfan Habib and Faiz Habib, 'A Map of India, 200 BC–AD 300', presented at the 51st session of the IHC, Calcutta, 1990, *PIHC*, 1991, pp. 103–14. (6) Irfan Habib and Faiz Habib, 'The Historical Geography of India, 1800–800 BC', presented at the 52nd session of the IHC, Delhi, 1991–92, *PIHC*, 1992, pp. 72–97. (7) Irfan Habib and Faiz Habib, 'Epigraphic Map of India, AD 300–500', presented at the 54th session of the IHC, Mysore, 1993, *PIHC*, 1994, pp. 832–46. (8) Irfan Habib and Faiz Habib, 'From Oxus to Yamuna, *c.* 600–750 CE', presented at the 55th session of the IHC, Aligarh, 1994, *PIHC*, 1995, pp. 52–82. (9) Irfan Habib and Faiz Habib, 'A Map of India, 600–320 BC', presented at the 56th session of the IHC, Rabindra Bharati University, 1995, *PIHC*, 1996, pp. 95–104. (10) Irfan Habib, 'Political Geography of Northern India, First Half of the Thirteenth Century', presented at the 58th session of the IHC, Bangalore, 1997, *PIHC*, 1998, pp. 206–17. (11) Irfan Habib and Faiz Habib, 'Mapping the Evolution and Diffusion of Humankind and India's Place in It', presented at the 59th session of the IHC, Patiala, 1998, *PIHC*, 1999, pp. 58–76. (12) Irfan Habib and Faiz Habib, 'India in the 7th Century: A Survey of Political Geography', presented at the 60th session of the IHC, Calicut, 1999, *PIHC*, 2000, pp. 89–128. (13) Irfan Habib, 'Imagining River Sarasvati: A Defence of Commonsense', presented at the 61th session of the IHC, Kolkata, 2000–01, *PIHC*, 2001, pp. 65–92. (14) Irfan Habib and Faiz Habib, 'Economic Map of India, AD 500–800', presented at the 62nd session of the IHC, Bhopal, 2001, *PIHC*, 2002, pp. 104–18. (15) Zahoor Ali Khan, 'Kali Nadi: The History of a River', presented at the 48th session of the IHC, Goa, 1987, *PIHC*, 1988, pp. 741–49. (16) Zahoor Ali Khan, 'Afghanistan and North-western India in the 11th Century: Mapping the Ghaznavid Empire', presented at the 61st session of the IHC, Kolkata, 2000–01, *PIHC*, 2001, pp. 262–66. (17) Zahoor Ali Khan, 'Geography of the Gahadvala Kingdom', presented at the 63rd session of the IHC, Amritsar, 2002, *PIHC*, 2003, pp. 243–46. (18) Zahoor Ali Khan, 'Sarasvati Theories and the Constraints of Geography', presented at the 64th session of the IHC, Mysore, 2003, *PIHC*, 2004, pp. 77–82.

presentations made at the Indian History Congress between 1986 and 1989, though the maps were shown during the presentations). Fortunately, some of these gaps can now be filled because more up-to-date maps are available in the author's monographs published in the now well-established *People's History of India* series.[5]

Thematically, too, the *Atlas* and the *Presentations* differ considerably. Schwartzberg states that the *Atlas* 'provides no more than an outline of the territorial aspects of the political history of the ancient period; for social, cultural, and economic history, it barely scratches the surface. On demographic history, it sheds virtually no light.'[6] Unlike this, there is no consolidated statement for the *Presentations*, which were dispersed and disparate by nature. However, even a casual content analysis is enough to suggest that their main focus is to identify processes of historical transformation through the demonstration of (a) changes in human geography: identifying human cultural movements in pre-literate times; (b) shifting centres of political power; (c) interlinks between archaeology, genetics and linguistics: dispersals of language groups/families, almost drawing linguistic maps of early India; (d) spread of the Indus Civilization and other protohistoric archaeological cultures up to *c.* 800 BC; and, most importantly, (e) economic products and activities of India. Though not unaware of the importance of social, religious and cultural histories, unlike Schwartzberg, Habib does not even scratch their surfaces. Providing a rationale for his efforts, he had, in the first *Presentation*, underlined:

> The *Historical Atlas of South Asia*, edited by Joseph E. Schwartzberg, Chicago and London (1978), marks a notable stage in the progress or research on the historical geography of ancient India. Its well printed maps and detailed explanatory text have cleared the decks for other cartographic endeavours.

---

[5] Irfan Habib, *Prehistory, A People's History of India 1*, New Delhi: Tulika Books, in association with Aligarh Historians Society, 2001; Irfan Habib, *The Indus Civilization, A People's History of India 2*, New Delhi: Tulika Books, in association with Aligarh Historian Society, 2002; Irfan Habib and Vijay Kumar Thakur, *The Vedic Age, A People's History of India 3*, New Delhi: Tulika Books, in association with Aligarh Historians Society, 2003; Irfan Habib and Vivekanand Jha, *Mauryan India, A People's History of India 4* (later renumbered as 5), New Delhi: Tulika Books, in association with Aligarh Historians Society, 2004; and Irfan Habib, *Man and Environment: The Ecological History of India, A People's History of India 36*, New Delhi: Tulika Books, in association with Aligarh Historians Society, 2010. As examples of updated maps (as compared to similar depictions in *Presentation* No. 6), see Map 1.1 ('The Lands of the Rigveda') and Map 2.1 ('Late Vedic Zone') in Habib and Thakur *The Vedic Age*. In the former, even earlier settlements of the tribes of Yadu, Bharata, Paravata, Srinjaya are shown with the suffix 1, of course outside the zone of the *Rigveda*. Cedi, too, has been taken out of the zone of the *Rigveda* but Maruvridha has been added. In Map 2.1, the bulge representing Kamboja has been taken out of the zone.

[6] Joseph E. Schwartzberg (ed.), *A Historical Atlas of South Asia*, Oxford/New York: Oxford University Press, 1992, p. XXX.

These are undoubtedly needed, for, without qualifying in any way one's admiration for the work of Schwartzberg and his colleagues, one may still regret the uniformly small scale of the maps and a frequently disputable choice of themes. Many gaps, therefore, require to be filled.[7]

Using Literary Texts

While both invoke literary texts as major sources for the representations of various themes, they differ in their overall approach to such texts. The *Atlas*, for example, is too text-oriented in several maps. Thus, subsection III.A is entitled 'India of the Vedas and the Epics', and has maps on 'Vedic India', 'India as Revealed in the Ramayana' and 'India as Revealed in the Mahabharata'.[8] Further, we get to see maps with captions such as 'India as Revealed by Panini's *Ashtadhyayi*', 'India as Revealed by the Kautilya *Arthashastra*' and 'Puranic India (Bharata)'.[9] Obviously, these tend to obfuscate the temporal aspects, which are *sine qua non* for any meaningful historical reconstruction. In contrast, not a single *Presentation* (out of fourteen) bears such nomenclature. To illustrate, *Presentation* No. 6, though based on the *Avesta*, the *Rigveda* and Later Vedic texts, is entitled 'The Historical Geography of India, 1800–800 BC'; similarly, *Presentation* No. 10, based essentially on Minhaj's *Tabaqat-i Nasiri*, bears the title 'Political Geography of Northern India, First Half of the Thirteenth Century'. Such examples can be multiplied.

While both Schwartzberg and Habib are familiar with the debates on the period of Kautilya's *Arthashastra*, especially the scientific work done by Thomas R. Trautmann,[10] Schwartzberg still dates it to the fourth century BC. He recognizes that 'Names indicated are those of identifiable peoples and places referred to by Kautilya in descriptive passages on the economy, polity and history of various regions and should not be construed as demonstrating his full knowledge of South Asian geography',[11] and yet he has no qualms in asserting: 'our ascribing them (peoples, places, and products cited) to the Mauryan period poses no insurmountable problem'.[12] Habib, on the other hand, after referring to major writings (right up to Trautmann's work) in 'Mapping the Mauryan Empire',[13] does not equivocate:

That historians should continue to use the *Arthashastra* to support or dispute

---

[7] Habib, 'The Economic Map of India, AD 1–300', p. 141.

[8] Schwartzberg, *Atlas*, p. 13, Pl. III.A.1(a); p. 13, Pl. III.A.1(b); and p. 14, Pl. III.A.2(a–c).

[9] Schwartzberg, *Atlas*, p. 16, Pl. III.B.2(b); p. 16, Pl. III.B.2(c); and p. 27, Pl. III.D.3(a).

[10] Thomas R. Trautmann, *Kautilya and the Arthashastra: A Statitistical Investigation of the Authorship and Evolution of the Text*, Leiden: E.J. Brill, 1971.

[11] Schwartzberg, *Atlas*, p. 16, Pl. III.B.2(c).

[12] Ibid., p. 168.

[13] Habib and Habib, 'Mapping the Mauryan Empire', pp. 57–58.

theories about the Mauryas is illustrative of a curious inertia among historians; it is surely not a reliable argument in its favour as a Mauryan source. We have, therefore, regretfully put the *Arthashastra* on one side, having already used its evidence for compiling our map on Indian Economy in the first three centuries of the Christian era. (*Presentation* No. 1)[14]

A few more observations need to be made on the way literary texts have been used in the *Presentations*. To begin with, texts in varied languages have been invoked without being too credulous about them. Thus we get to read: 'The *Milindapanho* was checked, but it did not yield any information of possible use for our mapping.' Most scholars have generally used Ptolemy's *Geographike Huphegesis* for early centuries of the Common era (even the *Atlas* has a map, Pl. III.C.5(d): 'The World According to Ptolemy, *c.* AD 150'). Habib, however, is candid in being cautious, since there is growing realization now that the extant Ptolemaic text probably incorporated material added by a Byzantine author of the tenth–eleventh century. Accordingly, he has 'made no attempt to show the large number of cities that the text lists unless these are otherwise attested' (*Presentation* No. 1).[15] The manner in which literary texts of different languages (Chinese, Persian and Arabic) have been used to map northwestern India and Afghanistan in the seventh–eighth centuries shows the discerning aspects of the overall approach. This *Presentation* is essentially based on the travelogue of Xuan Zhuang, the *Chachnama* and the accounts of Arab geographers. Not only does Habib go over the ground again (it was already traversed by Cunningham in his geography based on the account of the Chinese pilgrim), but he also offers notes on every place, territory, river or other feature shown on the map (125, all arranged alphabetically). Further, his efforts to corroborate Xuan Zhuang's account of the Turks with that of the *Chachnama*, and that of the old kingdom of Tokhara with the Arab geographers' accounts deserve appreciation (*Presentation* No. 8).[16] We may, however, add that the Diary of He-Cho, a Korean monk who visited India in the early eighth century, and left an account modelled along the lines of Xuan Zhuang and Yi Jing (I-tsing, AD 635–713), could also be used, especially to supplement information on the Arabs and Turks in northwestern India. It also throws light on economic products and inter-religious relations (especially between the Turks/Arabs and the Buddhists), and, therefore, could have been invoked in *Presentation* No. 14 with the same qualifying notices as are made on Xuan Zhuang.

---

[14] For other difficulties arising out of the nature of the text and problems of transferring the *Arthashastra*'s information to the map, see Habib's *Presentation* No. 1, 'The Economic Map of India, AD 1–300', pp. 141–42.

[15] Ibid., p. 143.

[16] Habib and Habib, 'From Oxus to Yamuna, *c.* 600–750 CE', p. 53.

On 'Boundaries' and 'Frontiers'

Since both the *Atlas* and the *Presentations* are essentially engaged in carto-graphic representations, and since delineations of centres, polities and politi-cal powers are the chosen themes of both, their relative approaches to the demarcation of 'boundaries' inevitably become points of departure. Schwartzberg prefers to use 'frontier' rather than 'boundary', because he thinks that the former connotes vagueness and instability, rather than defi-niteness and relative stability as conveyed by the latter. In several maps of the *Atlas*,[17] nonetheless, we see demarcation of the 'core' areas and the 'maxi-mum' limits/extent of the empires of numerous political powers ruling between *circa* 200 BC and *circa* twelfth century AD. Again, knowing full well that there is no consensus about the date of accession of the Kushana emp-eror Kanishka, the *Atlas* maps 'ten views of the limits of the Kushana Em-pire'[18] and simultaneously justifies its delineation of 'frontiers' of the empire thus:

> In these circumstances, it would be folly to put forward our own view of the maximum limits of the Kushana empire with any sense of certitude. We do, of course, have definite reasons for portraying each portion of the Kushana fron-tier in the particular position we have given it, and we have been more meti-culous than others in making the frontiers conform logically to physiographic constraints to expansion in many sectors and in avoiding alignments along modern political boundaries. We have also hedged our view by showing large areas as 'possibly included or tenuously held', a form of equivocation most other authors did not allow themselves.[19]

Another illustration of this kind in the *Atlas* would be the map entitled 'Political Flux on the Northwest Threshold of South Asia, *c.* 130 BC to AD 78 '.[20] This plate is based solely on the mapping undertaken by K. Walton Dobbins, who had worked on the find-spots, mint locations, and dates (known and supposed) of coins of individual polities or sovereigns. Schwartz-berg is aware of several ifs and buts involved in such data assemblage, and yet he has not hesitated to include as many as seventeen maps only to dem-onstrate that the states were in a constant flux and that there were remark-able shifts in a relatively short time-span.

Habib's approach to the delimitation of 'boundaries' is justifiably cauti-ous. In the recent past, the concept of 'empire' in the ancient world has been under the scanner. There has been considerable debate about the organiza-

---

[17] Schwartzberg, *Atlas*, p. 20, Pl. III.C.1(c); p. 25, Pl. III.D.1(b); p. 31, Pl. IV.1(c); p. 32, Pl. IV.2 (b–c).

[18] Ibid., p. xxxiii.

[19] Ibid., p. xxix.

[20] Ibid., p. xxxiv.

tion of what has hitherto been characterized as the Mauryan 'empire'. Romila Thapar, a major participant in this debate, cites Ainslee Embree's *India's Search for National Identity* (1972) to tell us: 'In the absence of cartography there can be no boundary lines bilaterally agreed upon. Frontiers are at best natural boundaries or else buffer-zones.'[21] Disagreeing with such an understanding, Habib stipulates:

> Cartography merely helps in the carrying out of military operations and administrative functions; it is not a prerequisite for them. Lists of villages where one levied tax or tribute would have served sufficiently to demarcate areas of sovereignty. There is nothing to show that the Mauryas were so primitive as to establish imperial or provincial boundaries. That we cannot restore them, except very loosely, derives only from the limitations of our sources. (*Presentation* No. 4)[22]

But this recognition did not blind him to note, in the context of the political geography of northern India in the first half of the thirteenth century: 'within the claimed limits of the Sultanate, there were large areas (*mawasat* – the rebel areas) which did not pay revenue or tribute or even failed to acknowledge that authority of the Sultan' (*Presentation* No. 10).[23]

Habib's reluctance to draw boundaries largely because of uncertainties of hitherto postulated chronologies and synchronizations of various political powers is granted. And yet, he does not conceal a certain arbitrariness in choosing some dynasties and excluding others for any period under consideration. This is especially noticeable in the *Presentations* based on epigraphic data. Strict 'adherence to the period-limits', therefore, became an expandable criterion (*Presentation* No. 7).[24]. Even while acknowledging that agreement on such an issue would be hard to obtain, a proposition made on the issue of mapping Kushana inscriptions needs to be analysed. Presenting an 'Epigraphic Map of India, AD 300–500', Habib is perplexed by the 'sparseness of inscriptions in Pakistan and Afghanistan, in contrast to their abundance in the preceding period (200 BC–AD 300)' (*Presentation* No. 7).[25] This forces him to recall R.G. Bhandarkar's view (first mooted in 1900) that the beginning of the Kanishka era may be dated to the third century AD, and to raise the question whether Kushana inscriptions have not been dated far too early. Habib's final word is: 'If Kushana chronology were to be moved downwards, our maps would certainly look different in the North-west as well as around Mathura, where inscriptions of Vasudeva, the

---

[21] Romila Thapar, Romila, *The Mauryan Revisited*, Kolkata: K.P. Bagchi, 1987, p. 3.
[22] Habib and Habib, 'Mapping the Mauryan Empire', p. 79.
[23] Habib, 'Political Geography of Northern India, First Half of the Thirteenth Century', p. 213.
[24] Habib and Habib, 'Epigraphic Map of India, AD 300–500', p. 834.
[25] Ibid., p. 835.

last great Kushana emperor, are concentrated.' Surely, this would not end
the problem, for the arguments in favour of and against this age-old proposition have been in the field for too long and need not be recalled. But
should the exercise of mapping be guided by its visual appeal?

Handling the 'Uncertain'

Habib is clearly not inclined to take liberty with the basic data. To illustrate, in constructing a map of India of the post-Mauryan five centuries
(circa 200 BC to circa AD 300), one of his concerns is to show the dynasty
and the name of the ruler together with the year/s (of an era/regnal year).
With the intention of keeping the nature of his map 'raw', he not only
refrains from converting the years mentioned in inscriptions of the period
into Christian years, but is also candid about his disinclination to draw
boundaries on the map. He adds: 'This is not because we do not believe in
their existence, but because in the present case the information on them is so
uncertain.'[26] As an illustration, his exposition of the 'Zone of the Rigveda'
may be pondered over:

> The boundary-line of the Rigvedic zone drawn on the basis of the above informa-
> tion (about rivers, seas, tribes, regions and mountains) must be considered as
> very rough. It does not necessarily mean that people of all areas in the zone
> spoke Rigvedic Sanskrit or that the zone as delimited by us defined the limits
> of the geographical knowledge of the Rigvedic people. Rather, it is to be seen
> in the light of the region with which the composers of the Rigvedic hymns
> were most familiar or most concerned. (Presentation No. 6)[27]

Though in a somewhat different context, Olivier Guillaume, who has
extensively studied Graeco-Bactrian and Indo-Greek history and numismatic
evidence of the times, has also evolved a methodology focusing on the need
for almost a complete demolition of extant notions about varied phases of
northwest India in the post-Mauryan centuries. He is particularly insistent
on being wary of such conclusions as have so far held the field on very
uncertain data. Equally, he is aware that 'stricter requirements for testing
would certainly lead us to relinquish a great deal of knowledge we think we
have on the BIG ('Bactro–Indo–Greek') kingdoms'. Significantly, without
being scared of such a prospect, he draws our attention to J. Stengers' following view of eighteenth-century cartography:

---

[26] Presentation No. 5: Habib and Habib, 'A Map of India, 200 BC–AD 300', p. 103. This
   argument has been reiterated in the context of the mapping of the subsequent two centuries
   (circa AD 300–500) as well as in Presentation No. 7 (Habib and Habib, 'Epigraphic Map of
   India, AD 300–500', pp. 834–37). Here, the pitfalls of drawing boundaries have been spelt
   out more explicitly and the need for being cautious underlined.

[27] Habib and Habib, 'The Historical Geography of India, 1800–800 BC', p. 82.

In the XVIIIth century also – and for me this is a striking precedent – they boldly scrapped many details that were found on the geographical maps (up to that time, the cartographers felt it was their duty to fill up these maps and to make them into ornate pieces of work). *They eliminated from cartography not only what was imaginary but also everything which was uncertain.* And this was a great step forward. (Emphasis added)[28]

There are, indeed, just too many examples in the *Atlas* where one would have wished the application of Stenger's view of eighteenth-century cartography. There is hardly any map in it where one does not see the cluttering of enormous details that clearly belong to the realm of the 'uncertain', if not completely speculative. To illustrate just a few: 'Probable Route of Rama between Sharbhanga-ashrama and Lanka (traditional and modern interpretations of the Epic)'; the legend in the context of Gandhara detailing King Pukkusati being friendly to Bimbisara and hostile to Chandapradyota; the legend in the context of Devapattana (Nepal), 'visited by Ashoka, who allegedly married his daughter, Charumati, to Devapala, builder of Devapattana'.[29] Examples of 'uncertain/unauthenticated' interpretations of epigraphic evidence being prominently displayed can also be given, similarly.

Locating Texts (Literary and Non-Literary) in Topographical Contexts

Evidently, both the *Atlas* and the *Presentations* rely heavily on textual and archaeological evidence, amongst others. However, it is the latter that tend to be more sensitive to the need of locating them in their topographical contexts. This becomes particularly crucial in determining the courses of rivers in the past, especially when attempts are being made by ideologically motivated scholars to overawe the average reader with so-called 'scientific data' obtained through sophisticated investigative and exploratory technology such as satellite/Landsat images. In this context, Habib underlines the importance of establishing and delineating detailed contours so as to verify the direction of the flow of old palaeo-channels. Only the contours can determine if they were actually running along, and not against, the slope of the ground. The relative advantages and pitfalls of satellite imagery are also pointed out.[30] The significance of the application of this method

---

[28] Cited in Olivier Guillaume, 'An Analysis of the Modes of Reconstruction of the Graeco–Bactrian and Indo-Greek History', *Studies in History*, New Series, Vol. II, No. 1, January–June 1986, p. 16.

[29] Schwartzberg, *Atlas*, p. 13, Pl. III.A.1(b); p. 15, Pl. III.B.1(b); p. 18, Pl. III.B.4(a).

[30] Irfan Habib, 'Methods of Historical Geography', in Bharati Ray (ed.), *Different Types of History*, Vol. XIV, Part 4 of *History of Science, Philosophy and Culture in Indian Civilization* (General Editor: D.P. Chattopadhyaya), Delhi: Pearson Longman, 2009, p. 400. In *Presentation* No. 3 (Habib and Habib, 'Mapping Archaeological Cultures, *circa* 1800–800 BC', p.

may be seen in *Presentation* No. 13, 'Imagining River Sarasvati: A Defence of Commonsense'. No wonder, it could conclude:

> There is no evidence in Geology or Geography that ever since the passage of the Pleistocene epoch there has been another river on the scale of the Indus running from the Himalayas through Haryana and the desert to the Rann of Cutch; or that the Yamuna and Sutlej have ever during Holocene flowed into the Thanesar stream, now identified as Sarasvati. We have seen too that the *Rigveda* when it calls Sarasvati mighty or great, by no means refers to this stream, or, indeed, necessarily to any earthly river. All claims built upon the greatness of River Sarasvati are, accordingly, nothing but castles in the air, however much froth may be blown over them. (*Presentation* No. 13)[31]

Following its lead, Zahoor Ali Khan, Habib's colleague, also rests his main argument on the delineation of contours for evaluating the so-called palaeo-channels of the now 'lost' Sarasvati mentioned in the *Rigveda*, and the drainage systems of modern rivers such as the Ghaggar–Hakra, Yamuna, etc., which have often been brought into service for buttressing pseudo-scientific claims.[32]

Another related methodological concern (in addition to the delineation of contours) may be seen in the delineation and use of isohyets (lines joining places of equal rainfall). The relationship of the limits of the Indus Culture with those of the drier zone of western India (in its pre-1947 sense) has often been emphasized by scholars of the Harappan/Indus Civilization in the recent past. Habib tries to resolve this issue by drawing up isohyets. Thereafter, his deductions are worth underlining:

> It will be seen that the 30-inch isohyet practically marks the boundary of the Indus zone towards the east; and the 40-inch isohyet is not penetrated at all. The only explanation we can suggest for this is that copper-wielding agrarian cultures did not have enough metal-tools to cut down the dense forests, which must have covered areas of heavy and medium rainfall. It was surely the generalization of iron which made the penetration of forested areas by agricultural communities possible. (*Presentation* No. 2)[33]

---

105), the Habibs did not show contours in the map 'in order to avoid undue crowding'. Regretting this omission, they have been generous enough to show the way out to the reader: 'since our map is drawn on the same scale (1:4 million) as Bartholomew's World Travel Map of the Indian Subcontinent, it can be fitted on to our map to understand the physiographic contexts of sites and cultures.'

[31] Habib, 'Imagining River Sarasvati: A Defence of Commonsense', pp. 86–87.
[32] *Presentation* No. 18, Khan, 'Sarasvati Theories and the Constraints of Geography'; see also *Presentation* No. 2, Habib and Habib, 'The Geography and Economy of the Indus Civilization', pp. 62–63.
[33] Habib and Habib, 'The Geography and Economy of the Indus Civilization', p. 61.

In another *Presentation*,[34] almost a sequel to the preceding one, the archaeological cultures dated between *circa* 1800 and 800 BC have been mapped. Here too, settlements are situated in specific environmental and technological contexts, and much is built on isohyets (40 and 60 inches). It is seen that no place in Afghanistan has 40 inch~s of rainfall. The distribution of sites, when set against isohyets, shows that:

> During this period there was very little penetration beyond the 40-inch isohyet and practically none beyond the 60-inch rainfall line. The western sea coast (the Konkan, Karnataka and Malabar coasts) were still to be cleared for agriculture, and, so too, much of the larger portion of the Gangetic alluvium lying under medium and heavy rainfall. Since iron was just beginning to be used (*c.* 1000 BC), this correspondence between isohyets and site distribution may reinforce the older view that it was not chalcolithic but iron-using communities which were responsible for clearing land in forest-infested areas. It is also to be asked whether the progress against forest was not hampered by absence of the shafted axe, which has been found only to the west of the Indus.

Using Epigraphic Texts

Epigraphic evidence has also been used with a critical eye. As for the four 'Hun' inscriptions of Toramana, Mihirakula and Khingala, it is rightly stressed that there is no epigraphic description of these rulers as 'Huna' or by any other dynastic name. The designation 'Shahi' found on two of these inscriptions (at Kura and Gardez) indicates, rather, Iranian (including Bactrian) affinities.[35] Map 1 faithfully records the inscriptional data only. Limitations of epigraphic evidence have not been papered off. A case in point would be the mapping of the economic landscape between *c.* AD 500 and *c.* AD 800. It is duly recognized in this context that the inscriptions that were found to be so important for the political mapping of India yield very little that could be of use for the economic geographer.[36] The other side of the coin is equally true. The use of inscriptions has not been given up for the cartographic delineation of the political geography of thirteenth-century north India, notwithstanding the fact that by then these texts on stone/ copperplates had begun to lose their pre-eminence. The find-spots, as well as the names of rulers, governors and chiefs mentioned in several inscriptions are shown in the accompanying map. Such data are found to complement the *Tabaqat-i Nasiri* (the principal text used for this map), to shed light on the alignment of political boundaries not otherwise established,

---

[34] *Presentation* No. 3, Habib and Habib, 'Mapping Archaeological Cultures, *circa* 1800–800 BC', pp. 105–07.

[35] *Presentation* No. 7, Habib and Habib, 'Epigraphic Map of India, AD 300–500', p. 835.

[36] *Presentation* No. 14, Habib and Habib, 'Economic Map of India, AD 500–800', p. 111.

and to help in reconstructing the political geography of the Indian king-doms beyond the limits of the Sultanate.[37]

Locating Sites

It goes without saying that that the *sine qua non* of any cartographic expo-sition should be exact location of places, regions, physiographic features, etc. The task becomes relatively more difficult for periods for which record-ed data are not foolproof. On more than one occasion, Habib boldly shares his serious misgivings on this score. Notwithstanding the availability of *Corpus Topographicum Indiae Antique, Part II: Archaeological Sites* (Leuven, 1990), a convenient atlas containing 1:2,000,000 maps covering archaeo-logical sites reported in print before the 1980s in the territories of India, Pakistan and Bangladesh,[38] and a few other publications giving coordi-nates,[39] he remained somewhat sceptical and found it imperative to correct the coordinates available in some of these publications. In another *Present-ation* Habib observes, and goes on to admonish as follows:

> For plotting the selected sites, we must continue to mourn the inadequate indications which archaeological reports often provide us with. The full pub-lished reports cover a very small number of sites. . . . We would urge all exca-vators and explorers to give rigorous indications of locations, in coordinates, banks (right/left) of rivers, distances from nearest railway station/administrat-ive centre 'as the crow flies' (not road distances) with compass directions. Co-ordinates need to be carefully read off the map and carefully printed.[40]

This is not just the outburst of a 'layman'. Similar misgivings and frustra-tion figure even in the recently published *Annotated Archaeological Atlas*

---

[37] *Presentation* No. 10, Habib, 'Political Geography of Northern India, First Half of the Thirteenth Century', p. 206. Another noticeable example of invoking epigraphic evidence of the late medieval period (twelfth–thirteenth-century north India) in an innovative manner may be seen in Zahoor Ali Khan's 'Geography of the Ghadavala Kingdom' (*Presentation* No. 17). His delineation of two curves, A–A and B–B, marking the territory where inscrip-tions of Govindachandra's successors are not found, is significant. He accounts for this recession of authority through 'some internal pressure'.

[38] *Presentatuon* No. 9, Habib and Habib, 'A Map of India, 600–320 BC', p. 95.

[39] As noted in *Presentation* No. 2, Habib and Habib, 'The Geography and Economy of the Indus Civilization', pp. 57–58.

[40] *Presentation* No. 3, Habib and Habib, 'Mapping Archaeological Cultures, *circa* 1800–800 BC', p. 104. It is somewhat surprising that some of the maps included in Habib's volumes published under the *People's History of India* series do not show latitudes and longitudes. To illustrate: Map 3.1 ('Double Harvest Agriculture, 2000–1500 BC') and Map 3.3 ('Language and Language Families') in Habib, *The Indus Civilization*, pp. 79, 95 respectively; Map 1.3 ('Africa: Human Origins in the Great Rift Valley'), Map 4.2 ('The Panjab: Major River Courses in 1400 and 1970') and Map 4.3 ('The Kaveri Delta') included in Habib, *Man and Environment*, pp. 14, 79 and 81 respectively.

of West Bengal, a product of deliberations at the Directorate of Archaeology and Museums, West Bengal; funded by the Department of Information and Cultural Affairs, Government of West Bengal; and finally executed by a team of historians, archaeologists and geographers under the auspices of the Centre for Archaeological Studies and Training, Eastern India (Kolkata). Projected to be published in four volumes, the first, dealing with *Prehistory and Protohistory* was published in 2005.[41] The editors of the volume note:

> The technical problems which had to be faced while plotting the find-spots or sites pertain to the cartography. A few of them may be mentioned here. The major technical problem was the outcome of inadequate or faulty recordings of the locations of artefacts or sites. In many cases the longitudes and latitudes were not given at all in the publications consulted; sometimes the coordinates given were obviously wrong; sometimes the name of a village would not match with that of the district. . . . It was found during such observations (field investigations) that one of the major anomalies in the available data is also that while the location may have been given in terms of a village name, the actual spot may have been an open upland away from the village. Identical village names in the same locality are of common occurrence, and in the absence of proper documentation, can be another source of uncertainty.[42]

The problem of an insufficient or wrong database is not confined to archaeological sites of prehistoric and protohistoric times. It hampers the cartographic work of historians of early historic times as well. It does not come as a surprise, therefore, when Habib outlines the difficulties in locating sites for the 'Epigraphic Map of India, AD 300–500' thus:

> One must continue to regret the rather casual way in which the exact sites are described (only tehsils or districts given after the mention of a site) in case of some inscriptions. Sometimes, as in respect of copper-plates, the difficulties are genuine: trace of the original find-spot has often been irretrievably lost. With stone or slab inscriptions fixed *in situ*, there ought surely to be a better system of recording location than what now prevails. However, at the scale of our maps (1 = 4m), the difficulties of precise location are not so great, and most are resolved by Quarter-inch sheets of the Survey of India. Yet some inscriptions could not be located on our maps because the information on their find-spots is not available.[43]

---

[41] B.D. Chattopadhyaya, Gautam Sengupta and Sambhu Chakrabarty (eds), *An Annotated Archaeological Atlas of West Bengal, Vol. 1: Prehistory and Protohistory,* Delhi: Manohar, in association with Centre for Archaeological Studies and Training Eastern India, Kolkata, 2005.

[42] Ibid., p. 18.

[43] *Presentation* No. 7, Habib and Habib, 'Epigraphic Map of India, AD 300–500', p. 834.

Some Prominent Themes in the *Presentations*

Languages, Language Groups and Scripts

Language groups/families, their movements and assimilations, and, in a similar vein, the dispersal of scripts through the millennia, constitute an important theme mapped in the *Presentations*. These are commented upon and delineated in more than half of them. One may begin with the mapping of the 'Evolution and Diffusion of Humankind and India's Place in It', where we are perceptively warned about the limitations of 'larger gene pools'. More importantly, the dubious nature of the genes–language link is also underlined: 'while people of particular regions, and, therefore, of similar genetic characteristics may speak the same language, the speaking of that language by no means requires those particular genetic characteristics'.[44]

Tracing the 'Language Movements' during the millennium between *circa* 1800 and 800 BC[45] and drawing up of a sort of 'Linguistic Map of India' with the help of Ashokan inscriptions[46] mark two major contributions on the theme under discussion. While the former focuses on the distribution of two major language families, viz. Dravidian and Indo-European, the latter essentially draws the zones of variations in dialects of Prakrit used in the Ashokan inscriptions. In all these forays, Habib is acutely aware of the futility of drawing any fixed linguistic boundaries, for 'old languages have died and new have arisen all the time'.[47] Schwartzberg too had reminded us of the Hindi proverb: '*Kosa kosa pai paani badale; chaar kosa pai baani*' ('Every two miles the water doth change and every four the dialect').[48]

Languages may spread because of human migrations. They can also be adopted and adapted by people other than the original speakers through acquaintance brought about by political conquests and cultural contacts. There must have been large numbers of languages that people spoke but which, being never written, have disappeared. Some of them might have left their traces in patterns of pronunciation or grammatical features in succeeding languages. Such survivals in the speech of later times (coming to us from written documents or current records of usage) can be mapped, the lines defining the area of survival being called an 'isogloss'.[49]

---

[44] *Presentation* No. 11, Habib and Habib, 'Mapping the Evolution and Diffusion of Humankind and India's Place in It', p. 71; where special attention has been drawn to Patrick Sims-Williams ('Genetics, Linguistics and Prehistory: Thinking Big and Thinking Straight', *Antiquity*, Vol. 72, 1998, pp. 505–27) making a spirited attack on excessive claims for genetics.

[45] *Presentation* No. 6, Habib and Habib, 'The Historical Geography of India, 1800–800 BC', pp. 72–76.

[46] *Presentation* No. 4, Habib and Habib, 'Mapping the Mauryan Empire'.

[47] *Presentation* No. 6, Habib and Habib, 'The Historical Geography of India, 1800–800 BC'.

[48] *Atlas*, p. 100, Pl. X.B.1.

[49] Habib, 'Methods of Historical Geography', p. 403.

Some useful historical examples of factors determining the spread or movement of languages have been cited by R.S. Sharma. Explaining the substratum of Dravidian speakers amongst Sanskrit speakers in the *Rigveda*, he refers to the dominance of the elite (Indo-Aryan chiefs and priests), and the relatively more productive mode of subsistence that was achieved through the use of the horse, war chariot, spoked wheels, rituals of the fire and the *soma* cult. An extremely valuable insight is provided by his fieldwork in Manbhum district in 1948, where he observes: 'The social dominance and numerical strength of the Bengali-speaking people in Purulia district let its Kurmi tribals give up Kurmali and adopt Bengali'.[50]

Almost all linguists, and following them, all historians and sensitive archaeologists, have noted the presence of Brahui, 'undoubtedly a Dravidian language', in Baluchistan, at least from the second millennium BC and certainly before the expansion of the Indo-European languages in South Asia. Habib does not go beyond David McAlpin's discovery of the links between Elamite and Brahui, and hypothetical reconstruction of 'Proto-Elamo-Dravidian'. This discovery makes it practically certain that a chain of Proto-Elamo-Dravidian languages existed in a wide arc from southwestern Iran to south India, well before 3000 BC. Since Dravidian compositions that have survived (including Tamil–Brahmi inscriptions and Sangam literature) date largely from the post-Mauryan times, Habib refrains from mapping their dispersal in the larger Indian subcontinent. The farthest that he has been able to go is to consider the possibility of the 'authors of the South Indian Neolithic cultures' as being the speakers of a 'Proto-Dravidian' language.[51]

It would not be out of place to bring into this context, R.S. Sharma's cartographic delineation of the 'Routes of the Historical Settlements of Dravidians in the Subcontinent'. He observes the presence of Dhangar (a dialect of the Dravidian Kurukh language) and its speakers (identified as the Dhangar tribe, later a caste) in the present-day mid-Ganga plains. His mapping shows the long, unilinear trek of Dravidian from the northwest (*circa* 3000 BC) to Sri Lanka (passing through southern Rajasthan and northern Maharashtra, *circa* 2000–1500 BC, and the Andhra Pradesh–Karnataka region, *circa* 1000 BC). But how about postulating another pocket of Dravidian speakers in the Narmada and Tapi Valleys that may have also radiated influences across central India and right up to the middle Ganga valley? Could it not be that some of the makers of the Black-and-Red Ware of the post-Harappan Chalcolithic cultures were carriers of these strains? And what does one make of recent reports about signs of the Harappan script figuring

---

[50] R.S. Sharma, *Advent of the Aryans in India*, Delhi: Manohar, 1999, Chapter 3, especially p. 59.

[51] Ibid., p. 51, Map 2, and Chapter 3.

on a neolithic stone axe from the Sembian-Kandiyur village near Mayiladu-thurai (Nagapattinam district, Tamil Nadu), and a sign akin to the Indus Valley's engraved in a cave at Edakkal (Wayanad district, Kerala)?[52]

Discussion of the movement of the Indo-European languages inevitably gets focused on the surviving linguistic evidences in two compilations, i.e. the *Rigveda* in the Indian/Indo-Aryan (the s-branch) and the *Avesta* in the Iranian (the h-branch, h substituting here for the Indic-s). Taking due cognizance of (a) reassessments of the period of the Gathas, the oldest portions of the *Avesta;* (b) precisions of Glott chronology; (c) the appearance of Indo-Aryan words, personal names and names of gods amongst the Mitanni in Hittite and Egyptian records of *c*. 1400 BC; (d) the Avestan and Rigvedic linguistic and other thematic affinities; and, above all, (e) the 'homeland' of the hypothetical Proto-Indo-European language still eluding us, the branching off of the Proto-Iranian and Proto-Indic has been rightly placed around 2000 BC. Further, this bifurcation is located in Transoxiana (area of the Andronovo culture). And from this base, as many as six movements/sub-movements have been mapped:[53] (i) 'centum' diffusion (Tocharian A&B) under pressure of the Proto-Indo-Iranian occupation of Transoxiana; (ii) Proto-Dardic (a branch of the proto-Indic, spreading through Afghan-istan and into Kashmir – the areas of the Gandhara Grave Culture of the Swat Valley dated by C-14 to middle and late second millennium BC); (iii) West Asian Indic (this split from the Proto-Indic within or north of Afghanistan, and then a westward movement); (iv) the movement of Indic proper, through Afghanistan into the Rigvedic zone; (v) possibly after the composition of the bulk of the *Rigveda* and around 1400 BC, the subse-quent movement of Proto-Iranian into the zone of the *Avesta;* and finally, (vi) from this wave the west Iranian and the Avestan branch off.[54]

Way back in 1986, while making his first *Presentation* of the series of maps at the Srinagar session of the Indian History Congress, Habib had cited an 'adequate map of the Mauryan empire despite the large amount of work done on Ashokan inscriptions' as an important gap that needed to be filled, despite Shwartzberg's *Atlas*.[55] This was therefore sought to be plugged

---

[52] As reported in *The Hindu* (Delhi edition) dated 1 May 2006 and 26 September 2009, res-pectively.

[53] *Presentation* No. 6, Habib and Habib, 'The Historical Geography of India, 1800–800 BC', p. 94, Map 1.

[54] Ibid., pp. 72–76.

[55] That such a lackadaisical attitude still persists should be apparent from a recent publication, which is otherwise a painstaking work of substantive archaeological significance: Lars Fogelin, *Archaeology of Early Buddhism*, Lanham–Toronto–New York–Oxford: Altamira Press, 2006. It has a map showing 'The Locations of Ashokan Rock Edicts' (ibid.: 25, Figure 2.2). It does not mention even a single site and, judging by the location of the dark black dots (supposedly indicating the spots of inscriptions), it is clear that the map is not confined to

by him in 1989, when he presented 'Mapping the Mauryan Empire' at the 49th session of the Congress (*Presentation* No. 4). One of the most arresting features of this presentation was the representation of languages, dialects and scripts prevalent during the time of the Mauryas. The *Proceedings* of the session[56] only included its text but, fortunately, we now have detailed maps on the subject in the monograph *Mauryan India*, in the *People's History of India* series.[57] As many as four dialects (A–D) of Ashokan Prakrit, some sub-dialects and their respective regions have been plotted on the maps. One of the highlights of these representations is the drawing up of the line of '*l*' isogloss, which separates the zones of the consonants '*l*' (Dialect 'A', used in all the Ashokan and other Mauryan-period inscriptions in the Gangetic basin and Orissa) and '*l + r*' (Dialect 'B', in central India and the southern parts of the Mauryan empire).[58]

The inference drawn by Habib from this is that within the large area enclosed by the '*l*' isogloss, the speakers of the local Indo-Aryan language or Prakrit must have inherited an inability to pronounce '*r*' from an older, presumably non-Indo-Aryan language, whose earlier existence here is thereby attested. As corroborative evidence for this inference, we may recall some allusions to *asura*s in the *Shatapatha Brahmana*, where they have been called *mlechchha*s because of their linguistic and other cultural specificities which included the making of *chamus*, i.e. circular, shallow and subterranean burial chambers. It is said in one of the passages (III.2.1.23) of this text that when the *deva*s and *asura*s were fighting for *bali* (sacrificial offering), power and territory, the latter were deprived of their power of speech. Therefore the *asura*s shouted '*helavah helavah*' and lost the fight. Sayana's commentary helps in reading this as a synonym of '*herayo herayo*' ('hey, enemy').[59]

Dialect 'C', represented by the Girnar version of the Rock Edicts, has certain Sanskritizing tendencies, which are still more visible in Dialect 'D' represented by the Mansehra and Shahabazgarhi inscriptions, written in the Kharoshthi of the North Western Frontier Province. The latter are taken to be the earliest known form of Gandhari Prakrit. The sounds were probably pronounced just as they were in the Iranic language written in Aramaic

---

'Rock Edicts' and includes sites of Pillar Edicts as well. Harry Falk (*Ashokan Sites and Artefacts*, Mainz am Rhein: Verlag Philipp van Zabern, 2006), though useful on documentation, is not very scientific in the mapping of data.

[56] Habib and Habib, 'Mapping the Mauryan Empire'.

[57] Habib and Jha, *Mauryan India*, Maps 2.1 to 2.4 and 3.2, pp. 55–58 and 152.

[58] See Map 3.4, entitled 'Ashokan Prakrit, *c.* 250 BC: The 'L' Isogloss', ibid., p. 104. The map and its discussion are also included in Habib, 'Methods of Historical Geography', pp. 403 and 405, Map 18.9.

[59] K.M. Shrimali, 'Bhasha, Sanskriti aur Rashtriya Asmita', General President's Address at the 12th annual session of the Uttar Pradesh History Congress, Bareilly, 2001, in A.K. Sinha (ed.), *Readings in Indian History*, New Delhi: Anamika Publishers, 2003, pp. 6–7.

script (the source of Kharoshthi). The Sanskritic affinities of Dialect 'D' possibly have something to do with the influence of the Iranic language under Achaemenian domination of the area. Habib drew a line (passing between Shahbazgarhi and Mansehra) showing the present region of Iranic languages (Pushtu, Tajik, etc.). Of such Iranic presence, Ashoka's own Aramaic inscriptions at Taxila and in Afghanistan are the best examples. It is perhaps not a mere coincidence (given the status of the language movements up to *circa* 800 BC, delineated above) that the Avestan element seems to be quite prominent among the Iranic words used in these inscriptions.

Ashokan edicts in Greek found at Kandahar – written in fine Greek script, and both in the pure Koine (RE XIII) and Attic (Athenian, in RE XII) dialects – provide an interesting landscape of the linguistic map of India of those times. Further, the growing knowledge of Tamil–Brahmi inscriptions (where Prakrit loan words amount to over 25 per cent of the vocabulary) enlightens the linguistic scene outside the Mauryan empire.

Three of the *Presentations* (Nos. 5, 7 and 12), based essentially on epigraphic evidence, cover almost a millennium: from *circa* 200 BC to AD 750. Of these, the last one was complementary to *Presentation* No. 8 which mapped the region between the Oxus and the Yamuna between *circa* AD 600 and 750, on the basis of accounts given by the Chinese traveller Xuan Zhuang and in Arabic and Persian texts. Mapping (unfortunately, the map accompanying *Presentation* No. 5 was not published in the *Proceedings*: Habib and Habib, 'A Map of India, 200 BC–AD 300') in the three *Presentations* under reference highlights several transitions taking place in the use of languages and scripts. First, there are inscriptions with a strong presence of Prakrit influenced by Sanskrit, and vice-versa. Second, while the zones of Brahmi and Kharoshthi were already known through Ashokan edicts, there were some aberrations here and there. To illustrate, the two 'Shahi' or 'Hun' inscriptions of Kura and Gardez, and the Shorkot inscription in the Kharoshthi zone are in characters of the Brahmi family. A question is raised: does this indicate a supplanting of the Kharoshthi script in the entire area, or merely a mis-dating of many Kharoshthi inscriptions to an earlier time? Third, Brahmi was also the vehicle of Tamil (heavily influenced by Prakrit) and of Eli (proto-Sinhalese), and Brahmi inscriptions in these two languages constitute two distinct zones (Tamil Nadu and Sri Lanka) in the immediate post-Mauryan centuries. Fourth, the persistence of Prakrit in certain areas of south India, in spite of its near-total ejection from north and central India, is an arresting feature. Fifth, Kannada marks its first occurrence in the fourth-century Halmidi pillar inscription of Kakustha(varman). Sixth, the tendency of Sanskritizing popular place names (Kankuj > Kanauj > Kanyakubja, based on the story of seven humpbacked princes in Xuan Zhuang), or of tracing Persian influences (via Arab-ruled Sind in the eighth century), say, in Gujarat (Gujar + suffix -*aat/jaat*, indicative of plural). All of these constitute substantive inputs of Habib's mapping initiatives. Even when dealing with later periods, say, the thirteenth century, for which mapping has been done essentially on the basis of Minhaj's *Tabaqat-i Nasiri* (*Presentation* No. 10), place-names figuring in their Sanskritized forms in the inscriptions are recorded accordingly. Almost in a similar vein and in the same spirit, Zahoor Ali Khan notes that the number of names surviving in Afghanistan from the pre-Islamic past (Gandhar, Tukharistan, Zabulistan, Kaikanan, etc.) is surprisingly large, and maps them accordingly.[60]

Mapping Economic History

'Economic history remains in general a field largely neglected by the map-makers'.[61] It is with such a conviction that Habib undertakes the mapping of enormously rich facets of people's economic activities through several millennia. As many as seven of the *Presentations* (Nos. 1–4, 6, 9 and 14) are either exclusively concerned with the delineation of data of economic significance, or undertake their representations as part of the historical or political geography of the Indian subcontinent. Occasionally, one sees almost a poetic synthesis of modesty personified and presumptuous sternness. Thus 'two laymen' try to traverse the vacant ground that seems to exist between detailed and specialist mapping, and the rather rough and general maps that lie scattered among books. Justifying their mapping of the geography and economy of the Indus Civilization, the Habibs claim: 'we are presumptuous enough to say that accurate mapping of so many Indus and contemporary culture-sites, the delineation of contours and isohyets, and, finally, the plotting of economic information, all on a single map to expose their relationships, may be found to be of some use'.[62]

In general, the data collected for mapping economic history take note of minerals and metals; precious and semi-precious stones; sea products – pearl fisheries; animals and animal products; forest produce, agricultural crops; spices and fruits; craft products; technology – e.g., ungeared *saaqiya* (modern 'Persian wheel'), steel-making, tie-and-dye ('*bandhana*'), silk-weaving, rotary querns, distillation, etc.; ports and trade routes (inland, riverine and overseas). In rare cases, such as that of the Indus Civilization, for instance, even estimates of population of urban settlements (Rahman Dheri: 12,000; Harappa: 40,000; Mohenjo Daro: 41,000) are included, and a process of deurbanization in the post-Indus millennium (*c.* 1800–800 BC) is indicated.

---

[60] *Presentation* No. 16, Khan, 'Afghanistan and Northwestern India in the 11th Century: Mapping the Ghaznavid Empire', p. 264.

[61] *Presentation* No. 1, Habib, 'The Economic Map of India, AD 1–300', p. 141.

[62] *Presentation* No. 2, Habib and Habib, 'The Geography and Economy of the Indus Civilization', p. 57.

The most regrettable aspect of the seven *Presentations* under reference is the non-inclusion of maps for four (Nos. 1–4) of them in the relevant *Proceedings* of the Indian History Congress.[63] Some of this lacuna can, of course, be made up with the help of volumes of the *People's History of India* series. The monographs entitled *The Indus Civilization, The Vedic Age* and *Mauryan India* provide easy access to the relevant maps.

A perusal of the maps, wherever they are available, shows that relatively speaking, the most complete ones are for the period *c.* AD 500–800.[64] Four maps accompanying this *Presentation* show even agricultural and pastoral products, along with crafts, mineral and marine products, etc; even the 'Economic Map' in *Mauryan India* does not show agricultural and forest products.[65] *The Vedic Age* has only one map on economic history, viz. 'Early Iron Age Sites'.[66] Map 2.1 showing 'The Indus Civilization' in the monograph of the same title, depicts mining of copper and silver, and areas of working in precious and semi-precious stones such as agate and lapis lazuli; but again, areas of agricultural products are not marked.[67] It seems that the four maps representing Eastern, Western, Northern and North-Western India during *circa* 600–320 BC have only incidental representation of economic data. Apart from showing some inland trade routes (carefully indicating the places on the route that could not be located), we notice the marking of cloth (Kashi), bronze utensils (Kosala, Ayodhya), lead and silver mining (Agucha and Zawar), and salt and gold-dust (Gandhara) in Maps 1 and 3.[68] Why is there this general reluctance to show agricultural and forest produce on the maps? Irfan Habib offers an explanation for the difficulties in mapping such information, provided by Xuan Zhuang:

> Unluckily, there is no hint furnished as to regions where each product was found, so that this information cannot be transferred to the map. However, one may have here one explanation why Xuan Zhuang seems to stop giving us particulars about regions within India that he has given on *en route*: he saw no great reason to do so since the products, etc., are already described in the general chapter on India.[69]

One wonders if this is a satisfactory explanation. Why, for instance, could

---

[63] Habib, 'The Economic Map of India, AD 1–300'; Habib and Habib, 'The Geography and Economy of the Indus Civilization'; Habib and Habib, 'Mapping Archaeological Cultures, *circa* 1800–800 BC'; Habib and Habib, 'Mapping the Mauryan Empire'.

[64] *Presentation* No. 14, Habib and Habib, 'Economic Map of India, AD 500–800'.

[65] Habib and Jha, *Mauryan India*, p. 120, Map 3.1.

[66] Habib and Thakur, *The Vedic Age*, p. 88, Map 3.2.

[67] Habib, *The Indus Civilization*, p. 23.

[68] *Presentation* No. 9, Habib and Habib, 'A Map of India, 600–320 BC'.

[69] *Presentation* No. 14, Habib and Habib, 'Economic Map of India, AD 500–800', p. 105.

not *yava* (barley) and *dhana/dhanya* be shown in the 'zone' of the *Rigveda*, or numerous agricultural crops mentioned in the later Vedic texts be included in the 'Late Vedic Zone'?[70] Similarly, the plough (terracotta model from Banawali) and the ploughed field (Kalibangan) are known from the Indus Civilization. A photograph of the twelfth-century BC ploughed field at Aligrama, Swat (Pakistan), has been published in *The Vedic Age.*[71] But none of these data figure in the available maps. Other comparable observations can also be made in respect of various animals mentioned in the *Avesta, Rigveda* and later Vedic texts.

Mapping of mining areas (copper, silver, gold, diamond, etc.), as well as of areas of working in precious and semi-precious stones, has generally been done in a convincing manner, notwithstanding an occasional oversight in referencing. For example, B.N. Mukherjee's *The Economic Factors in Kushana History* (1970) has been cited only partially in the context of diamond mines.[72] Apart from referring to medieval texts such as Taranatha's *Rgyagar-chos-hbyun, Ain-i Akbari* and *Tuzuk-i Jahangiri*, Mukherjee's main argument for locating those mines in eastern Malwa rests on the occurrence of the term *aakara* (literally meaning 'mine') in western Kshatrapa and Satavahana inscriptions of the first and second centuries AD. Habib seems to have missed that. While still on mining, we would also like to draw attention to a stimulating contribution by Marcia A. Fentress.[73] Its Map 2 and Appendix 1 list the distances of major stone and metal resources from Mohenjo Daro and Harappa, and delineate regional traditions that worked towards the urbanization process in the Indus Civilization. The accent here is clearly on areas of resource exchange, and the technological and commercial transactions contributing to that process.

Coins and Currency Systems

The mapping of numismatic evidence is rather weak, and methodologically too, somewhat questionable. It has been rightly observed that 'money is

---

[70] Cf. also Makkhan Lal, 'The Development and Dispersal of Agricultural Settlements in the Garga–Yamuna Doab (2nd and 1st Millennium BC)', presented at the 48th session of the IHC, Goa, 1987, *PIHC*, 1988, pp. 730–40. Covering the period between *circa* 1800 BC and *circa* AD 300, this contribution undertakes 'locational analysis' of 'agricultural settlements' in a micro area of the Ganga–Yamuna Doab. It delineates three stages in the development of such settlements, keeping in view the nature of available water resources. Regrettably, however, there is no reference to cropping patterns in the concerned area.

[71] Habib and Thakur, *The Vedic Age*, p. 7.

[72] *Presentation* No. 1, Habib, 'The Economic Map of India, AD 1–300', pp. 145–46.

[73] Marcia A. Fentress, 'Regional Interaction in Indus Valley Urbanization: The Key Factors of Resource Access and Exchange', in Sylvia Vatuk (ed.), *American Studies in Anthropology of India*, Delhi: Manohar, 1978, pp. 399–424.

absent' in both the *Avesta* and the *Rigveda*.[74] Barring perhaps the cartographic delineation in the first *Presentation* ('The Economic Map of India, AD 1–300'), there is not much depiction of data on coins. Even for the periods that witnessed prolific/reasonable use of money (e.g., *c.* 200 BC – AD 500), not much effort seems to have been made to harness existing information. Confessions like 'Our plotting of (Western) Satraps' Hoards is manifestly incomplete' notwithstanding, they leave much to be desired, especially when certain important inferences about 'distinct boundaries' of the emergence of 'three coinage zones' (Roman, western Kshatrapa and Kushana) have been forcefully made.[75] Further, one is tempted to assume that Habib got carried away by the lure of the gold. While the find-spots of even single Roman coins have been plotted and find-spots yielding ten or more such coins have received special attention, the coinage of the Satavahanas (contemporaries of the Romans) is not represented at all, for they did not have 'gold or silver' issues. Incidentally, the Satavahanas did issue silver coins with their portraits, though in small numbers perhaps, and these issues also carry legends that have great linguistic significance (a battleground for Tamil/Telugu chauvinists); and the Wategaon Hoard (Sangli district, Maharashtra) alone yielded as many as 700 lead coins of the dynasty. Do we take it that coins issued in baser metals/alloys such as copper, lead, tin, potin, etc. (as was done by the Satavahanas) do not deserve attention? Nor can the non-depiction of Satavahana coinage be justified, as has been done, on the ground that its zone 'overlapped parts of that of the western Satraps' silver and of Roman gold and silver'.[76] Finally, the contention that Roman gold and silver were melted for coinage of the western Kshatrapas and Kushanas, respectively, is a rather one-sided explanation and needed to be nuanced.

Presentation No. 14, 'Economic Map of India, AD 500–800', could also profitably use extant data on coins. It carries as many as four maps which do include Xuan Zhuang's statements about money materials in use. However, the evidence from the coin hoards has been left out because it was 'a separate enterprise in itself', though its value has been duly conceded.[77]

Notwithstanding the abovementioned reservations, one area of adequate and scientific representation of numismatic data concerns punchmarked coins,

---

[74] *Presentation* No. 6, Habib and Habib, 'The Historical Geography of India, 1800–800 BC', p. 85.

[75] *Presentation* No. 1, Habib, 'The Economic Map of India, AD 1–300', p. 153.

[76] Ibid.

[77] *Presentation* No. 14, Habib and Habib, 'Economic Map of India, AD 500–800', p. 114. More or less similar reluctance and rationale have been shown in plotting the urban settlements of the period *circa* AD 1–300, for which copious archaeological data is available. But harnessing this data is considered 'too vast to be undertaken by us' (*Presentation* No. 1, Habib, 'The Economic Map of India, AD 1–300', p. 144).

the earliest coins of India. *Presentation* No. 9, covering the period between *circa* 600 and 320 BC, carries four detailed area maps on Northern, North-Western, Eastern and Western India.[78] Since the mapping of the concerned numismatic evidence has been done in the context of the so-called sixteen *mahajanapadas* (great states), it takes cognizance of the hypothesis about the link between the emergence of metal money and the rise of states. Of particular interest here is the depiction of revenues paid by each province of the Achaeminid empire and the questioning of Herodotus' assumption about such revenues being paid in 'gold talents' by the empire's 'Indian' province. Habib has worked out that it was actually 360 silver talents.

In the context of punchmarked coins, we would also like to appreciative-ly recall Habib's contribution in the making of Map 1.2 ('Early Coinages: Major Findspots') that went into our monograph, *The Age of Iron and the Religious Revolution,* in the *People's History* series.[79] Since the precise chro-nology of more than 170 known hoards of such coins (with identifiable find-spots) is not available, it was impossible to locate them on the map, though many were indeed mentioned in the text. Habib drew my attention to the technicalities involved, viz., post-300 BC hoards of punchmarked coins could not be shown (in Map 1.2) because the chronological limits had to be the same as those of the sites of the Achaemenian and early Athenian coins that were also shown on the same map. As a partial solution, then, most of the places mentioned in the text, irrespective of precise period limits, were shown in the four larger regional maps (Maps 3.1 to 3.4),[80] with the hope that the reader will find the arrangement satisfactory.

Major Desideratum

Religion has been a significant, if not the central, aspect of human social and cultural life. New models of science, increasing concern with symbol-ism and belief, improved interpretive models and theories such as an eco-logical approach to religion, and a growing reconciliation between humanis-tic and scientific approaches have contributed towards making the study and representations of religions a viable and vibrant area of research. Carto-graphic presentations of this human behavioural aspect across world reli-gious systems has been picking up. *Buddhism: Its Origin and Spread in Words, Maps and Pictures,* and its companion volumes on Islam and Christ-ianity were published in London in the 1960s. Schwartzberg has given some

---

[78] Habib and Habib, 'A Map of India, 600–320 BC',

[79] K.M. Shrimali, *The Age of Iron and the Religions Revolution, c. 700–c. 350 BC, A People's History of India 3A* (later renumbered as 4), New Delhi: Tulika Books, in association with Aligarh Historians Society, p. 30.

[80] Ibid., pp. 82–85.

attention to these, both in exclusive terms and as components of cultural sites.[81] *Atlas of the World's Religions* (1999), edited by Ninian Smart, is a recent and fairly comprehensive example of this growing interest.

Non-depiction of religious developments in early India is one of the most serious desideratum of the *Presentations*. Barring the representation of the *stupas* at Piprahwa, Sarnath, Bharhut, Sanchi, Mirpur Khas and Amaravati, and that too 'with some degree of trepidation, knowing of the uncertainties involved',[82] there is not a single map on religious movements, centres, the course of their spread, etc. The Habibs are acutely aware of this:

> We have not attempted to show the religious affiliations indicated by the inscriptions, though in the bulk they relate to donations and gifts for religious and pious purposes. We hope to be able in future to add this information, since we realize its great significance for religious and sectarian history, whose geographical dimensions are not often adequately considered.[83]

Hopefully, this will not remain an empty promise and will be fulfilled in the very near future. Further, we hope that invocation of texts too will not remain confined to epigraphs and will get extended to other genres of texts as well. May we, in this context, recall our earnest plea, made more than two decades ago,[84] about undertaking a geography of Indian religions taking cognizance of the 'types of religions' and what has been called 'anthropology of the sacred'. Briefly, it was a proposition for an independent atlas of Indian religions in which mapping *per se* must have the objective of grappling with problems of the growth of Indian religions. We had spelt out several themes that could be a part of the cartographic delineations – for instance: the correlation and correspondence, if any, between the distribution of memorial stones, on the one hand, and of land grants, on the other. Is it a mere coincidence that both phenomena proliferated in the post-sixth century AD? Perhaps mapping the two can provide some answers.

Ideology in Mapping

How far can we go in making cartographic representations 'raw'? Can such an exercise be absolute, for, whatever the method employed, will it not ultimately be a 'representation'? Can such 'representations' be 'ideologically

---

[81] Cf. Schwartzberg, *Atlas*, Plates III.B.5, III.C.3(a), IV.3(a), IV.4 (a, b).
[82] *Presentation* No. 4, Habib and Habib, 'Mapping the Mauryan Empire'.
[83] *Presentation* No. 5, Habib and Habib, 'A Map of India, 200 BC–AD 300', p. 104.
[84] Krishna Mohan Shrimali, 'Religion, Ideology and Society', Presidential Address, Section I (Ancient India), 49th session of the IHC, Dharwad, 1988, *PIHC*, Section IV, 1989, pp. 75–83 and corresponding notes.

neutral'? If the history-writing of any period can only aim to be 'relatively objective', surely mapping historical times should also not sacrifice that goal. *Prima facie*, Schwartzberg's *Atlas* and Habib's *Presentations* have some indicators of the parameters within which they seem to have decided to bind themselves voluntarily.

To begin with, there is the issue of periodization. With the themes and chronologies clearly spelt out in the title of each *Presentation*, Habib makes his preferences clear. He does not show any special fondness for texts of any particular genre, or to apply any specific value-loaded categorizations/ nomenclatures. It is just a mapping of the Indian subcontinent or some specific regions thereof, within certain chronological limits. Neither his ideological predilections nor his personal views on various aspects of Indian history through the millennia are unknown. And yet, by and large, he has been able to not get swayed by them. The only exception is perhaps 'Imagining River Sarasvati: A Defence of Commonsense' (*Presentation* No. 13, with as many as seven maps), which, incidentally, was not a part of the thirteen-map series he had planned for representing early India. It was clearly provoked by the specific political change that came into being in India with the formation of the National Democratic Alliance government in New Delhi (1999–2004). As part of its 'Culture Policy', this government formulated an ideologically motivated 'Sarasvati Project' in the name of 'Cultural Nationalism'. The Project aimed at identifying archaeological bases for the course of the 'lost' Sarasvati river, whose paeans have been sung in the *Rigveda*. Ironically, support to it was extended by a Cambridge-based archaeologist who otherwise was busy espousing the so-called 'colonial Indology' (one of its components has been the unqualified debunking of Vedic literature).[85]

Given such a context, it is no surprise that Habib adopted a somewhat different mode; he tended to be polemical at times, though without sacrificing academic rigour. Mincing no words, he began his *Presentation* No. 13 thus: 'In the current official and quasi-official effervescence over new-found truths about our past, that keep coming in a stream from resident and, especially, non-resident oracles, the Sarasvati river has come to occupy a pre-eminent perch.'[86] Further: 'Giving a name amounts to half the battle, and if the Indus Civilization is to be rechristianed [*sic.*] "Sarasvati Civilization", name-capture, not argument, is the thing that matters.'[87]

---

[85] For Habib's scathing comment on this, see *Presentation* No. 1, Habib, 'The Economic Map of India, AD 1–300', p. 70; and for our critique of the paradigm of 'colonial Indology', see Krishna Mohan Shrimali, 'People's Archaeology and Archaeology for the People', Y.D. Sharma Memorial Lecture, *Puratattva*, No. 39, 2009, pp. 172–94.

[86] Habib, 'Imagining River Sarasvati: A Defence of Commonsense', p. 65.

[87] Ibid., p. 66. In a complementary contribution on the same theme, Zahoor Ali Khan also deals with 'the Sarasvati school' (so named by Habib in the above-mentioned *Presentation*) and

Such an overall disposition may be better appreciated if we put the *Atlas* under the scanner. Schwartzberg formulated his vision thus:

> We reject such simple, though formerly fashionable, schemata as 'Hindu', 'Mohammedan' and 'British' periods; or the transplanted European categories 'Ancient', 'Medieval' and 'Modern'; or the patently inapplicable Marxist stages of 'Slavery', 'Feudalism', 'Capitalism' and 'Communism'. Among the various periodization schemes put forward to date, our own most closely resembles that of the ten-volume *History and Culture of the Indian People* . . . under the general editorship of R.C. Majumdar. But while our approach is methodologically similar to that of the HCIP, our chronological breakdown and our period designations differ considerably.[88]

One wonders if there is something more to it. We may recall, in this context, that this well-known series of the post-independence years, viz., *The History and Culture of the Indian People*, popularly known as the Bharatiya Vidya Bhavan Series, was conceived and planned by the noted Hindu chauvinist K.M. Munshi, who was the founder of that educational society and had spearheaded the reconstruction of the Somanatha temple (destroyed by Mahmud Ghazni in the tenth–eleventh centuries) immediately after India's independence. The General Editor, too, was a known Hindu chauvinist. Of the planned ten volumes, as many as five (I: *The Vedic Age*; II: *The Age of Imperial Unity*; III: *The Classical Age*; IV: *The Age of Imperial Kanauj*; V: *The Struggle for Empire*) were devoted to the 'ancient' period (up to *c.* AD 1300), and only two (VI and VII) covered the more than four centuries of the *Delhi Sultanate* and the *Mughal Empire*. One century of the 'Hindu *padpadshahi*' of *Maratha Supremacy* (1707–1818) constituted Vol. VIII and the rest were concerned with *British Paramountcy and Indian Renaissance* (1818–1905, in two parts) and *Struggle for Freedom* (1905–47). The overall 'communal' bias of the entire series is well established. No wonder, the present-day 'cultural nationalists' accept this series as their role model. And the *Atlas* accepting its framework speaks for itself.

A few more illustrations from Schwartzberg would be no less appropriate. His following two positions also smack of an ideological orientation that is not dissimilar to that of Hindu chauvinists masquerading under the mask of 'cultural nationalism'. First, in a not very subtle manner, he hints at an equation between the Harappan culture and the corpus of Vedic texts.

---

concludes: 'Can one, therefore, make a plea to all, from geologists to politicians, to return to reason and geography in what has been so blatantly made into an emotional and propaganda issue?' (*Presentation* No. 18, Khan, 'Sarasvati Theories and the Constraints of Geography', p. 82).

[88] *Atlas*, p. xxvii.

The Primary themes of subsection III.A, 'India of the Vedas and the Epics' are growth of Aryan knowledge of the various regions of India and the development of a distinctive Ganga Culture in the course of Aryan Expansion. In time, it overlaps with section II of the atlas, 'Prehistory', which should be referred to for an analysis of the material aspects of the culture of the period as revealed by its archaeological remains.[89]

Second, the *Atlas* is keen on projecting the Hindu–Muslim divide, notwithstanding its rejection of nomenclature of periods in terms of religious identities. While referring to the 'Arab conquest of Sind in AD 711–12, anticipating a more widespread Islamic penetration and cultural confrontation', it underlines: 'Virtually throughout the period (eighth–twelfth centuries) various Muslim groups made incursions into northwest India and, occasionally much deeper, but the somnolent Hindu kings failed to perceive the looming crisis in store for them'.[90] And still more emphatically later, in his writing about the general course of developments in the same period (Section IV), we can easily recall Huntington's 'clash of civilizations':

Socially and religiously, the differences between the Islamic tradition and that of Hinduism were many and deep. Islam, a revealed and prophetic religion, seeks through proselytism to create a world community of the faithful (*Ummah*). Within that essentially egalitarian community, a sense of cohesion and self-consciousness are fostered by emphasis not only on a single deity (Allah), but also on a single prophetic teacher (Muhammad) and a single book (Qur'an). Hinduism, however, diverges strikingly from Islam in all the foregoing particulars, being highly assimilative and far more complex. The two world views could not easily be reconciled, and neither community, it may be said, ever fully understood the other. Hence, in contrast to the host of divergent regional interests *within* South Asia, the period under review witnessed the early stages of a new and enduring confrontation on a much larger regional scale – namely, that between the indigenous, primarily Hindu civilization of India as a whole and the exogenous and rapidly expanding civilization of Islam. (Emphasis in the original)[91]

What has been said above about Habib's handling of 'the Sarasvati school' could also be understood differently. Two modes of mapping must be differentiated here. One, take an ideological position and map accordingly – Schwartzberg's efforts betray this. Two, first map the relevant data and then draw historical inference/s. Habib's maps and the accompanying texts show the application of this. This is seen not only in the case of mapping the

---

[89] Ibid., p. 161.
[90] Ibid., p. xxviii.
[91] Ibid., p. 187.

'Sarasvati', but also in defining the 'Late Vedic Zone'. After plotting the rivers, tribes and regions, and mountains, Habib is struck by a palpably obvious feature, viz., 'the Late Vedic Zone . . . no longer included any territory west of the Indus (the Balhikas and Mujavants being deemed alien people)', and he draws the following inference:

> The withdrawal on the western side is interesting; and at present, Avestan geography best explains the phenomenon. All trans-Indus lands as well as Hepta-Hendu/Sapta-Sindhavah were regarded as part of Ahura Mazda's special creations listed in the *Vendidad*. . . . The Iranianization of the area (and Zoroaster's anti-'daeva' movement) might have been responsible for the permanent linguistic (and ritualistic) alienation of this area from the Indic zone – a divorce already reflected in the post-Rigvedic evidence.[92]

Tasks Ahead

We began this essay by drawing attention to an overall apathy towards cartographic representation of processes of historical developments. There are numerous reports on the contents of school textbooks produced by various states of the Indian Union. These reports rarely reflect on the maps included in such publications. Still less attention is paid to analysing maps in books and monographs used by students and researchers at a higher level. This can be a fruitful, even challenging, enterprise that may be undertaken soon. Meanwhile, we give below extracts from reviews of two recent textbooks on early Indian history for college/university-going students:

> The maps with their coloured physical base, are pretty to look at, but are unluckily so inaccurate and often so misleading that one wonders whether it is wise to have them at all. A few examples have to suffice here. Map 2.3 ('Major Palaeolithic Sites', p. 70) shows such well known sites as Kalpi, Baghor, Belan valley, Jhansi, Lalitpur, Mandasor, Bhopal, Rohri Hills, Las Bela, Nasik, Goa and Kurnool at spots hundreds of kilometres and, in some cases, regions away, from their correct positions. Mehrgarh, the earliest agricultural site in the Indian subcontinent, is differently positioned on maps 3.2 and 3.3 (pp. 107 and 109) and both spots are wrong. On map 7.1 (p. 328), the two important sites of Ashoka's rock edicts, Shahbazgarhi and Mansehra, are wrongly plotted: the former to the south of the Kabul river and the latter to the west of the Indus. In the latter case, the reader loses the sense that Mansehra could have

---

[92] *Presentation* No. 6, Habib and Habib, 'The Historical Geography of India, 1800–800 BC', p. 89.

been on the route to Kashmir. Even Khajuraho is wrongly plotted on map 10.4 (p. 566).[93]

Amongst salient features of the book is the inclusion of as many as 15 maps. Most of these are quite illustrative and serve very useful purpose. However, some cartographic lapses/lacunae stand out. In Map 5.1 showing 'Regions and states in ancient India' Pracya (the east) is plotted in the north-east hill areas, east of the Brahmaputra, whereas in the details below, it says: '*Pracya* meant all lands between *Prayag* and the Ganga delta'. Out of 15 maps, barring those which did not require inland boundary delineation (such as Maps 5.2, 7.2 and 11.2), Map 7.1 entitled 'Post-Mauryan kingdoms' (p. 129) is the only map of the Indian sub-continent where India has been shown headless, *i.e.,* without the modern Indian state of Jammu & Kashmir. . . . At one place in the text (p. 192) there is an allusion to Pallava inscriptions providing us with the details of the use and care of earthwork tanks in the context of accent on irrigation. The cross-reference to Map 9.1 is not relevant here, insofar as the map does not say anything about such tanks. We have reservations about the plotting of 'Pratiharas' in Map 11.1 depicting 'Major Indian kingdoms of the eleventh and twelfth centuries'. Did they really exist in this period as a 'major' power? The region where they are plotted in this map is known as Madhyadesha and surrounding areas, which has rightly been described in the corresponding text as occupied by their successors such as the Gahadavalas, Kalachuris and Chandellas. The 'Kalachuris' have also perhaps been plotted considerably in the southeastern location in the same map.[94]

These should serve as examples of how mapping should *not* be undertaken.

On a more positive note, historical studies of early India, as they stand now, have been able to generate colossal data across different regions in the Indian subcontinent. Availability of numerous micro-regional histories is also sufficiently rich. It is time that such accumulated data are harnessed to produce regional historical atlases. Reference has already been made above to *An Annotated Archaeological Atlas of West Bengal* (2005). This is indeed a very specialized product and more in this genre would be very welcome. We would also like to draw the attention of the readers to a more comprehensive mapping of a very large area of the Indian subcontinent. Entitled *Historical Atlas of South India from Prehistoric Times to 1600*

[93] Irfan Habib, 'Review' of Upinder Singh's *A History of Ancient and Early Medieval India: From the Stone Age to the 12th Century, Outlook,* 8 September 2008, p. 85.

[94] Krishna Mohan Shrimali, (2007b), 'Writing India's Ancient Past', Review Article on Burgor Avari, *India: The Ancient Past: A History of the Indian Subcontinent from c. 7000 BC to AD 1200,* Routledge, 2007, *The Indian Historical Review,* Vol. XXXIV, No. 2, July 2007, pp. 187–88.

CE, its alternative nomenclature could also have been *Historical Atlas of Peninsular India.*[95]

Inspired by such early works as those of Schwartzberg, Irfan Habib (*An Atlas of the Mughal Empire*) and Y. Subbarayalu's *The Political Geography of the Chola Country*, and at the same time feeling that they do not answer the needs of the specialist, the Laboratory of Geomatics and Applied Informatics of the French Institute of Pondicherry and the Department of Epigraphy and Archaeology of the Tamil University, Thanjavur initiated a collaborative project in 2002 to explore the possibility of developing a comprehensive historical atlas of South India *in digital format*. It is intended to be accessed on the Internet through a combination of maps, photographs, illustrations, texts and Geographical Information System (GIS) functionalities, a feature absent in the earlier works mentioned. It aims to create interest among the general public on the rich historical heritage of the region, and, on the other hand, stimulate collaboration among scholars working in history and archaeology. It seeks to provide a novel and more dynamic way of presenting historical knowledge related to a geographical region by providing more concrete tools to clarify various issues of historical significance. Thus, economic activities (hunting, gathering, pastoralism, agriculture at various levels, craft production, etc.), society (migrations of people, demography, religious movements), nature of state formation (e.g., segmentary state hypothesis), movements of art styles over time and space, settlements as part of water management and land-use patterns, etc., form the broad themes of the project. In 2005–06. Subbarayalu made a presentation at the 66th session of the Indian History Congress held at Santiniketan,[96] which attempts to reconstruct the historical geography of a large political region comprising the northern part of Tamil Nadu and adjoining Andhra districts from the third to the thirteenth centuries AD. Detailed mapping of socio-political micro-regions like *nadu* and *koottum* within the study area brings out some hitherto unnoticed features of the human geography. It suggests that the appropriate sense of *koottum* is a demarcated territory which could have been occupied by a pastoral clan in the beginning.

Beginning with the mapping of a micro-region of Pudukkottai (central Tamil Nadu), the scope was gradually extended to the entire state of Tamil Nadu and of Kerala, as well as two pilot areas in Andhra Pradesh and Kar-

---

[95] I am extremely grateful to Y. Subbarayalu, the scientific supervisor of the project and its major source of inspiration, for providing me a detailed note on the vision of this atlas, its periodic reviews, amendments in the project, progress reports, etc. The details given here are based on that note.

[96] Y. Subbarayalu, 'Mapping History of Tondaimandalam (North Tamil Nadu)', *PIHC*, 2007, pp. 120–24.

nataka. With the extension in the scope, new partners were also brought in. The new collaborating institutions are: Mahatma Gandhi University (School of Social Sciences), Kottayam, Kerala; Mangalore University (Post-Graduate Department of Studies in History), Mangalore, Karnataka; and Central University of Hyderabad (Department of History), Hyderabad, Andhra Pradesh. The members of the Core Group representing the collaborating institutions are: Professors Y. Subbarayalu, K. Rajan, Aloka Parasher Sen, Rajan Gurukkal, Kesavan Veluthat, D. Balasubramanian and D. Lo Seen.

As per the report on the progress of the *Historical Atlas of South India* till April 2008 and as envisaged in the project proposal, the entire area included from the present states of Tamil Nadu and Kerala has been put on maps. In addition to this, the mapping of two pilot areas that were selected in the states of Karnataka (Shimoga district) and Andhra Pradesh (Telengana district) has been completed. As a byproduct of this unique venture, we are fortunate in having two distinctive volumes entitled *Catalogue of Archaeological Sites in Tamil Nadu* (published by Heritage India Trust, Thanjavur, 2009), authored by K. Rajan and two young research scholars, V.P. Yathees Kumar and S. Selvakumar. Though these volumes are limited to the period from palaeolithic times to the early historic period, still, nearly 2,000 archaeological sites with their exact locations and photographs of prominent finds have been plotted in 69 maps. One hopes that the atlas project will bring out similar catalogues for other states as well.

The atlas is a computer application based on CD/DVD, and has been prepared using the latest Geographical Information technology. It can be accessed using popular browsers and is available on the Internet (http://www.ifpindia.org/ecrire/upload/ digital_database/ Site/historicalatlas/). It covers a vast time-span, from prehistoric times to AD 1600, and is organized into seven major periods, three encompassing prehistoric times and four, historical times. The atlas is built on a large database made up of nearly 7,000 historical places, and about 10,000 images collected from field surveys, archaeological reports, inscriptions and literature. It is so organized as to be a powerful tool for accessing and interpreting historical information by a major theme, by a period of time, or by a geographical zone or individual site. Facilities are provided for users to navigate and interact with, by querying, the vast historical and archaeological database by time, space and theme. In addition to the conventional method of indicating geographical information by self-explanatory symbols, the text and visual material (image files) are also linked to sites wherever necessary. Since it is web-based, periodic updating of the atlas will be quite easy and has been planned so.

What has been achieved by these two regional atlases needs to be replicated in other regions. The Archaeological Survey of India had promised only a fraction of what has been envisioned and achieved by the various universities in the four southern states. Its promise has remained on paper so far. Can we expect it to deliver now?

Another area where we would like to see more work done is concerned with the preparation of a sketch-map history of early India. This needs to be done in a format that is not only handy for students, but also becomes a useful teaching aid. About ten years ago, I was invited to deliver a lecture on 'Harappan Culture, the *Rigveda* and the Problem of the Aryans' to undergraduate students at a college of the University of Delhi. I had prepared two such sketch-maps that attempted to synthesize data from the relevant literary texts (the *Rigveda* and the *Avesta*) and archaeological evidence (see Maps 1 and 2). The response from the students as well as teachers was very encouraging. Such maps need not be technically very precise.

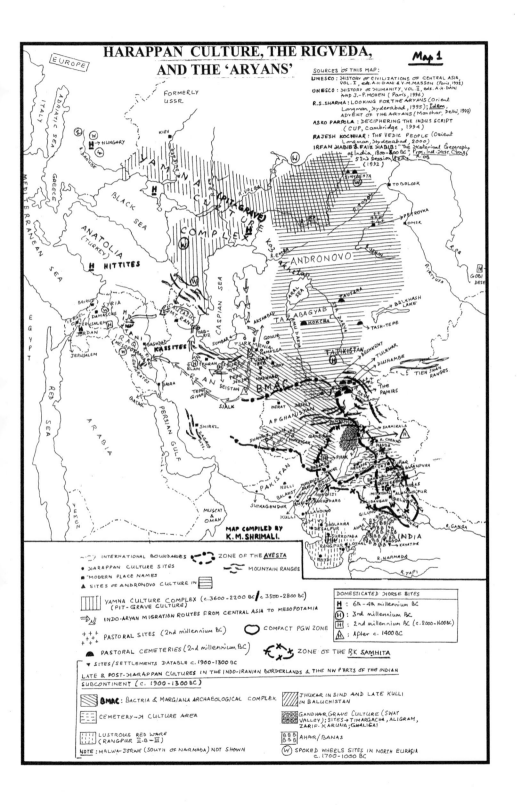

HARAPPAN CULTURE, THE RIGVEDA, AND THE 'ARYANS' — Map 1

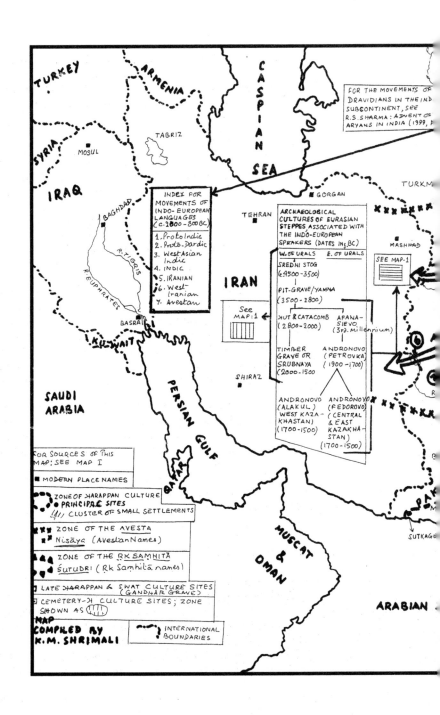

FOR THE MOVEMENTS OF
DRAVIDIANS IN THE IND
SUBCONTINENT, SEE
R.S. SHARMA: ADVENT OF
ARYANS IN INDIA (1999, P

INDEX FOR
MOVEMENTS OF
INDO-EUROPEAN
LANGUAGES
(c.2800 - 800 BC)

1. Proto Indic
2. Proto-Dardic
3. West Asian Indic
4. INDIC
5. IRANIAN
6. West Iranian
7. Avestan

ARCHAEOLOGICAL
CULTURES OF EURASIAN
STEPPES ASSOCIATED WITH
THE INDO-EUROPEAN
SPEAKERS (DATES IN c.BC)

W. OF URALS	E. OF URALS
SREDNI STOG (c.9500-3500)	
PIT-GRAVE/YAMNA (3500-2800)	
KUT & CATACOMB (2800-2000)	AFANA-SIEVO (3rd. millennium)
TIMBER GRAVE OR SRUBNAYA (2000-1500)	ANDRONOVO (PETROVKA) (1900-1700)
ANDRONOVO (ALAKUL) WEST KAZA-KHASTAN (1700-1500)	ANDRONOVO (FEDOROVO) (CENTRAL & EAST KAZAKHA-STAN) (1700-1500)

SEE MAP-1

See MAP:1

FOR SOURCES OF THIS MAP: SEE MAP I

■ MODERN PLACE NAMES

ZONE OF HARAPPAN CULTURE
● PRINCIPAL SITES
(/|/) CLUSTER OF SMALL SETTLEMENTS

ZONE OF THE AVESTA
■ Nisāya (Avestan Names)

ZONE OF THE RK SAMHITĀ
◆ Śutudrī (Rk Saṃhitā names)

■ LATE HARAPPAN & SWAT CULTURE SITES (GANDHĀR GRAVE)

■ CEMETERY-H CULTURE SITES; ZONE SHOWN AS (|||||)

MAP
COMPILED BY
K.M. SHRIMALI

INTERNATIONAL BOUNDARIES

TURKEY
ARMENIA
CASPIAN SEA
SYRIA
IRAQ
TABRIZ
MOSUL
BAGHDAD
R. TIGRIS
R. EUPHRATES
BASRA
KUWAIT
SAUDI ARABIA
PERSIAN GULF
QATAR
IRAN
TEHRAN
GORGAN
TURKM
MASHHAD
SHIRAZ
SHIRAZ
MUSCAT & OMAN
ARABIAN
SUTKAGE

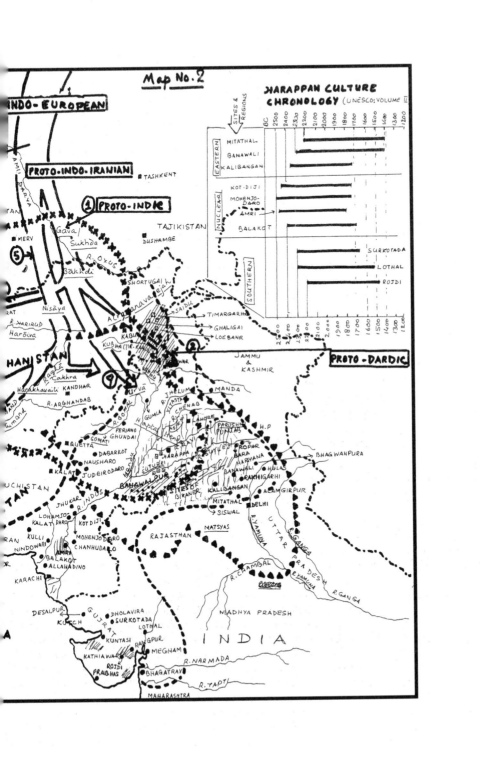

Map No. 2

HARAPPAN CULTURE CHRONOLOGY (UNESCO: VOLUME II)

SITES & REGIONS		BC	2500	2400	2300	2200	2100	2000	1900	1800	1700	1600	1500	1400	1300	1200
EASTERN	MITATHAL															
	BANAWALI															
	KALIBANGAN															
NUCLEAR	KOT-DIJI															
	MOHENJO-DARO															
	AMRI															
	BALAKOT															
SOUTHERN	SURKOTADA															
	LOTHAL															
	ROJDI															

2500 2400 2300 2200 2100 2000 1900 1800 1700 1600 1500 1400 1300 1200

INDO-EUROPEAN

PROTO-INDO-IRANIAN

① PROTO-INDIC

PROTO-DARDIC

Reflections on the Idea of Religious Tolerance

Early Nineteenth-Century Bengal

Sabyasachi Bhattacharya

Irfan Habib's writings on Emperor Akbar's policy of religious tolerance[1] are well known, and the impact of these writings can be seen in a wide area of intellectual work in our times including, most recently, Amartya Sen's work on the idea of justice.[2] As a tribute to Habib, it may not be inappropriate to recall his thoughts on the idea of religious tolerance in relation to reason in the history of Indian civilization, and to focus attention on one segment of that history. To begin with, we shall address in this paper a conceptual issue which demands attention in order that different kinds of tolerance may be distinguished. And then an attempt will be made to study a chapter in the intellectual history of Bengal in the early nineteenth century, in the light of the conceptual distinctions we propose regarding the attainment of a rational attitude of tolerance.

Tolerance in the present context evidently means willingness to be accommodative in the domain of religious belief systems and practices. This is usually translated into the quotidian language of social relationship as tolerance towards religious communities other than one's own. I shall argue in this paper that, both in relation to India's past as well as socio-political practices today (when obscurantist elements in India oppose and threaten tolerance), it is important to recognize that reason is only *one* of the sources of tolerance.[3] Not all votaries of tolerance are the same; they may arrive at the same position from diverse starting points and they may do so by routes

---

[1] Irfan Habib (ed.), *Akbar and His India*, Delhi: Oxford University Press, 1997.

[2] Amartya Sen, *The Idea of Justice*, London: Prenguin-Allen Lane, 2009, pp. 36–39.

[3] Irfan Habib, in his recent major work, *Medieval India: The Study of a Civilization* (New Delhi: National Book Trust, 2008), pp. 117, 183–85, makes a perspicacious distinction between religious toleration on 'empirical grounds' (e.g., vis-a-vis 'forming an ethnically and religiously composite nobility') and tolerance born of conviction, after the *ibadat-khana* discussions that 'all religions were to be tolerated, but did not need to be followed'. He appears to make a further distinction between the 'policy of equal treatment of all religions (as distinct from a simple policy of tolerance)'.

which are quite dissimilar. It will be neither necessary nor possible to give here illustrative historical examples, but the essence of the distinctions we make can be stated as follows.

Broadly speaking, it may be said that tolerance has three sources. First, *theistic universalism* allows one to regard all religions as equally valid for the true believers in them. Many variants of this idea have been propagated (at least from the times of the medieval Bhakti and Sufi saints onwards) right up to Mahatma Gandhi. The social effect has been laudable; it has helped maintain inter-community harmony. But this tolerance is not claimed to be founded on reason. Second, there are also instances of what may be called tolerance of *political equidistance*. That is to say, a parity between different social groups or religious communities is established by a display of equal treatment for all. Thus, for instance, in rituals of the Indian Republic or public shows of the major players in the politics of the day, it has become customary to pay homage to all religions – through recitation of the *Gita*, the Quran, the Bible, etc. A third source of tolerance is a *rationalist world outlook*. This is the secularism born of sceptical questioning of religious beliefs and practices. A rationalist may accord equal status to all belief and practices which are not founded on reason in his judgement.

These three types of tolerance are located in three different domains: theistic universalism in the domain of faith, the policy of equidistance in the domain of power, rationalist secularism in the domain of the critical interpretative faculty of the human mind. The enemies of these three types of tolerance are again different: orthodoxy and theistic monism oppose the first, communal particularism and exclusivism oppose the second, antirational or purportedly extra-rational obscurantism oppose the third. In real life these oppositions, needless to say, are interlinked, because in real life faith and power relationships, and ideational orientations are interlinked. Contradictions in any sphere, faith or power or reasoning, become multidimensional and spill over into other spheres.

In this paper, we examine the writings of the group known as Young Bengal of the late 1820s and 1830s, early participants in the so-called Bengal Renaissance. It may be argued that this was historically significant because it was a relatively rare instance of the third of the abovementioned categories, the rationalist approach. Influenced by David Hume's empiricism (acquired through the teachings of H.L.V. Derozio in Hindu College), a generation of educated youth questioned some of the hitherto unquestioned basic premises of Hindu religious and social practices. Evidence of this is available in the forums of the Young Bengal intellectuals, proceedings of the Society for the Acquisition of General Knowledge (1838–43) and some contemporary journals.

Needless to say, in Rammohan Roy's writings we see the seed of a new rationalism. At the same time, that was a rationalism which was different from the rationalism of Young Bengal. Roy claimed affiliation between his discourse of reason and the discourse of *yukti* (reason) in the Sanskritic tradition. A favourite quotation of his was a *shloka* from the *Brihaspati Smriti* (XII–5): 'Let no one found conclusions on the mere words of the Shastras. From investigations without reasons, religious virtue is lost.' This was Roy's translation, and in the words '*Yukti-heena vicharatu dharma-hani prajayate*', rang loud and clear the preference of reason over the authority of the Shastras. At the same time, we must remember that his rationalism was qualified in two ways. First, he often appealed to the *shastric* authority, e.g., in his famous campaign against the custom of *sati*. This dichotomy or inconsistency might have been due to the need Roy felt to convince his orthodox opponents and to debate the premises on the basis of the sources they accepted. Roy's rationalism was qualified by another factor: he remained a confirmed theist and indeed the founder of a religious system popularly known as the faith of the Brahma Samaj. He did not, unlike the Young Bengal intellectuals, pursue his rationalism to the ultimate point of atheistic challenge of religion itself.[4]

Soon after Roy's death, there developed in Bengal a more radical rationalism which questioned religious beliefs and *shastriya* (*shastric*) authority in a fundamental way. The Young Bengal school of thought, taught in Hindu College by a dark-hued Eurasian or Anglo-Indian, Henry Derozio (1809–31) by name, pushed rationalism well beyond the limits Rammohan had respected.

'Do you believe in God?', the famous scholar H.H. Wilson wrote to Derozio on 25 April 1831. Atheism, he said, was one of the 'rumoured charges against you' and that was one of the grounds on which Derozio was dismissed by the Managing Committee of Hindu College of which Wilson was a member.[5] Derozio did not declare his personal beliefs in his carefully drafted answer of 26 April 1831: 'I have never denied the existence of God in the hearing of any human being . . . but I am neither afraid, nor ashamed to confess having stated the doubts of philosophers. . . . Is it forbidden anywhere to argue upon such a question?'[6] Derozio also admitted that he used to teach his students the essence of David Hume's views on theism. The Scottish philosopher Hume had admirers and followers in India, among them one David Drummond. The latter was a Scottish free-thinker who

---

[4] Vide Satyendranath Pal, *The Rise of Radicalism in Bengal in the Nineteenth Century*, Kolkata: Manisha Granthalaya, 1991, p. 145.
[5] Thomas Edwardes, *Henry Derozio: The Eurasian Poet, Teacher and Journalist*, Calcutta: W. Newman, 1884, p. 62.
[6] Ibid., pp. 63–68.

had among the students in his school, Henry Derozio.[7] Later, Derozio made Hume's writings a major text in his teaching at Hindu College, much to the alarm of the conservative gentry who sent their sons to that college for just enough 'English education' to get government jobs. Not only did they raise in the Managing Committee the 'rumoured charge' of Derozio propagating atheism, but the English authorities also looked askance at the rationalism he instilled in the minds of his students. They were equally alarmed to read a short-lived journal, *Parthenon*, published by Derozio. The leading journal of the British in India, *John Bull*, said: 'give these native children but an inch of free discussion, they will soon take an ell'.[8] Such were the reasons why Derozio was dismissed from Hindu College and spent his last days in penury, eking out a living from journalism.

As regards the Hindu College products, *John Bull* proved to be right. Within the college they had little opportunity to pursue free thinking but in 1838 they set up the Society for the Acquisition of General Knowledge (SAGK hereafter) which had about 150 members, mainly alumni of that college. The papers presented in the 1840s at the meetings of that Society have survived since a few copies were printed between 1841 and 1843 in three volumes.[9]

The early alumni of Hindu College, taught by Derozio, are usually known as Young Bengal. They have had a bad press. Their outrageous conduct in defying social conventions was condemned both in their times and in our times. Barring some exceptions like Susobhan Chandra Sarkar (*Notes on the Bengal Renaissance*), they have been condemned for other reasons as well, for example, on the ground that they represented just the upper crust of the colonial bourgeoisie. It will be a waste of time to address and refute such simpleminded and mechanical application of supposedly Marxist theory. For the present, we shall limit ourselves only to the theme of reason and tolerance in the writings of the leading lights of Young Bengal, in the proceedings of the SAGK.

In the writings of the members of SAGK, four major trends of argumentation emerge. First, reason is posited against the authority of the Shastras. For instance, Mahesh Chandra Deb, Derozio's pupil and eventually an outcast from Hindu society due to his apostasy, wrote in January 1839 ('The Condition of Hindu Women') denouncing the Shastras: 'those religious codes

---

[7] Ibid., p. 4.

[8] *John Bull*, excerpted in *Asiatic Journal*, September 1830, p. 5, cited in Gautam Chattopadhyay, *Awakening of Bengal in Early Nineteenth Century: Selected Documents*, Calcutta: Progressive Publishers, 1965, p. XXII.

[9] Ibid., p. XXVIII.

of our countrymen which render their wives literally slaves in their body and mind'.[10] Or again, Pearey Chand Mitter (1814–1883), author of the first novel in the Bengali language and a founder of the British India Society, wrote in September 1839 ('State of Hindoostan under the Hindoos') of 'the gloom of superstition in which the Hindoo mind was enveloped, the frequent and reiterated scowlings of the Priestcraft on every freedom of enquiry and freedom of thought'.[11] Or consider what Krishna Mohan Banerjee, one of the few students of Hindu College who became a Christian convert, wrote ('Reforms, Civil and Social'):

> Civilization meets with a dead stop when it is not allowed to make any further progress than antiquity assigned to it. . . . It is therefore a point of peculiar importance to be constantly reminded of our natural right to think and act for ourselves and to study non-submission to any system which we may have discovered to be pernicious to the interests of humanity'.[12]

The second major theme was attack on contemporary social practices. Uday Chandra Adhya, who was, judging by his name, a member of the lower caste of gold merchants, wrote against the casteism endorsed by the British government in refusing admission of all except high-caste Hindus to study Sanskrit and the Shastras in Sanskrit College.[13] Mahesh Chandra Deb condemned, in his essay of January 1839, the 'Status Hindu Society Had Assigned to Women'.[14] K.M. Banerjee likewise said: 'It is impossible that a nation can take rapid strides to civilization while half the members that compose it are sunk in ignorance and degradation'.[15] A prejudice commonly observed in these writings about women was that it was contact with Muslims that brought about the concept of *zenana*, i.e. the incarceration of women in the home. But this notion was contested by some who found evidence of such incarceration in pre-Muslim texts (K.M. Banerjee belonged to that school of thought), while others attributed it to 'partly imitation [of the Muslim custom] and partly fear' in parts of India under 'Muslim rule'.[16] K.M. Banerjee, one of the Derozians who converted to Christianity, perhaps felt more free than others to speak critically of the Hindu social practices. For instance: 'What Brahmin can pretend that he strictly observes those duties the neglect whereof would, according to the Shastras, entail a forfei-

---

[10] Ibid., p. 97.
[11] Ibid., p. 156.
[12] Ibid., p. 185.
[13] Ibid., p. 29.
[14] Ibid., pp. 88–105.
[15] Ibid., p. 190.
[16] Pearey Chand Mitter believed so on the evidence of Mountstuart Elphinstone's *History of India*; ibid., p. 286.

ture of his dignity? Consider the bare-faced audacity of those who, while infringing the tenets of the Shastras themselves, dare to raise their voice against us'.[17] He was also the most forthright, being of high brahman lineage himself, against casteism. He roundly condemned the 'universally acknowledged caprice that has, without any countenance from the Vedas and Puranas, caused myriads of arbitrary division amongst us'. And again, of the institution of child marriage: 'The father who gives away his daughter without waiting until the dawn of reason in her, and the husband who marries her, are both culpable'.[18] Thus the Young Bengal intellectuals anticipated the issues to be taken up by social reformers from Vidyasagar onwards decades later, arguing on the basis of rational ethics.

Thirdly, another aspect of the new rationalism of early nineteenth-century Bengal was that is led to a critique of inequality – not only between castes or genders, as pointed out above, but also racial inequality. This tendency of thought no doubt owed a lot to David Hume, the American Tom Paine's (1737–1809) works like *The Age of Reason* (1793) and *The Rights of Man* (1791), or Edmund Burke's (1729–1797) impeachment speeches on misgovernment in India under Warren Hastings. We have contemporary evidence that these writings were in circulation at the time of the rise of the Young Bengal school of thought. There was, no doubt, an element of ambiguity in their attitude to the British who brought to India some of the ideas that inspired them. But a part of that ambiguity was a critical attitude to the inherent inequality of the white and black races in British India. Thus K.M. Banerjee, referring to an early proto-political association of 'enlightened' natives wrote:

> The British India Society may watch over your political interests and attempt to introduce a more liberal policy whereby the blacks are to be respected as much as the whites. . . . You must yourselves set to the task, or the work will never be finished. . . . Foreigners may at best aid and encourage you . . . [but] before you act your own parts, you cannot with good grace enforce your claims upon the sympathy of those that are abroad.[19]

There are few such direct assertions of racial equality as a principle in the proceedings of the SAGK, but that was a sub-text of the dramatic confrontation between critics of British rule in India and its defenders which was enacted in February 1843 when a member, Dukhina Ranjana Mookerjee, launched upon such a critique. The *Bengal Hurkaroo* reported that the speaker said that the British Indian government's 'courts [of law] were notoriously

---

[17] Ibid., p. 192.
[18] Ibid., p. 189.
[19] Ibid., p. 194.

and shamelessly corrupt' and a byword of 'instruments of oppression among the wealthy', that there was no 'effective check upon the abuse of power by the Company's Civil Servants', that the police system was one 'in which natives had least confidence', that British officers were unapproachable to the natives, and that 'the motives which had influenced the British in coming to these shores' were commercial. When he was about to elaborate the last point Captain D.L. Richardson, Principal of Hindu College, interrupted him to say that the speaker's views were biased, and that Richardson 'must close the door against all such meetings' since they encouraged 'treason'. To the credit of the 150 members present, they dismissed Richardson's objection; the speaker was allowed to continue his speech and at the end of the day Richardson, abashed, retracted his reprimand.[20] However that put to an end the use of Sanskrit College (run by the government) for SAGK meetings. This, however, is a rather rare instance of a confrontation, since the claim to equality was not so much in the political domain as yet in the 1830s and 40s.

Finally, the fourth characteristic of these Young Bengal writings was again a product of the new rationalism: their emphasis on science. For instance, in the year ending May 1841, of the eight papers read at SAGK, two were on physiology, one on physics and two were topographical accounts of districts where the authors lived. The same group brought out a biological science journal called *Bignan Sar Sangraha* (*Gleanings from Science*) in 1833, but we know of the journal only from reviews in other contemporary journals upon its publication.[21] Some of those who wrote papers at the SAGK on Indian history, for example, Pearey Chand Mitter, highlighted the scientific achievements recorded in Sanskrit texts on mathematics and astronomy. Russick Krishna Mullick (1810–1858), one of the students of Hindu College, became notorious in the Hindu community for his refusal to take the oath in a court of law by touching the 'holy waters of the Ganges'. When the British judge asked him to take the oath he said, in defence of scientific principles, 'I do not believe in the sacredness of the Ganges' – thus causing a minor crisis in the British judicial administration.[22] It was but a short step from Mullick to Akshay Kumar Datta (1820–1886) who earned greater notoriety a little later, for having propounded the following rationalist equation:

Prayer + Labour = Production
Labour = Production
Therefore, Prayer = Zero.

---

[20] Ibid., pp. 389–99.
[21] Ibid., pp. XXV, XXXI.
[22] Sibnath Shastri, *Ramtanu Labiri o Tatkalin Bargasamaj* (in Bangla), reprint, Calcutta, 1955, p. 150.

Finally, a question that needs to be raised is whether the rationalist thought trends outlined above were connected in any manner with social change in Bengal. Many historians, from Susobhan Sarkar (*Notes on the Bengal Renaissance*) onwards, have pondered over the question why the spirit of rationalism ran out of steam by the end of the nineteenth century. The triumph of *bhadralok* conservatism over Young Bengal is beyond question, although traces of the spirit of early rationalism were preserved in Akshay Kumar Datta and a few others. The theist universalism of Ramakrishna Paramahansa, or the enlightened nationalists' attempts to create a 'tolerance of equidistance' notwithstanding, the strength of Hindu orthodoxy carried all before it by the end of the nineteenth century. What accounts for the difference between the early nineteenth century, the era of Young Bengal, and the end of that century?

One answer to this puzzle, it may be suggested, is that in the decades immediately following, social conditions nurtured a kind of radicalism due to opportunities for social mobility. First, it is generally known that the first few decades after the establishment of the Permanent Settlement in 1793 were decades allowing for considerable social mobility due to the fall of the old zamindars who failed the test of the 'Sunset Law', i.e. the law requiring delivery of revenue before sunset on an appointed date. The composition of the landed gentry class altered, accommodating many new entrants as small zamindars and *taluqdar*s. Secondly, till the middle of the nineteenth century there was still some space for Indian merchants in the business world and hence a scope for social mobility, specially for the lower business castes. Some of the Hindu College boys were businessmen. Thirdly, as it happens in the process of colonial urbanization, waves of migrants from stagnating rural society came to rapidly urbanizing Calcutta and its environs, and that also promoted a kind of freedom from traditional social bonds.

These features of early nineteenth-century Bengal contrast sharply with the end of the century. By the 1880s and 1890s, a century after 1793, the zamindari system acquired a stability; the landlords' hegemony possibly engendered a conservative world outlook, the reverse of Young Bengal's spirit of rebellion which had occurred in a climate of rapid social change and turbulence. The path of business entrepreneurship was closed to natives by the end of the nineteenth century, and hence again acted as a constraint on social mobility. Thus, arguably, the transformation of the social order in Bengal and the transition from radical thinking to conservatism may not be unconnected. To the extent tolerance survived, it was not tolerance of reason, but the tolerance characteristic of traditional theistic universalism and the tolerance originating in the political calculus of equidistance.

A Marxist Medievalist in India's Stone Ages[1]

Vishwa Mohan Jha

In this essay I shall seek to discuss the more important of the academic and professional issues raised by Irfan Habib's books on ancient India,[2] published as a part of *A People's History of India*, a series sponsored by the Aligarh Historians Society. The series as a whole (and not just the ancient India part of it) is committed, in the Society's words, to 'the cause of promoting the scientific method in history, and resisting communal and chauvinistic interpretations'. Any discussion of this important commitment must be based on the series as a whole and in tandem with a range of themes of a very different order than those being covered here.

Irfan Habib (who is also the General Editor of the series) has so far authored/co-authored four books on ancient India in the series: *Prehistory* (2001); *The Indus Civilization* (2002); *The Vedic Age* (co-authored with the late Vijay Kumar Thakur, 2003); and *Mauryan India* (co-authored with Vivekanand Jha, 2004). Here we focus on the first three works, on the prehistory and protohistory of India; *Mauryan India* would be better appreciated, in our opinion, in the light of the volume in the series by K.M. Shrimali, *The Age of Iron and the Religious Revolution, c. 700–c. 350 BC* (2007), that comes between it and *The Vedic Age*.

These are no school textbooks, as is thought by Martha Nussbaum in an important study she did soon after they came out. A number of circumstances appear to have contributed to this impression. The books came at a time when the assault on history by the ruling National Democratic Alliance (led by the Bharatiya Janata Party) was in full swing in India. The 'old NCERT textbooks' of history (authored individually by Romila Thapar, R.S. Sharma and others, and published by the autonomous government organization, National Council of Educational Research and Training [NCERT]) had been removed after a slanderous attack, and replaced by 'new NCERT text-

---

[1] This essay owes its birth to the persuasion and inexhaustible patience of Rajendra Prasad, Managing Editor, *Social Scientist*.

[2] India will be used interchangeably with South Asia in this essay.

books' (authored individually by Makkhan Lal, Minakshi Jain and others). A textbook controversy followed that was spearheaded on the secularist side with distinction by Habib and his collaborators, which Nussbaum naturally could not afford to miss. The *People's History of India* project, with its commitment to scientific as against communal and chauvinistic history, had received generous funding from the Madhya Pradesh State Textbook Corporation which is generally concerned with school-level textbooks alone. It is therefore understandable why Nussbaum viewed Habib's books as school textbooks – 'a commercially published set of alternative textbooks'; an alternative, that is, to the 'new NCERT textbooks' that replaced the 'old NCERT textbooks'. The slimness of Habib's volumes (a mere 88 pages for *Prehistory*, for example) – which has tended to create the impression that these books, intended to be 'popular', provide less than adequate coverage for college- and university-level studies – may also have strengthened the view that they were brought out as rivals to the 'new' school textbooks.[3]

In Nussbaum's analysis, while the 'new' textbooks, like Makkhan Lal's, are no patch on Habib's textbooks, the latter, 'pedagogically, too . . . may be superior to the old NCERT books, which, by all accounts, were heavy and uninviting'.[4] However, in neither length nor level of treatment of the

---

[3] It is important to keep in mind the intended meanings of 'new' and 'old', because by the time Nussbaum's study was published, the swing in the political pendulum had led to yet another replacement of the 'new' books by newer ones that shared Habib's opposition to communal history, though not his particular vision of scientific history.

[4] Martha C. Nussbaum, *The Clash Within: Democracy, Religious Violence, and India's Future,* Cambridge, Mass.: The Belknap Press of Harvard University Press, 2007, pp. 271–72, 289. As Habib's books are so far from being school-level textbooks, Nussbaum's judgment raises interesting questions about the way the argument of pedagogy has been used in the textbook controversy in India, across ideologies. Her charge that the old NCERT books were dull and boring seems to feed on a curious bag of propaganda. The issue of writing 'interesting' textbooks – a pedagogical question – was raised only for the history textbooks, just as these books alone were targeted for hurting the sentiments of various communities. Books on other subjects were never subjected to this type of questioning. In other words, the same history books were sometimes said to be so dull that no one wanted to read them, and at other times so provocative that they could not be tolerated for a moment: dull books would normally pass unnoticed, unprovoked. Unlike the vociferous attack of the sentiments-getting-hurt issue, the other was mainly a whisper campaign (though it is possible to provide references). It was heartily fanned by a rival professional spirit on the hither side of the ideological divide as well. Thus one sees why a Teesta Setalvad, in a meeting organized against the 'new' books, mentioned the need for removing or reforming the 'old' ones on the ground that they were heavy reading, or why Nussbaum too underlined the point (though it was not very pertinent to her argument). It is doubtful, or at least debatable, that in readability or accuracy, pedagogically or otherwise, the old books have till date been superseded (for all the advice solicited of me and that I had to offer in the production of the newest textbooks!). There has no doubt been a great improvement in the quality of illustrations, but this is mostly due to technological changes in book production; quite rotten books these days would score in this respect over excellent ones of yesteryears. Plainly, advances in knowledge due to progress of research should have been reason enough to go in for a revision or

subject are the *People's History* books anywhere near the school textbooks.
They have been composed with a 'commitment to conciseness', so much so
that the author felt required to offer an explanation when, as compared to
88 pages of *Prehistory*, he offered a bulkier second volume of 124 pages![5]
This conciseness, it is seen, is accomplished, apart from through a certain
economy of style, by avoiding surveys of historiography and descriptions of
individual sites (instead of referring to tools and artefacts at every important, individual site of an archaeological culture, you save a lot of space if
you describe them at one place for the culture in general). To judge from the
explanations offered,[6] it was apparently for the same necessity of conciseness that the bibliographical notes at the end of chapters had 'necessarily to
be very selective'. Yet, for the time-span covered by them, the three volumes,
with a combined total of 320 pages, compare not too unfavourably with
the standard monographs in the field over the last quarter century or so.[7]
And, as we shall see, Habib says it differently from any of the authors he has
consulted. *Prehistory*, *The Indus Civilization* and *The Vedic Age* invite comparisons of a very different order than with the NCERT textbooks.

Habib points to students and general readers as the intended readership.
There is every reason – one being the space and attention given to bibliographical notes – to think that by the former he does not mean school- but
college-level (undergraduate and postgraduate) students. And while the
People's History series aims to be comprehensible at the popular level, it
seeks to be equally satisfying and stimulating to the specialist. Surely, a
specialist reader is being addressed when Habib offers the following explanation for his preferred spellings of 'Rigveda' and 'Ashoka':

---

replacement of the older books. Going by the rave reviews of Romila Thapar's *Early India* by
younger scholars from 2003 onwards, the decision in the immediately following years not to
request her to write a new book for NCERT, i.e. to replace her by new authors, could hardly
have been prompted by doubts about her ability to meet the needs occasioned by 'shifts in
thinking about history' (Neeladri Bhattacharya, 'Teaching History in Schools: The Politics
of Textbooks in India', *History Workshop Journal*, Vol. 67, No. 1, 2009, p. 105) that her
previous NCERT textbooks, among others, did not reflect, and which became the basis for
writing new textbooks. If the scholarly reception of *Early India* is any criterion – and that
should have been among the foremost for the decision-makers – Thapar was the fittest
person around for the task.

[5] Irfan Habib, *The Indus Civilization, A People's History of India 2*, New Delhi: Tulika Books,
in association with Aligarh Historians Society, 2002, p. ix.

[6] Irfan Habib, *Prehistory, A People's History of India 1*, New Delhi: Tulika Books, in association with Aligarh Historians Society, 2002, p. ix; Habib, *The Indus Civilization*, p. x.

[7] Puzzlingly, Nussbaum (*The Clash Within*, p. 272) also complains that the books 'have few
illustrations (presumably because of economic factors)'. Actually, with a total of 65 figures
(23+39+3), aided by 12 tables (4+5+3) and 23 maps (8+9+6), the books teem with them,
though one may complain about the poor quality of the photographs.

The quoted words are still too few to merit troubling the reader with separate explanations of the standard systems of transcription and transliteration. Since without such explanations, diacritical marks as well as the additional characters used by historical linguists drawing on IPA might not be understood, I have employed the English letters closest to the original sounds. I have, therefore, spelt 'Rigveda', not 'Ṛgveda'; and 'Ashoka', not 'Aśoka'.[8]

The general reader and the student could hardly have demanded this kind of explanation, which they may indeed have to struggle to understand! (It is a rare occasion when a technical term [IPA: International Phonetic Alphabet] has been left without explanation.)

The same specialist reader is invoked yet again in the Preface to *The Vedic Age*: 'we have followed the practice of Indologists in giving short references to the number of chapters and clauses in the texts [e.g. *Rigveda*, VII, 33 on p. 24, and *Atharvaveda*, III, 13] . . . where we felt the reader might like to have the assurance of authority in more specific terms'.[9] To the same end, Sanskrit words used in the sources are frequently referred to: e.g., *agi* for chariot-racing and *aksha* for dicing.[10] It also strikes one here that Habib and Thakur have not based their work only on the translations they refer to in the bibliography, but have regularly consulted the original works, if only to locate and interpret the key Sanskrit terms.

Let a Hundred Flowers Bloom: In Praise of Secondary Research and Tertiary Reflection

Irfan Habib's authorship raises crucial issues for the discipline of history, of the nature and implications of the boundaries created by specialization, as well as of the importance that is to be attached to a continuously growing body of secondary and tertiary works. How competent is Habib, a medievalist, to undertake a history of early, or for that matter modern, India? The question was implicit in one review of *Prehistory* by an archaeologist, which was above all an assessment of an outsider on her home turf.[11] This is a question that is of wider significance since we are wont to take shelter behind our professionalism and to be dismissive of an outsider's criticism precisely on the ground that he/she is an outsider, not a professional historian.

---

[8] Habib, *The Indus Civilization*, pp. ix–x.

[9] Irfan Habib and Vijay Kumar Thakur, *The Vedic Age, A People's History of India 3*, New Delhi: Tulika Books, in association with Aligarh Historians Society, 2003, p. vii.

[10] Ibid., p. 27.

[11] Nayanjot Lahiri, 'Short and Selective', Review of *Prehistory*, in *The Hindu*, Sunday, 4 November 2001.

The historian's primary sources are so varied and/or voluminous that specialization is a technical must for primary research. However, this is not the sense in which we are historians of ancient, medieval or modern India: we are so because the volume of information contained in secondary works is too vast for any one individual to master all of it. It is knowledge of secondary sources, rather than expertise in primary research, that makes one an expert in one rather than another branch of Indian history. I am a specialist in ancient Indian history because I have spent more time studying the secondary works on ancient than on medieval or modern Indian history.

The distinction between the two senses of specialization in history is especially difficult to remember for ancient and medieval Indian histories, given the limited range of primary sources for them: discussions of Mauryan India even at the school level bring in primary sources (like Ashoka's inscriptions or Megasthenes' account) on a scale that is unimaginable for, say, a discussion of Lord Curzon's India even at the postgraduate level. Yet it is easy to see that no one is a specialist in ancient Indian history from a primary research viewpoint: one is so only for a fragment of it. For the rest, each depends on the primary research of others. The dependence must grow through the progress of research, a good example of which is the manner in which archaeologists, in order to interpret the data unearthed by them, have come to depend on an array of experts from different fields.

All this calls for a better appreciation of the importance of secondary sources, *and of the tertiary research based on them (for this is what the knowledge of specialists in the second sense mostly amounts to)*, especially in ancient and medieval India studies where, for instance, it is probably easier to consult the *Rigveda* than to master the generations of scholarly efforts expended on it, and end up arguing for something that has already been proved to be right or wrong. Even eminent professional minds regularly fall for it. Thus B.B. Lal has argued recently, by producing references from the *Rigveda* as well as citing such formidable authorities as A.A. Macdonell and A.B. Keith[12], that the *pur* in the *Rigveda* means a town or a city.[13] One would not know, simply by looking at Lal's arguments, that his references as well as other references bearing on the issue have been the subject of a book-length study by Wilhelm Rau,[14] who has established that the term *pur* in the *Rigveda* does not refer to any urban centre.

---

[12] A.A. Macdonell and A.B. Keith, *Vedic Index of Names and Places*, Vol. II, London: John Murray, published for the Government of India, 1912.

[13] B.B. Lal, 'Aryan Invasion of India: Perpetuation of a Myth', in Edwin F. Bryant and Laurie L. Patton (eds), *The Indo-Aryan Controversy: Evidence and Inference in Indian History*, New York: Routledge, 2005, pp. 66 ff.

[14] Wilhelm Rau, *The Meaning of 'Pur' in Vedic Literature*, Abhandlungen der Marburger Gelehrten Gesellschaft, Munich: W. Fink, 1976.

Consultation of primary sources does not absolve an ancient or medieval historian from the *equally important* obligation of consulting secondary sources: a lapse on either count can be equally fatal. This needs to be said because an impression to the contrary is common among ancient Indian historians, at times with a palpable disdain for works based on secondary sources: if I know my *Arthashāstra* firsthand, I can afford not to bother too much about the others who have studied it, and I would always know better about ancient India from this text than someone who knows it only through others' studies in it.

In fact continuous attention to secondary works prevents us from becoming like José Arcadio Buendía, the character in Marquez's *One Hundred Years of Solitude* who nearly killed himself only to rediscover that 'the earth is round, like an orange'! Not everyone would of course be as gifted as José Arcadio, and may labour only to conclude that the earth is flat. In Lal's case, as he was probably aware of the arguments of Rau but would not address them, the explanation for the neglect would be ideological; but for a great majority of cases, it is a matter purely of (lack of) the required intellectual endeavour. Rau's principal claim to fame comes from the book he published in 1957 (*Staat und Gesellschaft im alten Indien nach den Brahmana-en-Texten dargestellt*), a year after D.D. Kosambi published his *Introduction to the Study of Indian History*. Rau's study of Later Vedic texts altered a number of received ideas and made new discoveries about Later Vedic India, a number of which were incorporated, with due acknowledgement, by Kosambi in the revised edition of his *Introduction*, published posthumously in 1975.[15] All this has generally been missed while the Later Vedic texts have been endlessly revisited by researchers without any one of them stumbling upon Rau's conclusions independently:[16] we have accordingly paid a not-inconsiderable price for our neglect of Rau and Kosambi.

All those who undertake sincere studies of secondary works in a field must be taken very seriously by those doing primary research in that area, for the former may have something to offer, by way of a new idea or a piece

---

[15] D.D. Kosambi, *An Introduction to the Study of Indian History*, revised second edition, Bombay: Popular Prakashan, 1975, pp. 106, 140–41. The revision has been completely missed in the commentaries on Kosambi's life and work. All the probable reasons for this cannot be discussed here but in a couple of cases at least, a basic reason is the inability to tell a reprint from a revised second edition. This, as I hope to show in a separate study, is by no means the most shocking of the treatment that Kosambi has been meted by a generally – but *only generally* – admiring posterity.

[16] Rau's work (*Staat und Gesellschaft im alten Indien nach den Brahmana-Texten dargestellt*, Wiesbaden, 1957) was referred to for its radical and new interpretation of *grāma* and *saṃgrāma* by Kulke (Hermann Kulke and Dietmar Rothermund, *A History of India*, Delhi: Manohar, 1986, pp. 39 ff) who has subsequently returned to it for a few more details.

of information, that did not occur to or was missed by the latter. And this could be a piece of information from a book everyone is consulting all the time, such as Macdonell and Keith's *Vedic Index of Names and Subjects*. Our examples this time are Kosambi and Habib. Kosambi,[17] who studied the *Rigveda* so insightfully, somehow could not trace more than one reference to *vaṇij* in it: the *Vedic Index* provides two in the entry under the name.[18] Habib, delving into original research, produces two quotes from the *Rigveda* to establish that '*bali* was thus an imposed tribute, and not voluntary offerings, as is so frequently asserted in textbooks'.[19] Actually, as the following quote from the *Vedic Index* under the entry '*bali*' shows, what Habib rejects through his own research as mere textbook wisdom turns out to have quite a respectable ancestry, just as Habib's own finding is anticipated by an equally time-hallowed scholarly understanding that was represented, among others, by Kosambi,[20] who calls it 'a *bali* tax, special prerogative of the chief . . . the first of all regular internal taxes':

> Bali occurs several times in the Rigveda and often later in the sense of tribute to a king or offering to a god. Zimmer thinks that the offerings were in both cases voluntary. He compares the notices of the Germans in Tacitus, where the kings of the tribes are said to receive gifts in kind as presents, but not a regular tribute. There seems to be no ground whatever for this view.[21]

Habib's interest in ancient Indian history pre-dates the *People's History* series. Quite early he tried to rekindle interest in the history of technology in early India, to which our response has varied from keen engagement to half-hearted attention to sheer indifference.[22] For some time, again, he has been

---

[17] Kosambi, *Introduction to the Study of Indian History*, 1975 edition, p. 91.

[18] Macdonnell and Keith, *Vedic Index*, p. 237.

[19] Habib and Thakur, *The Vedic Age*, pp. 14–15.

[20] D.D. Kosambi, *An Introduction to the Study of Indian History*, first edition, Bombay: Popular Book Depot, 1956, p. 94.

[21] Macdonnell and Keith, *Vedic Index*, p. 62.

[22] Vishwa Mohan Jha, 'Economy of North India', *A Comprehensive History of India*, Vol. IV, Pt. 2, New Delhi: Comprehensive History of India Society and Manohar, 2008, Chapter XXVI(c), pp. 280–81, 282–84. B.D. Chattopadhyaya, in immediate response to Habib's argument about the water-wheel that came to be known as *rahat*, made a significant contribution (ibid., pp. 280–81 and n. 118). Unfortunately, most of the technical points seem to be generally lost on ancient Indian historians. To take one example, the gear, by converting horizontal motion into a vertical one, made it possible to use animal power in operating the wheel and thus transformed the ancient water-wheel into the medieval Persian wheel. We imagine, however, that the function of the gear was simply 'to ensure a continuous flow of water', so that, in view of the references in early Indian sources to continuous flow of water from the wheel, early India is believed to have had 'something similar to the Persian wheel, if not exactly identical to it' (Upinder Singh, *A History of Ancient and Early Medieval India from the Stone Age to the 12th Century*, Delhi: Pearson Longman, 2009, p. 583). Likewise, Dilip Chakrabarti (*The Oxford Companion to Indian Archaeology*, New Delhi: Oxford

working on an atlas of ancient Indian history. From the parts of it that have been published in the form of articles in *Proceedings of the Indian History Congress*, it is evident that this work is based on a serious study of both primary and secondary sources. Habib, thus, has always had a good claim to being regarded a specialist in ancient Indian history.

It is easy to see that Irfan Habib has not simply read fat syntheses to re-gurgitate a slimmer version of them. He ranges widely to select his data, rethinks them to produce his own synthesis, and does not hesitate in the process to consult the original sources to offer his own original interpreta-tion of them. I for one, who specialized in ancient Indian history but can claim no specialist knowledge (in the first sense) for the period being cover-ed here, stand updated on more than one count, having learnt things I did not notice in other surveys of the periods covered by these three works. For instance, relying on James Mellaart's contribution in the *History of Humani-ty*,[23] I had been teaching my students that 'calibration has not yet proceed-ed beyond a true age of 9,200 years ago (which equals an uncalibrated raw date of 8,250 years BP)', and that the 'earlier "true" dates, older than 9,200 years ago, are therefore provisional'. Now I know this from Habib: 'Cali-bration based on tree-rings is now available for carbon dates up to 8000 BC, which is 9350 BC by calibration. Calibration based on coral deposits takes us to carbon date 18000 BC, which is 21650 BC by calibration.'[24] Scholars will no doubt find errors, of omission and commission, in the three books, but they will be ill-advised to ignore the rest for that reason, since, for every such error it is not difficult to point to an error of equal or more serious magnitude in similar undertakings by early Indian history specialists.[25]

University Press, 2006, p. 440) states: 'The mechanism of drawing water out of a well by setting inside it a wheel with a chain of pots around it and by rotating wheel by animal power was known and mentioned in the inscriptions as *araghatta* or *araghatta-ghatiyantra*.' Apart from noting that Chattopadhyaya, on whose work this statement is based, clearly rules out the use of gearing and thus of animal power in his references to the *araghatta*, one may wonder how a chain of pots around a water-wheel placed *inside* a well could have sent forth water *outside* it.

[23] James Mellaart, 'Western Asia during the Neolithic and the Chalcolithic (about 12,000–5,000 years ago)', in S.J. De Laet (ed.), *History of Humanity*, Vol. 1: *Prehistory and the Beginning of Civilization*, Paris: UNESCO, 1994, p. 425.

[24] Habib, *Prehistory*, p. 45.

[25] The non-mention of an important book in his readings by Habib is thus more than matched by the failure to include Langhnaj by a professional archaeologist (Dilip K. Chakrabarti, *India: An Archaeological History*, New Delhi: Oxford University Press, 1999) in his survey of Indian archaeology. Similarly, unlike what Habib believes, 'Sudās' cannot mean a 'good slave (of gods)' (Habib and Thakur, *The Vedic Age*, p. 19); it came to have that meaning only later and after it became a different word altogether, i.e. 'Sudāsa'. Kosambi, who noted that the earlier name 'Sudās' came to be written later as 'Sudāsa', thought that 'the earlier form

Archaeologists should have more than one reason to welcome Habib's foray into their field. It has helped *inter alia* to redress their long-term and perfectly reasonable complaint of neglect by historians. In view of the negligible position of and/or regard for prehistory in earlier surveys (single or multi-volume) of Indian history,[26] we must not miss the significance of the decision to have a separate volume on prehistory in the *People's History* series, instead of seeing prehistory as a brief introductory ritual that must be performed, however perfunctorily, before one can address more important issues of India's past. There has since been a heartening all-round rise in historians' awareness of the importance of this earliest past of ours, as exemplified in the work of Upinder Singh,[27] though the old tradition continues

---

means "the good giver"' (*Introduction to the Study of Indian History*, 1975 edition, p. 94). Actually, the word in the *Rigveda*, when it did not mean the name of the king, was used in the sense of 'worshipping the gods well', but which Sāyaṇa glossed as 'bestowing rich gifts' (Monier Monier-Williams, *A Sanskrit–English Dictionary*, reprint, Delhi: Motilal Banarsidass, 1990; first published in 1899: q.v. *sudās*). Lest anyone should make capital out of this, ancient Indian historians need a sobering reminder of how an error on a key issue in Sharma's *Material Culture and Social Formations in Ancient India* – on how important pastoralism was in the Early Vedic period – is being repeated by us till date. Following a statement of Sharma, we all believe that the term for the cow in the *Rigveda* is *gau*, which in different declensions occurs 176 times in its Family Books (R.S. Sharma, *Material Culture and Social Formations in Ancient India*, New Delhi: Macmillan, 1983, p. 24; Krishna Mohan Shrimali, 'Index "A" [Pāli, Prākrit, Sanskrit and Allied Words]', ibid., p. 242; D.N. Jha, *Holy Cow: Beef in Indian Dietary Traditions*, New Delhi: Matrix Books, 2001, p. 28; Singh, *History of Ancient and Early Medieval India*, p. 189). Actually there is no *gau* in Sanskrit and the correct term is *go*, one of its declensions being *gauḥ*. The pains Habib has taken to get his facts right is seen, among other things, in his use of the correct form *vaṇij* rather than *vaṇik* (a declension of *vaṇij*) that is commonly used by ancient Indian historians.

[26] A notable exception is R.S. Sharma's 'old' NCERT textbook, which, irrespective of the problems of detail, was one of the first books to give an important place to prehistory. The pioneer was of course D.D. Kosambi who, in his overview of Indian history, devoted more pages than any previous historian to the prehistoric past of India, and was fully alive to the latest developments in prehistoric archaeology. However, it would be idle to expect him to offer summaries of the available body of knowledge in prehistory (he has actually been berated for this by less discerning critics) for he did not aim to do that, and actually does not do so for any period of Indian history covered in the later chapters of both his *Introduction* and *Culture and Civilization*. His was an exercise in the elaboration of his own interpretations: no detail is ever mentioned that is not a part of an argument that is typically his own. He can, and should, be faulted empirically only when he ignores or misconstrues data that were available at his time and that affect his argument adversely. There is more than one instance of this, and not only for the prehistoric period: one is his misinterpretation of King Bhoja's lake as an irrigational project (Vishwa Mohan Jha, 'Malwa under the Paramaras: A Study in Economic and Political History', unpublished M. Phil. dissertation, Department of History, University of Delhi, 1988, pp. 11–12; Jha, 'Economy of North India', pp. 277–78).

[27] The Aligarh Historians Society's decision is of course a part, and a product, of a longer and multifarious process of the gradual rise in the historian's awareness of prehistory's importance. Singh's source of inspiration (in *History of Ancient and Early Medieval India*) does not, for example, seem to be Habib's works, which do not find a place in her bibliography.

through updated and enlarged versions of earlier surveys, for example, those by Romila Thapar and Hermann Kulke.[28]

The medievalist in Habib does from time to time break through his narratives on ancient India to provide parallels and reference points. Thus the

---

[28] Through the successive editions of his work (co-authored with Dietmar Rothermund), Kulke manages to do without the Palaeolithic and Mesolithic, and, excepting Mehrgarh, has little to say about the Neolithic and Chalcolithic periods as well (cf. Kulke and Rothermund, *A History of India*, pp. 1–2 and Map 1.1). The case is only slightly better with Burton Stein, whose general disregard for prehistoric matters is evinced in statements such as: 'So-called "middle stone age" societies appeared between 40,000 and 10,000 years ago, followed by those using microlithic tools, first found around 15,000 years ago' (Burton Stein, *A History of India*, second edition, edited by David Arnold, Chichester: Wiley-Blackwell, 2010, p. 39). Romila Thapar gives a more detailed and therefore more revealing treatment of Indian prehistory in her chapter on 'The Antecedents', in *Early India from the Origins to AD 1300*, London: Allen Lane, 2002. For the earlier part of the prehistoric story, one notices a string of tell-tale statements over the about-8-page account of the Palaeolithic, Mesolithic, Neolithic and Chalcolithic periods (ibid., pp. 71–79). (1) Palaeolithic sites are stated to have been first discovered in the northwest and only later in the rest of South Asia: 'The initial studies focused on the north-west, in terraces of the Soan River and in the Potwar Plateau. Since then, sites have been found scattered across the subcontinent' (ibid., p. 71). Actually, as the Allchins note in their popular introduction to Indian pre- and proto-history (*The Rise of Civilization in India and Pakistan*, New Delhi: Foundation Books by arrangement with Cambridge University Press, 1988, pp. 35–36), the first Palaeolithic tools in the subcontinent were discovered in 1863 in Bruce Foote, a full 70 years before their discovery in the Potwar Plateau (the Soan River is a part of the Potwar Plateau). In fact the outstanding significance of the early discovery in South India – 'only three years after they were first recognized in Europe' (Bridget Allchin and F.R. Allchin, *The Origins of a Civilization: The Prehistory and Early Archaeology of South Asia*, Viking, 1997, p. 45) – has been a matter of celebration among Indian archaeologists, as noted by the Allchins in their earlier work: 'During the past decade Indian archaeologists have celebrated the centenaries of two great events: the foundation of the Archaeological Survey, and the discovery by Bruce Foote in 1863 of the first Indian Palaeolithic artifact from lateritic deposits near Madras' (Bridget Allchin and F.R. Allchin, *The Birth of Indian Civilization*, Harmondsworth: Penguin Books, 1968, p. 21). (2) Little importance is placed on the antiquity of the Palaeolithic period, which is dated 'from before 30,000 to about 10,000 BC' (Thapar, *Early India*, p. 72). The 'before' has been known, since the 1980s, to date from about two million years ago (Allchin and Allchin, *Rise of Civilization in India and Pakistan*, p. 36). Further, the Mesolithic period is dated by Thapar 'between the tenth and the fifth millennia [BC]' (*Early India*, p. 73). Actually, the beginning of the Mesolithic period in India is known to be more than twice as early. (3) While describing pebble tools, the Allchins regularly specified the type(s) of pebble in question: 'pebbles of quartz' (*Origins of a Civilization*, p. 44); 'a whole range of jasper, agate and other kinds of chalcedonic silica . . . usually obtained in the form of pebbles from river gravels' (*Rise of Civilization in India and Pakistan*, p. 74) ; 'pebbles and rocks of the same kinds of rock – chiefly quartzite', 'pebbles of jasper' (ibid., pp. 44–45, 86), 'quartzite pebbles', 'pebbles of jasper', 'quartz pebbles' (*Birth of Indian Civilization*, pp. 62, 92, 97). Going by the following statement, however, pebbles would not simply be stones of a particular size, surface and shape (small, smooth, rounded), but, like quartz and agate, of a particular composition: 'change from using pebble-stones to a different kind of stone, such as quartz, chert, agate, chalcedony and suchlike' (Thapar, *Early India*, p. 72). (4) Using flakes as tools is a Mesolithic technique, and is never associated with Palaeolithic tool-making. Flakes, blades, parallel-sided blades and burins are referred to *only* as Mesolithic tools (ibid., pp. 72, 79). (5) For the

'wandering *vaṇij*' of the *Rigveda* reminds him of the medieval *banjara*;[29] the significance of place-names in ancient India is explained with reference to those from Mughal India; discussions of spinning hark forth to the medieval spinning wheel; and so on. All this calls attention to parallels that would not generally occur to historians of early India, and is welcome for that reason, even when done sometimes at the cost of depriving the readers of the more relevant, ancient historical contexts of the issues in question. The absence of the spinning wheel is about as significant for early India as the spinning jenny's absence is for medieval India; it would be historically significant only if it is shown to bear on a given historical situation. The reference to the medieval *banjara* in the context of a single merchant from a different context should be more in terms of a contrast than a lineal connection, on pain of shifting attention away from the function of merchants in tribal societies.

In their treatment of details, originality of argument and boldness of interpretation, the three volumes constitute, to use a well-worn phrase, a welcome contribution to the growing literature on the subject. A number of themes of irreplaceable importance to students of the field are dealt with, one realizes with some surprise, for the first time in a general survey of Indian history: methods of dating in prehistory, the archaeological method (cf. the section on the archaeological sources in the innumerable introductions to early Indian history by its specialists), historical geography, etc. (though the sequence in which they occur is a bit odd at times, like placing the archaeological method in *Indus Civilization* rather than in *Prehistory*). No controversy is ever referred to without the author taking a clear stand.[30]

Neolithic period, animals are stated to have been 'used additionally for traction and for transportation' (ibid., p. 76). This is generally considered to be a post-Neolithic development. (6) Early Harappan, as well as Nal and Kulli cultures are included as part of the Neolithic scene (ibid., pp. 77–78). Generally, they are known as Chalcolithic cultures. It is also not easy to understand a number of other statements in Thapar's rapid survey, as for example, when people are stated to have become more sedentary *because of* increasing population density: 'A higher density of population in places where agriculture was practised might also have brought about a more sedentary population' (ibid., p. 75). Later in the same chapter, however, she provides a quite serviceable survey of the other Neolithic and Chalcolithic cultures of South Asia (ibid., pp. 88–94). The reason for the above-noted treatment of the earlier phases thus is probably due to indifference to the concerned themes; the issue certainly is not one of competence.

[29] Habib and Thakur, *The Vedic Age*, p. 10; actually it is *Rigveda* 5.45.6 and not 5.145.6.

[30] Mutual neglect – often through a mistaken sense of mutual respect – of competing hypotheses and interpretations has unfortunately become rather endemic in South Asian studies. Apart from its deleterious effect on higher studies and research, this leaves teachers of undergraduate courses with the option either of making research an indispensable part of their teaching in order to form their own judgement, or creating non-existent 'debates' out of uncertainties and/or mutually unrecognized differences in the discipline's repertoire, and resorting to according-to-this and according-to-that historian types of histories.

Habib's works, along with some other recent studies, provide an opportunity to forefront a number of crucial issues that have not been paid much attention in early Indian history. For instance, it is not possible to discuss the significance of surplus production in ancient Indian social formations on the basis of most of the available surveys of Indian archaeology because they have had little use for it: probably the only time Dilip Chakrabarti refers to 'surplus' in his archaeological history of India is in the context of the disposal of 'surplus water' through the Harappan drainage system.[31] The continuing relevance of Gordon Childe's work, the concept of diffusion, the importance of technology as a motor of social change, and the importance of anthropology to understanding the past are among the other issues that I wish to discuss here with reference to Habib's three works.

For at least two reasons it is necessary to emphasize the importance of Habib's labours in early Indian history. First, the critique I offer in the following pages would otherwise paint a completely negative picture, which is not what I intend to do.[32] However – and this is the second reason – that is exactly how my remarks may be understood and used, and not just by ideologists. Given the lie of the professional land, academic exchanges between South Asianists do not exactly lack in acerbic irrelevance (and Habib, it has to be said, is not one who would take things lying down or pull a punch should an opportunity present itself), which has tended over the years to affect the most dispassionate of observers, however momentarily.[33]

---

[31] Chakrabarti, *India: An Archaeological History*, p. 167.

[32] On the contrary, it is precisely through a critique that I intend to pay respect, not just to the lifetime of Irfan Habib's critical labours but to the tradition of which he is a part, where, in the words of Karl Marx as reminded to us by E.P. Thompson, 'to leave error unrefuted is to encourage intellectual immorality' (E. P. Thompson, *The Poverty of Theory: or an Orrery of Errors*, Merlin Press: London, new edition, 1995, p. v). Habib reputedly refuses to be associated with anything that will encourage, in the post-Stalinist vocabulary, a 'cult of personality'. I should like to present my essay as a tribute to that sentiment as well.

[33] A relatively mild, and ultimately edifying, instance of this is seen in the bibliographical essay of the Metcalfs in their *Concise History of India*, where Habib's *Agrarian System of Mughal India* is called a classic within quotes, while other studies, such as the one by Ranajit Guha, are called true classics, i.e. without quotes (Barbara D. Metcalf and Thomas R. Metcalf, *A Concise History of India*, Cambridge: Cambridge University Press, 2002, pp. 302, 304, 307). However, in the first chapter of the same book, no such reservation is seen in the reference to Habib's work (ibid., p. 20), and, more important, in the second edition of the book, the quote marks are removed (Metcalf and Metcalf, *A Concise History of India*, second edition, Cambridge: Cambridge University Press, 2006, p. 311). The quotes in the first edition were probably used in a moment of absent-mindedness, yet are significant in reflecting an insinuation analogous to the one noted by P. Hardy for the same book by Habib (P. Hardy, *The Muslims of British India*, Cambridge: Cambridge University Press, 1972, p. 265). For a juicy snippet of 'who are the best Indian historians?' (and, by default, who are not), see Rukun Advani, 'The History Jungle', *The Hindu*, Sunday, 26 May 2002.

Palaeolithic Tools: Lower, Middle and Upper

It is common knowledge that tools of earlier phases continued to be made and used through the development of Palaeolithic stone tool technology. What needs equal emphasis is the fact that stone tools that typify a later stage could also be, and were, made in the earlier periods as well. This is now being noted with increasing frequency. For instance, while earlier scholars believed that only core tools were produced in the Lower Palaeolithic period and flake tools only from the Middle Palaeolithic period, it is now realized that 'both the sharp-edged flakes and the sharp-edged cores . . . were probably used as tools' from the very outset of the Lower Palaeolithic period.[34] This had indeed been foreseen quite early by Grahame Clark and Stuart Piggott:

> The manufacture of hand-axes, and still more perhaps of chopping-tools, led inevitably to the production of flakes, some of which were large enough to serve for tools. This has often been overlooked in the past, in all probability owing to limitations in most of the evidence available to archaeologists: many of the lithic assemblages of Middle Pleistocene age have been sorted by river action and weathering of various kinds, and a large proportion of the lithic material in museums has been abstracted from geological deposits on a highly selective basis by collectors intent on securing well-worked specimens.[35]

The Allchins confirmed this bias in sampling for India as well, underlining the importance of flake tools in the Lower Palaeolithic period at length:

> Flakes, whether as by-products of the manufacture of core tools or as the main objective of the tool makers, are an intrinsic part of the hand axe industries in India, as in many other parts of the world. Some collectors have overlooked them, but they are present at factory sites and in river gravels to be found by anyone who looks for them.[36]

While, despite the Allchins, the Lower Palaeolithic continues to be defined exclusively in terms of core tools,[37] Habib takes full cognizance of the

---

[34] Carol Ember, Melvin Ember and Peter Peregrine, *Anthropology*, tenth edition, London: Pearson Education, 2002, p. 104; Brian M. Fagan,, *People of the Earth: An Introduction to World Prehistory*, tenth edition, Upper Saddle River, New Jersey: Prentice Hall, 2001, p. 63.

[35] Grahame Clark and Stuart Piggott, *Prehistoric Societies*, London: Penguin Books, 1965, pp. 44–45.

[36] Allchin and Allchin, *The Rise of Civilization in India and Pakistan*, p. 46.

[37] A failure to appreciate the shift in definition has led not only to uneven portrayals of the period, but also to some contradiction within a scholar's framework of analysis: 'Early palaeolithic tools were fairly large core tools made of quartzite or other hard rocks. They include chopping tools, handaxes, and cleavers' (Singh, *History of Ancient and Early Medieval India from the Stone Age to the 12th Century*, p. 68). In Table 2.2, p. 67 and on p. 74

importance of flakes in this period, and describes and illustrates the 'pebble flake' as a characteristic Lower Palaeolithic tool.[38] Further, the importance of flakes in the Late Acheulian repertoire is not only duly underlined, but also linked, quite imaginatively, to hominid evolution: 'more dexterous' hands of the 'less robust' (i.e. gracile) species of *Homo erectus* made it possible to produce the lighter, more graceful, Late Acheulian flake tools, such as at Bhimbetka.[39] The likelier explanation, however, is somewhat prosaic: the locally available stone 'tends to occur in large blocks' which could hardly have been used as core tools.[40]

Next, two types of Middle Palaeolithic cultures in India are distinguished by Habib: 'Nevasan' and Levallois. The Nevasan culture, seen over central and south India but also at a few sites in the northwest, is marked by the 'flake-blade';[41] also once called 'flaked blade', it is the same as the 'blade-flake' of others. The remaining Middle Palaeolithic cultures of India, e.g., at Sanghao Cave, are marked by tools made by the Levallois method (also called Levallois–Mousterian or Mousterian, in the same sense[42]), in which a

---

(ibid.), also, Lower Palaeolithic is said to be a period of core tools, including hand-axes, cleavers and chopping tools, and distinct from the Middle Palaeolithic period of flake tools. However, later the cleaver is defined as 'a flattish tool made on a broad rectangular or triangular flake, one end of which has a broad and straight cutting edge' (ibid., pp. 69, 645). The definition of the cleaver as a flake is obviously not kept in mind when including it as an example of a core tool in the definition of the Lower Palaeolithic. It is true that cleavers are well known to be *both* core and flake tools in India as well as outside; as core tools they are just like hand-axes, with the difference that they have a wide cutting edge at the end instead of a point. The issue, however, is not the factual accuracy of the cleaver as a core tool, but the hiatus between its inclusion as a core tool in the definition of the Lower Palaeolithic and its definition as a flake tool. This illustrates a fairly common way in which definitions can refract our thinking. A second example is the double use of the term 'backed blade' by Habib, once to define the Upper Palaeolithic, next as part of the definition of the Mesolithic. The just cited Table 2.2 (ibid., p. 67) also shows the Lower, Middle and Upper Palaeolithic periods to correspond to the Lower, Middle and Upper Pleistocene epochs respectively. This is too neat. As the Middle Pleistocene lasted from about 730,000 to about 130,000 years ago (Habib, *Prehistory*, p. 26; Peter Bogucki, *The Origins of Human Society*, Oxford: Blackwell, 1999, p. 31), it is obvious that the Lower Palaeolithic spanned the first two divisions of the Pleistocene, while the Middle Palaeolithic dates only from towards the end of the Middle Pleistocene and mostly belongs, together with the Upper Palaeolithic, to the Upper Pleistocene.

[38] However, there is some confusion, at least in my mind, about his terminology. It seems all right to speak of 'pebble cores and flakes' (Habib, *Prehistory*, p. 25), but misleading to refer to flake tools as 'flaked pebble tool industry' (ibid., p. 24): a flaked pebble would be a core tool, not a flake one. It is likewise confusing to speak of the core tool as 'the main flaked pebble' (ibid., p. 25); that would make pebble flake tools (rightly so called generally: ibid., p. 23, fig. 2.3) 'the other or subsidiary flaked pebbles'!

[39] Habib, *Prehistory*, p. 27.

[40] Allchin and Allchin, *The Rise of Civilization in India and Pakistan*, p. 40.

[41] Habib, *Prehistory*, pp. 27, 30–31, 34–35.

[42] Thus the site of Mula Dam is stated in the text as having Mousterian tools (ibid., pp. 36, 75), but is shown in the maps as a Levallois-tool site.

variety of 'flakes of desired shape' were made by preparing the core suitably.[43] It may be noted that Levallois–Mousterian means not one specific technique but two ways of preparing the core for flake production: in the Levallois technique the core is tortoise-shaped, and in the Mousterian, disc-shaped. There could be cores of other shapes as well.

However, this distinction between the Nevasan Middle Palaeolithic with the flake blade, and the Levallois Middle Palaeolithic sites with a variety of other flake tools, is not sustained by the evidence we have, at least on the authority of the Allchins, a major source of Habib's account. The flake blade is just one of several types of flake tools at Nevasan sites, not the most important of them, and is not exactly absent at non-Nevasan sites. At Sanghao Cave, for instance, 'cores and flakes of triangular outline are seen in small numbers . . . and parallel-sided blade-flakes are more numerous'.[44]

Habib seems to think that the other flake tools at Nevasan sites were products not of the Levallois–Mousterian technique but of the earlier pebble-flake tradition. This, at least, is the best inference one can draw from his note to Fig. 2.6.[45] Here, of the eleven Nevasan tools illustrated by the Allchins,[46] the first eight are reproduced. No. 3 is a flake blade, which is taken by Habib as a 'marker of Middle Palaeolithic', while no. 7 'shows',

---

[43] Ibid., pp. 29, 30–31, 34–35, 36–37.

[44] Allchin and Allchin, *The Rise of Civilization in India and Pakistan*, p. 52.

[45] Habib, *Prehistory*, p. 28.

[46] Allchin and Allchin, *The Rise of Civilization in India and Pakistan*, p. 49. The illustration is originally from Bridget Allchin's study, 'The Indian Middle Stone Age: Some New Sites in Central and Southern India' (*Bulletin of the Institute of Archaeology*, Vol. 2, 1959, pp. 1–36). As Bridget Allchin ('Middle Palaeolithic Culture', in A.H. Dani and V.M. Masson (eds), *History of Civilization of Central Asia*, Vol. I: *The Dawn of Civilization: Earliest Times to 700 BC*, Paris: UNESCO, 1992, p. 69) has pointed out, it was in this paper that the Nevasan culture was first defined by her, though the name 'Nevasan' was given to it by Sankalia five years after Allchin's work: the site had of course been excavated in the mid-1950s by H.D. Sankalia and S.B. Deo, followed by the publiation of a massive report. Unfortunately, however, Bridget Allchin's work has gone unacknowledged generally as all the credit tends to be given to Sankalia (K. Paddayya, 'Paleolithic Cultures', in *Encyclopedia of Archaeology*, edited by Deborah M. Pearsall, 2008, pp. 769; Singh, *History of Ancient and Early Medieval India from the Stone Age to the 12th Century*, p. 75), although a good part of the blame for this must go to the Allchins' own sense of grace and modesty, whereby they must refer to Sankalia's contribution but generally skip their own in their own work (Allchin and Allchin, *The Rise of Civilization in India and Pakistan*, p. 47). In her review of Sankalia's *Prehistory and Protohistory in India and Pakistan* (*Man*, New Series, Vol. 1, No. 1, 1966, p. 111), however, Allchin did point out, as courteously as possible, his tendency to place 'throughout emphasis . . . upon work done by Indians as opposed to that of outsiders'. These 'outsiders' included, as Kosambi had already noted in his review of the same book ('Archaeological Review 2', reprinted in D.D. Kosambi *Combined Methods in Indology and Other Writings*, compiled, edited and introduced by B.D. Chattopadhyaya, Delhi: Oxford University Press, 2007 edition [not specified by the publisher, but seen in the Editor's note on p. 829], pp. 835, 836), Childe, Mortimer Wheeler and F. R. Allchin.

according to him, 'continuance of pebble-flake industry'.[47] However, no. 7 shows no continuance of the pebble-flake tradition but is the type of core from which flake blades like no. 3 were prepared. In their note to the illustration, the Allchins call no. 7 as well as nos. 4 and 5 'struck cores',[48] and in the text they explain that while nos. 4 and 5 were 'cores of the well-known "tortoise" type [i.e. Levalloisian type]', no. 7 exemplifies 'cores of another type, made by removing one or two flakes from a suitable pebble to provide a striking platform, from which thick but sometimes approximately parallel-sided blade-flakes were then struck off'.[49]

The Nevasan Middle Palaeolithic was thus distinct from the other Middle Palaeolithic cultures neither in the presence of the flake blade nor in the absence of the Levallois technique. In fact, there were more than two types of Middle Palaeolithic cultures in South Asia; for instance, apart from the Nevasan, two others were Luni and Rohri.[50] The differences between the Nevasan and the Luni industries have been located, not in their respective flake production techniques but in their relationships with the previous Lower Palaeolithic cultures, in 'percentage of reworked flakes', and in the range and variety of flake tools.[51]

The presence of blades in the Middle Palaeolithic period creates a further problem for Habib for the definition of the Upper Palaeolithic, which is traditionally defined as the period when blades and burins came to be produced. Sometimes, when the presence of burins alone but not of blades in the Middle Palaeolithic is noted, the Upper Palaeolithic is seen as a period when blades were made for the first time and when burins began to be made in still larger numbers than earlier.[52] Having defined the flake blade as the hallmark of the Nevasan industry, Habib sees the distinguishing trait of the Upper Palaeolithic in the backed blade.[53] However, what he calls backed blades are actually not backed blades but simply blades. He speaks of 'backed

---

[47] Habib, *Prehistory*, p. 28.

[48] Allchin and Allchin, *The Rise of Civilization in India and Pakistan*, p. 49, fig. 3.6.

[49] Ibid., p. 48.

[50] Rohri Hills region in Upper Sind is indicated in Map 2.2 by Habib (in *Prehistory*) as marked by 'flake-blades', i.e. a Nevasan Middle Palaeolithic culture. This runs foul of the Allchins' description of the site as having a distinct Middle Palaeolithic identity, marked by longer tools and carefully selected nodules as cores that required almost no preparation (Allchin and Allchin, *The Rise of Civilization in India and Pakistan*, p. 56; Bridget Allchin, 'Middle Palaeolithic Culture', p. 75). A Middle Palaeolithic culture resembling the Nevasan culture has been located in the Karachi area in Lower Sind (ibid., p. 76), but one does not know if this is what is meant by Habib.

[51] Allchin and Allchin, *The Rise of Civilization in India and Pakistan*, pp. 53–54.

[52] Singh, *History of Ancient and Early Medieval India from the Stone Age to the 12th Century*, pp. 74, 76.

[53] Habib, *Prehistory*, pp. 32–33.

blades with parallel edges', defining them as 'thin, double-edged prismatic flakes'.[54] Apparently, by 'backed blade' here is meant a flake, one cutting edge of which has in the back, or is backed by, a second, parallel cutting edge. This is not a backed blade, but a blade in general or a parallel-sided blade. A blade is by definition parallel-sided, but the term 'parallel-sided blade' is helpful in distinguishing it from a 'backed blade', which means a different thing to archaeologists. It means a blade that has been blunted on one side to provide a single cutting edge. The backed blade, as a secondary development of the blade technology, is indeed the second of the three elements of the Upper Palaeolithic industry in its classical definition, along with the blade and the burin:

> A second innovation was the employment of a steep, almost vertical, retouch for shaping such products as knife-blades, projectile heads or insets for composite tools, the twin objects of which were to concentrate on the strongest, thickest part of the blade and to blunt edges, either for ease of mounting or as a protection to the finger.[55]

The customary usage of the terms[56] is employed in Habib's book itself in the note to Fig. 2.9 illustrating microliths from Mahadaha, where nos. 1 to 9 are called 'parallel-sided blades' and nos. 10 to 21, 'blunted backed blades'.[57]

As it happens, unlike the blade and the burin which are known from the earlier period as well, the backed blade as a tool-type remains, perhaps till date, a distinctive Upper Palaeolithic feature.[58] So is all that we need to be clear about the nature of the backed blade, which may then be retained as *the* defining element of the Upper Palaeolithic? I should like to think, however, that identification of a technological stage must rest primarily on the technique of production rather than on the types of tools alone. Thus flake tools were made in the Lower Palaeolithic period but not by the prepared-core method, and blades and burins were made in the Middle Palaeolithic period too but not by the method typical of the Upper Palaeolithic period, which is therefore better understood in terms of a particular type of pre-

---

[54] Ibid., p. 32.

[55] Clark and Piggott, *Prehistoric Societies*, pp. 55–56.

[56] As seen for India, for instance, in A. Ghosh (ed.), *An Encyclopaedia of Indian Archaeology*, Vol. I, New Delhi: Munshiram Manoharlal, 1989, pp. 32 ff.

[57] Habib, *Prehistory*, p. 39.

[58] Robert Jameson ('Backed Blade', in Ian Shaw and Robert Jameson, eds, *A Dictionary of Archaeology*, Oxford: Blackwell, 1999, p. 100), having defined the backed blade as a 'flint blade with at least one edge blunted by secondary retouch, apparently to allow the tool to be handled more comfortably', states that 'backed blades were first produced in the early Upper Palaeolithic'.

pared core rather than a type or two of tools.[59] The central importance of this Upper Palaeolithic core-type, cylindrical in shape, has regularly been duly described by specialists, though they may not always have adequately conveyed its definitional centrality.[60] This cylindrical core is by far the most economical of both labour and material: a fully struck (i.e. fully utilized) Middle Palaeolithic core is probably identified much more readily than a fully struck Upper Palaeolithic cylindrical core, which would be reduced to a rather small, nondescript lump.

The Mesolithic in South Asia

Irfan Habib's discussion of the development and significance of Palaeolithic cultures in South Asia is admirably located in a world-historical context. This is missing from his account of the Mesolithic cultures,[61] apparently because of his concern with dates as well as the advocacy of diffusion. He notes the very early dates for the Sri Lankan Mesolithic (34,000 and 28,000 years ago), and, on noting again a very early but later than Sri Lankan date for the Mesolithic culture at Patne in Maharashtra, wonders about a northward diffusion,[62] before sketching out the salient features of other Indian Mesolithic cultures.

Recognition of the Sri Lankan Mesolithic as 'perhaps' the earliest in the world and suggestion of its diffusion to the rest of South Asia have implications for the rest of the world. Habib falls short of fleshing these out.[63]

---

[59] The origins of a method typical of one period would of course be found in the preceding one. Thus the beginnings of the prepared-core technique are seen in the Lower Palaeolithic period in India (Allchin and Allchin, *The Rise of Civilization in India and Pakistan*, p. 46).

[60] Clark and Piggott, *Prehistoric Societies*, p. 56; Allchin and Allchin, *The Rise of Civilization in India and Pakistan*, pp. 57, 58; A. Ghosh (ed.), *An Encyclopaedia of Indian Archaeology*, Vol. I, pp. 32, 35. For illustrations, Allchin and Allchin, *The Rise of Civilization in India and Pakistan*, p. 59 fig. 3.9, nos. 10 and 11; Fagan, *People of the Earth*, pp. 125 fig.4.4, 127 fig. 4.5; Ember, Ember and Peregrine, *Anthropology*, p. 143 fig. 9-3; Supriya Varma, 'Early Societies', in *Themes in World History*, New Delhi: NCERT, 2006, p. 21.

[61] Habib, *Prehistory*, pp. 38–43.

[62] Ibid., p. 38.

[63] By keeping silent about the world-historical context of the Mesolithic, Habib skirts more than one problem that arises with such an early date for the Sri Lankan Mesolithic: why should the South Asian Mesolithic cultures bear no relation to the advent of the Holocene as all other Mesolithic cultures are believed to do, and what are the implications of such early South Asian dates for a narrative of diffusion based simply on dates, both for the much later Mesolithic cultures of West Asia as well as for the eastward diffusion of the Neolithic? Northwest India would thus receive its Mesolithic culture from Sri Lanka and the Neolithic revolution from West Asia!

A similar, even more compelling issue for world history waits to be worked out. This is the implication, for hominid migrations out of Africa, of the dates of the earliest Palaeolithic tools in South Asia. Although the Allchins hinted at it (*The Rise of Civilization in India and*

However, there is no reason why microliths could not have been made independently at various centres if 'the flake blade' could come up all over the world without much diffusion ('the apparently independent appearances of the flake blade in many parts of the world'[64]). Since microliths are made by breaking down blades into smaller units, the case for diffusion is still weaker for them than it is for the flake blade.[65]

We shall presently see how considerable misrepresentation of the ideas of Gordon Childe continues to prevail all round, mainly because of our inability to see through the misinterpretation of Childe by a few dominant voices. In fact, the manner in which Childe has been read by both his critics and followers is just one example of a fairly widespread intellectual tendency. Another instance of the same tendency is the way in which Habib's own work has been read: he has been attributed, and then criticized for, things that he never says or implies. Thus, in an example singled out by a critic to illustrate his 'unsure grip on the subject [of prehistory]', Habib is seen as associating Mesolithic cultures with the Holocene epoch, and when Habib calls these cultures 'transitional', he is believed to be saying that all these

---

Pakistan, pp. 18–19), this is not generally recognized. Singh thus refers once to the migration of *Homo erectus* from Africa to other parts of the world *after* 1.7 million years ago (mya) and then to about 2.8 mya, between 2.4 and 2 mya, and 2.01 mya as the dates for the earliest stone tools in South Asia, without noting their necessarily mutual bearing (*History of Ancient and Early Medieval India from the Stone Age to the 12th Century*, pp. 62, 68). Habib seems to note the problem but does not come to grips with it (*Prehistory*, p. 25). Burjor Avari alone gives the problem due attention and offers an explanation that would come naturally to a non-expert: 'it would be imprudent to be too categorical with the dates' (Burjor Avari, *India: The Ancient Past*, London: Routledge, 2007, p. 23). In support, one may refer to the revision of the date of the famous skull discovered by Richard Leakey from 2.6 mya to 1.8 mya (Bogucki, *The Origins of Human Society*, p. 36). There could be a problem at the African end as well where 'the dating of the fossil record is sometimes out of sync with the dating of the archaeological record' (ibid.).

Developments in the field have been so rapid and so scanty is the fossil record for the period, that the overall picture can dramatically change with a single discovery, revision in date or reworking of a linkage; experts underline the limited shelf-life of the conclusions being provided by them, which could be as brief as a few months (ibid., p. 30). But it is not easy to follow the specialist literature, so one tends to fall back on (at least wonder about) whatever relevant data one runs into. The issue would be resolved in one way if an archaeologist's reference to 'the first human occupation of India dat[ing] back to about a million years' (Shereen Ratnagar, *Makers and Shapers: Early Indian Technology in the Home, Village and Urban Workshop*, New Delhi: Tulika Books, 2007, p. xi) is a revision of the earlier dating and not a mistake, but in quite another way with the new information supplied by another archaeologist, that tool-making began with the Austropithecines and not necessarily with *Homo habilis* (Varma, 'Early Societies', p. 20); it is not clear if either is aware of the significance of her datum for our problem.

[64] Habib, *Prehistory*, p. 27.

[65] It may also be relevant to remember, as Childe once observed tersely, that 'not all microliths are Mesolithic' (Gordon Childe, 'The New Stone Age', in Harry L. Shapiro, ed., *Man, Culture, and Society*, revised second edition, New York: Oxford University Press, 1971, p. 97; first edition 1956 – Childe's article was retained from the first edition).

cultures lasted only till the coming of the Neolithic.[66] It is important not only to see that Habib has wrongly been attributed both these, but also to trace the roots of the attributions – both of which lead us back to Childe, the first via Lewis Binford.

Holocene and Mesolithic, both appear in Habib's narrative but quite independently of each other. Holocene dates from about 10,000 years ago,[67] while Mesolithic cultures in South Asia are dated back to 34,000 years ago. Habib has been quite alive to the importance of environmental factors as well of the need for utmost caution in reconstructing their history, even though he could have done with still more caution.[68] He is of course also aware of the epoch-making importance of the coming of the Holocene, and duly underlines it. It is again the importance of the difference between the Holocene and the Pleistocene that apparently prevents him from interpreting Palaeolithic cultures in terms of their present-day floral and faunal setting, a tendency to which historians of early India, following the glib remarks of the excavators of Bhimbetka, often succumb, even though the Allchins demurred in some detail.[69]

---

[66] Lahiri, 'Short and Selective'.

[67] Habib, *Prehistory*, p. 8.

[68] On p. 24 of *The Indus Civilization*, as he argues against the view that the Indus basin received heavier rainfall than it does now, it is pointed out that the heavier rainfall thesis 'is also inconsistent with the drainage system at Mohenjo Daro and Kalibangan which could not have withstood any heavier rainfall than the area now receives'. In fact, assuming that the weather conditions did not change between then and now, the drainage system of the cities must have been designed to withstand a much heavier rainfall than the area receives on an average. This is due to the extreme variability of rainfall in arid zones, both over years and for any given year. The following sample for the Indus basin says it all: 'As for aridity and its concomitant variability, Drigh Road (Karachi), with an average rainfall of about 8 in. (203 mm.) recorded in five successive years 13.52, 0.69, 9.41, 20.82 and 6.97 in. – c. 343, 18, [239], 528, and 177 mm. Almost it never rains but it pours; Karachi has recorded 12 in. (305 mm.) in 24 hours' (O.H.K. Spate and A.T.A. Learmonth, *India and Pakistan: A General and Regional Geography*, Bungay, Suffolk: Methuen, 1967, p. 508).

[69] Given the persistence of the tendency (Thapar, *Early India*, pp. 71–72; Singh, *History of Ancient and Early Medieval India from the Stone Age to the 12th Century*, p. 71), it is crucial to see the point made by the Allchins: 'The excavators [of Bhimbetka] point out that today the surrounding countryside is well supplied with edible wild plants, still extensively used by local communities, who depend upon them for a significant part of their diet, and that within living memory it was rich in wild life. Larger game animals . . . are now rare, but fish are regularly caught in rivers and streams. There is no reason to presume that precisely the same resources were available during any period of the Stone Age, and indeed there is every reason to suppose that conditions varied considerably from one period to another, as pointed out in the previous chapter. However, these observations are interesting, although perhaps more relevant to Mesolithic ecological studies. The absence of surviving organic remains in the occupation deposits in the rock shelter emphasizes the importance of making a comprehensive investigation of all faunal and other organic remains in the implementiferous deposits, such as those in the Narbada valley 25 km to the south, and of attempting to relate the cultural and climatic phases represented in the rock shelters to stratified alluvial deposits' (Allchin and Allchin, *The Rise of Civilization in India and Pakistan*, p. 40).

However, at no point does Habib try, even remotely, to relate Holocene with Mesolithic cultures. It is easy to see why. His interest in the theme of diffusion makes him pause at the earliest evidence of the Mesolithic in South Asia (34,000 years ago): if you insist on the significance of the first date of the Mesolithic, you cannot possibly relate its advent to something that happened more than a score millennia later.

It is easier yet to see why one should just assume that everyone must necessarily relate Mesolithic cultures to the advent of the Holocene. The two have been so closely and regularly intertwined in the literature that the critic could easily be excused for missing that Habib mentions both without linking them. Holocene, or its synonym 'post-Pleistocene', has actually been built into the definition of the Mesolithic, as in the following statement of Singh: 'The term mesolithic is generally used for post-Pleistocene (i.e. Holocene) hunting-gathering stone age cultures marked by the use of microliths.'[70] However, the term 'post-Pleistocene', given wide currency through its use by Lewis Binford, creates many difficulties for understanding the climatic contexts of the Mesolithic cultures of West Asia and other places as well. One may thus refer to the rampant confusion on this count in Brian Fagan's *People of the Earth*. In Chapter 7 on the Mesolithic, in the section named 'The Holocene (after 10,000 BC)', it is stated: 'Palaeoclimatologists divide the earliest part of the Holocene . . . into two parts.' One is called 'Bølling-Allerod Interstadial (*c.* 14,700 to *c.* 12,500 years ago)', the other 'Younger Dryas Interval (*c.* 12,950 to 11,650 years ago)'.[71] It is remarkable that a scholar like Fagan should be unable to see how any part of the Holocene can have dates like 14,7000, 12,500 or 12,950 years ago, if the Holocene itself begins after 10,000 BC.[72] In fact these two periods belong to the long period of the gradual end of the Pleistocene epoch, which began around 18,000 years ago. Mesolithic cultures began to emerge *not after the end of the Pleistocene but during this long phasing out of the Pleistocene* (the Pleistocene–Holocene boundary, or Late Glacial times), a fact that was clearly grasped and stated by earlier archaeologists like Childe and Braidwood before Mesolithic cultures came to be circumscribed by concepts like post-Pleistocene and post-Glacial.

As to the Mesolithic being a 'transitional' period, conceptually, Mesolithic does imply an intermediate stage between Palaeolithic and Neolithic, and it

---

[70] Singh, *History of Ancient and Early Medieval India from the Stone Age to the 12th Century*, p. 82.

[71] Fagan, *People of the Earth*, p. 206.

[72] Leaving aside the overlap of a precise 450 years between the two divisions, such miscalculation being endemic to the book: on the dates given here, Younger Dryas is said to be a '1100-year-long-cold snap'; on p. 256 we see a reference to 'the 1000 year-long Younger Dryas, between about 10,500 and 10,000 BC'!

is sufficient that this should have happened in *some* cases, just as 'proto-history' by definition means a stage between prehistory and history even when the next stage did not follow.[73] Archaeologists are quite correct to speak of the Early Harappan phase as transitional to the Mature Harappan stage even when several Early Harappan sites continued to flourish parallel to Mature Harappan ones.

The argument may be located in a wider context as a legacy of the famous dilemma whether Mesolithic or Neolithic is a stage or an age. For, it was on the ground of the continuing survival of hunter-gatherers and primitive farmers, and their coexistence with the later societies – the same ground on which Habib's use of the term 'transitional' has been objected to – that Childe would always argue that it is better to speak of the Neolithic or the Mesolithic as stages rather than ages.[74] It was with this point about the Neolithic being a stage rather than an age that Childe ended his 1956 essay in Shapiro's *Man, Culture and Society*, having used the term 'stage' consistently throughout the essay:

> In conclusion, it may be well to repeat that the Neolithic Stage, though usually called an Age, does not represent a definite period of time. It began in Hither Asia perhaps 7000 years ago, but in Denmark probably no more than 4500. In Australia it never began at all. It survived in the Americas, except in

---

[73] Thus when D.P. Agrawal (*The Archaeology of India*, New Delhi: Select Book Service, 1982, p. 4) describes the protohistoric period in India as 'transitional between prehistory and history', or when Singh (*History of Ancient and Early Medieval India from the Stone Age to the 12th Century*, p. 648) defines protohistory' as 'a segment of the past that is transitional between prehistory and history', the *conceptual* validity of the definition would stand despite the fact that the Harappan civilization was 'transitional' between prehistory and not history but prehistory again, or that the civilization itself will transit into history as soon as there is a historiographical transition to successful deciphering of the script. What is meant by a person who uses the term 'transition' is more pertinent here than the meaning in the mind of the critic. We should try to ensure that a potentially loaded term does indeed carry the implication: the critic in this case hardly made the attempt, as the point about the continuity of the Mesolithic sites of Bagor and Langhnaj that she refers to was duly noted by Habib too (Lahiri, 'Short and Selective'; Habib, *Prehistory*, p. 62). It would, for instance, be rather easy, on an analogous ground, to accuse the Allchins of having an extremely unilinear, teleological and evolutionist view of prehistoric India, on the basis of the choice of titles of their works: all of Indian prehistory is oriented towards either the 'birth' or the 'rise' of the 'origins' of Indian civilization! However hard they may find it to explain their choice of words, they do not need to answer the charge that is thus levelled: so absurd is it. Yet it is by the same kind of logic that similar charges are being thrown about, right, left and centre, in much of the ongoing historiographical judgments in early Indian studies. Conversely, one may consciously think of Indian prehistory in unilinear terms without using any loaded term (and, as it happens in this case, without making much effort and being able to demonstrate it): 'If at the end of this book, one is left with a sense of the archaeological direction to Bharatavarsha, I shall consider this humble endeavour of mine successful' (Chakrabarti, *India: An Archaeological History*, p. xvi; see also ibid., p. 338).

[74] For example, Gordon Childe, *Social Evolution*, London: Watts & Co., 1951, p. 20.

Peru, till the advent of the Europeans; in the Pacific to the nineteenth century; in parts of New Guinea till today. But in the Near East it gave place to a new technological stage, the Bronze Age, over 5000 years ago, in the Mediterranean basin not much later, in Denmark by 1500 BC, even in north Russia about 1000 BC.[75]

The point made by Childe continues to dominate archaeological thinking, and sometimes makes for somewhat curious situations: scholars subscribe to the point about the stages and yet cannot help speaking of the Neolithic or Bronze Age. Thus Ratnagar: '"Neolithic", "Iron Age", etc., are terms denoting stages of development rather than chronological divisions.'[76]

Yet it is possible to get around the dilemma and see, despite Childe, the sense in which we may speak of the Mesolithic or Neolithic or Bronze Ages. There was a time when there was no Neolithic or Bronze Stage anywhere in the world, and a time when there was a Neolithic Stage but no Bronze one, just as for a considerable span there was a Bronze Stage but no Iron one. In the world context, therefore, it is possible, and rewarding, to speak of a Neolithic Age and a Bronze Age, with the proviso that in all these ages there would be survivals of earlier ages. The concept of an age, in other words, is defined by the absence of the next stage but not denied by the presence of earlier ones; the concept helps us to see that the Industrial Age has arrived.

The Neolithic Revolution and Vere Gordon Childe

Habib's account of the Neolithic cultures in India centres conceptually on Childe's idea of the 'Neolithic Revolution'. Childe is credited with noting the relationship between the coming of a new type of (Neolithic) stone tools and changes in material life:

> Man's stone tools in the earlier times were made by striking stone against stone. . . . At a very late stage they began to be supplemented by ground tools. . . . The famous archaeologist V. Gordon Childe (1892–1957) noted that these Neolithic or New Stone age . . . tools were associated with very important changes in man's material life. . . . Childe argued that once Neolithic tools began to be made, they would in turn make it easier to cultivate the soil.[77]

Habib reserves for these tools the designation of 'Neolithic techniques', and it is with their appearance and diffusion that he associates the story of

---

[75] Gordon Childe, 'The New Stone Age', p. 111.
[76] Ratnagar, *Makers and Shapers*, p. 13, n. 6.
[77] Habib, *Prehistory*, p, 48.

the origins and spread of food production in India.[78] Conceptually this technique is distinguished from the processes of domestication: 'Other developments would take place, not directly attributable to Neolithic technique, but certainly to agriculture'.[79] It is the virtual absence of ground stone tools that has led to the denial of the Neolithic in Sri Lanka.[80]

Habib's representation of Childe's Neolithic Revolution, and the attendant correspondence of Neolithic tools with food production, are fairly widely shared. Thus Ratnagar thinks that ground and polished tools came to be made and used only in the Neolithic period after the flake tools of hunters, even though she attaches greater significance to the fact of food production: 'With the coming of agriculture began the use of groundstone or polished-stone tools, heavy duty tools mounted on wooden handles, for cutting down vegetation to clear the land, and for tilling the soil.'[81] For Singh too, ground and polished stone tools were 'innovations in stone tool technology' that came with the Neolithic period, and were 'related to shifts in subsistence strategies', i.e. 'advent of food production'.[82]

Earlier, Jacquetta Hawkes had believed that polished axes and adzes were used for cultivation too, though she was fully aware that these were first made in the Mesolithic period, and were tools for felling trees and working wood. She referred to 'the axe and the adze – both of which, but more particularly the adze, were *probably* often used also as hoes' (emphasis added).[83]

---

[78] Ibid., pp. 49 ff.

[79] Ibid., p. 49.

[80] Habib and Thakur, *The Vedic Age*, p. 84.

[81] Ratnagar, *Makers and Shapers*, pp. 143–44, also 7, 14.

[82] Singh, *History of Ancient and Early Medieval India from the Stone Age to the 12th Century*, p. 97.

[83] Jacquetta Hawkes, *Prehistory*, Vol. I, Part 1 of *History of Mankind: Scientific and Cultural Development*, New York: Mentor Books, 1965; first published in 1963, p. 421. Two pages later, she imagines she had 'shown' this: 'it has been shown that both adze and axe blades were used as hoes by the early farmers' (ibid., p. 423). The belief continues to be shared by Ratnagar, who thinks that the same tool was used for felling trees as well as digging the soil: 'At the Neolithic stage groundstone "axes" were used for clearing vegetation and for preparing the ground for seeds, breaking up the soil with repeated vertical movements impacting on the ground' (*Makers and Shapers*, p. 17). On pages 16 and 287 of her book, however, Ratnagar thinks that the two functions were performed separately by two different types of tools: the one that prepared the ground was the hoe, and it is guessed that one type of groundstone axe 'could have been used as a hoe'. The hoe's movement is more likely to be tilted than vertical, and therefore adzes with a plano-convex cross-section rather than axes with symmetrical cross-section would seem better candidates for possible use as a hoe – though ethnographic and later historical evidence must also be brought in. Identification of hoes in stone age contexts in India tends to be problematic. Statements like 'discarded axes might have served as hoes' (K.S. Ramachandran, in A. Ghosh, ed., *An Encyclopaedia of Indian Archaeology*, Vol. I, New Delhi: Munshiram Manoharlal, p. 66), remind one of Kosambi's critique of Sankalia's statement about 'ploughing with a digging stick' (Kosambi, 'Archaeological Review 2', pp. 836–37).

Consistently enough, Habib, who is fully aware that direct evidence for cultivation of food-grain dates only from the second phase of the Southern Neolithic,[84] and also that the mere presence of querns at sites like Bagor or Chopani Mando is no evidence for cultivation, as distinct from gathering of wild grains,[85] would nevertheless argue that cultivation was being practised in the first phase of the Southern Neolithic too even if 'no grains have been found', evidently because there ground axes have been found along with rubbing stones and querns.[86]

In fact Childe spent his life arguing to the contrary, namely that his Neolithic Revolution was defined only by food production, quite independently of any particular type of tools. Let us begin with *Man Makes Himself* and *What Happened in History*, the two works of Childe that Habib refers to.[87]

In *Man Makes Himself*, Childe makes an emphatic denial of any necessary relation between ground and polished stone tools and food production as such: 'forests had replaced the tundras and steppes of the Ice Ages. Man was obliged to deal with timber. The response to this stimulus was the creation of the "polished stone celt" (axe or adze), which *to the older archaeologists was the distinctive mark of "neolithic times"*' (emphasis added).[88]

> But, though neolithic celts are almost invariably found in the oldest settlements of simple food producers, it is not certain that the implement is really a result of the new cconomy. Axe-like tools are found, for instance, on the Baltic, long before there are any indications of farming. The models there seem to be provided by implements of bone and antler, also sharpened by polishing. Ground stone axes and adzes were certainly used by some denizens of the North European forest who still bred no animals for food and cultivated no plants. And outside Europe, many typical food-gatherers, including even the aborigines of Australia, used ground stone axes. On the other hand, the

---

[84] Habib, *The Indus Civilization*, p. 92. Cf. Singh, *A History of Ancient and Early Medieval India*, p. 127, where it is argued in the context of the first phase of the Southern Neolithic that 'millets seem to have been the staple crop, but grains of pulses and seeds of *ber* have also been found'; and ibid., p. 236, where it is pointed out for the second phase that 'horse gram and *ragi* were the new grains in this period'.

[85] Habib, *Prehistory*, pp. 62, 64.

[86] Ibid., p. 67.

[87] Habib, *Prehistory*, p. 71. Despite my best efforts, I have not been able to find copies of the first editions of Childe's *Man Makes Himself* (1936) and *What Happened in History* (1942), to which Habib refers. However, I feel assured by Childe's insistence, in the revised editions I have consulted – Gordon Childe, *Man Makes Himself*, third revised edition, London: Watts & Co., 1956, p. vii; Gordon Childe, *What Happened in History*, revised second edition, Harmondsworth, UK: Penguin Books, 1954, p. 11 – that he changed nothing in the basic arguments.

[88] Childe, *Man Makes Himself*, p. 88.

Natufians of Palestine, who certainly reaped something, presumably a cereal, with sickles, possessed no axes. *The ground stone celt is not therefore an infallible sign of the neolithic economy.* (Emphasis added)[89]

The same point is made in *What Happened in History*: 'Archaeologists take the polished stone axe as the hall-mark of a neolithic equipment. But it is not quite unknown to savages and not invariably employed by barbarians whose economy is or was neolithic.' In fact he furnishes specific evidence for it a few paragraphs later, when it is seen that the pre-pottery neolithic stage at Jericho was without ground stone axes while the one at Jarmo did have them.[90]

Childe went on to do everything within his powers to iterate his interpretation. In yet another piece, he associates polished stone celts with Mesolithic rather than Neolithic cultures: 'Many recent "savages" [i.e. hunting-gathering bands] including not only many Red Indians but also some Australian aboriginal tribes used polished stone celts; indeed the economy of modern savages is generally more like that of European Mesolithic groups than that of their Palaeolithic precursors'.[91] It is also pointed out how ground and polished stone tools, which began to be made by the Mesolithic hunter-gatherers, were a product of transferring to the relatively hard rocks, the process of sharpening by grinding and polishing that was first devised for bone tools.[92]

In fact, all stone age societies that practise food production are to be regarded as Neolithic, without reference to any tool-type: 'The polished stone celt – axe- or adze-blade – used to be regarded as the criterion of the higher, Neolithic stage, *which is here defined by food-production*' (emphasis added).[93] Again: 'What the archaeologists call the Neolithic Stage and the ethnographers term barbarism is characterized by "food-production" – the cultivation of edible plants or the breeding of animal for food or the combination of both activities in mixed farming.'[94] And: 'Naturally the

---

[89] Ibid., p. 89.
[90] Childe, *What Happened in History*, pp. 57, 59.
[91] Childe, 'The New Stone Age', p. 98.
[92] Ibid. This clear connection between sharpening and grinding of bone and antler tools, and ground and polished stone tools, is sufficiently emphasized in *Man Makes Himself*, as seen in the lines just cited, although there Childe also speculates about the possible connection with grinding of grains and friction with sandy soil in the course of cultivation (Childe, *Man Makes Himself*, pp. 88–89). Habib seems to draw on these speculations in his explanation of the possible origins of neolithic tools (Habib, *Prehistory*, p. 48). In fact, the usefulness of ground stone tools for woodworking, apart from felling trees, is widely evidenced, as in Archaic Americans' (Archaic cultures/peoples of eastern North America) rich repertoire of ground stone tools.
[93] Childe, 'The New Stone Age', p. 98.
[94] Ibid., p. 99.

Neolithic Revolution – the transition from pure hunting and collecting to farming – was really a complicated process.'[95] Thus over three pages, it is defined thrice.[96]

When Childe called the Neolithic a technical revolution or referred to 'Neolithic techniques', he did not mean ground and polished stone tools, but the technical – as distinct from the economic – aspects of cultivation and/or stock-breeding:

> Food-production constituted a real economic and technical revolution. Firstly [i.e. economically], it put society potentially in control of its own food supply. . . . Secondly [i.e. technically], plant-cultivation and stockbreeding for the first time put men in control of sources of energy other than human muscle power . . . plants and animals are, to borrow a phrase from Leslie A. White, 'biochemical mechanisms', and by breeding or cultivating them they make these mechanisms work for them.[97]

The spread of 'Neolithic techniques' meant such things as taking the seeds and animals to places other than their original habitat, and introducing cultivation and stock-breeding in those areas.[98]

For those who have noted his redefinition of the Neolithic (e.g., Possehl[99]), Childe is generally thought to have offered it first in *Man Makes Himself* (1936), but actually he had been developing the idea in the 1920s. As he

---

[95] Ibid., p. 100.

[96] For good measure, the novelty of Childe's definition of the Neolithic was further highlighted in the second edition of the same volume by R.A. Gould ('The Old Stone Age', in Harry L. Shapiro, ed., *Man, Culture, and Society*, revised second edition, New York: Oxford University Press, 1971, p. 50): 'Thus when Childe spoke of the "Neolithic Revolution" he did not mean a change from chipped to ground stone tools but a shift from a hunting to a horticultural economy.' A peculiarity of Childe's terminology may be noted here. For the Neolithic period, i.e. before the coming of the plough, he would not use the term 'agriculture' for plant domestication. His reason lay in the etymology of the term agriculture. It is with the coming of the plough that, he argues, 'the plot gives place to the field, and agriculture (from Latin *ager*, "a field") really begins' (Childe *Man Makes Himself*, pp. 122–23; see also Childe, *What Happened in History*, p. 89, and 'The New Stone Age', p. 101). For the pre-plough period, he prefers to call it simply farming or cultivation of cereals. This strained interpretation, however, is not followed by Childe himself, as when he refers to the 'agricultural nomadism' and 'agricultural botany' of the Neolithic people (Childe, *What Happened in History*, pp. 64, 70). It is also undesirable because it perpetuates, in a way, the contrast in the earlier literature between 'vegetatively-propagated horticulture' of the primitive peoples and the advanced 'seed-propagated agriculture', rooted in an unfounded prejudice ('"horticulture" was easier to learn, and therefore, *should* come first; the "savages" would not at first be capable of planting seeds!': Jack R. Harlan, 'Plant Domestication: An Overview', in De Laet, ed., *History of Humanity*, Vol. 1: *Prehistory and the Beginning of Civilization*, 1994, p. 379).

[97] Childe, 'The New Stone Age', pp. 99–100.

[98] Ibid., pp. 100–02.

[99] Gregory L. Possehl, *Indus Age: The Beginnings*, Philadelphia: University of Pennsylvania Press, 1999, p. 394.

was to point out in his 'Retrospect', this – 'adopting food-production as the differentia of the Neolithic', 'for originally the beginning of food-production has been supposed to coincide with that of stone polishing' – was his major original contribution, something 'distinctively Childeish'.[100] Childe has been read so hurriedly and so much in terms of one's own preconceptions that, even when his redefinition of the Neolithic is correctly noted, misunderstanding and underappreciation on other counts remain. Thus Possehl:

> The Neolithic was defined as the era within which ground stone tools and pottery made their first appearance in local archaeological sequences. The great synthesizer of Old World archaeology, V. Gordon Childe, reversed this definition, when he proposed the Neolithic as the period within which humans first used domesticated plants and animals and settled into villages (Childe 1936). This shifted the definition from a technological stage to one relating to *the settlement and subsistence system* of a people. *For some time*, it was thought that Childe's new Neolithic was probably coincidental with the appearance of ground stone tools and pottery; *but as we learned more* about human prehistoric life it has become clear that there are many parts of the world where the initial appearance of domesticated plants and animals is uncorrelated with particular types of material culture. (Emphasis added)[101]

Possehl notes, correctly, that Childe did not define the Neolithic Revolution in terms of ground and polished stone tools, but mis-ascribes to him the view that the Neolithic Revolution is defined both by food production and the permanence of settlements.[102] Childe, in fact, never failed to stress what he aptly dubbed the 'agricultural nomadism' of early Neolithic societies.[103] He was equally conscious of the possibility of abundant wild resources permitting a higher population density of hunting-gathering communities, and even sedentism. He identified the tendency to sedentism among European Mesolithic societies, pointing out how some of them

---

[100] Gordon Childe, 'Retrospect', *Antiquity*, Vol. XXXII, 1958, p. 70. The surprising thing, as Childe noted in his *Social Evolution* (pp. 18–19), was that the new understanding – which replaced Lubbock's definition of the Neolithic in terms of the polished stone tool – should have taken so long in developing, for Lubbock's schema was not being supported by 'stratigraphic observations' as early as 1899. Childe also acknowledged his debt to Grafton Elliot Smith in developing his own idea of the Neolithic Revolution: 'So in 1925, adopting an idea advanced by Elliot Smith ten years earlier, from the three current criteria (polishing of stone, or modern fauna, or domestic animals and cultivated plants) I selected "food-production" as distinguishing the Neolithic from the earlier Palaeolithic and Mesolithic' (ibid., p. 22).

[101] Possehl, *The Indus Age*, p. 394.

[102] Gregory L. Possehl, *The Indus Civilization: A Contemporary Perspective*, New Delhi: Vistaar Publications, 2002, p. 23.

[103] Childe, *What Happened in History*, p. 64; 'The New Stone Age', pp. 101–02.

independently discovered the technique of making pottery.[104]

Permanence of settlements is not the defining element in Childe's account of the Neolithic Revolution, as it is in Possehl's. The views of Possehl on this matter are a bit curious, in view of the importance that archaeologists generally attach to Mesolithic sedentism. These archaeologists, however, err in claiming this as revolutionary new knowledge, unknown to scholars of bygone days such as Childe. Colin Renfrew states in a recent review of the literature:

> It is time now to turn again to the first of these great changes in human life that Gordon Childe identified nearly seventy years ago. Over the past couple of decades, research in western Asia . . . has taken the origins of agriculture back much earlier than had been thought. . . . What has *now* become much clearer, however, is that the appearance of settled village life did not follow upon the establishment of a secure agricultural regime, *as had earlier been thought*; it preceded it. The evidence is clear that sedentism preceded farming, although it was dependent upon the availability of abundant wild food resources. In one of the earliest known case, the Early Natufian culture in the Levant – which was still based upon foraging, well before the cultivation of cereal crops – there developed what were perhaps the world's first settled villages. (Emphasis added)[105]

That settled life was possible and existed before food production, and that food production did not necessarily mean permanent settlement, was known to archaeologists at least since *Man Makes Himself* (1936), when it was put forth in terms that can scarcely be clearer: 'The adoption of cultivation must not be confused with the adoption of a sedentary life'.[106] It was pointed out how the hunter-fishers of Canada in the nineteenth century and the Magdalenians in Pleistocene times led a settled life, while the lives of a number of farming communities in Asia, Africa and South America were marked by 'nomadism'.[107] As already seen, the tendencies to sedentism with the abundance of wild resources were regularly noted thereafter by Childe; a particularly striking instance emerged from 1950 when the Mesolithic Ertebølle people were found to be not just leading a settled life, but also making pottery.[108]

---

[104] Childe, *What Happened in History*, pp. 48, 50, 52; 'The New Stone Age', p. 99.

[105] Colin Renfrew, *Prehistory: The Making of the Human Mind*, London: Weidenfeld and Nicolson, 2007, p. 142.

[106] Childe, *Man Makes Himself*, p. 71.

[107] Ibid., pp. 58–59, 64, 71–73. By neglecting these considerations, like Possehl, Ratnagar draws too tidy a contrast between the nomadism of hunter-gatherers and the settled village of food producers (Ratnagar, *Makers and Shapers*, p. 14).

[108] Childe, *Social Evolution*, pp. 81, 168. They also made ground-stone implements, besides microliths.

Neglect and/or misunderstanding of Childe's definition of the Neolithic have been responsible for a truly pervasive confusion in the identification of stone age sites in India. Instead of identifying the Neolithic in terms of a food-producing stone age culture, we continue to employ the criterion of ground and polished stone tools. As a result, food-producing sites in south India with evidence of animal domestication are dubbed Neolithic because of the presence of ground and polished stone tools, but food-producing sites with similar evidence of animal domestication in central India (e.g., Bagor and Adamgarh) are categorized as Mesolithic for want of ground and polished stone tools there and the presence of microliths. By our terminology, food-producing, pre-pottery Jericho would be Mesolithic, and food-producing, pre-pottery Jarmo Neolithic![109] Without the small find of ground tools from there, one can only wonder about the name we would have given to Mehrgarh, as the site is dominated by blade tools.

It is not only in South Asia that Childe's bequest has been trivialized. In one of the more poignant ironies of his legacy in archaeology, archaeologists in the Soviet Union (and those under their influence in East Europe and Central Asia) failed to learn from Childe's definition of the Neolithic, and went on using polished pottery and/or stone tools as the criteria for identifying an archaeological culture as Neolithic, while the western archaeologists would criticize Soviet archaeologists for their outmoded concept but refuse to acknowledge that their own concept of the Neolithic was Childe's. The tone was set early by Clark and Piggott in the contrast they drew between the discredited Marxian concept of the Neolithic and the superior concept of it in 'western archaeological thought':

> In the nineteenth and the early twentieth centuries archaeologists took the use of pottery as one of the distinguishing marks of a 'Neolithic' assemblage of material culture, and thus appeared to make a technological distinction be-

---

[109] In 'An Aside on the South Asian Mesolithic' in his *Indus Civilization* (p. 31) Possehl raised the problem of definition of the Mesolithic without however suggesting a way out: 'Confusion over the definition of the Mesolithic – settlement and subsistence versus typology – has muddled much writing on Indian sites with microlithic technology. Some writers seem to imply, or even state, that if a tool assemblage contains microliths, it is thereby Mesolithic.' However, it does not seem to be true that there is any 'confusion over the definition of the Mesolithic' and that 'some writers' alone define the Mesolithic in terms of microlithic technology; Possehl does not cite any scholar who defines the Mesolithic otherwise, and there probably is none. South Asianists seem to have been quite consistent in defining the Mesolithic in terms of microliths, just as they have been in defining the Neolithic in terms of ground and polished stone tools. Probably, it is truer to say that the South Asian definition of the Mesolithic should have created a confusion, which it has not, in its implications for the definition of the Neolithic as a food-producing phase. The issue raised by Possehl was well taken care of by Childe's definition of the Neolithic, combined with the sense (as explained above) in which we can speak of the Mesolithic or Neolithic Age as distinct from a Stage.

tween stone-using cultures otherwise comparable save in this feature. This criterion is still employed in Russian archaeology, presumably owing to its association with Morgan's, and hence Engels's, theories of social evolution. With the recognition of other possible distinguishing factors, and with the more precise documentation made possible by cooperation with the natural sciences, western archaeological thought moved from a technological to an economic model, and made the distinction between Neolithic and other stone-using cultures in terms of subsistence economics: a Neolithic culture must of necessity be based on some form of food production, normally involving the domestication of animals and the cultivation of wild plants.

This new concept led to the recognition of the existence of prehistoric cultures that had an agricultural basis but did not manufacture pottery, and, conversely, of cultures with a hunting and food-collecting basis of Mesolithic type which, nevertheless, included pottery as a characteristic trait.[110]

Strangely, here and elsewhere, they completely black out Lubbock's definition based on the use of ground and polished stone tools, and even more, continue to subscribe to the discredited earlier view as the 'formal' definition of Neolithic.[111] Above all, there is no hint whatsoever that the new definition in 'western archaeological thought' is mainly the contribution of a Marxist called Gordon Childe, who, despite all his modesty, liked to claim the new definition as 'distinctively Childeish'. The success of Clark and Piggott in this has been quite remarkable, as the problem of defining the Neolithic continues to be seen in almost exactly similar terms, with East European and Central Asian usages being contrasted to the 'Western European definitions . . . focusing on subsistence economy as the defining criterion', and without the remotest hint at Childe's fundamental contribution.[112]

It remains to underline the precise sense in which Childe used the term 'revolution'. He has been both defended and attacked for using the word in the sense of a relatively sudden occurrence. Irfan Habib is naturally a defender, and on good reasoning: even if it was no overnight event, it did occur in a relatively much shorter span of time than the previous changes in prehistory.[113] However, in Man Makes Himself, Childe was perfectly clear that

---

[110] Clark and Piggott, Prehistoric Societies, p. 156.

[111] Ibid., p. 145. 'Based as they were on mixed farming, the Jarmo people were not formally speaking Neolithic, since they did not make pottery.' Cf. ibid., p. 144.

[112] Robert Jameson, 'Neolithic', in Shaw and Jameson (eds), A Dictionary of Archaeology, 1999, p. 423.

[113] Habib, Prehistory, p. 50. On the same reasoning, Gamble has defended the use of the term for the 'Human Revolution' of the Upper Palaeolithic period (Clive Gamble, Archaeology: The Basics, second edition, London and New York: Routledge, 2008, p. 159). Once again, the chapter 'Time Scales' in Childe's Man Makes Himself is a memorable statement of the underlying idea, and remains probably the best introduction to it.

he did not mean it that way: 'The "neolithic revolution" was not a catastrophe but a process'.[114] 'The neolithic revolution . . . was the climax of a
long process. It has to be presented as a single event because archaeology can
only recognize the result; the several steps leading up thereto are beyond the
range of direct observation'.[115] He knew the point could bear repetition:
'Naturally the Neolithic Revolution – the transition from pure hunting and
collecting to farming – was really a complicated process actually spread over
many centuries and perhaps millennia.'[116]

For his concept of Urban Revolution too, Childe sought to obviate any
misconstruing of the term 'revolution': 'The word "revolution" must not of
course be taken as denoting a sudden violent catastrophe; it is here used for
the culmination of a progressive change in the economic structure and social organization of communities.'[117]

The clarification hardly helped, however, even when it succeeded. The
word 'revolution' sort of jarred, almost rankled. Even when his sense of it
was perfectly understood and appreciated, Childe would yet be criticized
for '*potential* distortions involved in the use of the term' (emphasis added)
by Robert McC. Adams, who insisted that 'the more common usage of the
word "revolution" . . . implies aspects of conscious struggle', and 'any implication that such was generally the case . . . is certainly false'.[118]

More on the Neolithic: Milk, Wool and Pottery

Like many others, Irfan Habib too subscribes to the view that after the
Neolithic revolution, domesticated animals became a source of supply of

---

[114] Childe, *Man Makes Himself*, p. 99.

[115] Ibid. p. 105.

[116] Childe, 'The New Stone Age', p. 100.

[117] Gordon Childe, 'The Urban Revolution', *The Town Planning Review*, Vol. 21, No. 1, April
1950, p. 12.

[118] Robert McC. Adams, *The Evolution of Urban Society: Early Mesopotamia and Prehispanic
Mexico*, London: Weidenfeld & Nicolson, 1966, p. 9. A still more symptomatic case relates
to 'planning'. Galbraith, having brought out with hallmark acuity how there could be no
corporate capitalism without long-term comprehensive planning, noted how planning became nevertheless a bad word once it came to be associated with communism: 'Until the end
of World War II, or shortly thereafter, planning was a moderately evocative word in the
United States. It implied a sensible concern for what might happen in the future and a
disposition, by forehanded action, to forestall avoidable misfortune. . . . With the Cold War,
however, the word planning acquired ideological overtones. The communist countries not
only socialized property, which seemed not a strong likelihood in the United States, but they
planned, which somehow seemed more of a danger. . . . Modern liberalism carefully emphasizes tact rather than clarity of speech. Accordingly it avoided the term and conservatives
made it one of opprobrium' (J.K. Galbraith, *The New Industrial State*, Pelican Books, 1967,
p. 32).

'both milk and meat'.[119] This requires a bit of a qualification, in view of both the commonality of the assumption that milk as much as meat was the aim of domestication, as well as the reactions that references to meat-eating in early South Asia sometimes provoke. It is now known, thanks to the work of Andrew Sherratt and others on the 'secondary products revolution', that initially animals were domesticated not for milk or wool primarily, but for meat. As Sandor Bökönyi has pointed out, it is possible to distinguish two phases of the Neolithic period in this respect:

> Up to the end of the Early Neolithic, domestic animals had only one use (apart from their sporadic use as sacrificial animals, hunting companions, herd or watch dogs and so on): to supply meat. Then their secondary uses, to provide milk, wool, draught power, and so on were discovered. This was almost another 'revolutionary' step and started a 'domestication fever' in the second half of the Neolithic.[120]

This had indeed always been suspected.[121] The suspicion was especially strong for wool, given that 'in most wild sheep the coat is hairy and only a thin down represents what becomes wool [through selective breeding of domesticated sheep]'.[122] Now we know the reason behind this: 'a sudden mutation that stopped the yearly change of wool fibres'.[123]

Following the current usage, Habib's references to pottery-making assume distinctions that are only seemingly self-evident and hence call for an explanation. The search for the explanation helps to focus on a problem area of some significance. The first pots were of course hand-made, and one type of hand-made pottery is stated to have been made on 'some kind of a crude turn-table'.[124] In the references to wheel-made pottery, a distinction between two types of the potter's wheel is seen in the frequent mention of the slow wheel and the fast wheel.[125] However, neither the turntable in the hand-made pottery tradition, nor the difference between the slow and the fast potter's wheel is explained anywhere.[126] This creates difficulties. For

---

[119] Habib, *Prehistory*, pp. 49–50.

[120] Sandor Bökönyi, 'Domestication of Animals from the Beginnings of Food Production up to about 5,000 Years Ago', in De Laet (ed.), *History of Humanity*, Vol. 1, 1994, p. 394.

[121] Childe, *Man Makes Huimself*, p. 79.

[122] Childe, *What Happened in History*, p. 56.

[123] Bökönyi, 'Domestication of Animals', p. 391.

[124] Habib, *Prehistory*, p. 67.

[125] Habib, *The Indus Civilization*, pp. 5, 80, 91; Habib and Thakur, *The Vedic Age*, p. 81.

[126] In fact, Habib's account of the Swat Valley creates a definite impression, although this may not have been intended, that three types of wheel (slow, fast and faster) were used there over time: 'It [i.e. Swat or Ghalighai Culture IV, *c.* 1800–1400 BC] has pottery turned on both slow and fast wheels' (Habib, *The Indus Civilization*, p. 83); and then: 'Pottery continued to be refined [in the following period, around 1200 BC] as it began to be made on faster wheels,

instance, when the first evidence of the potter's wheel at Mehrgarh is discussed, it is contrasted with the earlier hand-made pottery, but one is not told whether it was the slow or the fast wheel.[127]

Habib draws on an established practice, however, and one that continues after him. Chakrabarti made the same unexplained distinction between the slow and the fast wheel in his references to the slow wheel, and generally mentioned simply 'wheelmade' pottery.[128] Singh refers occasionally to pottery made by 'the turntable method', the 'slow wheel' and 'a fast-moving wheel',[129] without explaining the nature of the supposedly three types, and, equally crucially, without specifying exactly which of the two wheels is meant on the occasions when she simply refers to 'wheel-made', 'wheel-thrown' or 'wheel-turned' pottery.[130]

For proper clarity about the major techniques of pottery-making, one must begin with the basic distinction between hand-made and wheel-made pottery. At an early stage in the hand-made tradition, a device called the 'turntable' or *'tournette'* began to be used. Then came the potter's wheel, of which there were two main types, one of which was set in a pit and was moved by the potter's foot, the other being known as the 'hand-operated [with a stick]' or 'spun' wheel. The main points were summed up neatly by Gordon Childe:

> All Neolithic vessels have been built up by hand, aided only by a leaf or mat on which the lump of clay might stand, and smoothing tools of wood or bone. By Old Kingdom times, however, the Egyptians were utilizing a pivoted disc that would revolve readily as the pot was being shaped. It is sometimes called the *tournette*. But by 3000 BC Sumerian potters were already using the true wheel that will spin fast. The lump of soft clay is placed on the centre of, or on a tray connected by a sort of axle to the centre of, a horizontal wheel. The latter can be made to rotate rapidly by the potter's foot or by an assistant. A lump of clay of the proper consistency thus set spinning almost automatically assumes a cylindrical form; all the potter's hand has to do is to give the gyrating mass the required contours. By the use of this device ten or twenty vessels can be modelled, and that more symmetrically, in the time required for building up one by free hand. On the other hand, with the adoption of the

---

so that grey-black wares changed into grey ware' (Habib and Thakur, *The Vedic Age*, p. 75). The use of the 'faster' wheel in itself could not possibly have *caused* the change in pottery's colour, as may appear from the last statement: for a brief account of the factors that affect the colour of pottery, see Childe, *Man Makes Himself*, pp. 91–92.

[127] Habib, *Prehistory*, p. 54.

[128] For example, Chakrabarti, *India: An Archaeological History*, pp. 225, 236–37.

[129] Singh, *History of Ancient and Early Medieval India from the Stone Age to the 12th Century*, pp. 120, 125, 238, 247.

[130] Ibid., pp. 105, 106, 158, 370, 467.

wheel, pottery tends to become a factory product and to lose much of its individuality.[131]

The technical and other points have since been elaborated many times over, accompanied by significant advances in our knowledge of them. For our purposes, the distinction between the potter's wheel and the *tournette*, the 'pivoted disc' or turntable, is crucial. The first thing to note is that the term 'slow wheel' refers to neither of the just noted two types of potter's wheel (foot-wheel and spun-wheel), but to the turntable or *tournette*. As the turntable is different from the true potter's wheel in vitally important respects, the use of the term 'slow wheel' for the turntable tends to blur these differences and hence should be avoided. Lack of clarity about this has indeed been responsible for much vagueness and confusion in South Asian studies.

Unlike the true potter's wheel, a *tournette* does not have any movement of its own. It is *meant* not to rotate on its own but to stop after the hands are taken off it: the movement of the device in itself thus imparts no shape to the clay being turned.[132] The *tournette*, in other words, is a type of device for rotating the clay on its working surface as it is fashioned by the hand. Indeed sometimes even unpivoted platforms, like a rounded stone or a piece of pottery, that were used for turning the clay around are called *tournettes*.[133] However, these are better distinguished in the literature as 'proto-*tournettes*'. The coming of the pivoted platform that could be freely rotated to get the different sides of the vessel being made was no doubt an improvement on the rounded stone or piece of pottery: a *tournette* facilitates the work and imparts a certain symmetry to a vessel that may not have been easy to achieve earlier. Nevertheless, it is clear that the *tournette* belongs to the hand-made pottery tradition.

In a true potter's wheel, the fast-moving wheel transfers its own inertia to the clay, imparting to it a basic shape which can then be worked upon by the potter's hands. The wheel turns the clay, exerting on it a centrifugal force; a shape is thus 'thrown', and so we have wheel-turned or wheel-thrown pottery. It speeded up the process of production manifold. It has also been observed that the two techniques were actually very different in their implications for social organization, with the *tournette* apparently

---

[131] Gordon Childe, *The Bronze Age*, Cambridge: Cambridge University Press, 1930, pp. 50–51. The chronology would vary of course with time and space.

[132] This point tends to be missed in modern experiments with ancient specimens of *tournettes*, when it is shown that with strenuous effort they can be made to throw some small vessels.

[133] Hans J. Nissen, 'The 'Ubaid Period in the Context of the Early History of the Near East', in Elizabeth F. Henrickson and Ingolf Thuesen (eds), *Upon This Foundation: The 'Ubaid Reconsidered*, Copenhagen: University of Copenhagen, 1989, p. 251. (The article could be accessed only in part on Google Book Search.)

making much less demands on changes in the existing set-up than the true potter's wheel.[134]

Sometimes the qualitative difference in the production process between the *tournette* or turntable or 'slow wheel', on the one hand, and the potter's wheel, on the other, is sought be conveyed by the distinction between the 'turning' of the turntable and the 'throwing' of the wheel. Thus, with reference to early food-producing cultures such as at Mehrgarh, it is stated that 'wheel-turned pottery later gave way to wheel-thrown pottery'.[135] Given

---

[134] Among other things, the role of women in pottery-making faded into the background with the coming of the potter's wheel. It has also been pointed out that 'while the *tournette* was readily accepted within a short span of time over wider areas of the ancient Near East, the acceptance of the potter's wheel was restricted to Mesopotamia and parts of northeast Syria' (ibid., p. 249).

[135] Thapar, *Early India*, p. 76. A wholly unexpected thing about Thapar's book came to my notice, thanks to the incidental fact of my non-possession of a personal copy. I first consulted the first, hardbound edition of the book published by Allen Lane, London, in 2002, and the next time, the paperback edition published by Penguin India in 2003 – both from my college library. I discovered that the latter is not a reprint of the former, as one would suppose from the publication details. In the sentence that I have just quoted, 'wheel-turned pottery' has been replaced with 'hand-turned pottery' in the Penguin India edition; also, more than one sentence has been added to the author's Preface, which however remains dated 2001, the year before it was published by Allen Lane. The chronological table has also been rearranged with a view to making it more systematic. I checked the internet for other editions of the book, and in the one published by the University of California Press in 2004, purportedly a reprint again, I found on the acknowledgment page (xi), evidence of further, somewhat hasty retouching. In the first two editions, Professor Nilakanta Sastri's name was mis-spelt as 'Nilakantha Sastri' on this page, where we also have a more visible typo: *The Principle Upanisads* in place of *The Principal Upanisads*. In the California edition, Sastri's name is corrected, but the latter typo remains. Fortunately, the pages I have referred to in this essay are displayed on the Google preview of the California edition, and those citations remain unchanged, except for the one already noted. I have not been able to compare the three editions for anything else, but I mention all this to forewarn the unsuspecting reader/researcher.

It remains unclear whether the changes were made by the author or the publisher. In case the additions to the Preface of the Penguin India edition was made by Thapar herself, it helps to accentuate the dilemma among historians as to what they should do with pre and proto-history. In the Preface to Thapar's *A History of India* (1966), it was stated: 'The history . . . [in the book] begins with the culture of the Indo-Aryans and not with the prehistoric cultures of India. There is already a useful study of Indian prehistory and proto-history in the Pelican series (Stuart Piggott, *Prehistoric India*), and there is no point in repeating the same material.' *Early India*, however, has a full chapter on the theme. Its Allen Lane edition states: 'An introduction already exists to the pre-history and proto-history of India in the volume by F.R. and B. Allchin, *The Birth of Indian Civilization*, revised in 1993, also published by Penguin.' In the Penguin India edition of *Early India*, this is expanded thus: 'An introduction already exists to the pre-history and proto-history of India in the volume by F.R. and B. Allchin, *The Birth of Indian Civilization*, revised in 1993, also published by Penguin, as well as *The Origins of a Civilization* by the same authors and published by Viking in 1997 (Penguin, 1998). I have therefore given only a brief overview of pre-history and proto-history.' The least one can say is that the overview can by no means be charged with 'repeating the same material'! And point out, as a further confirmation of the point made

the evidence for the 'slow wheel' in the early layers of Mehrgarh,[136] this presumably seeks to represent the distinction of 'turning' by the 'slow wheel' and 'throwing' by the 'fast wheel'. Generally, however, both 'wheel-turned' and 'wheel-thrown' pottery are taken to mean the same thing, i.e. wheel-made pottery. 'Turning' and 'throwing' have in fact been used synonymously for describing the same process (pot-making on the wheel) for too long to make their divergence desirable. Matters are hardly helped when 'turning', in a further spin on it, is invested with a yet another meaning for pot-making.[137]

The four divisions – pottery made by hands alone, with the help of the *tournette*, and with two types of the wheel – were regularly employed by the Allchins in their overviews of South Asian archaeology; they preferred the term 'turntable' to '*tournette*' and additionally pointed out the distinct provenances of the two types of potter's wheel ('foot-wheel' and 'spun-wheel') in South Asia, with the spun-wheel in use mainly to the east of the Indus.[138]

---

earlier (above, n. 28) about a certain indifference of attitude to things prehistoric, that the alleged revision of *The Birth of Indian Civilization* – the original raison d'être of the brevity of the overview – was never undertaken. What appeared in 1993 was a reprint of the old book with a new preface, where the Allchins describe their initial disinclination about the idea of the reprinting and how they were eventually persuaded by David Davidar of Penguin India of the continuing relevance of their 1968 classic. Only one change was made in the 1993 reprint: 'The change that we have made is the removal of the list of C14 dates at the end of the original book' (Allchin and Allchin, *The Birth of Indian Civilization*, p. 8).

136 Possehl, *The Indus Civilization*, p. 90.

137 'Sometimes, after throwing, a pot is put back on the wheel for thinning of the walls with small steel blades set in wooden handles . . . which is called "turning". But turning is less common in South Asia than lifting the pot off the wheel' (Ratnagar, *Makers and Shapers*, p. 40).

138 Bridget Allchin and F.R. Allchin, *The Birth of Indian Civlization*, Pelican Books, 1968, pp. 287–88, 292–93, 331; *The Rise of Civilization in India and Pakistan*, pp. 110–11, 125, 197, 199, 266, 317, 323. Ratnagar (*Makers and Shapers*, p. 40) states in her informative study of early Indian technology: 'F.R. Allchin and B. Allchin report (1982: 199) the rare occurrence of wheels controlled by the foot (they are set in a pit and connected by an axle to a light turntable) in Pakistan.' Foot-wheels, however, are anything but a rare occurrence. Not only are they dominant in Pakistan but are fairly widely prevalent (also known as pit-wheel, kick-wheel or double-wheel) over a large area outside Pakistan. The Allchins do not seem to be pointing to the alleged rarity on the cited page. They state: 'The foot-wheel is still in use in Sind and parts of the Punjab, Saurashtra, and the North West Frontier Province, in contrast to the Indian spun-wheel found east of the Indus, and may be taken with some degree of certainty to be a legacy of this period. The modern foot-wheel closely resembles those which are found right across Iran and into Mesopotamia, both today and probably in ancient times' (Allchin and Allchin, *The Rise of Civilization in India and Pakistan*, 1982 edition, p. 199). In fact elsewhere in the same book, they venture to suggest that 'the pottery of the entire Indus system' during the Early Indus period was 'predominantly made on the foot-wheel' (ibid., p. 162). For a well-illustrated study of traditional pot-making in Pakistan, see Owen S. Rye and Clifford Evans, *Traditional Pottery Techniques of Pakistan: Field and Laboratory Studies*, City of Washington: Smithsonian Institution Press, 1976.

It was also by and large clear that in the broad distinction between hand-made and wheel-made pottery, pottery made on the turntable belonged to the former category. Although in general descriptions scholars sometimes distinguish pottery made on the turntable from hand-made pottery, what is really meant is the distinction between pottery made on the turntable and other types of hand-made pottery, i.e. hand-made pottery that is made on the turntable and hand-made pottery that is not. The following references will help to clarify the point: (1) 'There is a limited range of types, all hand-made or built on simple turntable.'[139] (2) 'This pottery is hand-made, probably built on some kind of turntable.'[140] (3) 'Almost the whole range is hand-made; the turntable and the dabber and anvil are the two main techniques employed.'[141]

Over the years, the term 'slow wheel' seems to have replaced 'turntable' or '*tournette*' as the preferred substitute in South Asian studies. The synonymy of the terms, though sometimes noted,[142] would seem to have generally faded away, so that a scholar who runs into an odd reference to the 'turntable' or '*tournette*' in the literature is apt to think, as Habib and Singh apparently do, that it is different from the 'slow wheel'. It is better to retain the term '*tournette*' or 'turntable' rather than 'slow wheel', not only because its qualitative difference from the true potter's wheel is conveyed by the former better than 'slow wheel', which appears to make its difference from the 'fast wheel' a matter merely of degree, but also because the term 'slow wheel' tends to create a good deal of unnecessary confusion.

Thus Habib calls the pottery of south Indian Neolithic cultures 'entirely hand-made' with a turntable being used in the process: 'Pottery was entirely hand-made, but some roundness was imparted to it by its being rotated slowly, on some kind of a crude turn-table (not the fast-moving potter's wheel).'[143] In Singh's account, this is referred to as the use of the 'slow wheel', and with time there was 'a slight increase in the amount of wheel-made pottery'.[144] The same pottery is thus referred to as hand-made by one author and wheel-made by the other. For the site of Chirand, the usages are swapped. For Singh, 'most of the pottery [at Chirand] was handmade, though

---

[139] Allchin and Allchin, *The Rise of Civilization in India and Pakistan*, pp. 110–11.

[140] Ibid., p. 125.

[141] K. Paddayya, in Ghosh (ed.), *An Encyclopaedia of Indian Archaeology*, Vol. I, p. 227.

[142] Jane R. McIntosh, *The Ancient Indus Valley: New Perspectives*, Santa Barbara: ABC-CLIO, 2008, pp. 61, 416; K.S. Ramachandran, in Ghosh (ed.), *An Encyclopaedia of Indian Archaeology*, Vol. I, p. 247; V.N. Misra, in Ghosh (ed.), *An Encyclopaedia of Indian Archaeo-logy*, Vol. II, p. 36.

[143] Habib, *Prehistory*, p. 67.

[144] Singh, *History of Ancient and Early Medieval India from the Stone Age to the 12th Century*, p. 125.

there were some examples of the turntable method';[145] for Habib, 'The pottery is mainly handmade but with lustrous burnishing and painting; and some wheel-turned ware also occurs'.[146] For Neolithic Koldihwa, Singh refers to three varieties of hand-made pottery: 'The pottery was handmade, and consisted of three varieties – net-marked or cord-marked pottery; a plain red pottery; and a black-and-red ware.'[147] Of these varieties, however, the red ware is known to have been produced on the slow wheel,[148] so that it would not be surprising if someone refers to both hand-made and wheel-made pottery at Koldihwa.

Clearly, it is the use of the term 'slow wheel' for the turntable that has been responsible for the confusion, illustrated here by the examples of Habib and Singh as both end up calling the same kind of pottery wheel-made as well as hand-made. In a way, this is natural: pottery made on the slow wheel is apt to be described as wheel-made, and this in turn abolishes the distinction between hand-made and wheel-made pottery. It needs to be noted that in this Habib and Singh in fact follow distinguished professional archaeologists. In making the following statement, M.K. Dhavalikar did not remember that the slow wheel is but another name for the turntable so that the pottery made on it is hand-made, not wheel-turned: 'The pottery is wheel-turned, possibly on a slow wheel.'[149] K.S. Ramachandran refers in the same book to the same kind of pottery as 'hand-made' and 'wheel-turned' alternately: 'The pottery of the Neolithic folk is entirely handmade in the technique of the anvil and dabber . . . or of turning on a turntable'; 'The whole assemblage . . . is wheel-turned, possibly on a slow wheel or turntable.'[150]

Diffusion, Diffusionism and Childe

In a note on 'the methods of archaeology', Irfan Habib points out how diffusion was once a very important method of explanation among archaeologists, notably Childe; it was then heavily criticized by advocates of New or Processual Archaeology and finally has come to be appreciated once again

---

[145] Ibid., p. 120.

[146] Habib, *Prehistory*, p. 65.

[147] Singh, *History of Ancient and Early Medieval India from the Stone Age to the 12th Century*, p. 110.

[148] K.V. Soundara Rajan, in Ghosh (ed.), *An Encyclopaedia of Indian Archaeology*, Vol. I, p. 53.

[149] M.K. Dhavalikar, *Indian Protohistory*, New Delhi: Books and Books, 1997, p. 139.

[150] K.S. Ramachandran, in Ghosh (ed.), *An Encyclopaedia of Indian Archaeology*, Vol. I, pp. 67, 247.

by archaeologists.[151] It is with reference to this point that the following statement is made in his bibliographical note: 'Despite the passage of time, many of Childe's basic propositions retain their validity and are receiving fresh attention, after a phase in which he was much criticized for "diffusionism".'[152] Accordingly, diffusion is regularly employed by Habib to account for change.

Diffusion is generally distinguished from migration, in that it refers to the adoption in one culture of the features of another and not their physical movement from one place to another, though migration is recognized as an important mode of diffusion. Occasionally, Habib conflates the two: migration is meant once when diffusion is spoken of ('modern man's diffusion from Africa'[153]), and at another place, both migration and diffusion are meant by 'diffusion' ('Africa to India: Diffusion of the Human Species and Tool Cultures', Map 2.1[154]). Generally, however, he does distinguish between 'diffusion of techniques' and 'human migrations', limiting diffusion to 'spread of techniques, languages or ideas',[155] and describing movements of people as migrations.[156]

The case for diffusion is argued on the basis of priority of dates – something seen later at one place than at another is interpreted as having diffused from the latter place. We have seen this for the Mesolithic cultures of Sri Lanka and Maharashtra. It is also suggested for the diffusion of rice cultivation and cord-impressed hand-made pottery from China, Vietnam and Thailand via Assam to eastern India and beyond: 'It would seem, then, that the Vindhyan Neolithic, with its cord-impressed pottery, was the terminal point of diffusion from an eastern source, of which the Assam sites and Pandu Rajar Dhibi, Period I, may mark two important stages.'[157] By Period II at Pandu Rajar Dhibi, the presence of 'wheel-turned pottery' suggests diffusion from the west: 'This kind of pottery . . . could be the result of an infusion of technique from the Indus basis, where it was found 2,000 years earlier.'[158]

Dates, again, are the reason why Habib excludes diffusion and allows independent development in the case of the southern Neolithic: 'So far as we can judge, the sole Neolithic culture that was probably entirely indi-

---

[151] Habib, *The Indus Civilization*, pp. 20–21.
[152] Ibid., p. 21.
[153] Habib, *Prehistory*, p. 32.
[154] Ibid., pp. 30–31.
[155] Habib, *The Indus Civilization*, pp. 20, 21.
[156] Habib and Thakur, *The Vedic Age*, pp. 3, 15, 16, 47.
[157] Habib, *The Indus Civilization*, p. 64.
[158] Ibid.

genous in its origins was that of the south.'[159] This obviously is based on the earlier dates for the southern Neolithic than those for the Neolithic–Chalcolithic cultures that intervene between it and those of the northwest and north India. However, I would like to know if wild sheep were indigenous to the region, for if they were not (as seems to be the case[160]), they must have been brought to the region from outside, denting their indigenity. Independent domestication of the wild goat would also seem doubtful if the existing views of it – that one West Asian variety spread eastwards from about 8000 BC while the domestication of the East or South Asian one dates only from 2000 BC, if not as late as AD 1000 – are correct,[161] for in south India the evidence of their domestication dates from *c.* 3000 BC.

It is commonly agreed that dates by themselves cannot establish the case for diffusion: it is the distribution of wild flora and fauna, and genetic make-up that tell us which variety at Mehrgarh was locally domesticated and which was brought from outside.[162] However, dates alone are commonly invoked to destroy a case for diffusion. The example of the south Indian Neolithic suggests that this need not hold always.

It is in the case of iron technology in south India that Habib's defence of diffusion gets unnessarily strong. In his reconstruction of the eastward diffusion of iron technology, we get a commendably critical presentation of the extant evidence of iron-using cultures. The picture is spoilt by the very end of his diffusional tale, the case of Karnataka. Note the downplaying of the early dates here, as well as the energetic defence of diffusionism:

> Quite remarkably, in Karnataka iron-use seems to have begun earlier than in most parts of India, except perhaps the borderlands. For its Period II, where iron objects first occur, Hallur, on the Tungbhadra, has carbon dates yielding a range of 1385–825 BC. The neighbouring site of Komaranahalli has TL dates for its iron-using megalithic period that range from 1440 to 930 BC. A floor date for the beginning of iron-use around 1000 BC or even earlier, therefore, is not unreasonable. Such an early date rules out transmission from northern India. On the face of it, a direct transmission from West Asia to south

---

[159] Habib, *Prehistory*, p. 67.

[160] The following distribution of wild sheep excludes south India: 'Wild sheep lived along the same [mountain] chains as [wild goats], but in three distinct varieties. The mouflon survives in the Mediterranean islands and the hill country of Hither Asia from Turkey to Western Persia; east of the mouflon, in Turkestan, Afghanistan, and the Punjab, is the home of the urial; still farther east, in the mountains of Central Asia, lives the argal' (Childe, *Man Makes Himself*, p. 76).

[161] McIntosh, *The Ancient Indus Valley*, p. 59.

[162] See ibid., pp. 58–60. Also, Dorian Q. Fuller, 'Neolithic Cultures', in *Encyclopedia of Archaeology*, edited by Pearsall, 2008, pp. 756 ff; Avari, *India: The Ancient Past*, p. 35.

India is also unlikely, since no other commercial or cultural contacts are evident. Yet, it cannot also be ruled out. Copper-smelting itself was a weak industry in the south Indian Neolithic, so that an indigenous development of the complex process of iron-smelting and carburization in south India seems even more improbable.[163]

To be sure, we need to exercise the utmost caution in ruling out diffusion in the case of iron metallurgy, in view of the unusual complexity of the process. Habib rightly emphasizes this, so that 'it is difficult to conceive of the discovery being made independently of each other in different cultures'.[164] We need to note, however, the rather big jump from this statement to the following conclusion: 'Diffusion from *one* source, therefore, has great probability on its side' (emphasis added).[165] The improbability of too many centres of discovery need not exclude the possibility of the discovery at more than one place. It was on similar grounds that Isaac Newton accused Gottfried Leibniz of plagiarizing his discovery of calculus, but we know (as did Newton) that this complex branch of mathematics was thought up independently at two places in Europe in the seventeenth century.

More than a word needs to be said about Habib's point about the renewed recognition of the importance of diffusion as an explanatory tool among archaeologists. It is true that scholars like Ian Hodder see considerable merit in the concept, but that does not mean, as Habib seems to think, that they thereby also approve of what they think were Childe's views on the matter. Kevin Greene, in his *Archaeology*, referred to by Habib in his bibliography, does reaffirm the value of the concept of diffusion, but is careful to distinguish it from Childe's 'diffusionism', which remains discredited.[166] As he puts it very clearly, the problem with earlier proponents like Childe was that they took diffusion for granted, instead of as something that requires demonstration:

> The problem lay not in the *idea* of diffusion, for the history of technology provides many well-documented examples of invention followed by diffusion, but in the way that it was accepted as a fundamental fact, rather than as a theoretical proposition that might be supported or refuted by further evidence.[167]

This judgment of Childe's ideas on diffusion is widely shared. As it happens, it overlooks the bulk of his writings on the issue, and is based on a

[163] Habib and Thakur, *The Vedic Age*, p. 90.
[164] Ibid., pp. 86–87.
[165] Ibid., p. 87.
[166] Kevin Greene, *Archaeology, an Introduction: The History, Principles and Methods of Modern Archaeology*, third edition, London: Routledge, 1995, pp. 162–67.
[167] Ibid., p. 163.

flatly wrong interpretation of a horribly narrow reading of Childe's posthumously published essay, 'Retrospect'. The roots of the judgment go back to the works of Renfrew (Greene's point of reference) who, from 1972 onwards, has continually pointed out the fallacy of Childe's views on diffusion: 'We can no longer accept that the sole unifying theme of European prehistory was, in the words of Gordon Childe, "the irradiation of European barbarism by Oriental civilization".'[168] The charge has never ceased to be repeated. To continue with Renfrew, Childe is stated to have 'practised a "modified diffusionism", accepting the view of Montelius that the story of European prehistory was, as Childe later put it, "the irradiation of European barbarism by Oriental civilization"'; and one is told again how the new radiometric dates 'hold up for scrutiny the entire "diffusionist" assumption of what Childe had called the "irradiation of European barbarism by Oriental civilization"'.[169]

Incredible as it may seem, what has made Childe a diffusionist to such a large number of persons is this phrase – 'the irradiation of European barbarism by Oriental civilization' – that he wrote in his 'Retrospect'. Since it came from Childe's own reflections on the lifetime of his work, the expression is taken to capture his standpoint accurately. Thanks to the unquestioned influence of Childe on the profession, this view is further taken to have been pervasive till it was questioned by Renfrew. Renfrew himself does not seem to have got much beyond this expression, and the influence of this patriarch has made it a piece of household wisdom in the archaeological community. Gamble, for instance, refers to this statement by Childe to establish his lifelong adherence to diffusionism: 'He was to later write of his early syntheses that "the sole unifying theme was the irradiation of European barbarism by Oriental civilization" . . . [citing Childe, 'Retrospect', p. 70], and he directed his considerable powers of archaeological synthesis and philological analysis to showing this was indeed the case.'[170]

Renfrew critiqued Childe's diffusionism also for its naiveté. According to him, Childe both accepted the 'principle' of *ex oriente lux* and, in explaining culture change in Europe, simply 'assumed' that it must have occurred through diffusion. In both he did no more than just follow Oscar Montelius, although Renfrew puts it to Childe's credit that he did not subscribe to and avoided the theory of ancient Egypt as the source of all diffusion.[171] It has

---

[168] Colin Renfrew, *The Emergence of Civilization: The Cyclades and the Aegean in the Third Millennium BC*, London: Methuen, 1972, p. xxv.

[169] Renfrew, *Prehistory*, pp. 33, 48.

[170] Clive Gamble, *Origins and Revolutions: Human Identity in Earliest Prehistory*, New York: Cambridge University Press, 2007, p. 11; Renfrew, *The Emergence of Civilization*, pp. 57–58.

[171] Renfrew, *Prehistory*, pp. 33, 42, 48.

since been almost customary to represent Childe's diffusionism in these terms. Thus Gamble: 'Europe, he [Childe] claimed, fell under the light from the east, *ex oriente lux*.'[172] And thus Greene: 'Childe, like Montelius and others before him, made an assumption that all innovations or improvements observed in European prehistory must have originated in those areas where civilizations flourished at the earliest date.'[173]

In fact, it was as an exercise in self-criticism that Childe mentioned the idea of 'the irradiation of European barbarism by Oriental civilization' in 'Retrospect'; he pointed out that this was not his original idea but 'a traditional dogma in Britain' to which he subscribed in his early work, and dissociated himself from it completely, calling it 'childish' rather than 'Childeish':

> The sole unifying theme [of *The Dawn of European Civilization*, first edition, 1925] was the irradiation of European barbarism by Oriental civilization, a traditional dogma in Britain my faith in which had been consolidated as much by a reaction against the doctrines of Kossinna and Hubert Schmidt . . . as by the Diffusionist thesis of Elliot Smith and Perry which at the time was arousing quite sectarian passions among anthropologists and prehistorians.
>
> . . . I looked with over-credulous eyes for footprints of Steppe horsemen in the marshes of the Pripet. . . . This was childish, not Childeish.[174]

Emancipation from the irradiation theme entailed two tasks: developing a critical attitude to diffusionism and establishing the distinctive identity of prehistoric Europe from the available data. The first was relatively easy and began early: 'the sea voyagers who diffused culture to Britain and Denmark in the first chapters in the first *Dawn* (1925) . . . were relegated to a secondary position in the second edition of *The Dawn* (1927)'.[175] The second task – demonstrating 'the individuality of prehistoric Europe'[176] – was more demanding and hence an extended affair, in the course of accomplishing which Childe incurred a major intellectual debt to C.F.C. Hawkes' *Prehistoric Foundations of Europe*.[177] It is with some satisfaction that Childe looks upon his last book, *The Prehistory of European Society*, as an epitaph to the irradiation theme: 'It is a final answer to those who told us: "the true prelude to European history was written in Egypt, Mesopotamia and Pales-

---

[172] Gamble, *Origins and Revolutions*, p. 11.
[173] Greene, *Archaeology, an Introduction*, p. 162. This statement describes a figure representing the diffusionist argument as advocated by Montelius and Childe (ibid., figure 6).
[174] Childe, 'Retrospect', p. 70.
[175] Ibid.
[176] Ibid., p. 73.
[177] Ibid., p. 74. Cf. Childe, *The Prehistory of European Society*, Harmondsworth: Penguin Books, 1958, p. 8.

tine while the natives of Europe remained illiterate barbarians"'.[178]

Yet Childe was also able to successfully salvage the valuable idea of diffusion from the mishmash of diffusionism. For all the advantages of discarding 'migrationist hypotheses', independent development by itself will simply not do: 'Yet I just had to admit migrations and the impact of foreign cultures: the internal development of Scottish society in accordance with "universal laws" simply could not explain the archaeological data from Scotland; reference to Continental data actually documented the solvent effects of external factors.'[179]

A major about-face on another key assumption of diffusionism occurred in the 1930s. Childe argued, as the following passage in his *The Most Ancient East* (1929) shows, for the typically diffusionist view that there could not have been more than one centre of invention of things like metallurgy and food production:

> If it is so hard to identify the original cradle of metallurgy, how can we hope to locate the first centre of food-production? Speculation here becomes almost uncontrolled guess-work, that is positively harmful. Yet such a centre is more than a methodological postulate. It would at least be absurd to suggest that men began cultivating plants whose range in nature is quite limited, like wheat and barley, at several independent centres in that circumscribed region. It would be hardly less fantastic to assume that the domestication of cattle, sheep and swine happened more than once. The common traits of what is not very happily termed the 'neolithic culture' are too numerous to deny some unity behind it.[180]

By *Man Makes Himself* (1936), he had outgrown his belief in the invention-only-once-thence-diffusion-all-around idea. He noted the enormous variation in the staple diet of humans in the world ('rice, wheat, barley, millet, maize, yams, sweet potatoes'), variations within an animal or foodgrain population, such as three varieties of wheat and wild sheep, and the very

---

[178] Ibid. This anti-diffusionist argument was in fact central to Childe's last book, *Prehistory of European Society*: 'The central object of this book is to show that even in prehistoric times barbarian societies in Europe behaved in a distinctively European way, foreshadowing, however dimly, the contrast with African or Asian societies that has become manifest in the last thousand years.'

[179] Childe, 'Retrospect', p. 73. To appreciate its significance, we need to contrast this statement with the plight of later British archaeologists antipathetic to diffusion: 'By the 1960s British archaeology was placed into a curious state, for many prehistorians considered that the major technological and social changes had resulted from independent development and internal evolution, rather than having been introduced by immigrants or invaders' (Greene, *Archaeology, an Introduction*, p. 163).

[180] V. Gordon Childe, *The Most Ancient East: The Oriental Prelude to European Pre-history*, New York: Alfred A. Knopf, 1929, p. 228.

wide provenance of all these.[181] Even for the beginning of wheat and barley cultivation, he would say no more than this: 'The questions where cultivation started and whether in one centre or in several are still undecided.[182]

In an article that he had written the previous year (1935), Childe underlined the need for establishing (as against simply assuming) the case for diffusion by ruling out the ever-present possibility of independent invention: 'similarities in material culture can nearly always be explained away as parallel adjustments evoked by a similar environment'.[183] Any theory of diffusion based on 'superficial resemblances and abstract arguments' will not do, as when '"polished, stone celts" were cited as constituting a common trait uniting remote cultures quite regardless of how the "celt" was mounted or whether it was used as an axe, an adze or a battle-axe'; 'Scientific prehistory cannot be satisfied with such abstractions'.[184] In *What Happened in History*, his discussion of the importance of diffusion in human history makes the fullest allowance for the importance of independent inventions and the inner dynamics of societies, and has little room for what is understood and criticized as diffusionism.[185]

A difference in dates by itself meant nothing to Childe in this context. In his time pottery was regarded as providing a very good case for diffusion. He argued against this with a concrete example:

> The possibility of independent invention can never be ruled out *a priori*; in some cases it has to be admitted. In 1950, it certainly seems that pottery appeared in Northern Europe before any Neolithic farmers had advanced far enough north to impart the art to local savages, but yet too late to be the progenitor of Egyptian or Mesopotamian ceramics. If so, the discovery – or rather the discoveries – involved must have been at least twice.[186]

It was for the Neolithic cultures that Childe insisted on the importance of diffusion, in terms that are unexceptionable:

> These cultivated cereals are derived from annual grasses that grow wild in rather dry and elevated steppe country. Possible cradles are Syria–Palestine

---

[181] Childe, *Man Makes Himself*, pp. 67–71, 76–77.

[182] Ibid., p. 69.

[183] V. Gordon Childe, 'Changing Methods and Aims in Prehistory', in Thomas Carl Patterson and Charles E. Orser Jr. (eds), *Foundations of Social Archaeology: Selected Writings of V. Gordon Childe*, Walnut Creek, California: Altamira Press, 2004, p. 41; reprinted from *Proceedings of the Prehistoric Society*, Vol. 1, No. 1, 1935. The article could be accessed only in part on Google Book Search.

[184] Ibid., p. 40.

[185] Childe, *What Happened in History*, pp. 27–29.

[186] Childe, *Socail Evolution*, p. 168.

with Iran and Cyrenaica, Abyssinia, and western China. So cereal cultivation cannot have originated independently in temperate Europe, upper Asia, or the tropics. Wild sheep again occur in North Africa, Hither Asia, Iran, and central Asia and could only be domesticated there. Beyond this, we are not justified in making any assertion as to where the farming began, though recent discoveries do point rather explicitly to the hill countries of and bordering the Fertile Crescent to the cradle of wheel and barley cultivation.[187]

For Mesolithic cultures, he emphasized the fact of adaptation as against diffusion. Even as to whether the distinctive carpentry tool-kits of the European Mesolithic people were to be found among the other Mesolithic peoples, he did not pose the question in terms of diffusion: 'There is at present no evidence to show whether other societies in the Mesolithic stage created independently or possessed such efficient carpenters' tools'.[188]

It needs to be noted that Childe did not call himself a diffusionist. In fact he made it a point to distinguish his critical espousal of diffusion from diffusionism, of which he identified a number of varieties. One was the 'extreme diffusionism' (commonly known as 'hyper-diffusionism' these days) of W.J. Perry and Elliot Smith, another was that of 'the Austrian culture-historical school of ethnographers' and so on. Far from aligning himself uncritically with the votaries of *ex oriente lux* and Montelius' scheme of dates based on diffusionist assumptions, Childe was the first to identify (and thus to distance himself from) Montelius as a diffusionist, sound the necessary warnings, pinpoint the diffusionist assumption, and underline the importance of absolute dating as the only way out:

> The great masters of Continental prehistory – Montelius and Sophus Müller – were no less diffusionists. . . . Their systems of chronology assume diffusion as a methodological postulate; for they are based on the assumption that types, invented in the East Mediterranean area, were transmitted to the North and there adopted. The appearance of a type in a datable context in Greece or Egypt therefore provides a limiting date for its appearance in Denmark or Sweden.[189]

---

[187] Childe, 'The New Stone Age', p. 100.

[188] Ibid., p. 98. The 'only once' idea of invention and subsequent diffusion that is sometimes ascribed to Childe's viewpoint during the 1940s and 1950s (Shereen Ratnagar, *Bronze Age Civilizations*, Block 2 of the course MHI-01, 'Ancient and Medieval Societies', School of Social Sciences, Indira Gandhi National Open University, New Delhi, 2004, p. 5) needs to be qualified by the foregoing. In some other respects too, Ratnagar limits the development of Childe's ideas to the 1940s and 1950s, inexplicably neglecting his earlier work, especially *Man Makes Himself* (Shereen Ratnagar, *Understanding Harappa: Civilization in the Greater Indus Valley*, New Delhi: Tulika Books, 2001, p. 11).

[189] Childe, 'Changing Methods and Aims in Prehistory', p. 40.

Before accepting similar devices, employed by two cultures, as proofs of diffusion, it is essential first of all to determine the chronological relations of the respective cultures. A choice between the war-cries *Mirage Orientale* ['the oriental mirage'] and *Ex Oriente lux* ['from the east light'] can only be justified finally to science when *an entirely independent system of chronology* can be applied equally to the Aegean and the Baltic. (Emphasis added)[190]

Not unnaturally, therefore, Childe was among the first to recognize, in the revised edition of *What Happened in History*, the significance of absolute dating made possible by the radiocarbon revolution; he compares, for the origins of food production, the dating based on diffusionist assumptions with that based on the Pleistocene epoch and the historical horizon as twin *termini*, and the radiocarbon method respectively.[191]

We can now not only see why the standard criticisms of diffusionism that are current these days should not apply to Childe, but also expect him to have made the criticism himself in the first place. A major weakness of diffusionist theories is said to be their inability to take into account the actual mechanisms of historical change. Thus Singh:

These theories appear to offer an explanation, but actually do not explain anything at all. Technologies or cultural transformation do not get transported and transplanted into new areas in a simple or automatic way. *There has to be a need and acceptance for them in the recipient culture.* . . . Mere awareness of a different way of life does not lead to people changing their ways of doing things or living their lives.[192]

Childe makes the same point in his *Social Evolution*:

For no society can adopt from another a device unless it fits into the culture already developed by that society. For instance, a negro tribe in tropical Africa cannot adopt transport in automobiles unless it has the technical skill and equipment to construct roads, a political system to maintain and police them, and an economic system to secure and distribute petrol. Moreover, a need for transport, faster and more economical of labour than porterage must be socially recognized. Just the same sort of conditions would hold good for the adoption of wheeled carts by a preliterate society inhabiting the forests of temperate Europe.[193]

---

[190] Ibid., p. 41.
[191] Childe, *What Happened in History*, pp. 57–58.
[192] Singh, *History of Ancient and Early Medieval India from the Stone Age to the 12th Century*, p. 139.
[193] Childe, *Social Evolution*, p. 37.

What Childe was preaching here in 1951, he had long been practising, since 1936 (*Man Makes Himself*) at least, and in a manner that remains, in most respects, exemplary.[194]

A second reason why diffusionism is not acceptable these days is this: 'Diffusionist theories often take up superficial resemblances between cultures and ignore the differences. They then hold up the superficial resemblances as very significant and as "proof" of diffusion.'[195] Childe went in for a detailed criticism of diffusionism on the same count and openly sided with functionalists like A.R. Radcliffe-Browne on this issue (although he faulted them for their ahistorical perspective). He expansively and repeatedly rebutted 'the loose arguments of the sort often used by many diffusionists and still more . . . the "shreds and patches" conception of culture implicit in their argumentation. Diffusionists – and others too – went about picking bits out of various cultures, divorcing them from their context and function, and comparing these lifeless isolates.'[196]

When we name Childe a diffusionist because he employed the idea of diffusion, we resort to an age-old ploy of intellectual laziness that was quite in vogue in Childe's time as well, and which he himself helped to bring out through a discussion of what he termed 'an illusionary antithesis between "evolutionism" and "diffusionism"', in his celebrated essay 'Archaeology

[194] For an account of the numerous ways in which the reception of diffusion is determined by the home contexts of the potentially recipient cultures, see Childe, *Man Makes Himself*, pp. 168–78. The idea about degradation (ibid., p. 177), under the obvious diffusionist influence of Perry and Elliot Smith, was not only rapidly superseded in his later writings, as for example when he referred to the Europeans' multiple improvements upon the technological inventions of the Orient, but was also held up for regular ridicule as an essentially theological thesis.

[195] Singh, *History of Ancient and Early Medieval India from the Stone Age to the 12th Century*, p. 139.

[196] V. Gordon Childe, 'Archaeology and Anthropology', *Southwestern Journal of Anthropology*, Vol. 2, No. 3, 1946, p. 246. About the same time, Bronislaw Malinowski was making the same points in detail, in several works, for anthropologists. 'The empirical study of diffusion reveals to us that the process is not one of indiscriminate give and accidental take but is directed by definite forces and pressures on the side of the donor culture and well-determined resistances on the part of the recipients. We shall find also that diffusion cannot be studied at all in field work unless we realize that the units of transformation are not traits or trait complexes but organized systems or institutions' (B. Malinowski, *The Dynamics of Culture Change*, edited with an introduction by Phyllis M. Kaberry, New Haven: Yale University Press, 1945, p. 19). With his open acknowledgment of Malinowski's influence, it is not surprising that Childe's ideas should have a lot in common with this senior contemporary's simultaneous rebuttal of diffusionism and advocacy of diffusion as a 'dynamic process'. It is also relevant to note here that there is nothing particularly Marxist about the idea of diffusion; anti-diffusionism, in fact, was the ruling credo in the USSR before it was denounced by Joseph Stalin (Gamble, *Origins and Revolutions*, p. 10).

and Anthropology'.[197] He cites Leslie White[198] to describe how diffusionists in Britain completely misrepresented the works of scholars like Henry Maine, Herbert Spencer, Lewis H. Morgan and Edward B. Taylor, making them out to be evolutionists simply because they spoke of evolution. Childe further points out how, having created this 'bogey of a one-sided evolution', the diffusionists countered it with 'an equally one-sided postulate of diffusion'.[199] It is truly ironical that Childe himself should have become a victim of the same process of bogey creation.

Surplus and Technology

On the question of surplus, one argument of Irfan Habib is that there is a gap between the coming of agriculture and surplus production. He states in *Prehistory* that the Neolithic communities did not begin producing a surplus from the very outset, but did so only 'in time'.[200] The argument is elaborated in *The Indus Civilization*. The 'ability' to produce surpluses for bringing about the 'Urban Revolution' comes later, with inventions such as the plough:

> Such a situation [i.e. urbanism] could only be brought about when peasants grew more food than they needed for their bare subsistence, or, in other words, produced a surplus. Such ability did not *immediately* come about when agri-

---

[197] This essay is but a small sample of how seriously Childe took anthropology. Sherratt must have been in a tearing hurry when he referred to the shallowness of Childe's interest in and familiarity with anthropology ('curious ragbag anthropology'), and, accusing him of neglecting the ethnography of New Guinea, explained it as a result of 'a rather narrow, and perhaps even insecure, Eurocentrism' (Andrew Sherratt, 'Childe: Right or Wrong', in *Economy and Society in Prehistoric Europe: Changing Perspectives*, Edinburgh: Edinburgh University Press, 1997, pp. 491, 505 n. 13). One example alone – the bibliography of *Man Makes Himself* – will serve to show up the rashness of the charge. No archaeologist is likely to outdo Childe in the preponderant importance he attaches to anthropology in this short list. 'For neolithic economics', for example, all we are asked is to 'see Firth, *Primitive Economics of the New Zealand Maori*, London, 1929; Thurnwald, *Economics in Primitive Communities*, London, 1932; and Malinowski, *Argonauts of Western Pacific*, London, 1922; and *Coral Gardens and their Magic*, London, 1935' (Childe, *Man Makes Himself*, pp. 239–40). In fact, it may not be easy to come up with a stronger single statement of method about the importance of anthropology to archaeology than Childe's in his 'Retrospect' (p. 74): 'The archaeological data are . . . the fossilized remnants of behaviour patterns repeatedly illustrated in ethnography and written records.'

[198] Leslie White, '"Diffusionism vs. Evolution": An Anti-Evolutionist Fallacy', *American Anthropologist*, Vol. 47, 1945, pp. 339–56.

[199] Childe, 'Archaeology and Anthropology', p. 245.

[200] Habib, *Prehistory*, p. 50.

culture first began to be practised during the 'Neolithic Revolution'. A further set of developments was necessary to increase agricultural production. (Emphasis added)[201]

This, however, is negated by his alternative view: that, 'with agriculture, Neolithic communities began to produce surpluses'.[202]

And for Habib, wherever there is a surplus, there is exploitation. He states in the Preface to *Prehistory* that Chapter 3 of the book, on the Neolithic Revolution, 'describes mainly the coming of agriculture, and the beginnings of exploitative relationships'.[203] In the same chapter, about the very first phase of Mehrgarh, even before the coming of pottery, one reads first of the 'possibility' that 'some structures were large store-houses'; then about crafts like basketry, cloth-weaving, and bead- and bangle-making; and then: 'These craft products and the large storage facilities for grain suggest the existence of social differentiation, in which the rich and the powerful could claim a large share of the surplus produce and, in exchange for such produce, obtain relatively expensive craft products.'[204]

As with the Neolithic revolution, the works of Childe remain the sole conceptual anchorage for Habib's account of the Urban revolution. This exposes his work and therefore calls for a return to the criticisms to which Childe has been subjected on this count. The most basic of these is of technological determinism. With an 'exclusive preoccupation with technology', Childe's work could not but give rise to 'the purely technological and mechanistic view of the emergence of civilized societies from the barbaric peasant communities'.[205] Sometimes this is explained as a result of his flawed method. Childe attached excessive importance to archaeological evidence and hence to the role of technology: 'Both works ['The Urban Revolution' and *New Light on the Most Ancient East*] emphasize archaeological rather than textual findings, leading to a corresponding interpretive stress on technological aspects of change.'[206]

Technological determinism in turn made surplus production largely a function of productivity, i.e. efficiency, of agriculture. Increased surpluses were further supposed to have brought about the Urban revolution. Adams believes that Childe 'never' dealt with these issues which nevertheless inform his writings, and argues for the primacy of social institutions, just the opposite of what Childe is supposed to have held.

---

[201] Habib, *The Indus Civilization*, pp. 1–2.
[202] Habib, *Prehistory*, p. 56.
[203] Ibid., p. ix.
[204] Ibid., pp. 51, 52.
[205] Clark and Piggott, *Prehistoric Societies*, p. 175.
[206] Adams, *The Evolution of Urban Society*, p. 9, n. 2.

Next we may consider the nature of agricultural 'surpluses' insofar as they may have been a precondition for the Urban Revolution in Mesopotamia and Mesoamerica. . . . But does the exploitation of a given environment by a given agricultural technology, implying a potential level of productivity from which actual consumption can be subtracted to define the surplus available for reallocation, actually help to engender the ideologies and institutional contexts that are required to mobilize the surplus? Is there an inherent tendency for agriculturalists to advance in productivity toward the highest potential level consistent with their technology, that is, to maximize their production above subsistence needs and so to precipitate the growth of new patterns of appropriation and consumption involving elites freed from responsibilities for food production? Gordon Childe, although never dealing with these issues, appears to have thought so. Karl Polanyi and his collaborators have argued persuasively to the contrary . . . noting that actual agricultural surpluses are always defined and mobilized in a particular institutional setting and that it is precisely the growth of the collective symbols and institutions of the primitive states that can explain the conversion of peasant leisure into foodstuffs in urban storehouses.[207]

Then, as against Childe's assumed notion of surplus based on increases in productivity in per capita terms, Adams brings in as a more satisfactory alternative the concept of 'gross surplus', working on a suggestion of Martin Orans. This concept, along with his critique, has earned him worldwide appreciation. The short entry on 'urban revolution' in the *Encyclopaedia Britannica* credits him with introducing the importance of social factors in the advent of the revolution. Drawing upon him among others, in India the terms of the debate were set in 1973 by A. Ghosh as between the technological and the institutional explanation of surplus,[208] which continue to be followed till date though mainly with reference to the original argument of Adams.[209] Historians have also come to subscribe to Adams's concept of

---

[207] Ibid., p. 45; see also p. 12.

[208] Ghosh, *The City in Early Historical India*, Shimla: Indian Institute of Advanced Study, 1973, pp. 19–21, 24, 25. Cf. Sharma, *Material Culture and Social Formations in Ancient India*, pp. xv, 12.

[209] It is thus with reference to Adams that Romila Thapar states: 'To argue that the technical feasibility of a surplus was sufficient to start a chain reaction which automatically led to state formation would be too mechanical an interpretation of the change. Surplus is . . . not an event but a process, as has been rightly suggested' (*From Lineage to State*, p. 77 and n. 25). More recently, Upinder Singh has noted the contrast Adams draws between Childe's technology-based explanation of the emergence of civilization and his own emphasis on social factors (*History of Ancient and Early Medieval India from the Stone Age to the 12th Century*, p. 134). See also the discussion in Ranabir Chakravarti, 'Appendix' to B.D. Chattopadhyaya (ed.), *A Sourcebook of Indian Civilization*, Calcutta: Orient Longman, 2000, pp. 582–84. Shereen Ratnagar asks: '. . . but if "surplus" is conceived as output over

'gross surplus',[210] implicitly accepting thereby not only the novelty of his idea but also its superiority over the Childean concept critiqued by him. Acceptance of this kind of judgment is also implicit among Marxist scholars, some of whom find Childe offering a mechanical interpretation of the past,[211] while others like Habib think they are following the tradition of Childe in privileging technology over other factors of social change.

In stating his belief about Childe 'never dealing with these issues', Adams makes it clear that he did not note any of the numerous ways in which Childe described his views on the role of technology and the concept of surplus. A study of these statements by Childe leads us to conclude that he had presented a more nuanced and richer view of the issues than is covered by Adams' exposition of the concept of 'gross surplus'.[212] In order to see that, we must first carefully note each of the following points Adams makes about his concept of gross surplus:

> What really matters . . . is not the margin between per capita production and consumption, which implies improving 'efficiency' as the major factor in change and which is inherently incalculable from the usual archaeological–historical data. At least from the viewpoint of understanding sociocultural change, the crucial variable, instead, is the *gross* amount of deployable wealth or 'surplus'.
>
> There are several advantages to conceptualizing the problem in these terms. First, it calls attention to the fact that a chain of processes is involved in mobilizing 'surpluses' in any sociocultural context rather than merely the attainment of a margin between production and consumption on the part of the primary producers. The accumulation of surplus is at least facilitated by improvements in technological–transport facilities not directly related to agriculture at all (e.g. boats and carts), and, in any case, involves the elaboration

---

and above what *can be consumed* – which is a faulty definition – the question would arise why any society should produce unnecessary quantities of food' (*Understanding Harappa*, p. 137, emphasis added). This, as it happens, is not only a faulty definition of surplus but seems to be nobody's definition as well. Surplus-generating producers are normally seen as living at subsistence levels, underfed and undernourished: not many would doubt their ability to consume more than they did.

[210] B.D. Chattopadhyaya, 'Urbanization in Early Medieval India: An Overview', in Sabyasachi Bhattacharya and Romila Thapar (eds), *Situating Indian History: For Sarvepalli Gopal*, New Delhi: Oxford University Press, 1986, p. 28.

[211] 'Childe's understanding of Marxism remained one-sided, and his interpretations of prehistory and antiquity essentially mechanical' (Neil Faulkner, 'Gordon Childe and Marxist Archaeology', *International Socialism: A Quarterly Journal of Socialist Theory*', Issue 116 (online), 2007).

[212] Because of the focus on retrieving Childe's views with a view to assessing his critiques and comparing them with the concept of 'gross surplus', the other related issues, such as problems with Childe's ideas as retrieved here, will not be considered.

of complex institutional mechanisms, not merely for assuring production of a surplus by the peasantry, but also for concentrating and reallocating it. Equally important, the concept of gross surplus directs attention to the political or religious centres of the society, urban or otherwise. It was in those centres, after all, that its utilization resulted in the formation of the new classes and groups of specialists, as well as the monumental structures and luxuries associated with them, by which we identify the Urban Revolution in the first place.

Emphasis on gross surplus rather than per capita surplus serves other functions as well. It suggests, for example, that an increase in the gross size of population and territorial unit may offer *at least* as strong a stimulus to the Urban Revolution as putative increases in 'efficiency'. Trends toward territorial aggrandizement, political unification, and population concentration within the political unit accordingly can be interpreted not merely as expressions of the outcome of the Urban Revolution but as functionally interrelated processes that are central to it.

Calculated as gross amounts of deployable wealth rather than per capita ones, the significance of surpluses changes from an implied independent factor of change to a component in an interdependent network of cause and effect. Extensions of territorial control, new forms of political superordination, and a multiplicity of technological advances all may have had as much effect on the size of the surplus as improvements in immediate agricultural 'efficiency', while the deployment of the surplus, however it was formed, obviously had important reciprocal effects on these other factors. Further, to emphasize the inter-dependency of surpluses with a host of political, economic, and technological institutions, it may be noted that agriculture received organizational inputs from the institutions that emerged during the course of the Urban Revolution.[213]

A review of Childe's writings on the subject may begin with his view that all food-producing societies must necessarily produce surplus. This is well described in *Man Makes Himself*. A surplus has to be produced – through the simple facts that 'a crop must not be consumed as soon as it is reaped', nor livestock 'be indiscriminately slaughtered and devoured' – for several reasons:

1. 'The grains must be conserved and eked out so as to last till the next harvest, for a whole year.'
2. 'And a proportion of every crop must be set aside for seed.'
3. 'The young cows and ewes at least must be spared and reared to provide milk and to augment the herd or flock.'
4. 'The surplus thus gathered will help to tide the community over bad seasons; it will form a reserve against droughts and crop failures.'

[213] Adams, *The Evolution of Urban Society*, pp. 46–47.

5. The tendency to multiply is another important reason why surpluses will be needed, by increasing acreage and pasturage if necessary: 'It will serve to support a growing population.'

6. 'Ultimately, it may constitute a basis for rudimentary trade, and so pave the way to a second revolution.'[214] That is to say, the producers may like to exchange their surplus for a semi-precious stone or some other object that they may fancy.

For one who is brought up on a particular reading of Childe, it may be difficult to believe that for him none of this meant that this inbuilt tendency towards surplus production will automatically throw up a civilization by shelling out the mandatory minimum. He argues to the contrary in fact:

> Now the farmers in the Nile valley or Mesopotamia could easily produce the requisite surplus. They would, indeed, produce so much above their immediate needs as to provide against bad season. But why should they do more? Man, it is argued, is a lazy beast and prefers a simple life to luxuries earned by unremitting toil.[215]

Childe then goes on to discuss the possible ways in which the farmers could be bent to the will of the surplus expropriators. 'Conquest would certainly constitute one means of overcoming this inertia.' 'But theories that regard it [i.e. military conquest] as an essential precondition of the second revolution must be regarded with reserve.' And so on.[216]

The surplus that is needed to support the Urban revolution is a different type of surplus: it is 'social surplus'. Defined as 'the food above domestic requirements',[217] the concept of 'social surplus' is important and helps us to distinguish it from the domestic surpluses, which in a sense are common to all societies (everywhere people have this obligation to procure over and above what they consume when a child is born or a family member is incapacitated). With the concept of social surplus regularly employed by Childe, one also sees that the contradiction in Habib's simultaneous affirmation and denial of surplus in all neolithic societies is but a small paradox: neolithic societies must produce a surplus, they need not produce any 'social surplus'.

In a word, the producer must both be enabled by productive forces and be compelled/induced by production relations to produce the social surplus for sustaining civilizations. Childe seldom tired of emphasizing that peasants would not produce simply because they can by virtue of their labour, or

---

[214] Childe, *Man Makes Himself*, pp. 82–83.
[215] Ibid., pp. 131–32.
[216] Ibid., pp. 132–36.
[217] V. Gordon Childe, 'The Birth of Civilisation', *Past and Present*, No. 2, November 1952, p. 3.

improvement in productivity, or favourable natural factors: 'to judge by the practice of subsistence farmers today, neolithic peasants would have been disinclined to produce regularly more than was needed to support themselves and their dependents; to obtain a surplus regularly some inducement or pressure would be needed.'[218] Mere availability of technology, for all its importance, will not give you a civilization, without the necessary 'economic organization and social framework'. In *What Happened in History*, Childe makes these points again and again.

> Society persuaded or compelled the farmers to produce a surplus of foodstuffs over and above their domestic requirements, and by concentrating this surplus used it to support a new *urban* population of specialized craftsmen, merchants, priests, officials, and clerks.[219]

> The worst contradictions in the Neolithic economy were transcended when farmers were persuaded or compelled to wring from the soil a surplus above their own domestic requirements, and when this surplus was made available to support new economic classes not directly engaged in producing their own food. The possibility of producing the requisite surplus was inherent in the very nature of the Neolithic economy. Its realization, however, required additions to the stock of applied science at the disposal of all barbarians, as well as a modification in social and economic relations.[220]

> Communities like Sialk III and the comparable al'Ubaid villages in Syria, as well as others similarly equipped on the plateau of Asia Minor, in Cyprus, and in peninsular Greece, disposed of all the technical knowledge and apparatus of civilization. The economic organization and social framework were alone deficient. During the thousand odd years of the Chalcolithic Age the peoples of the Near East had made discoveries pregnant with revolutionary consequences – the metallurgy of copper and bronze, the harnessing of animal motive power, wheeled vehicles, the potters' wheel, bricks, the seal. Even before 3,000 BC these achievements were being diffused at least to the Aegean and to Turkistan and India.[221]

> Metallurgy, the wheel, the ox-cart, the pack-ass, and the sailing ship provided the foundations for a new economic organization. Without it [i.e. the economic organization] the new materials would remain luxuries, the new crafts would not function; the new devices would be just conveniences.[222]

---

[218] V. Gordon Childe, 'The Bronze Age', *Past and Present*, No. 12, November 1957, p. 6.
[219] Childe, *What Happened in History*, pp. 30–31.
[220] Ibid., p. 77.
[221] Ibid., pp. 82–83.
[222] Ibid., p. 97.

In his classic 1950 essay, 'The Urban Revolution', invoking a comparative perspective, Childe discounted altogether the factor of technological development.

> . . . some three millennia later [than the Sumerian, Egyptian, and Indus civilizations] cities arose in Central America, and it is impossible to prove that the Mayas owed anything directly to the urban revolutions of the Old World. Their achievements must therefore be taken into account in our comparison, and their inclusion seriously complicates the task of defining the essential preconditions for the Urban Revolution. In the Old World the rural economy which yielded the surplus was based on the cultivation of cereals combined with stock-breeding. But this economy had been made more efficient as a result of the adoption of irrigation . . . and of important inventions and discoveries – metallurgy, the plough, the sailing boat and the wheel. None of these devices was known to the Mayas; they bred no animals for milk or meat; though they cultivated the cereal maize, they used the same sort of slash-and-burn method as neolithic farmers in prehistoric Europe or in the Pacific Islands today. Hence in the minimum definition of the city, the greatest factor common to the Old and the New will be substantially reduced and impoverished by the inclusion of the Maya.[223]

It was not only for surplus production that Childe located the significance of technological competence in its social contexts. In general too, for him, technology by itself did not say anything about its importance in any society. The man who is so often imagined to be a technological determinist wrote as follows:

---

[223] Childe, 'The Urban Revolution', p. 9. It is not easy to measure, still less to explain, the extent to which certain representations of Childe affect our reading of him. Habib does not refer to this piece for his account of the emergence of civilization (Habib, *The Indus Civilization*, pp. 1–4), and the resulting difference between him and Childe is palpable. Childe, as just seen, brought in the evidence of the New World to keep out a number of technical inventions from his discussion of the Urban revolution, while Habib keeps out the New World to retain the importance of technology. But this is one of the two works of Childe that Adams cites to fault him for the 'interpretive stress on technological aspects of change'. As it happens, the only time Childe brings metallurgy, the plough, the sailing boat and the wheel into his 1950 essay is in the above context, where he excludes them all from 'the minimum definition of the city'. However, such is the power of Adams' critique that what he fails to note in Childe continues to be missed by others. For example, here is what is made of Childe's viewpoint in an extended discussion of his ten features of urbanism based *exclusively* on the same 1950 essay: 'The various hypotheses that have been put forward to explain the rise of the world's first cities are reflective of how different scholars view and understand the unfolding of historical processes. Childe emphasized the importance of technological and subsistence factors such as increasing food surpluses, copper–bronze metallurgy, and the use of wheeled transport, sailboats, and ploughs' (Singh, *History of Ancient and Early Medieval India from the Stone Age to the 12th Century*, p. 134).

For instance, in the narrow valley of Egypt, whose habitable land was seldom even two miles away from the admirable highway of the Nile, wheeled vehicles would not be anything like as useful as on the steppes of North Syria, which lack natural waterways. The fact that wheeled carts were used in the latter area fifteen hundred years earlier than in Egypt does not mean that Egypt was more 'backward' than Syria.[224]

Childe believed that being a Marxist obliges one to go beyond technology.[225] Those who are mere archaeologists may understandably assign 'a determining role' to technology that figures so dominantly in their records, but if they are Marxists too, they must give due weight to production relations as well. It is in this context that his following statement in 'Retrospect' may be understood:

Since 'means of production' figure so conspicuously in the archaeological record, I suppose most prehistorians are inclined to be so far Marxists as to wish to assign them a determining role among the behaviour patterns that have fossilized. They can do so even in the U.S.A. without invoking the 5th Amendment, since it was to the 'mode of production' ('means' plus 'relations') that Marx attributed such a dominating influence. By 1936 I had advanced beyond this in so far as I insisted on the need for *concentrating the surplus* to accomplish the Urban Revolution and so recognized the Hegelian rationality of the political and religious totalitarianism that characterized the ancient Oriental States. (Emphasis added)[226]

The words in italics – 'concentrating the surplus' – point to a key aspect

---

[224] Childe, *Social Evolution*, pp. 14–15.

[225] Childe, 'Archaeology and Anthropology', p. 250.

[226] Childe, 'Retrospect', p. 72. This should take care of Adams' charge that Childe allowed himself to be swayed by his archaeological sources, to the neglect of textual sources, into laying an 'interpretive stress' on technological factors. The charge about the neglect of textual sources is simply not true, as may readily be seen from Chapter VII ('The Revolution in Human Knowledge') of *Man Makes Himself*. Childe is also criticized for exaggerating the scope of archaeological sources by including exact and predictive sciences, such as mathematics and the calendar, as a feature of urbanism that may be seen in the archaeological record, on the ground that these sciences are 'not directly deducible from the archaeological data' (Singh *History of Ancient and Early Medieval India from the Stone Age to the 12th Century*, p. 134). As against this, one may draw attention to the two archaeological artefacts – 'clay account tablets from Erech showing the oldest Mesopotamian writing', and 'Maya glyph giving date formula and numerals' – that Childe illustrated in his 'Urban Revolution' (Plate 2, fig. 5; and p. 14, fig. 16), as well as point out that the existence of some of the sciences are perfectly deducible from other archaeological sources too, such as the earliest Egyptian monuments: 'But it is plain from the results achieved and attested in the monuments that the Egyptians under the early dynasties were already successfully applying the simple arithmetical and geometrical rules illustrated by examples in the later "mathematical papyri"' (Childe, *What Happened in History*, p. 127).

of Childe's concept of surplus. He took into full account the importance of increasing productivity, as one has to in contexts like that of Ancient Sumer where 'the soil was so fertile that a hundred-fold return was not impossible'.[227] In general, however, it was not the increase in per capita productivity that he emphasized; the concept that occurs as a refrain in his writings is 'concentration' of surplus from the mass of producers. This idea – 'concentration' at one place of the small quantities of surplus produced severally by a large number of people – closely resembles, in critical respects, the notion of 'gross surplus' (just as the need for persuading or compelling peasants to produce surpluses for non-food producers anticipates the distinction Paul Baran drew between 'potential surplus' and 'actual surplus' in his critique of capitalism[228]). For example, in the 1950 essay, it is not the importance of increasing technical efficiency or per capita productivity in the generation of social surplus, but the 'concentration of social surplus' that is repeatedly stressed. 'Each primary producer paid over the tiny surplus he could wring from the soil with his still very limited technical equipment as tithe or tax to an imaginary deity or a divine king who thus concentrated the surplus'; 'Truly monumental public buildings not only distinguish each known city from any village but also symbolize the concentration of social surplus'; 'Hence in Sumer the social surplus was first effectively concentrated in the hands of a god and stored in his granary'; 'But naturally priests, civil and military leaders and officials absorbed a major share of the concentrated surplus and thus formed a "ruling class".'[229]

Naturally, thus, transport is seen to play a crucial role in the concentration of surplus, as it does in Adams' account of mobilization of gross surplus: 'Moreover the rivers that water the crops, are at the same time moving roads on which bulky goods, like food-stuffs, can economically be transported so that the produce of farms scattered over a wide area can readily be gathered at a single centre.'[230] The surplus would increase as much with population growth and expansion of political domain, as it would with improvements in productivity.

A common idea underlies concentration of surplus as well as improvement of productivity. This is the total quantity of surplus that may be increas-

---

[227] Childe, *What Happened in History*, p. 98.

[228] Paul A. Baran, *The Political Economy of Growth*, Penguin Books, 1957, Chapter Two. To me, Childe's and Baran's works furnish two excellent examples of the 'progressive' and 'fettering' role of relations of production: the coming of the Urban revolution helped actualize the productive potential of society, the persistence of capitalism fetters optimal actualization of society's productive potential. 'Productive potential' does not refer to material production alone.

[229] Childe, 'The Urban Revolution', pp. 11, 12, 12–13.

[230] Childe, 'The Bronze Age', p. 6.

ed by either or both. Through an insight remarkable for an archaeologist of his time, Childe came to also emphasize the critical importance of the total quantity of surplus by pointing out that the mere existence of social surplus need not translate into exploitative relationships, class formation and the emergence of civilization. What matters in the end is the quantity of surplus, whether it is obtained due to soil fertility, technological development, or concentration through growth of population or political domain:

> It was not however the concentration, but the quantity concentrated that was decisive. A Polynesian chief is able to concentrate a certain surplus, and it enables him to feast the peasants who assemble to build a canoe or a meeting house; it is not sufficient for the gigantic work of building civilization. In Sumer, where the alluvial land is so fertile that a plot of 7/8 of an acre under irrigation would support a family of five, accumulation presumably began in the remote prehistoric temples, and increased with the expansion of population and the improvement of techniques until the critical point was reached. This should be definable numerically in tons of grain and gallons of milk, though the prospects of such definition seem very remote. In Egypt, on the contrary, the requisite quantity seems to have been reached almost catastrophically by a series of campaigns extending over at most three reigns which made the war-chief of the Falcon clan in Upper Egypt master of the whole Nile valley, entitled to receive all the surplus produce of its peasantry.[231]

A very rich, complex and growing literature on the production and uses of surplus, inequality and exploitation in tribal societies has since been available to students of anthropology and archaeology. Amidst all its uncertainties and controversies, there does exist a consensus that social surpluses do not amount necessarily to class division and exploitation. Chris Harman sums it up admirably in his *People's History of the World*:

> Those people with high status had to serve the rest of the community, not live off it. As Richard Lee notes, there were the same 'communal property concepts' as in hunter-gatherer societies: 'Much of what tribute the chiefs receive is redistributed to subjects, and the chiefs' powers are subject to checks and balances by the forces of popular opinion and institutions'. So among the

---

[231] Childe, 'The Birth of Civilization', p. 4. Childe also noted how among the Maori of New Zealand and the Kayan of Borneo, 'even chiefs worked on their lands' (ibid., p. 3). In a different context, i.e. the distinction between full-time and part-time specialization (Childe, 'The Urban Revolution', pp. 6–7, cf. Childe, 'Retrospect', p. 71), the same point is made for chiefdoms: 'The social surplus is not big enough to feed idle mouths' (Childe, 'The Urban Revolution', p. 7). It is the bigness of the social surplus that is thus meant later in the article, in the following statement: 'Owing to the low efficiency of Neolithic technique, the surplus produced was insignificant at first, but it could be increased till it demanded a reorganization of society' (ibid., p. 13).

Nambikwara of South America, 'Generosity is . . . an essential attribute of power', and 'the chief' must be prepared to use the 'surplus quantities of food, tools, weapons and ornaments' under his control to respond 'to the appeals of an individual, a family or the band as a whole' for anything they need. This could even result in the leader having a harder time materially than those under him. Thus, among the New Guinea Busama, the clubhouse leader 'has to work harder than anyone else to keep up his stocks of food. . . . It is acknowledged he must toil early and late – 'his hands are never free from earth, and his forehead continually drips with sweat'.[232]

It may now be seen that mere surplus production and practising of crafts in Mehrgarh should not be assumed to mean 'exploitative tendencies'. The complexity of the Vedic evidence also argues against easy conclusions. One may thus point, as against Habib's arguments about class divisions and surplus appropriation in the Vedic times,[233] to the evidence for countervailing tendencies that he omits to discuss or seeks to explain away too summarily – such as the office of *bhāgadugha* in the Later Vedic period which is generally understood to be 'distributor of shares' but is guessed to mean 'paymaster' by Habib,[234] ignoring the significance of the term *bhāga* in the Vedic literature that was so radically opposed to its later sense of surplus expropriated from the producers. It was the attention to the countervailing tendencies that enabled Kosambi to see the Rigvedic king, the recipient of *bali*, as the 'apportioner [and not the appropriator] of surplus within the tribe'.[235]

Prehistoric Society

Irfan Habib refers to anthropology and comparative history as major aids in the interpretation of archaeological data.[236] However, he almost completely refrains from using anthropology, while making rather sparing use of comparative history. In this last section, we note how fuller attention to these would have made Habib's labours more fruitful.

Anthropology helps us guard against evolutionary speculation. Thus Childe noted that the digging stick or dibbler and hoe are used by different peoples in various parts of the world for primitive farming.[237] It may thus

---

[232] Chris Harman, *A People's History of the World*, London: Bookmarks Publications, 1999, pp. 15–16.
[233] Habib and Thakur, *The Vedic Age*, pp. 12, 14–15, 44.
[234] Ibid., p. 44.
[235] Kosambi, 'Stages of Indian History' [1954], in Kosambi, *Combined Methods in Indology and Other Essays*, p. 62.
[236] Habib, *The Indus Civilization*, p. 20.
[237] Childe, 'The New Stone Age', p. 101.

be misleading, without adducing the required ethnographic evidence, to see digging sticks as some kind of 'primitive hoes',[238] or to refer to *both* the hoe and the digging stick as being used simultaneously by the Indian peasants in pre-plough times.[239]

In terms of stages of political evolution, the stage before the state is better called 'chiefdom' rather than 'principality' by which Habib designates the supposedly pre-state Early Indus cultures[240] – though the use of the term 'chiefdom' by other scholars is an improvement but in name, for want of any detailed demonstration of any feature of the Early Indus cultures as resembling any salient feature of known chiefdoms. We assume that the state appeared only with the Mature Harappan stage, so the earlier one must have been a chiefdom.

Theory is always an aid to generalization but equally, also, a warning against too-easy generalizations. Thus war, anthropological theory tells us, is not a specific attribute of civilizations alone. It seems somewhat facile, therefore , to say, as Habib does in his account of the Helmand Civilization, that 'with the rise of the state, there also came war, and the suffering it brings'.[241] In fact as Childe describes in some detail, on the combined testimony of archaeology and ethnography, warfare inhered in the very process of the expansion of Neolithic cultures.[242] One could also bring up all the references to wars in the Vedic literature, were it not for the uncertainty one feels about Habib's views on this count. Habib does not say that Early Vedic society was a state society but he does not deny it either, nor, in his discussions of the Later Vedic polity, does he say anything about the direction in which political institutions were moving.

Anthropology would also make suspect the significance of the negative evidence regarding tribal endogamy. It is repeatedly noted that 'there is no proof of endogamy, or marriages being restricted to within the tribe'.[243] For tribes, almost by definition, must be assumed to be endogamous unless there is good, positive evidence to the contrary, and that can only be a very special case. Above all, anthropological work on the many modes of non-market exchange helps us understand more fully the significance of a host

---

[238] Habib, *Prehistory*, p. 48.

[239] Habib and Thakur, *The Vedic Age*, p. 47.

[240] Habib, *The Indus Civilization*, p. 12.

[241] Ibid., p. 8.

[242] Childe, *What Happened in History*, pp. 73–75. It was again in terms of warfare that Childe preferred to explain abrupt changes in archaeological cultures, say, from Halafian to al 'Ubaid (ibid., p. 96). All this, together with the other references to warfare and conflict of classes, is patently kept out of mind when scholars like K.V. Flannery and Sherratt criticize Childe for ignoring the importance of warfare, and explain it as probably a result of his pacifism (Sherratt, 'Childe: Right or Wrong', p. 494).

[243] Habib and Thakur, *The Vedic Age*, pp. 12, 21.

of terms in the *Rigveda* that denote forms of exchange other than market exchange. Very early, R.S. Sharma presented a mass of evidence for such terms, and although he did not provide a systematic account of how all these form parts of a system/systems of non-market exchange, he did draw attention to a very important segment of the Early Vedic economy and tried to find parallels for them in later Indian society;[244] still earlier, Kosambi had drawn on ethnography to make the fine point that 'free barter is not known to primitive societies in their earlier stages'.[245] Habib, however, does not go beyond the market paradigm; for him, all distribution is a matter either of market exchange (this includes barter) or of surplus extraction.

It is the assumption of market exchange that prevents Habib from a proper appreciation of the significance of the shift from hand-made to wheel-made pottery. He states:

> At the very end of Period II [at Mehrgarh], around 4000 BC, came the potter's wheel, a technological device imported from West Asia where it had appeared around 5000 BC. On this horizontal wheel, the pots could be rotated in order to speedily receive symmetrical shapes that were unimaginable when pottery was made by hands alone. It was thus a truly time-saving invention, which could make pottery cheap and accessible to all.[246]

There is no question of the hand-made pottery becoming cheap for it was not usually an item of sale and purchase; nor of it becoming accessible for it was already so as it was made in all households. The context in which mass production of wheel-made pottery occurred had significance of a different type. Since it was time-saving, and since the material and equipment were inexpensive, the coming of the potter's wheel made it redundant for women-folk to devote so much of their time and effort to the task of pot-making. For the first time, the potter's wheel *created* a market for pots; it is not that

---

[244] Sharma, *Material Culture and Social Formations in Ancient India*, pp. 39–46.

[245] Kosambi, *The Culture and Civilization of Ancient India in Historical Outline*, Delhi: Vikas Publishing House, 1965, p. 32.

[246] Habib, *Prehistory*, p. 54. The radiocarbon dates for Mehrgarh do not allow for easy conclusions about the chronology of its various phases. Generally, however, they have tended to push the dates back. Habib has apparently drawn his data from this shifting scenario, which has resulted in a bit of incongruity. In *Prehistory*, p. 54, 4000 BC is given as the date for the end of Mehrgarh II, the duration of which is stated two pages earlier to be from 5000 to 4000 BC. Two pages later, however, the pottery of Mehrgarh III is stated to be 'datable to *c.* 4300–3800 BC' (ibid., p. 56); the incongruity remains unnoticed and therefore unexplained, when the two are brought together, one on top of the other, in Table 3.1, Mehrgarh II being dated 5000–4000 BC and Mehrgarh III, 4300–3800. Another instance of this is seen in the dates for the ploughed field at Aligrama: in the text, it is stated to be eleventh century BC (Habib and Thakur, *The Vedic Age*, pp. 6, 75); and in the illustration, twelfth century BC (ibid., p. 7, fig. 1.1).

before its invention pottery was costly and not easily accessible to all.[247]

Deducing political unity from archaeological evidence is a tricky exercise, but it must be said to the credit of experts in the field (such as Shereen Ratnagar) that they have been able to work out a fairly reasonable case for it for the Mature Harappan Civilization. The uniformity of weights and measures, for instance, does seem to presuppose a political authority that introduced and enforced it. Habib draws on this scholarship in his account of the Harappan political system. Before that, however, he adds one more criterion in the case of the Helmand Civilization. He argues that the quantities of agricultural surplus the cities of this civilization, particularly Shahr-i Sokhta and Mundigak, required would have had to be met by the agrarian resources of the entire area (rather than some part of it), and so the entire area must have been governed by a single state:

> The territory of the state must have been large enough to extract enough surplus from the agricultural zone in order to sustain the towns. It is tempting therefore to regard the area of the Helmand civilization, which by 2600 BC was fairly homogenous in nearly all aspects of culture, as being under a single state, with Shahr-i Sokhta as the capital and Mundigak a subordinate seat of power.[248]

The problem with this argument is as follows. Why should the mobilization of surpluses for the twin Helmand cities that were separated by about 400 km have needed a single state? After all, cities of the Sumerian civilization far closer to one another than these two cities made do with a multiplicity of states. Although the uniformity of material culture across the Helmand Civilization is mentioned, the argument for the single state is not really made on this basis. For doing that, one will have again to vet one's arguments against comparable examples from other civilizations, as also against the evidence for uniformity before 2600 BC in the Helmand zone itself. Not every kind of uniformity of material culture will translate as political unity,

---

[247] The potter's wheel also drastically reduced the number of persons involved in the craft. In *The Indus Civilization*, however, while inferring the social implications of various crafts from archaeological finds, Habib misses out on the mass production of pottery due to the potter's wheel, along with the varying chances of survival of different types of material. The conspicuous presence of pottery in archaeological records leads him to think that after agriculturists, potters were the most numerous in Harappan society: 'Among the "consumer goods" industries, one of the most visible, and possibly employing the largest number outside of agriculture, was the potter's craft' (Habib, *The Indus Civilization*, p. 32). Habib provides the contradiction himself as he moves to discuss, supposedly, the next most important occupation: 'Next to pottery, we may expect textiles to be the craft engaging large numbers of people. Numerous spindle-whorls of terracotta and frit (unglazed vitreous paste) are found in Indus settlements, showing that hand-spinning was widespread, presumably as a woman's chore *in each household*, rich and poor' (ibid., p. 34, emphasis added).

[248] Habib, *The Indus Civilization*, pp. 6, 8.

for then we will have to interpret the 'cultural integration' of the area during 3200–2600 BC[249] as the result of some political unification.

We need also to take issue with the logic that where there is a cart drawn by bullocks, there has to be also a plough pulled by them: 'the use of the plough, for which no actual evidence is available but which may be legitimately inferred from the use of the humped oxen . . . for draught, as attested by the incised sketch of a bullock cart'.[250] It was apparently by the same logic that earlier scholars like Leonard Woolley postulated the use of the plough in the Indus Civilization.[251] It is true that both the cart and the plough resulted from the same type of harnessing of the same animal, and that both were linked to agrarian production. However, use of animal motive power for transport is no guarantee of its use for tillage or vice versa, any more than the potter's wheel allows us to assume the presence of cartwright's (or that the early evidence of camels pulling carts can be taken as evidence that they were used to pull the plough as well). There were centuries in Bronze Age Egypt, for instance, when cattle pulled the plough and the potter turned out pots on his wheel, but no two wheels were joined by an axle supporting a cart to which an animal was yoked. Very often, the presence of a wagon could be linked to contexts very different from agrarian production; as Piggott points out in the European context, it could be meant primarily for elite use as 'prestige equipment'.[252] In sum, the presence of the wheel opens up a possibility for the presence of the plough in an area, but it does not necessarily guarantee it. (The example of the New World, where wheeled toys were used but not wheeled transport, is another reason for caution.)

One must also beware of exaggerating the scale and pace of the spread of plough agriculture. Knowledge of the plough did not lead to wholesale replacement of hoe cultivation in any area, the evidence from Mesopotamia being particularly instructive.[253] The gender associations of hoe and plough cultivation are regularly noted in the literature, but their implications for the spread of the new technology do not seem to have been pondered over.

---

[249] Ibid., p. 4.

[250] Habib and Thakur, The Vedic Age, p. 80.

[251] Leonard Woolley, The Beginnings of Civilization, Vol. I, Pt. 2, of History of Mankind: Cultural and Scientific Development, New York: Mentor Books, 1963, p. 226. Indeed, the mere presence of bulls in the Harappan Civilization has been taken as evidence for the plough: 'Representations on seals and terracotta sculpture indicate that the bull was known, and archaeologists extrapolate from this that oxen were used for ploughing' (Jaya Menon, 'Bricks, Beads and Bones: The Harappan Civilization', in Themes in Indian History – Part 1, Vol. I, New Delhi: NCERT, 2007, p. 3). I am grateful to Ranjan Anand of Zakir Husain College (Evening), University of Delhi, for this reference.

[252] Cited in Sherratt, Economy and Society in Prehistoric Europe, p. 15.

[253] Ibid., p. 16.

Did the social institutional context of hoe cultivation immediately give way to that of plough cultivation? It seems unlikely, and the complications involved in it may have been a more important obstruction to the spread of the new technology than the expenses involved.

Gender, the blurb to *The Vedic Age* emphasizes, commands 'special attention' in the work. The book does address the issue in some detail though without exploring the complexity of the matter, such as when only one of the two significant forms of the term *dampati* is referred to.[254] Perhaps the bigger issue is the almost complete silence over gender-related developments in the other two volumes.[255] The neglect of anthropology is particularly unfortunate here; it is because of this that gender becomes a central concern only from the Vedic archaeology, for without anthropology, the issue can hardly be addressed on the basis of archaeological material alone. It was mainly on the basis of anthropological parallels that Childe described how the coming of the plough, the potter's wheel and the cart 'cut away the economic foundations of mother-right';[256] without their benefit, Habib's references to these technologies remain bereft of their transformational significance for social relations.

It is with the linguistic aspect of the gender issue, on which again Habib takes an explicit stand, that I should like to conclude this essay. Childe was very alive to the issue of gender, yet would not apply its logic to vocabulary and, after Marx, named his book *Man Makes Himself*. Obviously, 'man' to him represented the other members of the species as well. Habib continues the tradition, as seen from the table of contents from *Prehistory* onwards and throughout. The four sections of Chapter 2 in that book are thus entitled 'the evolution of the *human* species', 'early *man* in India', 'the Anatomically Modern *Man*' and 'the modern *human* in India'. In the Preface we are told that the book 'describes the earliest ages of *human* life in India', of which 'Chapter 2 provides the story of *man*'. And so on.

Habib knows what he is doing and seeks to justify it thus:

> It should be made clear that the use of the word 'man' or pronoun 'he', when what is intended is a reference to members of the hominid species in general, including women and men, is a concession to idiomatic usage. No particular emphasis on the masculine element should be assumed from such use.[257]

Not to recognize his reasoning would amount to disrespect; to allow it to go unchallenged is not to recognize the contribution of the feminist movement to clarity of thought.

[254] Habib and Thakur, *The Vedic Age*, p. 13.
[255] Cf. Habib, *Prehistory*, p. 48, on the role of women in plant domestication.
[256] Childe, *What Happened in History*, p. 94.
[257] Habib, *Prehistory*, p. x.

Appeal to idiomatic usage, we submit, does not always justify the choice of words. If 'early human in India' is acceptable idiomatic usage, 'early man' in India' must properly mean only one segment of what is sought to be denoted by 'early human in India'. The same will hold for the use of 'mankind'; 'humankind' is an old enough usage (dating from 1594) to make undesirable the use of 'mankind' in the same sense, even if the latter dates from the thirteenth century. Notions of correct idiom are changing. Anatomically Modern Man (AMM), employed by Habib, has for some time been replaced by Anatomically Modern Human (AMH). The issue of idiom occurs only in the case of the singular pronoun, when a choice has to be made between 'he' and 'she'. The use of the plural 'they' easily takes care of this and for this reason is preferred; it is to obviate the use of the singular pronoun that scholars speak of 'humans' or Anatomically Modern Humans in the plural.[258]

Old habits die hard, linguistic ones in particular,[259] but it is a great achievement of the feminist movement to have ensured correct usage. A big sign of the achievement in the discipline of history is seen in the shift of the UN vocabulary: its earlier world history series was called *History of Mankind*, its later one is styled *History of Humanity* (Habib is one of the editors, and contributors, in the new series). It is not easy to capture the passionate commitment of the feminist movement that has made it possible, but a glimpse (my favourite) may be seen in the following quote from Felix Pirani's Preface to Bertrand Russell's classic, *ABC of Relativity*, which shows how a gender-insensitive expression became, latest by 1985, plain wrong English:

> This book first appeared in 1925 . . . some revision was necessary for the second and subsequent editions. For the second and third editions I carried out these revisions with Bertrand Russell's approval. . . . Russell died in 1970. Further revisions in 1985 for the fourth edition . . . were entirely my responsibility. I again altered a number of passages to agree with present knowledge, and did my best to renounce the convention that the masculine includes the feminine, acceptable, or at least tolerated, sixty years earlier, but now no longer so. I felt that Russell, who was a pro-feminist ahead of his time, would have approved of this renunciation.[260]

---

[258] Dictionaries recognize this shift. Thus *The Concise Oxford Dictionary*, tenth edition, has the following on the relevant meanings of 'he': 'used to refer to a person or animal of unspecified sex (in modern use, now largely replaced by "he or she" or "they")'; 'any person (in modern use, now largely replaced by "anyone" or "the person")'.

[259] For example, Ratnagar, *Makers and Shapers*, p. 12, n. 1: 'It has been argued . . . that man may be a tool maker but we cannot give stone tools the central place in human development. . . . Man is essentially a self-mastering, self-designing, and social animal.'

[260] Felix Pirani, 'Preface' to Bertrand Russell, *ABC of Relativity*, Routledge: London and New York, 2002; reprinted in 2009, p. vi.

A Historian among Archaeologists

Jaya Menon

Irfan Habib is one among a rare group of historians who have attempted to move beyond the confines of a particular period in which they specialized. Seminal to the world of medieval history, he has forayed into the sphere of ancient Indian history with a series of articles and books. Since I cannot with ease discuss ancient history, I will largely deal here with the sphere of archaeology.

The general perception is that archaeology is a discipline that focuses only on a particular time-period, that is, the ancient, going by the traditional division of the study of history in India. This made Irfan Habib point out, in a speech at the inauguration of the Centre for Archaeological Studies and Training in Kolkata, that archaeologists tend to focus on prehistory and protohistory at the expense of historical and medieval archaeology. In reality, of course, one can archaeologically analyse sites of vastly different time-depths, such as of the Stone Age or of the colonial period or even of the present, as in modern material culture studies. Part of the reason for the misconception lies in the attitude of archaeologists themselves. The focus of archaeology in India has largely been to recover early remains or evidence of major human developments, such as the beginning of civilization or the domestication of a crop like rice or the independent invention of iron-working, all of which have been used to further neo-nationalist aspirations. Indian archaeologists have thus tended to concentrate on earlier periods and disdained working on later periods, claiming that much is already known about the latter from textual sources. However, it should be more than clear that much of what one learns from the texts is at the larger, more general level of processes or structures, while archaeology provides us with a glimpse into quotidian living. Thus both sources give vitally important and different pieces of evidence, and it would be unfortunate to use the archaeological evidence to merely corroborate what is written in the texts.

At the same time, it is also unfortunate that much of what currently goes in the name of archaeology of later periods (such as 'medieval archaeology') is in fact a study of architecture, whether these are forts, palaces, tombs, mosques, temples or bridges. There is a huge unrealized potential for undertaking excavations at medieval sites to uncover the material remains of later periods of history. Hardly any information is available about the artefacts, for example, that were used for various purposes in medieval times, or the different types of ceramics that were produced and used. Moreover, the usual tendency when dealing with past periods for which one has multiple sources, is to privilege the textual over the archaeological. Thus time-frames that are a construct of history are unquestioningly carried over into archaeological analysis under the assumption that material culture was transformed along with changes in the polity.

It was all the more significant, therefore, when archaeology was brought centrestage in Aligarh, in the medieval-centric Department of History at Aligarh Muslim University. This was largely due to the involvement of Irfan Habib in the case being argued before the Lucknow Bench of the Allahabad High Court, over the issue of whether the mosque, known as Babri Masjid, was built in Ayodhya after first destroying an early medieval temple dedicated to the birthplace of the god Rama. This necessitated excavations at the site in the year 2003, which was undertaken by the government body responsible for the heritage of the country, the Archaeological Survey of India. Several research students travelled to Ayodhya to witness this historic enterprise. Students of history who had little idea of how an excavation is conducted, who had little knowledge of the intricacies of stratigraphy and who had always assumed that archaeology was a source for history, had a first-time exposure to a discipline using a complete different methodology. This, against the backdrop of the unfair contempt that historians usually tend to have for archaeology, dismissing it as a less analytical discipline than history, and as one that belongs more in the realm of the sciences than the social sciences. Subsequently, during my six years at Aligarh, I have rarely seen an academic subject being discussed so animatedly by students as were the excavations beneath the floor of the Babri Masjid. Perhaps it was the underlying historical issue that resonated with them.

If one is to try and analyse some of Irfan Habib's multifaceted interests, what stands out is his fascination for geography and cartography. For several issues of the *Proceedings of the Indian History Congress*, he and Faiz Habib prepared maps on chronological periods falling within the ancient period along with explanatory articles.[1] The maps and articles were not

---

[1] Irfan Habib and Faiz Habib, 'The Geography and Economy of the Indus Civilization', in *Proceedings of the Indian History Congress* (hereafter *PIHC*), 1988, pp. 57–65; Irfan Habib and Faiz Habib, 'Mapping the Mauryan Empire', *PIHC*, 1989–90, pp. 57–79; Irfan Habib and Faiz Habib, 'A Map of India, 200 bc–Ad 300, based on Epigraphic Evidence', *PIHC*, 1990, pp. 103–14; Irfan Habib and Faiz Habib, 'The Historical Geography of India 1800–800 bc', *PIHC*, 1992, pp. 72–97; Irfan Habib and Faiz Habib, 'Epigraphic Map of India AD

published in strict chronological order, with maps on the evolution and diffusion of humankind, and on Neolithic sites, coming at the end of the series. The articles accompanying the maps are useful as they provide full references for the sources of various periods that are the concern of particular maps. The style of cartography follows Habib's pathbreaking atlas of the Mughal empire in its attention to detail. The maps are extremely useful also because all the relevant information is encapsulated within the borders of each map. One usually expects only basic information such as rivers or mountain ranges or site locations, though it should be mentioned that even this is not always adhered to with even eminent archaeologists often putting on their maps only site names and a few major rivers and little else, leaving sites in many cases swimming on a blank page. In Habib and Habib's map on the Indus civilization, one finds useful data on raw materials such as copper, silver, jade, agate, lapis (though steatite could also have been mentioned), isohyets, crops and archaeological cultures.[2] The map on Mauryan India is an illustration not only of historical geography, but also of cultural, linguistic and economic geography.[3] The maps dealing with archaeological periods show type-fossils and radiocarbon dates. It is encouraging to know that all these maps are soon to be published in a single volume as an atlas of the ancient period.

The 1988 article by Habib and Habib in the *Proceedings of the Indian History Congress* requires some comment.[4] In a section on categorization of sites by culture, the authors bring both Early and pre-Indus sites together into one category, noting that

> this is because we have been compelled to lump under this category all sites of cultures which do not show Mature Indus characteristics, and (a) which are either chronologically earlier than Mature Indus culture or (b) whose levels underlie Mature Indus levels, though they themselves do not, on present evidence, go beyond the beginning of the Mature Indus Culture in point of time.

There is a problem with the first assumption here, that this category of sites does not show Mature Indus characteristics. An absence of Mature Indus characteristics should be the case with pre-Harappan (or pre-Indus) sites, but not with Early Harappan (or Early Indus) sites. The very defini-

---

300–500', *PIHC*, 1994, pp. 832–64; Irfan Habib and Faiz Habib, 'From the Oxus to the Yamuna, *c.* 600–*c.* 750', *PIHC*, 1995, pp. 52–84; Irfan Habib and Faiz Habib, 'A Map of India 600–320 BC', *PIHC*, 1996, pp. 95–104; Irfan Habib and Faiz Habib, 'Mapping the Evolution and Diffusion of Humankind – and India's Place in It', *PIHC*, 1999, pp. 58–76; Irfan Habib and Faiz Habib, 'Mapping Neolithic India', *PIHC*, 2008, pp. 1302–09.

[2] Habib and Habib, 'The Geography and Economy of the Indus Civilization'.

[3] Habib and Habib, 'Mapping the Mauryan Empire'.

[4] Habib and Habib, 'The Geography and Economy of the Indus Civilization'.

tion of Early Harappan implies that materially there are points of convergence with the Harappan even while there are some/several new elements. Whereas the definition of pre-Harappan implies that there is no similarity in artefacts. A similar situation prevails with Late and post-Harappan. While the former culture should have some material elements in common with the Harappan, the latter should be completely different from the Harappan. Thus it is important that there should be no conflation of the identities of pre-Harappan and Early Harappan cultures.

The maps dealing with periods in ancient India provide information on each period to the student in graphic form. Another set of books being written by Irfan Habib primarily for students is in the *People's History of India* series. Eight volumes have been published in this series so far, of which five deal with various periods of ancient Indian history. One cuts across historical periods, being a study of human interaction with the environment over time.[5] The project under which these textbooks are being written is sponsored by the Aligarh Historians Society. The involvement of Irfan Habib can be seen in the fact that he has solely or jointly authored all but one of the five volumes dealing with ancient India,[6] as well as three others relating to later periods.[7] Aspects that stand out in my mind about the *People's History* series (and there too, especially if one looks at the sections on archaeology) are Habib's interest in technology (ranging from agricultural technology to writing), and in language and its development. On the whole, one finds a preference for dealing with economic features and structures, as seen, for example, in *Mauryan India*, where 20 pages are devoted to the economy, 8 to society and 9 to religion. His note in *The Indus Civilization* is very useful for students, particularly in trying to understand the development of the abstraction that writing is. He also shows a great interest in agricultural technology. Much attention is devoted to irrigation, tillage techniques, even to the probable discovery of castration. Much less focus, if at all, barring iron metallurgy, is given to craft technology, particularly what he calls the 'precision crafts'. Is that because he considers the latter too elitist?

---

[5] Irfan Habib, *Man and Environment: The Ecological History of India*, A People's History of India 36, New Delhi: Tulika Books, in association with Aligarh Historians Society, 2010.

[6] Irfan Habib, *Prehistory*, A People's History of India 1, New Delhi: Tulika Books, in association with Aligarh Historians Society, 2001; Irfan Habib, *The Indus Civilization*, A People's History of India 2, New Delhi: Tulika Books, in association with Aligarh Historiar.s Society, 2002; Irfan Habib and Vijay Kumar Thakur, *The Vedic Age*, A People's History of India 3, New Delhi: Tulika Books, in association with Aligarh Historians Society, 2003; Irfan Habib and Vivekanand Jha, *Mauryan India*, A People's History of India 4 (later renumbered 5), New Delhi: Tulika Books, in association with Aligarh Historians Society, 2004.

[7] Irfan Habib, *Indian Economy 1858–1914*, A People's History of India 28, New Delhi: Tulika Books, in association with Aligarh Historians Society, 2006; Irfan Habib, *Technology in Medieval India, c. 650–1750*, A People's History of India 20, New Delhi: Tulika Books, in association with Aligarh Historians Society, 2008; Habib, *Man and Environment*.

The *People's History of India* series relies on multiple sources to reconstruct different aspects of the past. For periods without texts, the reliance is on archaeological evidence, while both texts and archaeology give pointers to understand other, later periods. Thus Habib is able to write about crops and animal domestication using archaeological evidence,[8] and for later periods, using both archaeological and textual evidence.[9] Irfan Habib is not an archaeologist, nor is he an ancient historian for that matter. But as a historian he makes use of the discipline of archaeology to investigate the inventions, development, and transfers of technologies or ideas over time and space. One of his prime concerns regarding technology is to investigate where a certain technique or product was first found, much on the lines of Joseph Needham. For example, in the case of cotton, the Mohenjodaro specimen is pointed out as being one of the earliest examples, the other being from Jordan some time before 3000 BC.[10] So also are cited the evidence for bread-making or the use of the cart.[11] Following Gordon Childe, Habib tends to prefer diffusion as an explanation for the presence of several innovations. The technology of castration, '[a] major discovery, which could, by the very complexity of it, have scarcely been made simultaneously at more than one place',[12] and its probable spread is explained through diffusion. Diffusion is also seen as useful in downplaying the role of environmental determinism.[13]

Irfan Habib does not shy away from several polemical issues that have dogged the study of ancient history in India. The attempt to correlate the archaeological evidence of the Harappan Civilization with the textual tradition of the *Rigveda* is discussed in Note 2.2 in *The Indus Civilization*;[14] he has also written on the issue of the Sarasvati river and its significance.[15] The attempt at creating an 'epic archaeology' finds attention in Note 3.1 in *The Vedic Age*[16] and also in an article published in *Social Scientist*.[17] While claims for the earliest domestication of rice in the world are discussed, as at Lahuradewa,[18] surprisingly, proclamations of early iron in India, going back to *c.* 1800 BC, are not.

---

[8] Habib, *Man and Environment*, pp. 27–31.

[9] Ibid., pp. 48–59.

[10] Habib, *The Indus Civilization*, p. 34.

[11] Ibid., pp. 11, 9–10.

[12] Habib, *Man and Environment*, p. 32.

[13] Ibid., p. 22.

[14] Habib, *The Indus Civilization*, pp. 71–74.

[15] Irfan Habib, 'Imagining River Sarasvati: A Defence of Commonsense', *Social Scientist*, Vol. 30, Nos 1–2, 2001.

[16] Habib and Thakur, *The Vedic Age*, pp. 92–94.

[17] Irfan Habib, 'Unreason and Archaeology: The "Painted Grey Ware" and Beyond', *Social Scientist*, Vol. 25, Nos 1–2, 1997.

[18] The issue is given short shrift in Habib, *Man and Environment*, p. 28.

For the student of ancient India, some of Irfan Habib's references dealing with the medieval period are invaluable. One can note in this context, Shams Siraj 'Afif's descriptions of wild asses in the Sirsa tract in about AD 1400, as well as Babur's description of the rhinoceros in the region of Peshawar in about 1526–30.[19] Even while both these extracts are presented in the section of the book dealing with medieval India, their immense significance for the ancient period cannot be lost on the reader.

It appears that Habib is highly critical of New Archaeology, his main disagreement being its rejection of diffusion. But before we get into this, it would be useful to look at the issue from another viewpoint. As is well known, the main practitioners of New Archaeology were Lewis Binford in the US and David Clarke in Britain. The main proponent of what preceded New Archaeology, the so-called Culture–Historical school, was V. Gordon Childe, an Australian by birth but who did most of his work in Britain.

What are the main points stressed by New Archaeology or the Processual school?

(1) An emphasis on cultural evolution: that societies can be classified on a scale from simple to complex, and that societies evolved from one stage to another. This is a perspective taken largely from anthropology.

(2) Culture is seen as an extrasomatic means of adaptation to the environment.

(3) A stress on systems thinking and systems analysis. Culture is a system with inter-relating sub-systems.

(4) A stress on generalization. There may be different types of pottery styles or burial rites, but the underlying social system could have similarities.

(5) An emphasis on explanation. It is not enough to just describe tha data; one need to analyse them.

(6) Explanations are primarily through the scientific method. One needs to proceed beyond facts and their detailing, to understanding the linkages between facts. This can be done by using the scientific, hypothetico-deductive method.

(7) Culture should be seen as a process rather than as a set of events, with the implication of studying long-term changes.

(8) Part of the scientific method is the rejection of intuition. This is seen particularly in the area of classification and especially in the work of David Clarke.

(9) An emphasis on variability. This is primarily to understand archaeological material in statistical terms. If earlier emphases had mostly been on the

[19] Habib, *Man and Environment*, pp. 105, 106.

larger, urban sites, New Archaeologists pointed out that one cannot understand, say, a major urban civilization, without looking at its rural infrastructure and without knowing just how many rural sites there were on the
ground. To understand variability, New Archaeology looks at sampling theory
and techniques, and explores methods of random and systematic sampling.

(10) An emphasis on functionalism. The primary division by Binford of
archaeological material (artefacts) into technomic, sociotechnic and ideotechnic types means looking at their functions. Yet, he also pointed out that
the meanings of artefacts need not be so neatly compartmentalized; thus a
copper axe seemingly belonging to the technomic category, if found in a
burial, could be seen as ideotechnic. Important here is the context of archaeological finds.

New Archaeology found a larger breeding ground in the US than it did in
Britain. It has been suggested that the difference lay in the fact that in the
US, archaeology is much more directly related to anthropology; in fact,
most archaeologists are housed in anthropology departments. In the UK, on
the other hand, archaeology has greater links with history. It has also been
pointed out that in Britain, the cultural continuum is greater from a prehistoric past to the Roman world to the present, unlike in America where the
historical horizon is closer, tending to go back just to the colonies.

Barring one or two points, the divergences between the Culture–Historical school and New Archaeology seem more apparent than real. Some of
the points raised by New Archaeology had already been enunciated by Childe.
This in itself is not surprising as knowledge always builds on (and also
rejects) knowledge. There is a general tendency to think that New Archaeology entirely rubbished the Culture–Historical school, but that is not entirely correct. There may not be an explicit recognition of the debt to traditional archaeology within New Archaeology, but there are several startling
convergences. Let us look at some of these.

(1) Culture, according to New Archaeology, is man's extrasomatic means
of adaptation to the external environment. Now, let us see what Gordon
Childe wrote in *What Happened in History*:

> The human species is not physiologically adapted to any particular environ-
> ment. Its adaptation is secured by its extracorporeal equipment of tools, clothes,
> houses and the rest. By devising suitable equipment a human society can fit
> itself to live under almost all conditions. Fire, clothing, houses and an appro-
> priate diet enable men to endure arctic cold and tropic heat equally well.
> Material culture is thus largely a response to an environment: it consists of the
> devices evolved to meet needs evoked by particular climatic conditions, to
> take advantage of local sources of food and to secure protection against wild
> beasts, floods or other nuisances infesting a given region. Different societies

have been prompted to invent different devices and to discover how to use different natural substances for food, shelter and tools.[20]

(2) New Archaeology's emphasis on functionalism. Childe had marked a difference between what he called ethnically persistent traits that were spatially limited, and permitted people to be identified and traced in the archaeological record, from functionally efficient traits that diffused from culture to culture. According to Trigger, Childe was one of the first archaeologists to introduce explicitly functional considerations into the study of archaeological data.[21] This can be seen from Childe's functional classification in his book, *A Short Introduction to Archaeology*.[22] The importance given to function in his classification of objects can also be seen in his *What Happened in History*.[23]

(3) New Archaeology's use of generalization as a means towards explanation. One can agree with Renfrew that Childe's concepts of Urban Revolution, Neolithic Revolution and the Bronze Age are generalizations.[24] These terms, now considered classic, were attempts to understand at a general level, developments that took place in human society. One can see these in Childe's *Man Makes Himself*[25] and *What Happened in History*. Childe's classic paper on the urban revolution in the *Town Planning Review* of 1950, in which he outlined ten criteria for estimating urbanism was also a case of generalization.

(4) There are two additional points to be noted here. First, Renfrew makes the suggestion that in delineating ten interlocking factors in his *Town Planning Review* article, Childe came close to a systems analysis, so much a part of the Processual school.[26] Second, in his discussion of the Neolithic revolution, Childe reiterated that it was a process – something that New Archaeology was later to lay stress on. He wrote in *Man Makes Himself*: 'The neolithic revolution . . . was the climax of a long process. It has to be so presented as a single event because archaeology can only recognize the result, the several steps leading up thereto are beyond the range of direct observation.'[27] Similarly, he pointed out in *What Happened in History*: 'The thousand years or

---

[20] V. Gordon Childe, *What Happened in History*, Harmondsworth: Penguin, 1942, pp. 21–22.
[21] B.G. Trigger, 'Childe's Relevance to the 1990s', in D.R. Harris (ed.), *The Archaeology of V. Gordon Childe*, Chicago: Chicago University Press, 1994, p. 12.
[22] V. Gordon Childe, *A Short Introduction to Archaeology*, New York: Collier, 1956, pp. 29–31.
[23] Childe, *What Happened in History*, p. 19.
[24] C. Renfrew, 'Concluding Remarks: Childe and the Study of Culture Process', in D.R. Harris (ed.), *The Archaeology of Gordon Childe*, Chicago: Chicago University Press, 1994.
[25] V. Gordon Childe, *Man Makes Himself*, third edition, Wiltshire: Moonraker Press, 1981.
[26] Renfrew, 'Concluding Remarks', p. 127.
[27] Childe, *Man Makes Himself*, p. 94.

so . . . immediately preceding 3000 BC were perhaps more fertile in fruitful inventions and discoveries than any period in human history prior to the sixteenth century AD. Its achievements made possible that economic reorganization of society that I term the urban revolution.'[28] In no way can a thousand years be considered an event; this too has to be seen as a development, a process.

(5) Regarding laws as a means of explanation, let us see what Childe wrote in an article in the *Southwestern Journal of Anthropology*, interestingly entitled 'Archaeology and Anthropology':

> Since 99% of human history is prehistory, and only illiterate societies exist or have existed in sufficient numbers and with sufficient independence to provide the basis for reliable induction, this method offers the brightest prospect for reaching general laws indicative of the direction of historical progress. . . . I suggest that one pre-eminent task for anthropology is just to establish such directional laws or directional tendencies, so that we can determine in what direction culture progresses.[29]

(6) New Archaeology, particularly David Clarke's emphasis on classification. Clarke's explicitly laid out principles and formulations for classification were a brilliant piece of work. It can be easily pointed out that the inspiration was Gordon Childe. It is well known that Childe conceived of classification of a culture in terms of artefacts, types and assemblages. In his later work, Childe also realized, importantly, that 'it would be rash to try to define precisely what sort of social group corresponds to the archaeologist's "culture"'.[30] In *A Short Introduction to Archaeology*, he further wrote: 'The restriction of archaeology to types means, of course, the exclusion of individual actors from archaeological history. Such history cannot aspire to be biographical, and archaeologists are excluded from the school of "great man" history.'[31] This was also specifically pointed out by Clarke: that an archaeological culture should be best seen in terms of the entities of attribute, artefact-type, assemblage and culture, rather than a people or ethnic group.

The attempt here is not to point out that Childe was a New Archaeologist in disguise! There was one major area of contention between the two schools of thought and that centred on diffusion. Throughout *What Happened in History*, Childe made several references to traits, ideas, techniques, materials and people diffusing from one place to another. Phenomena, like

---

[28] Childe, *What Happened in History*, p. 69.
[29] Cf. Renfrew, 'Concluding Remarks', p. 126.
[30] Childe, *What Happened in History*, p. 20.
[31] Childe, *A Short Introduction to Archaeology*, p. 15.

urbanism, too diffused. New Archaeology, particularly in the US, reacted against diffusionism. Binford caricatured diffusion as 'an aquatic view of culture', meaning that:

> archaeologists saw the map of the prehistoric world as being a little like a large pool of water. When an innovation was made for whatever reason in a given place, it would tend to spread through the process of 'influence' or diffusion in all directions, like the ripples from a stone dropped in the pool. In any given location, then, one would see cross-cutting 'ripples' of influence.[32]

For Childe, the main areas of geographical interest were the Near East and Europe. When he did deal with the Far East or with India, it was mainly to illustrate his urban revolution and its spread. In fact, he was quite dismissive of the advances made in the New World. But it must be realized that Childe was working at a time when very little of the archaeological past was known. Cultures, as he saw them, had been little delineated, and with his exceptional memory, he was able to build up regional sequences and in turn illustrate his point about diffusion.

New Archaeology reacted violently against diffusion and the tendency was to completely dismiss all external influences as explanations for cultural change. The attempt, instead, was to project most developments, whether in Neolithic domestication or in technologies or in ideas, as indigenous to different regions, and in turn as independent centres of invention or development. This trend has of course, particularly recently, had unfortunate right-wing consequences, with attempts to locate most advances within rather than seeing them as coming from outside. At the same time, we should remember that the initial reaction to diffusion was seen, particularly in England and Europe, as stemming from racist ideas of all advances as originating from the Near East.

Childe was no racist, though unfortunately he did, in his early work, talk of a superior physique and a superior language. The diffusionism of his later work was permeated by a desire to counteract the rise of racism and nationalism in archaeology, and to 'absolve his own guilt over his previous adherence to the Aryan hypothesis'.[33] It does appear that much of anti-diffusionism was intended to fuel nationalistic tendencies and we quote Michael Rowlands here:

> Archaeology has been used by politicians in Serbia, Croatia and Macedonia to justify and resist territorial ambitions through claims of prior origin. . . .

---

[32] M. Johnson, *Archaeological Theory*, Oxford: Blackwell, 1999, p. 19.
[33] M. Rowlands, 'Childe and the Archaeology of Freedom', in D.R. Harris (ed.), *The Archaeology of V. Gordon Childe*, Chicago: Chicago University Press, 1994, p. 42.

Archaeologists are often the first to celebrate building justifiable pride in a specific cultural tradition. Many archaeologists also today recognize the importance of regional traditions as a means of structuring research, often within individual countries. It is part of a reaction against generalizing goals . . . and is linked to post-processualist (and one can include postmodernist) claims to multiple readings of the past. The fact is that claims to primordial origins can be and are used to justify ownership of land that an ethnic group or state claims to have held from 'time immemorial' or to adopt policies of domination and expansion over neighbouring peoples. The renaming or suppression of archaeological cultures and the redrawing of maps and boundaries in prehistory are all too familiar strategies.[34]

This applies all too distressingly to the Indian context where archaeology, particularly from the 1990s, has focused on discerning where the country stood first, whether it be the earliest Neolithic 'civilization' or the earliest evidence of rice domestication.

New Archaeology was obviously wrong in completely and outrightly rejecting diffusion. There need not be independent centres for each and every technique or process. In fact, Childe's conception of a Bronze Age with few borders where there was considerable mobility of craftsmen, traders, diplomatic expeditions and so forth, has been widely considered a brilliant analysis of the particular structures of that age.

The problem with diffusion is that it would have been better to leave it at the general level that Childe conceived, rather than, as recently, getting into the specifics of radiocarbon dates, and through these, figuring out the origins and directions of diffusion. The basic problem one would have is with radiocarbon dates themselves and with hinging entire hypotheses on them. It is not a given that the mere presence of C-14 dates will solve all our problems. One can give the instance of C-14 dates from the site called Jodhpura in Rajasthan to illustrate this point. At Jodhpura, there is a sequence of eight radiocarbon dates. Of these, there are two pairs of two dates each that are rejected because they are from the same layer and same trench, but are inconsistent in that they do not agree with each other. One date cannot be accepted as it is too early for the Black and Red Ware Culture. One date is rejected because the Black and Red Ware Culture did not continue till 380 BC. Only two dates are more or less consistent with each other and have been accepted. It does seem, therefore, that C-14 dates are accepted largely only because they fit in with preconceived chronologies. There appears to be very little objectivity here.

One can end by saying that there was much that was achieved with New

[34] Ibid., p. 44.

Archaeology and that all was not rotten with the world of New Archaeology. If we include specialized studies of plants and animals or soils in our archaeological analyses, or work out settlement pattern studies, site catchment analyses, nearest-neighbour analyses, rank-size hierarchies, and so forth, it is primarily because of the efforts of New Archaeology. Perhaps a major lack among New Archaeologicals is that they try to be too objective (if one can actually fault that), bringing archaeology a little too close to the pure sciences for comfort. Childe, and the passion with which he wrote, are clearly a contrast.

One must finally reiterate Irfan Habib's contribution not only to the field of medieval history, but also to other spheres of history. He has the ability to bring his historian's mind, unflinching secularism and phenomenal memory to the study of different parts of our past, and to move between them with equal felicity.

Medieval India

Agrarian System of the Mughals and the Eighteenth Century

Satish Chandra

By his wide-ranging and meticulous research, Irfan Habib has added greatly to our understanding of medieval Indian society, especially of the agrarian system: not only how it operated from above, but its effects on the life and living patterns of the vast majority of the peasants.

He has shown how once a class state replaced the tribal oligarchies (*vis*), the bulk of the cultivators were heavily oppressed. During medieval times, they were condemned to live at near-subsistence levels, or what Habib calls 'the barest minimum needed for existence'.[1] Irfan Habib has thus put to rest many a theory of a golden age in the past when milk and honey flowed! However, two questions have arisen from his seminal work. Did all cultivators (excluding those holding superior rights in land) live at the same margin of subsistence? And what, if any, were the elements of growth and change in such a society?

There has been a lot of controversy around these two issues. It would be useful to first note Habib's own comments on the flight of peasants from their lands, which was highlighted by Bernier and has been often quoted. He does consider the flight of peasants, the increasing pressure on them and peasant rebellions as causes for the decline of the Mughal empire; he says:

> The main fact attested by a number of observers is that the flight of the peasants from their lands was a common phenomenon, and that it was apparently growing in momentum with the passage of times. . . . with vast areas still unploughed, peasant migrations were probably a general feature of the agrarian life of our period.[2]

Habib questions any rapid increase of cultivation in the empire, except in

---

[1] Irfan Habib, *The Agrarian System of Mughal India, 1556–1707*, second revised edition, Delhi: Oxford University Press, 1999, p. 364. See also Irfan Habib, 'The Peasant in Indian History', in *Essays in Indian History: Towards a Marxist Perception*, New Delhi: Tulika Books, 1995, pp. 109–60; first published in *Social Scientist*, Vol. 11, No. 3, March 1983.

[2] Habib, *Agrarian System of Mughal India*, p. 392.

some areas such as modern east Uttar Pradesh, Bihar and east Bengal.[3] But he does not postulate a decline of the area under cultivation. He basically upholds the concept of 'stagnation' or slow growth, which was the result of the existing social relations and the administrative system reared on them.

In other words, Irfan Habib's theory of agrarian crisis has to be seen in the Marxist sense where the crisis of a class system is based on growing social contradictions within it. In the feudal system, where the ruling class subsists on extraction of surplus labour from the peasantry, such a crisis took the shape of an agrarian crisis.

In such a phase, limited agrarian growth was not ruled out. Habib points to the introduction of new crops, such as tobacco and maize, during the seventeenth century. There was also growth of cash-crops such as indigo, cotton, sugarcane, etc., to cater to the growing exports.[4] Shireen Moosvi notes that population grew at an annual rate of 0.21 per cent, and since there was no rise in the prices of food crops during the seventeenth century, cultivation would have expanded sufficiently to cater to the increased demand: 'But the actual rate of expansion at 0.23 per cent is nonetheless above the annual population growth of 0.21 per cent found for the entire period 1601–1871.'[5] It has also been pointed out by Nurul Hasan that the production of rabi crops, such as wheat, increased in the territories of Amber, and that this could have been possible only if there was a reasonable investment in agriculture.[6] The main agencies and beneficiaries of this growth were the *khud-kasht* and the village zamindars. In the process, a small percentage of the *khud-kasht* became prosperous or rich.[7] This highlighted social tensions in the village, with rich *khud-kasht* (called *mahajans*) loaning money to the poor or *khiraji* peasants, sometimes to pay for the land revenue demand or during famines, by mortgaging their lands and fore-

[3] Ibid., pp. 21, 22; Irfan Habib, 'Potentialities of Capitalist Development in the Economy of Mughal India', in *Essays in Indian History: Towards a Marxist Perception*, New Delhi: Tulika Books, 1995, pp. 183–84.

[4] Habib, *Agrarian System of Mughal India*, pp. 42–43, 50.

[5] Shireen Moosvi, *People Taxation and Trade in Mughal India*, Delhi: Oxford University Press, 2008, p. 7 This means agricultural production expanded sufficiently to cope with the population and the growing towns.

[6] S. Nurul Hasan, Khursheed Nurul Hasan and S.P. Gupta (2005), 'The Pattern of Agricultural Production in the Territories of Amber (1650–1750)', in S. Nurul Hasan, *Religion, State and Society in Medieval India*, edited by Satish Chandra, Delhi: Oxford University Press, 2005, p. 186.

[7] Satish Chandra and Dilbagh Singh, 'Structure and Stratification in the Village Society in Eastern Rajasthan', in Satish Chandra, *Essays on Medieval Indian History*, Delhi: Oxford University Press, 2003, pp. 159–67. Also see Satish Chandra, 'The Role of the Local Community, the Zamindars and the State in Providing Capital Inputs for the Improvement and Expansion of Cultivation', in *Essays on Medieval Indian History*, Delhi: Oxford University Press, 2003.

closing them as the opportunity arose.[8] However, neither all of these nor the peasant rebellions changed the agrarian system or the existing social relations.[9]

While agriculture stagnated, or grew slowly, there was scope for considerable growth of commercial elements within this system. Irfan Habib says: 'commercial activity could prosper best under an imperial system with its uniform methods of tax collection and administration, and its control of the routes'. He does not think, however, that this development threatened the existing system. These activities strengthened imperial power and reinforced the economic foundations of its existence. Habib concludes: 'Unlike the feudal lord of Western Europe, the Mughal jagirdar might not have needed to harbour any fear of money and trade undermining his power.[10]

It is precisely this aspect that has been countered by a number of scholars, both foreign and Indian. Thus we have the 'firm theory' (Karen Leonard), the 'mercantilist state theory' (Burton Stein) and the theory of 'portfolio capitalism' (Sanjay Subrahmaniam). They all emphasize the growing power of the moneyed interests, mainly commercial, and their growing distance from the Mughal state and its successor states or *riyasat*s. They also argue that these elements sought the support or help of the foreign trading companies, and, in some cases, joined hands with them to topple Indian state governments (as in Bengal). These theories have been examined in detail and need not detain us here.[11] However, Bayly's theory of the rise of 'intermediate groups' between the revenue-based state and the mass of agrarian society, from whom, he says, were 'ultimately recruited the Indian middle class', needs further examination.[12] He adds:

Eighteenth-century north India possessed what might be called an 'intermediate economy'. It functioned not at the level of the bazaar of the large town, nor in the village periodic mart (*hath*) where peasants exchanged petty commodities amongst themselves, but in the fixed gentry seat (*qasbah*) and the small regulated market (*ganj*). Its products were medium quality clothes, specialist fruit and vegetables and milk products; its services, provisioning and

---

[8] Dilbagh Singh, 'The Role of the Mahajans in the Rural Economy in Eastern Rajasthan during the Eighteenth Century', *Social Scientist*, May 1974, pp. 20–31.

[9] Habib, *Agrarian System of Mughal India*, p. 405; Satish Chandra, 'The Eighteenth Century in India: Its Economy and the Role of the Marathas, the Jats, the Sikhs and the Afghans', in *Essays on Medieval Indian History*, Delhi: Oxford University Press, 2003, pp. 101–02.

[10] Habib, *Agrarian System of Mughal India*, p. 304.

[11] Athar Ali, 'Recent Theories of Eighteenth Century India', in P.J. Marshall (ed.), *The Eighteenth Century in Indian History: Evolution or Revolution*, Delhi: Oxford University Press, 2008, pp. 90–99.

[12] C.A. Bayly, *Rulers, Townsmen and Bazaars: North Indian Society in the Age of British Expansion, 1770–1870*, Cambridge: Cambridge University Press, 1987, p. 6.

carrying for local magnates and moving armies; its motive force was the distribution of local political power expressed in revenue assignments.[13]

This was nothing new. The rise of *qasbah*s and *mandi*s was a feature of India under Mughal rule. Growth of an 'intermediate economy' would mean a move towards capitalism by establishing an economy between feudalism and capitalism. However, Bayly says: 'the contention that it is possible to see the sprouts of capitalism arising out of India's mercantile economy in the years 1600–1800 does not seem convincing'.[14] He also mentions that there 'emerged a unified merchant class wielding overt political power'.[15] This proposition does not have any solid evidence to back it. The case of Jagat Seth in Bengal cannot be used to cover the entire country. Also, Jagat Seth had his rival in Khwaja Wazid, the Armenian. The merchant class was unified in the sense that it could send goods and money across long distances, and even to countries outside India, through the *hundi-bima* (insurance) system. But this was an old system which gradually developed under the Mughals.[16]

During the first half of the eighteenth century, the economy showed both growth and decline. There was considerable commercial and artisanal growth in Bengal, largely on account of the operations of the European trading companies. On the basis of a careful study, Om Prakash concludes:

> The trade carried on by the Dutch and the English East India companies from Bengal during *c.* 1630–1720 (prior to the emergence of a colonial relationship) generated a significant increase of income, output, and employment in the region. The estimate of Rs 34 million per annum provides some idea of the magnitude of the increase in income and output on this score. The companies' procurement of textiles and raw silk would have sustained approximately 87,000 to 111,000 full-time job equivalents, accounting for 9 to 11 per cent of the total workforce engaged in the textile manufacturing sector of the province of Bengal.[17]

This pattern of growth cannot, of course, be applied to the rest of India, any more than Ashin Dasgupta's study of the decline of Surat and Gujarat can be applied to the rest of India. Although Delhi was devastated by the raid of Nadir Shah, it recovered quickly and remained a busy commercial

---

[13] Ibid., p. 52.

[14] C.A. Bayly, 'Rise of Corporations', in P.J. Marshall (ed.), *The Eighteenth Century in Indian History: Evolution or Revolution*, Delhi: Oxford University Press, 2008, p. 163.

[15] Ibid., p. 138.

[16] Sushil Chaudhury, *From Prosperity to Decline: Eighteenth Century Bengal*, Delhi: Manohar, 1995.

[17] Om Prakash, *Bullion for Goods: European and Indian Merchants in the Indian Ocean Trade, 1500–1800*, Delhi: Manohar, 2004, p. 282.

resort till 1772.[18] Punjab too recovered under able governors, and eastern Rajasthan under Sawai Jai Singh. The growth in Awadh was uncertain due to the rise of some powerful zamindars and the Rohillas.[19] Under the Marathas, in the areas held directly by the Peshwa, agriculture was revived and expanded following the Mughal model;[20] but this was a revival after a long period of war.

P.J. Marshall writes: 'In general, however, economic activity in India seems to have been more and more robust and deep-seated than used to be supposed'.[21] This certainly is a revision of the earlier British view of India's economic decline in the eighteenth century, and of the anarchy which justified the British conquest. However, in our present state of knowledge and till more regional records have been studied, it would be difficult to strike a balance between the theories of growth and of decline.[22]

In Bayly's work, as also that of many British historians, the *entire* eighteenth century is portrayed as one of continuation, with the East India Company assuming the form of some of the successor Mughal regimes. Thereby an attempt is made to portray the Company's rule or the British colonial regime as the legitimate successor of the Mughals, and to say that by standing forth as the rulers of all of India, they reunified the country! In any historical phase, many elements of the previous phase are bound to be continued. The task of the historian is to note the new elements and the discontinuities while not losing sight of the continuities. Much has been written about the misuse of the *dastak* system by the British, and of oppression by their *gumashta*s and agents.[23] These are sought to be brushed aside by those who lay emphasis on continuities.

---

[18] *Maasir-ul-Umara*, II, translated by Beni Prasad, Calcutta, 1952, p. 273; Satish Chandra, 'Cultural and Political Role of Delhi, 1675–1725', in R.E. Frykenberg (ed.), *Delhi through the Ages*, Delhi: Oxford University Press, 1980, pp. 208–17.

[19] Muzaffar Alam,, *The Crisis of the Empire in Mughal North India, Awadh and the Punjab*, Delhi: Oxford University Press, 1980, pp. 92–102. According to Iqtidar Siddiqi (*The Rohilla Power in the Eighteenth Century*, Delhi, 1994, pp. 202 ff), the Rohillas, despite marauding, did extend and improve cultivation.

[20] Frank Perlin, 'Of White Whale and Countrymen in the Eighteenth Century Maratha Deccan', *Journal of Peasant Studies*, V, 1978, pp. 172–327, quoted in P.J. Marshall (ed.), *The Eighteenth Century in Indian History: Evolution or Revolution*, Delhi: Oxford University Press, 2008, pp. 18–19.

[21] Marshall (ed.), *The Eighteenth Century in Indian History*, p. 13.

[22] For Irfan Habib's views on the subject, see his 'The Eighteenth Century in Indian Economic History', in Marshall (ed.), *The Eighteenth Century in Indian History*, pp. 110–19.

[23] See Mir Qasim's letter to the Council at Calcutta, dated 23 March 1765, and the views of Vansittart on the subject: Vansittart, *Narrative*, III, quoted in *A Comprehensive History of India*, Vol. IX: 1712–1772, edited by A.C. Banerjee, D.K. Ghosh, Delhi, 1978, pp. 681–82. Also see S. Bhattacharya (ed.), *The Cambridge Economic History of India*, Vol. II, Cambridge: Cambridge University Press, 1983, pp. 289–95). Marshall (*The Eighteenth Century*

While painting a picture of overall growth during the first half of the eighteenth century, Marshall writes: 'If a clear case be established for continuing economic growth over large parts of India during the first half of the eighteenth century, optimism about the second half of the eighteenth century is more questionable.'[24] While this is a typical British understatement, it should, however, be welcomed as a new approach by a colonial scholar.

In substance, we might conclude that the elements of growth, mainly in the trade and manufacturing fields and the infrastructure reared upon these, which had developed under the aegis of the Mughals, were so strong that they were not seriously disrupted, except in some areas, during the first half of the eighteenth century. That political disintegration of the Mughal empire did not seriously affect the major trade routes is upheld by Irfan Habib, who shows that insurance rates during the first half of the century did not rise but were more or less stable.[25] In this context, the word 'stagnation', which mainly applies to the agrarian sector but is sometimes used for the entire economy, is perhaps no longer appropriate.

---

in Indian History, p. 13) says: 'The activities of Indian merchants were to some degree constricted as the Company established monopolies, or brought weavers and spinners under their control.' The harsh methods used for the purpose is blurred over. He goes on to say: 'However, a large part of Bengal's commerce remained beyond the reach of the Company or of private British merchants. But as the Company's rule extended, merchants, spinners and weavers and cultivators received a serious setback.'

[24] Marshall (ed.), The Eighteenth Century in Indian History, p. 18.

[25] Irfan Habib, 'The Eighteenth Century in Indian Economic History', in Marshall (ed.), The Eighteenth Century in Indian History, pp. 104–05.

Religion in Medieval India

J.S. Grewal and Indu Banga

Irfan Habib is one of the few Marxist historians who have taken the study of religion rather seriously. He has edited a volume entitled *Religion in Indian History*,[1] to which he has contributed an article on Kabir in addition to his Editorial Introduction. His *Medieval India: The Study of a Civilization*[2] relates not only to the polity, economy, social order, science and technology, or to literature and the arts, but also to religion. The space devoted to religion is more than the space given to literature and the arts put together.

The 'medieval' period in this book covers more than a millennium, from AD 600 to 1750. This whole period is divided into early medieval (600–1200), India under the Sultanates (1200–1500) and Mughal India (1500–1750), each marked by some distinctive developments. More space is given to the last 250 years than to the earlier 900 years. Irfan Habib has an explanation:

This is not only because these two and half centuries, being nearest to us, should be of greater interest to us, but also because owing to the large amount of primary source materials, archival records, extensive historical narratives, an enormous number of books surviving in manuscripts, accounts of foreign travellers and European commercial records, we know much more about these centuries than for the entire preceding millennium.

The detail and depth in which it is possible to treat these 250 years is not possible for the earlier 900. In short, it is best 'to write more on what we know more about'.[3] Evidently, historical knowledge is based on credible evidence.

In his Introduction to *Religion in Indian History*, Habib gives a broad definition of religion, to cover 'all modes of human thought or action

---

[1] Irfan Habib (ed.), *Religion in Indian History*, New Delhi: Tulika Books, in association with Aligarh Historians Society, 2007.

[2] Irfan Habib, *Medieval India: The Study of a Civilization*, New Delhi: National Book Trust, 2008.

[3] Ibid., pp. vii–viii.

designed to cause or cajole a natural, or supernatural being, or force, or mechanism, to confer some benefit on, or ward off some harm from, the individual or group in this life or the conjectured existence beyond'. This definition includes not only the worship of God or gods, but also nature worship, cults of human gods, and philosophical religions like Buddhism and Jainism. In his article on Kabir, Habib talks of Kabir's humanistic and ethical concerns. He underlines that 'all religion is founded on basic premises that are ultimately not subject to the scrutiny of reason'. But the historian's approach to, and understanding of, religion has to be strictly rational.[4]

As for Karl Marx, so too for Irfan Habib, religion is 'the sigh of the oppressed creature, the heart of the heartless world, just as it is the spirit of a spiritless situation. It is the opium of the people.' Religion seems to meet a vital psychological need. However, Habib does not go all the way with Marx: his view, that man makes religion and religion does not make man, ignores the fact that 'once made by man, religion also influences human conduct, and, to that extent makes man'. Furthermore, religion is subject to change in the same manner as all other mental constructs.[5]

Habib makes two points on the theoretical and historical issues involved in the search for the roots of religion. The first is that, by and large, religions tend to accommodate their ethical codes to existing social circumstances. A religion, or certain aspects of a religion, may become popular as they adjust better to the changes in the economic or social order. Protestantism, for example, was seen by Marx as more suited to the conditions of rising capitalism. Max Weber saw it as the very source of 'the spirit of capitalism'. In any case, when a religion suits a particular form of social order, it also helps to sustain and reinforce it. Habib elaborates this point with reference to the caste system. He argues at some length that the caste system did not arise from the brahmanical ideology of purity so much as out of internal social processes in which economic and political changes played a major role. Furthermore, it was not the simple process of brahmanization that gave rise to the caste system: 'Buddhism and Jainism also contained ideological baggage with which the caste system could be explained, justified and lived with.' The second point made by Habib is that 'the roots of religion' lie in the woeful conditions in which a religion emerges. This is clearly recognized in the remark made by Marx that to abolish religion, it was necessary first to abolish the useful conditions of society.[6]

Medieval India, as presented by Irfan Habib, was marked by remarkable changes in the realms of politics, economy, society and technology, as much

---

[4] Habib (ed.), *Religion in Indian History*, pp. xi–xii.
[5] Ibid., p. xii.
[6] Ibid., pp. xiii–xiv, xviii–xxiii.

as by important changes in the realm of religion: the decline of Buddhism and Jainism, the resurgence of brahmanical Hinduism, the emergence of *bhakti* cults within Hinduism, the spatial spread of Islam and its internal developments, and the rise of the popular monotheistic movement. Habib takes notice of the social features of all these developments on the basis of primary source materials as well as the work of other scholars in the field. Therefore his statement on religion becomes important for understanding the history of religion in medieval India. In the following three sections we restate his position with regard to Hinduism, Islam and the popular monotheistic movement. We give our own appreciative critique in the last section.

The Chinese travellers of the early seventh and the early eight century register a strong presence of the Theravada and Mahayana forms of Buddhism in India. In the early eleventh century, however, Alberuni could find no Buddhist scholar in the northwest of India. The monastery at Nalanda survived various political upheavals only till the thirteenth century. Tantric tendencies developed within the Mahayana, with a marked emphasis on the efficacy of incantations (*mantras*), finger positions (*mudras*) and rites. The Bodhisattva Avalokiteshvara was made into a divine personage and his consort Tara became popular as the goddess of compassion. The Buddhists coexisted largely peacefully with the brahmanical schools, but there were acts of persecution in which they were the main sufferers. In its Tantric form, Buddhism survived only in Ladakh.[7]

In the early centuries of medieval India, the Jains were small in numbers but there were among them a few prolific exponents of the Jain philosophy. Later, the main area of their strength was Gujarat but they were found elsewhere too. Jain religious literature was composed in several languages, like Sanskrit, Prakrit, Braj, Kannada and Gujarati, but it was largely repetitive or hagiological. Both the Shvetambara and Digambara Jains flourished in the Vijayanagara empire. Jain priests claimed exceptional proximity to Akbar and his court. The Jain laity consisted mainly of trading communities.[8]

The decline of Buddhism and Jainism meant the triumph of brahmanisim. The epigraphic evidence and architectural remains of early medieval India point to increasing prosperity of the brahmans and their cults. One source of their strength were the *Dharmashastras*, which prescribed rituals and social laws for the laity. The basic texts of the *Smritis* had been composed by the sixth century. The commentaries and compendiums prepared in the early medieval period elaborated the rites and rules, and the religious basis

---

[7] Ibid., pp. 25, 28–29.
[8] Ibid., pp. 29, 94, 174–75, 184.

of the caste system. The connection of brahmanism with the caste system tended to become more and more close. The Mimamsa, the Samkhya and the Vedanta found able exponents, respectively, in Kumarila, Vachaspati Mishra and Shankaracharya, with emphasis in their works on the Vedic ritual, the autonomous working of the transmigration of souls and the path of knowledge. Irfan Habib underlines the importance of the Vedantic thought propounded by Shankaracharya. He was able to reconcile his highest Truth with the multiplicity of beliefs and rituals of orthodox brahmanism. He offered an ideological framework for 'unity in diversity' that could provide a basis for 'Hinduism' to evolve henceforth into a single, and increasingly monotheistic, religion over the centuries till the modern times.[9]

The proximity of Islam during the period of the Sultanates helped monotheism to move towards a more central position within 'Hinduism'. The very concept of religion underwent a change. To the Arabs and Iranians India was Hind and Indians were Hindus. With the rise of Muslim communities in India, the term 'Hindu' came to be applied to non-Muslim Indians. Muslims began to talk of the religious beliefs of Hindus, putting them in one docket. The label 'Hindu' was appropriated by some of the non-Muslim Indians and they began to think of their religion as a single, broadly identifiable faith, starting the process of transformation of various brahmanical traditions into 'Hinduism'. The compilation of certain legal and philosophical texts helped to provide the basis for such a comprehensive view of 'Hinduism'. A late fourteenth-century collection of all philosophic systems (*Sarvadarshana Samgraha*), which presents the Vedanta as the most perfect of all the systems, includes the Charvakas, the Buddhists and the Jains even though they are regarded as erroneous.[10]

The anonymous author of the *Dabistan*, in the mid-seventeenth century, noted that there were numerous religions, and countless faiths and customs, among Hindus. Here, 'Hindu' is a non-Muslim Indian but it is difficult to speak of Hinduism as 'a single body of doctrine'. However, 'all the basic elements of Higher or Orthodox Hinduism' are outlined in the *Ain-i Akbari* as well as the *Dabistan*. The traditional doctrines of the *Smriti* schools were reasserted in digests and commentaries. These works made no noteworthy deviation from the position adopted in the earlier *Smritis* in respect of the supremacy of brahmans and caste rules; they repeated and elaborated the restrictions imposed on the lower castes and women. One extreme view was that brahmans alone were the 'twice-born' because kshatriyas and vaishyas had fallen among the ranks of the shudras.[11]

[9] Ibid., pp. 25–28.
[10] Ibid., pp. 86–87.
[11] Ibid., pp. 169–70.

The increasing influence of the Vedanta of Shankaracharya was a marked feature of Hinduism during the Mughal period. It permeated a number of schools and sects. The work called *Vedantasara* exhibits an admixture of Samkhya principles, and the work called *Samkhyasara* admits the truth of Vedanta. A similar reconciliation of Vedanta with Shaivite beliefs seems to have been developed by a prolific writer of the sixteenth century. Equally remarkable was the increasing influence of Tantrism. Tantric literature received considerable additions during this period in north India.[12]

Another important aspect of brahmanism was the increasing emphasis on devotionalism (*bhakti*). Vishnu and his incarnations, especially Krishna–Vasudeva, became objects of emotional fervour through worship of images and devotional lore. Alberuni treats the *Bhagavad Gita* as the central philosophical and moral text of the Hindus. The Alvars in the south used Tamil for a distinctly devotional Vaishnava cult. Jayadeva's *Gita-Govinda* in Sanskrit was inspired by the love of Krishna. The cult of Shiva was a rival of Vaishnavism within the brahmanical fold. Besides Puranic Shaivism, the older worship of Shiva as Pashupati became popular. The Nayanars gave a theistic thrust to the worship of Shiva through their devotional songs. Their path was open to all, irrespective of caste. Thus Shaivism developed its own *bhakti* tradition. Durga became the fountainhead of Tantrism. Tantric influences were propagated through literature related to various goddesses. The esoteric nature of many Tantric rites tended to conceal or overwhelm the ethical and moral elements extolled in the Tantric texts.[13]

Ramanuja, who was opposed to Shankaracharya's interpretation of Vedanta, emphasized the importance of *bhakti*, and established a Vaishnava tradition which was followed by Madhava and Vallabha. The sixteenth and seventeenth centuries were essentially centuries of Vaishnavism. The Rama cult was propagated by Tulsidas through his *Ramcharitmanas* in the Awadhi dialect, giving a popular garb to the original *Ramayana*. In his fervent verses of devotion, a just Rama as the incarnated deity becomes God in full control of destiny. Tulsidas was a firm believer in the *Dharmashastras* and regarded 'popular monotheism' with its Shudra leaders as a sign of the degradation of *kaliyuga*.[14]

Krishna as an incarnation of Vishnu became important as an object of devotion. The cult was initiated in Bengal by Chaitanya, the devotee assumed to be a companion of Krishna at Vrindaban, who associated Radha with Krishna and re-enacted in his mind the sports (*lila*) of Krishna for communion with God. The devotee's love was cherished by Krishna. The successors

[12] Ibid., pp. 170–71.
[13] Ibid., pp. 26–27.
[14] Ibid., pp. 28, 171.

of Chaitanya at Vrindaban, the *gosvamins*, gave a philosophical basis to
the cult in their Sanskrit works and outlined its rituals. Right of worship
was not denied to the lower classes, though the devotees followed the caste
ritual as householders. The Sahajiya sect (eighteenth century) introduced
Tantric practices. A parallel Vaishnava sect was founded in Assam by
Shankaradeva who avoided image worship and laid emphasis on an Absolute, Personal God to whom all devotion was to be directed in the form of
love for Krishna.[15]

Vallabhacharya propagated a religion of grace (*pushtimarga*). Surdas,
who owed allegiance to this sect, wrote in Braj about the *lilas* of Krishna
with Radha and others as manifestations of the Lord's supreme powers. The
sect became popular in Gujarat and Rajasthan with excessive adoration of
the descendants of Vallabhacharya, who himself came to be regarded as an
incarnation of Krishna. Hita Harivamsha founded the sect of Radha-
Vallabhis, assigning a more crucial position to Radha.[16]

Both Unitarian and conservative elements were combined in the Vaishnava
movement in Maharashtra. Eknath expounded the principle of *bhakti* and,
though a brahman, allowed men of all castes and women to assemble for
singing the praises of God. Tukaram, a shudra peasant, addressed himself to
Vithoba, the Lord of Pandhari, but his God (called Allah too) tends to be
closer to the Rama of the monotheists. Ramdas propagated the worship of
Rama as God, upheld the holiness of brahmans and their deities, and organized *maths*. The Dasakuta movement in Karnataka was marked by devotional ecstasy for Vitthala, the deity of Pandharpur, who was accessible to
the lowly.[17]

Irfan Habib refers to the Siddhanatha tradition, going back to Gorakh-
nath, and combining various Shaivite, Shakti and Yogic beliefs in a kind of
Tantric mysticism propagated by hosts of mendicants. Among 'other sects',
he refers to logic and dialectics (*nyaya* and *tarka*), which continued to attract attention through the compilation of textbooks and commentaries.
The author of the *Dabistan* refers to the beliefs of the Charvakas, but he
does not name any text or votary of the sect for his source. Possibly, their
ideas were heard by word of mouth or derived from texts of their opponents.[18]

Irfan Habib gives more space to Islam than to 'Hinduism'. The arrival of
Islam marked a major alteration in the religious contours of early medieval

[15] Ibid., p. 172.
[16] Ibid., pp. 172–73.
[17] Ibid., p. 173.
[18] Ibid., pp. 88, 174.

India. Strongly monotheistic, Islam emphasized the absolute unity and power of God along with hostility to any kind of image worship. It shared with Judaism and Christianity much of their lore about earlier prophets, and belief in Satan and the Day of Judgement. It stressed the individual human being's obligation to obey God. The code by which Muslims were to conduct relations among themselves and with others was based on revelations embodied in the *Qur'an*, supplemented by the Prophet's own statements and practices collected in the *Hadis*. To these sources were added the use of analogy and elaboration by jurists. Some Arab customs and Jewish rituals were incorporated in the Islamic code (*shari'a*). A notable stress was laid on contractual obligations and on some elements of reform, like the condemnation of female infanticide and the assignment of a share in inheritance to a daughter (though equal only to half the share of the son). Islamic law permitted slavery and concubinage, but considered liberating slaves to be a meritorious act. It laid stress on charity too.[19]

With the conquest of Sind in the early eighth century, strong Muslim communities were established in a fairly large part of India. About the mid-tenth century, the Muslims in Multan came to owe allegiance to the Fatimid Caliph in Egypt and the Muslim rulers of Multan came to be known as Qaramita (Carmathians). This designation was given to the Isma'ili branch of the Shi'as. They were destroyed by Mahmud of Ghazni.[20]

A far more important development within Islam was that of Sufism or Islamic mysticism. The woman saint Rabi'a of Basra, in the late eighth century, had laid stress on love (*'ishq*) of God as the only valid reason for obeying him. Its logical corollary was the rejection of Paradise as the goal of ethical endeavour, and an aspiration for annihilation (*fana*), or elimination of self, through union with God. By the eleventh century, Sufism had become a recognized component of Islam. 'Ali Hujwiri's *Kashfu'l Mahjub*, written in the eleventh century at Lahore in Persian, marked the maturity of Sufism as a systematic body of beliefs and practices; it was also a firm announcement of the arrival of Sufism in India. The *'ulama* (scholars), who were the spokesmen of orthodox Islamic theology, made peace with the mysticism of the Sufis by 1200. The latter, on their part, respected the domain of theology. The one major practice of the Sufis that still caused disputation was *sama'*, or the public recitation of love-poetry addressed to God in Sufi assemblies.[21]

The increasing authority assigned to the *shaikh* or *pir* over his disciples led to the formation of various orders (*silsilah*s) among the Sufis. At his

[19] Ibid., pp. 29–31.
[20] Ibid., p. 32.
[21] Ibid., pp. 32–33, 82.

khanqah as the centre of Sufic activity, the *pir* imparted instruction, and held conversations and *sama'* (assemblies); his chosen assistants gave amulets; and a free kitchen (*langar*) was organized with unsolicited gifts (*futuh*). Regular gifts and land grants were scorned by many of the Sufis but some were not so particular. Individual *pirs* appointed deputies called *khalifas* who guided disciples of their own and appointed their own *khalifas* after the *pir*'s death. The two most influential Sufi orders in the thirteenth and fourteenth centuries were the Suhrawardi at Multan and the Chishti at Delhi and other places. The most famous Chishti saint, Shaikh Nizamuddin, whose conversations were recorded by Amir Hasan Sijzi in his *Fawaidu'l Fawad*, represented the pre-pantheistic phase of Sufism in its classical form. Sufism began to turn pantheistic due to the influence of Ibn al-'Arabi through the Persian poets earlier, and the efforts of Ashraf Jahangir Simnani in the early fifteenth century. This development synchronized with the increasing influence of Shankaracharya's school of Vedanta within brahmanical thought.[22]

The pantheistic doctrines and speculations of Ibn al-'Arabi seriously disturbed the comfortable arrangement within which orthodox theologians accepted Sufism as a permissible discipline so long as it met the formal requirements of the law and rituals of Islam. The bold views of al-'Arabi were a logical elaboration of the Sufic concept of communion with God. His doctrine of the 'unity of existence' (*wahdat al-wujud*) steadily gained adherents in India, despite opposition. The doctrine seemed to offer a good explanation of diversity in a country like India where Islam coexisted with Hinduism. This situation led to inner questioning.[23]

Ibn al-'Arabi's proposition of the Perfect Man (*insan al-kamil*) idealized the *shaikh* as 'a microcosm in whom the One is manifested'. This vision supplemented or reinforced the concept of *mahdi* whose arrival was a part of the popular Muslim belief. The first indication of the new intellectual turbulence was the Mahdawi movement, started by Saiyid Muhammad of Jaunpur in the late fifteenth century. The sect survived in spite of its denunciation by theologians. Another sect with similar millenary tendencies was started by Bayazid (Mian Raushan) in the late sixteenth century among the Afghans. The Raushaniya militancy led to a long war with the Mughals and the sect was suppressed.[24]

For Hindu–Muslim relations in medieval India, the attitudes of the Muslim rulers are seen as relevant by Irfan Habib. The Arab rulers in Sind worked out a system of coexistence with conquered non-Muslim peoples. The Hindus in Sind were deemed to be 'people of the book', at par with Jews and

---

[22] Ibid., pp. 82–83.
[23] Ibid., p. 83.
[24] Ibid., pp. 181–82.

Christians. So long as they paid the tax (*kharaj*) and poll tax (*jizya*), a large degree of tolerance was extended to them and their places of worship. The grants given by earlier rulers to brahmans out of state revenues were continued. Even the disabilities imposed on the outcaste communities of the pastoral Jats were confirmed. Nevertheless, in a brahmanical text composed in Sind, the Muslims were regarded as *mlechha*. Muizuddin of Ghor stamped the image of Lakshmi on some of his gold coins. But the Delhi Sultans took away the exemptions given to brahmans. In the fourteenth century, however, Hindus began to be appointed as governors and commanders. Sultan Muhammad Tughluq extended protection to Jain priests, played *holi* and consorted with *yogis*. Many temples were destroyed, especially during military campaigns, but temples continued to be built afresh, sometimes with official patronage.[25]

Irfan Habib discusses Akbar's 'supra-religious sovereignty' in the context of changes within Islam. The origins of the upheaval in thought under Akbar can be traced to the impulses of pantheism and the Messiah cult. In the 1570s, Shaikh Tajuddin, a protagonist of Ibn al-'Arabi, introduced his principal concepts in Akbar's court at Fatehpur Sikri. Shaikh Mubarak, who had read Ibn al-'Arabi and the illuminationist (*ishraqi*) doctrines, gained in influence at the court; he was suspected of Mahdawi inclinations. In any case, Akbar's direction for the compilation of a history of the first millennium of Islam (*Tarikh-i Alafi*) reflected his awareness of the popular belief in the need of renewal after the first millennium. The reformer was identified with Akbar in the *mahzar* of 1579: the leading Muslim theologians at his court signed the declaration that Akbar, in his position as a just sultan, was entitled to exercise limited powers of interpretation and elaboration of Muslim law, which was to be binding on all Muslims. Further debates and discussions in the *'ibadat-khana* at Fatehpur Sikri made it clear to Akbar that no single interpretation of Islam was correct and no single religion could be wholly true. It was for him, as the chosen man of God, to assist in the realization of Absolute Peace (*sulh-i kul*), to prevent idle strife between the votaries of different religions and factions. All religions were to be tolerated. Habib points out that there is no evidence for the label '*Din-i Ilahi*' for what Akbar prescribed for an elite corps of disciples; he did not wish to institute a new religion. In consonance with his views, in the 1580s, the followers of all religions in Akbar's empire were given full freedom of religious expression, conversion and construction of places of worship. It is not easy to find a parallel to this policy in the contemporary world. Habib goes on to add that the policy of tolerance was also politically useful.[26]

---

[25] Ibid., pp. 31–32, 83–84.
[26] Ibid., pp. 183–86.

Akbar's proclaimed belief in pantheism and *sulh-i kul* had some significant ideological consequences. Among other things, it generated a fresh interest in reason and science, and fostered a movement among Muslims towards the study of brahmanical texts and of Vedanta. A number of Sanskrit works were translated into Persian. This movement reached its culmination in Dara Shukoh who was immersed in Islamic mysticism through his attachment to the Qadiriya Sufis, Mian Mir and Mulla Shah Badakhshi. In his *Majma'ul Bahrain* ('The Mingling of Two Oceans'), Dara Shukoh explains the major terms and concepts used in Hindu spiritual discourse to show an identity between Hindu and Muslim seekers of God. His *Sirru'l Asrar* ('The Great Secret') is a faithful rendering of 52 *Upanishads*. The wide circulation of the *Dabistan*, giving a dispassionate account of all religions of the world, reflected the spirit of the times.[27]

The freedom of religious discussion accorded to all by Akbar assisted in the transformation of Shi'ism from a 'heresy' into a recognized variant of Islam. A Shi'a theologian argued that there was no need to conceal Shi'ite beliefs even though dissimulation was permitted by the law. He openly defended the Shi'ite position against Sunni criticism. Shi'a immigrants from Iran held high offices in the Mughal empire. Haidarabad in the Deccan, and Lucknow and Faizabad in Awadh, became important centres of Shi'ite learning during the seventeenth and eighteenth centuries.[28]

Sunni orthodoxy responded in various ways to the challenges posed by the free airing of views regarded hitherto as heterodox. Shaikh Ahmad Sirhindi wrote a refutation of the Shi'as (*Risala dar radd-i rawafiz*). He was hostile to Akbar's policies of tolerance, and expressed bitter opposition towards Hindus and their beliefs. In 1600 he became a disciple of the Naqshbandi mystic Baqi Billah, increasingly concerned with Ibn al-'Arabi's theories of *wahdat al-wujud* and *insan al-kamil*. Sirhindi's theory of *wahdat ash-shuhud* underlined that in the final stage the seeker saw only God and nothing else. Rigorous conformity to the *shari'a* was as necessary for a mystic as for others. He put forth his theory of *qaium*, the Perfect Man chosen by God as his vice-regent. This function was identified with yet another, the renovator of Islam in its second millennium (*mujaddid-i alif-i sani*). Both the offices were combined in Shaikh Ahmad himself.[29]

Abdu'l Haqq Muhaddis, a recognized authority on *hadis*, fully accepted the Sufic tradition of *wahdat al-wujud* in opposition to Ahmad Sirhindi. Aurangzeb patronized the descendants of Shaikh Ahmad but did not accept his extreme views. He supported traditional and legal Islam, and commis-

[27] Ibid., pp. 186–88.
[28] Ibid., pp. 188–89.
[29] Ibid., pp. 189–90.

sioned a massive compendium of the opinions of jurists on diverse matters, systematically arranged as the *Fatawa-i 'Alamgiri*. In the eighteenth century, Shah Waliullah adopted an orthodox Sunni position with regard to the Shi'as and translated Shaikh Ahmad's anti-Shi'a tract into Arabic. He was harsh on non-Muslims too, who were to be hewers of wood and drawers of water under an ideal *shari'a* regime. However, he accepted the Sufic heritage of Islam and himself assumed the position of a guide (*murshid*). He propounded an 'inspired' reconciliation of the theories of *wahdat al-wujud* and *wahdat ash-shuhud*. After the decline of the Mughal empire, the element of pantheism in Indian Islamic thought seems to have receded to the background.[30]

A kind of 'popular monotheism' began to emerge during the early medieval period. In the Virashaiva or Lingayat system of Basava in Karnataka, there was only one God, caste distinctions were denied, women were given a better status and brahmans no longer monopolized priestly functions. The popular character of the system was indicated by the use of Kannada as the medium of expression. A parallel trend was visible in Tamil Nadu where the Siddhars sang of one God in Tamil, and criticized caste, brahmans and even the doctrine of transmigration of souls. Monotheism was transmitted to the north by Namdev and Ramanand. The former was a calico printer from Maharashtra who preached a rigorous monotheism, and opposed image worship and caste distinctions. Ramanand was a brahman follower of Ramanuja who preached at Varanasi, and is seen as the preceptor of most of the leading monotheistic preachers of the early sixteenth century.[31] Kabir came to be associated with him.

In his article titled 'Kabir: The Historical Setting', Irfan Habib makes the general statement that religion has been 'an undoubted component of human civilization in its various stages of evolution'. He goes on to add:

> The time is past – if ever there was one, except in the case of a very simplistic variant of Marxism – when one could dismiss religion as either too insignificant a factor in history or, alternatively, see its various forms as mere reflexes of social environments, which could themselves be narrowed to a few standard 'modes'.[32]

Historical complexities go far beyond any straightforward, unilinear schemes. Religion has played its role not only in acting on behalf of the

---

[30] Ibid., pp. 190–91.
[31] Ibid., pp. 87–88.
[32] Ibid., p. 142.

ruling classes to justify the suppression of popular revolts, but also in rallying rebels.

Habib enunciates another general principle for the historian of religion:

> No historian can regard any religion or any religious belief as *ipso facto* true or untrue, or as absolutely original or God-given, not bearing marks of precedent or external influences nor susceptible to change or evolution. For purposes of its historical significance, as against its theology, any religion or religious system has to be seen as it was understood by its followers (and different groups of them), as well as by outsiders, at each different point of time. How it is understood by the believers now is only a matter of interest for contemporary history, not for earlier epochs.

These two principles are enunciated as being relevant for understanding 'the genesis of the ideas of Kabir' and 'the monotheist movement of the late fifteenth and early sixteenth century'. Kabir was 'a unique representative' of this movement.[33]

Habib points out that it is customary to use the word 'Hinduism' to cover the varied systems of beliefs and social customs in ancient India, but that this was anachronistic. In his view, the creation of 'Hinduism' out of the framework of social custom and ritual, and of the various earlier schools of brahmanical thought, 'seems to occur practically with the diffusion of Islam in India', a process that has continued into modern times. The view of some modern writers that Islam brought to India 'a fresh wind of equality' is erroneous. In the entire range of medieval Islamic literature, there is no word of criticism against the caste system, the theory of pollution or the oppression of untouchables. The sanction for full-fledged slavery and concubinage in Islamic law is enough to modify the view of equality in historical Islam.[34]

However, there was a difference between the social inequalities sanctioned by Islamic law and those of the Indian caste system. Upward or vertical mobility was restricted in both, but the caste system hindered horizontal, or inter-craft and inter-professional, mobility. The relative flexibility of Islam could possibly make the economies of Muslim polities more open to technological change, especially those that could be absorbed within the framework of manual crafts. Moreover, hierarchy in Islam among free men tended to be based on the possession of wealth and political power rather than birth. Whereas the feudatories in the structure of 'Indian feudalism' were practically hereditary potentates, the *iqta'* holders under the Sultanate were far more dependent on the Sultan's will. The establishment of the Delhi

[33] Ibid., p. 143.
[34] Ibid., pp. 143–44.

Sultanate was accompanied by certain social and economic changes. There is no specific evidence that any previous rules of caste were deliberately overthrown or abolished by the new regime. However, there was a simultaneous process of expansion of communities of Muslims among whom caste could not legally be the basis of hierarchy. Paradoxically, the immediate consequence of enslavement was 'liberation' from caste. To the caste-free core of the Muslim population of immigrants and slaves were added free converts, possibly in groups. When such group conversions occurred, caste customs and barriers continued until, in course of time, the increasing influence of the *shari'a* began to dilute the strength of earlier customs. Kabir appears to have been a member of such a weaver community in transition.[35]

Irfan Habib argues further that it was the demand for craft and urban labour, rather than any pull of an egalitarian faith, that attracted some artisan groups to Islam. A large number of new people were added to Muslim communities due to the urban demand for craft goods, the flow of wealth into towns, and the marked expansion of trade and urban expansion as well as new techniques of several kinds. In the domain where old occupations remained unaffected by the limited changes in craft technology, the caste system could continue with its own rigidities. Among the groups affected by the new economic and social pressures, however, an element of instability was introduced due to questioning of the old barriers of caste and religion.[36]

Habib looks upon the low-caste, artisan character of the monotheist movement as an indicator of its origins. Namdev was a petty calico printer, Kabir was a low-caste weaver, Ravidas was a carrion remover, Sain was a barber and Dhanna was a Jat peasant. This list is extended to include Guru Nanak as a petty trader or accountant, Dadu as a cotton carder and Haridas as a Jat slave. They all rejected the distinctions of caste in an emphatic manner. Tulsidas was disturbed by the fact that shudras had become religious preachers, and even more so by their wholesale rejection of Hinduism and Islam. The immense radicalism of such wholesale rejection of Hinduism and Islam in bold preaching addressed directly to the poor was unprecedented in the history of India. It was unique, perhaps, till then in the world.[37]

Habib stresses the point that Kabir was recognized in the sixteenth century as a 'monotheist' (*muwahhid*), and not as a Muslim or a Hindu. Abu'l Fazl in 1595 and Nabhaji in 1600 testify to this – they do not locate Kabir's thought in any single tradition. He himself refrains from mentioning any

[35] Ibid., pp. 144–46.
[36] Ibid., pp. 146–47.
[37] Ibid., pp. 147–48.

teacher or precursor. There is no credible evidence for regarding Namdev, Ramanand and the Shaivite yogis, or Shankara's Vedanta, as sources of influence on Kabir. There is no trace of pantheism in Kabir's thought; monotheism is trenchantly and repeatedly proclaimed. God is one and God is everywhere. 'It would seem, therefore, that what existed on the periphery of ancient Indian philosophy, became with Kabir the centre of everything.' One can detect here a strong influence of Islam.[38]

Habib goes on to add that the issue of the influence of Islam on Kabir is not at all a simple one. Muslim theology or its vocabulary does not figure in the language used by Kabir in any significant way. He rejects the *Ka'ba* and the mosque. The Sufi theme of love as the cornerstone of the man–God relationship is weak. God's position as the Judge, which is perhaps the most central element in non-Sufic Islam, is predominant in Kabir. This idea of Divine Judgement of human thought and deed comes essentially from Islam. However, Kabir goes beyond this. He preaches a monotheism that transcends the limits of orthodox Islam by insistence on total surrender to God and rejection of all rituals. 'The unity of God becomes for Kabir the means of comprehension of the unity of man.' His rejection of the concept and practice of purity and pollution, and of conventional modes of worship and all ritual, is explicit and absolute. The lowly, penniless devotee of God became 'the apostle of humanity' for the common man.[39]

Finally, Irfan Habib expresses great appreciation for the personal response of Kabir and other like-minded preachers:

> Tracing Kabir to his various ideological contexts and sources is important. Equally important, however, is to see his action as essentially a negation of some gross inequities of our culture, and not a mere synthesis of its divergent elements. I have attempted in this modest contribution to examine the circumstances, material, social and ideological, amidst which the thought of Kabir and other like-minded preachers took shape. But the radicalism of the response was their own achievement, not simply a 'determined' one. Their vision and boldness is a precious national heritage whose relevance is not bound by time.[40]

In his *Medieval India*, Habib emphasizes that Kabir made a change of substantive proportions in the Indian mode of religious thought. His com-

---

[38] Ibid., pp. 148–51.
[39] Ibid., pp. 151–53.
[40] Ibid., p. 153. This article by Irfan Habib is based on a lecture he delivered at New Delhi on 30 December 1992 as part of *Anhad Garje*, a festival organized by Sahmat (Safdar Hashmi Memorial Trust); it was first published in *Social Scientist*, Vol. 21, Nos 3–4, March–April 1993.

positions can be seen as 'a distilling of Vaishnavite, Nath-yogic, even Tantric beliefs to obtain a rigorous monotheism parallel to Islamic', or, alternatively, as 'a rigorous acceptance of the logic of the monotheism of Islam, while rejecting its theology, with the exposition necessarily offered in a language that those outside the culture of Islam could understand'. Strong arguments can be put forward for both the views, but 'in whatever manner Kabir came to espouse the views he proclaimed, his contemporaries were deeply struck by their boldness and vigour'.[41]

He refers to some of Kabir's ideas which we have already mentioned, and goes on to state that Kabir's audience was the common man, the artisan, the peasant and the village headman; his similes and metaphors came from their life and travails, and his language was the tongue they spoke. He was influenced by some of the prejudices in his environment against women. Still, he found a new dignity for the poor and the downtrodden. Ravidas (or Raidas) and Sain regarded Kabir as their precursor. A similar position was adopted by Dadu. The Satnamis in Haryana owed explicit allegiance to Kabir. However, their sects tended in time to develop rituals of their own, and to introduce notions and institutions taken from traditional religion, notably the ascription of *avatar* status to their original preceptor and a caste-like status to the monotheistic community itself. Even a brahman parentage came to be sought for the weaver Kabir. 'Such a reshaping of the original message of the masters is a testimony to the strong roots of ritual and the caste-order in those times; and our times are, perhaps, no different.'[42]

Irfan Habib was familiar with the Sikh movement at the outset of his academic career, in 1958, when he wrote his doctoral thesis on the agrarian system of Mughal India.[43] His treatment of 'Sikhism' in *Medieval India* is comprehensive but short. He covers the whole period from Guru Nanak to Ranjit Singh in five paragraphs. Therefore, every statement he makes becomes important.

Now recognized as one of the religions of the world, Sikhism began as a sect (*panth*) in the sixteenth century, 'more or less on the pattern of other sects of the contemporary popular monotheistic movement'. Its founder, Guru Nanak, was a Khatri, and belonged to an accountant and mercantile caste of the Punjab. The scripture of the Sikhs compiled by Guru Arjan in 1604, known as the *Guru Granth Sahib*, includes the compositions of Guru Nanak and his successors, those of the Muslim saint Shaikh Farid, and of

---

[41] Habib, *Medieval India*, pp. 175–76.
[42] Habib, *Medieval India*, pp. 176–78.
[43] See Irfan Habib, *The Agrarian System of Mughal India, 1556–1707*, second revised edition, New Delhi: Oxford University Press, 1999, pp. 397–98.

other saints like Namdev, Kabir and Ravidas. It is said to be similar in this respect to the compilations of the Dadu-panthis. Habib concludes that there was a strong sense among Guru Nanak's followers till the early seventeenth century, that they belonged to 'a general monotheistic movement, with only some differences of both nuance and substance separating its different components'.[44]

Guru Nanak believed in one God who was formless and omnipresent, and who could not be represented in a physical form. Image worship and ritual were thus condemned. The relationship between God and the devotee was intensely personal; the devotee was to serve God in humility and love, to obtain his grace. Ethical conduct, especially kindness to fellow human beings, was strongly emphasized. Guru Nanak condemned the arrogance of birth, the cult of ritual pollution and differences of caste. The salvation aimed at was *nirvan* or *sach khand*, the true abode, when man at last realizes God.[45]

'It is not clear', says Irfan Habib, 'to what extent Guru Nanak gave an organizational form to his sect, nor whether the word Guru used in his compositions, e.g. in *Japji*, means God or spiritual guide.' However, two processes appeared soon enough. First, a line of Gurus was established, each successor having the status of an incarnation of the same perfect spirit. Total obedience to the Guru was expected from every Sikh by the Guru. The second process was the expansion of the sect among the Jatts or peasants of the Punjab. The Gurus were all Khatris, but their principal lieutenants, the *masand*s, were mostly Jatt already in the seventeenth century. These two developments laid the ground for a third, the acquisition of armed power. A conflict with the Mughal authorities could not be long avoided after the martyrdom of Guru Arjan in 1606. The military power of the Guru reached its apex under Guru Gobind Singh, who sought, in 1699, to weld his followers into a militant community ('Khalsa') by prescribing a common baptism for men of all castes and appointing the items everyone had to carry, including the dagger or the sword which was part of the public bearing of a professional soldier of the time.[46]

Immediately after Guru Gobind Singh's death at Nander in the Deccan, his disciple Banda Bahadur returned to the north and raised a massive plebian rebellion. Many fresh converts and discontented zamindars joined the Sikhs, who operated over large portions of the Punjab and Haryana plains. The rebellion was ultimately suppressed and Banda was executed in 1716. This was followed by a period of demoralization and division. Recovery began

---

[44] Habib, *Medieval India*, pp. 178–79.
[45] Ibid., p. 179.
[46] Ibid., pp. 179–80.

with the collapse of the Mughal power under the impact of Nadir Shah's invasion in 1739 and the later repeated invasions of Ahmad Shah Abdali. Sikh *dals* and *misals* led by individual chiefs (*sardars*) became increasingly powerful. Many of them came from peasant or artisan stock. A semblance of unity was sought through the annual 'sarbat khalsa' at Chak Guru (Amritsar), but dissensions grew apace and each chief tended to carve out a separate territory for himself. The process was at last checked by Ranjit Singh who established a traditional kingdom in the Punjab, ostensibly in the name of the Khalsa.[47]

Looking back, we find that Irfan Habib's definition of religion is comprehensive enough to include all modes. However, it appears to dwell on hopes and fears as the roots of religion, to the virtual exclusion of any role for humanistic or altruistic concerns. In the realm of ethics too, he does not appear to entertain the possibility of altogether new values being enunciated and espoused. His approach to religion is essentially sociological, underscoring the relevance of social, economic and political factors for the origin, growth and decline of religions. He does not ignore religious ideology or theology, but the social orientation of religion remains more important to him as a historian.

Habib takes a comprehensive view of all important developments within what is now called 'Hinduism', taking into account the increasing strength of the Vaishnava, Shaiva and Shakta systems at the cost of Buddhism and Jainism. He makes a point of fundamental importance: that the presence of Islam, and the gradual but increasing acceptance of the Vedanta of Shankaracharya, started a movement within 'Hinduism' towards monotheism. The rise of *bhakti*, especially the cults of Krishna and Rama, was another major development towards devotional theism. Equally important is the distinction made by Habib between Vaishnava *bhakti* and popular monotheism. The only aspect of 'Hinduism' that is ignored by him is the ascetical tradition within Shaivism and Vaishnavism. The *jogis*, *sannyasis* and *bairagis* are seldom conspicuous in his treatment of 'Hinduism'.

Islam in medieval India was neither a static nor a monolithic system. Habib takes into account the importance of orthodox and legal Islam, the presence of Isma'ilis in medieval India, and the changing position of Shi'as within Islam. The changes within Sufism were relevant for the rise of millenarian movements. The tension between *wahdat al-wujud* and *wahdat ash-shuhud* did not actually end in the triumph of the latter during the Mughal period. Subsequently, pantheism became less important. More rel-

---

[47] Ibid., pp. 180–81.

evant for medieval India were the developments related to Hindu–Muslim relations. There was a mixed policy of accommodation and discrimination before Akbar introduced an exceptionally wide-ranging policy of tolerance, motivated essentially by religious and humanistic impulses but helpful for political consolidation too. Thus, hardly any significant development within Islam is left out.

Habib looks upon popular monotheism as a phenomenon distinct from all contemporary systems of religious belief and practice. Its salient features are underscored. Kabir is treated as the best and the most influential representative of the movement. His social position, religious affiliation, and sensitivity to the sufferings of the poor and the downtrodden account for Kabir's creative response to his historical situation. In his perceptive and extremely meaningful analysis of Kabir, Habib does not fail to note Kabir's gender bias. He rightly points out that the 'sects' which appear to have arisen under Kabir's influence later became brahmanized, like the Kabir-panthis. However, he does not notice Kabir's appreciation for renunciation and mendicancy, and his total lack of interest in institutionalization.[48]

In placing Sikhism within the popular monotheistic movement, Irfan Habib underlines the distinction of Sikhism from the contemporary systems but emphasizes the importance of the features it shares with the movement as a whole. However, it needs to be emphasized that Guru Nanak claims a divinely ordained mission for himself in the compositions which underscore the originality of his system. Furthermore, there are important differences even between Kabir and Guru Nanak with respect to their conception of God, concept of *hukam* and conception of liberation. Guru Nanak's rejection of renunciation, his commitment to social obligations and his concern for others (*parupkar*) distinguish him from Kabir even more.[49] Significantly, in his attitude towards women, Guru Nanak presents a total contrast to Kabir.[50]

Irfan Habib states that Guru Nanak's position with regard to organization is not clear. Here again, the evidence of Guru Nanak's own compositions clearly shows that a socio-religious fraternity had come into existence under his formal guidance as the Guru. His compositions were used for worship in the *dharamsal* (gurdwara) which was open to both men and women, and where a community kitchen (*langar*) was established for all. Before his death he installed one of his disciples in his place as the Guru,

---

[48] For a comparative study of Kabir and Guru Nanak, see J.S. Grewal, *The Sikhs: Ideology, Institutions and Identity*, Delhi: Oxford University Press, 2009, pp. 3–21.

[49] J.S. Grewal, *Lectures on History, Society and Culture of the Punjab*, Patiala: Punjabi University, 2007, pp. 126–27.

[50] J.S. Grewal, *Guru Nanak and Patriarchy*, Shimla: Indian Institute of Advanced Study, 1993, pp. 16–21.

thus founding the Sikh institution of Guruship. The doctrine of the *Guru-Granth* can be traced to his equation of the *shabad* with the Guru, and the doctrine of *Guru-Panth* to his decision to instal a disciple in his place during his lifetime. Guru Nanak referred to his path as the '*Gurmukh Panth*' to claim its distinctiveness from others.[51]

The *Guru Granth Sahib* is similar to, but also different from the Dadu-panthi anthologies. As mentioned by Irfan Habib, it includes the compositions of a well-known Sufi like Shaikh Farid whose identity as a Muslim is well recognized. There is no such composition included in the Dadu-panthi anthologies. The *Guru Granth* also contains the compositions of the Bhatts and Dums, and a secular composition called the *Ragmala*. Therefore, the character and significance of the *Guru Granth Sahib* is different from all other anthologies of medieval India.[52] Guru Arjan, who compiled the *Granth*, is emphatic about the distinct identity of the Sikhs in relation to Hindus and Musalmans. In fact, he talks of *halemi raj*, the whole dispensation of Guru Nanak and his successors, as the sole means of redemption in the *kaliyug*.[53]

Irfan Habib's view that the institution of Guruship and the presence of Jatts in the Sikh Panth politicized the Sikh movement minimizes the importance of the ideological, institutional and financial organization of the Sikh Panth before the time of the sixth Guru, Hargobind. This background, rather than the mere presence of Jatts among his followers, would account for his response to the intervention of the state in the affairs of the Sikh Panth. It may also be pointed out that Guru Gobind Singh did not simply create a militant fraternity, but also enunciated the ideal of sovereign rule (*raj karega Khalsa*).[54] Significantly, the coins struck by Banda Bahadur within two years of the tenth Guru's death bear an inscription that declares the sovereignty of the Khalsa. The undercurrent of this ideal is evident in the political struggle of the Khalsa for fifty years after the death of Banda

---

[51] J.S. Grewal, *History, Literature and Identity: Four Centuries of Sikh Tradition*, Delhi: Oxford University Press, forthcoming, chapter 1.

[52] For a discussion of the structure of the *Guru Granth Sahib*, see J.S. Grewal, *A Study of Guru Granth Sahib: Doctine, Social Content, Structure and Status*, Amritsar: Singh Brothers, 2009, pp. 168–84.

[53] For a discussion of *halemi raj*, see Grewal, *History, Literature and Identity*, chapter 5.

[54] The *Nasihatnama*, a manual of instructions attributed to Bhai Nandlal, and recently placed in the period between the institution of the Khalsa by Guru Gobind Singh in 1699 and his death in 1708, ends with the prophecy '*raj karega Khalsa*' ('Khalsa shall rule'). For a discussion and translation of this work, see Karamjit Kaur Malhotra, 'The Earliest Manual on the Sikh Way of Life', in Reeta Grewal and Sheena Pall (eds), *Five Centuries of Sikh Tradition: Ideology, Society, Politics and Culture*, Delhi: Manohar, 2005, pp. 55–81. For other contemporary evidence on this idea, see Grewal, *The Sikhs: Ideology, Institutions and Identity*, pp. 22–41.

Bahadur. When the Khalsa established their sovereign rule again in the late eighteenth century, they used the same inscriptions on their coins as the ones used by Banda on the seal and coin of his time.[55]

To sum up, Irfan Habib is a Marxist who differs significantly from Marx in according religion an important place in the evolution of human civilization. Apart from being a mental construct, religion for Habib is also a vital social phenomenon subject to change. He takes note of shifts and convergences from the early medieval to the end of the Mughal period. For him, the evolution of an increasingly monotheistic and inclusive religion called 'Hindu' was as much a product of Shankara's unity-in-diversity ideology, as of the proximity of Islam in the Sultanate period. As an altogether new development in the history of medieval India, Islam is treated in all its complexity, with critical notice taken of Akbar's ideas and efforts, and their bearing on sectarian and ideological developments within Islam and its relations with non-Muslims. While emphasizing the similarities of popular monotheistic movements in medieval India as the product of antecedent forces and external stimuli, Kabir is seen as its best representative. He is treated in the context of changes in technology and craft production, urban growth, social mobility and ideological change. He is rightly presented as neither Hindu nor Musalman. Guru Nanak is bracketed with Kabir at the cost of some basic ideological and institutional differences between them. Notwithstanding this limitation, no other historian has dealt with complex religious developments and a society in flux over nearly a millennium in so few words, and with such understanding, depth and objectivity, as Irfan Habib.

---

[55] Indu Banga, 'Raj-Khalsa: Ideology and Practice', *Journal of Punjab Studies*, Vol. 15, Nos 1 and 2, Spring–Fall, 2008, pp. 33–63.

Once More unto the Breach

Money Matters in the Writings of Irfan Habib

Najaf Haider

When critics disagree, the artist is in accord with himself. – Oscar Wilde

In one of the appendices to Irfan Habib's *Agrarian System of Mughal India*,[1] the reader will find a concise description of the currencies of the Mughal empire and their exchange rates, based mostly on untapped sources. Even though it constitutes a separate subject on its own and appeared as such in a reputed journal of the Aligarh History Department[2] in the run-up to the first edition of the book (published in 1963), the appendix on coinage closely followed the tenor and technique of the book. As in the rest of the book, Habib first documented the structure of the Mughal currency system and then analysed its implications.

It is remarkable for an appendix to mark a breakthrough in the historiography of a well-known theme. Early studies of money in India had been the preserve of numismatists, rooted in the physical analysis of coins to highlight their antiquity, artistic importance, political and genealogical significance, and their relevance for the identification of place-names. For the numismatists, coins epitomized money and metrology represented monetary history. Habib's full-blown essay on money placed the literary and numismatic evidence in a wider context, and raised questions directly relevant to monetary history in particular and economic history in general.[3] Much like Marc Bloch,[4] Irfan Habib considered money to be a motor as well as an indicator of change. The objective of his investigation has been to explore

---

[1] Irfan Habib, *The Agrarian System of Mughal India (1556–1707)*, second revised edition, Delhi: Oxford University Press, 1999, pp. 432–49.

[2] Irfan Habib, 'The Currency System of the Mughal Empire', *Medieval India Quarterly*, IV, 1961, pp. 1–21.

[3] Irfan Habib, 'The Monetary System and Prices', in Tapan Raychaudhuri and Irfan Habib (eds), *The Cambridge Economic History of India*, Vol. 1, *c.* 1200–*c.* 1750, Cambridge: Cambridge University Press, 1982, pp. 360–381.

[4] Marc Bloch, 'The Problem of Gold in Middle Ages', in *Land and Work in Medieval Europe, Selected Papers by Marc Bloch*, translated by J.E. Anderson, London: Routledge and Kegan Paul, 1967, p. 186.

the extent to which money was a means of capital accumulation and a possible factor of change. Along the way, he meticulously prepared a model of monetary economy that is broad in scholarship and deep in insight. It is a delight and honour for me to respond to Habib's writings on money, although a short piece like this will never plumb the wealth of his work. Happily, its richness still leaves a sufficient intellectual overlap to allow a beatnik to beat his drums, raise issues of common concern and, hopefully, make some addition to its scholarly assessment. Three important points emerge in Habib's writings on money in Mughal India, viz., transition to a tri-metallic system dominated by one currency; magnitude of money supply combined with credit; and changes in prices, wages and interest rates.

From Copper to Silver

The first point is about a change in the pattern of currency circulation. In Indian history, currency regimes have given way to one another – precious metal currencies to base or mixed metal, and vice-versa. The first transition in medieval India took place in the thirteenth century when the Delhi Sultanate introduced precious metal coinage (*tanka*s of pure gold and silver) that had fallen into disuse for quite some time. The Sultanate itself went over entirely to base metal currencies from the late fourteenth century.[5] The third big transition took place in the second half of the sixteenth century, although signs of it were already apparent with the introduction of pure silver coins of Central Asian standard (*shahrukhi*) by Babur and Humayun, and, above all, of *rupiya* by Sher Shah Sur in AD 1540. Akbar inherited the tri-metallic coinage of Sher Shah (gold *muhr*, silver *rupiya*, and copper *paisa* or *dam*) of uniform weight and purity, and gave it wider circulation. Still, the best part of the sixteenth century signified continuation of the traditions of the late Delhi Sultanate, of billon (*tanka i siyah*) and copper. At the turn of the seventeenth century, a transition took place that made silver the principal medium of exchange. Gold was used for high-valued transactions and copper as small change.

The point Irfan Habib makes about the shift in the currency composition was elaborated in an insightful essay through a study of the various levels at which money was used in Mughal society.[6] The distinction between the two currency regimes was useful for better comprehension of the changes that

---

[5] Najaf Haider, 'Coinage and Silver Crisis', in Irfan Habib (ed.), *Economic History of Medieval India (1200–1500)*, New Delhi: Pearson, 2010 forthcoming.

[6] Irfan Habib, 'A System of Trimetallism in the Age of "Price Revolution": Effects of the Silver Influx on the Mughal Monetary System', in John F. Richards (ed.), *The Imperial Monetary System of Mughal India*, Delhi: Oxford University Press, 1987.

took place in the Mughal monetary economy as a result of new commercial and institutional arrangements. Transitions are always difficult to explain, particularly when documentation is scarce, with some statistics lost forever and others buried in archives as yet inaccessible. Habib however hinted at the complexities of the transition by pointing to the prevalence of a dual price and wage structure, and the problem of exchanging goods and services in multiple currencies.

He also offered a two-fold explanation of how the transition may have taken place: one empirical, the other conjectural. Empirically, it has been established beyond doubt that Mughal India received large quantities of silver from the middle of the sixteenth century (see below). However, we are still not quite clear about the process of distribution of the newly arrived silver in commercial and fiscal circuits, although we know that the rupee began to be minted in large quantities from the last quarter of that century. Habib's explanation of the mechanism by which the rupee displaced copper was complicated by the assumption (*à la* Moreland) that silver depreciated in value due to its abundance. Posing the problem in the context of a market that was free to determine the rates of currencies, he states:

> The puzzle, therefore remains: why then should Gresham's Law have still applied; why is it that silver, as it depreciated, did in fact drive out copper? One may, perhaps, suggest a possible explanation if one excepts the assumption that, while in the sixteenth century the basic money in which prices, wages, debts and tax obligations were specified was copper (*tankas/dams*), there was at the same time little or no hesitation in accepting payment in silver (rupees) at rates of conversion current in the market. As large quantities of silver were imported, these must have been bought by merchants and shroffs at prices naturally lower than the standard rate of 1 rupee to 40 *dams*. Upon getting the silver coined, they would have been willing, in their turn, to re-exchange it for copper at a discount; coined silver would thus enter circulation, spurred on by the discount.[7]

The argument is sound in so far as merchants and moneychangers did buy silver from foreign merchants and got it minted.[8] How it reached the end-user and replaced copper is yet to be mapped out. An alternative explanation of the expansion in silver circulation seems to be that it happened because the metal in fact appreciated in value.[9] This was due partly to a rise

---

[7] Ibid., p. 157.

[8] Najaf Haider, 'Precious Metal Flows and Currency Circulation in the Mughal Empire', *Journal of the Economic and Social History of the Orient*, Special Issue on 'Money in the Orient', 39, 1996, pp. 326–35.

[9] Najaf Haider, 'The Quantity Theory and Mughal Monetary History', *The Medieval History Journal*, Vol. 2, No. 2, 1999, p. 347.

in the monetary demand of silver (as an efficient medium of exchange, it was coveted much more than copper), and partly to a corresponding fall in the demand for copper as a currency at a time when there was a surplus of demonetized copper in the market (each rupee of 11.5 grams replaced 835 grams of copper in a single transaction based on official rate of exchange).[10] It was at this stage that prices, at least of industrial and export goods (such as indigo), began to be quoted in rupees. Indian merchants expected to gain from the sale of their products in silver (if they later exchanged it for copper), whereas foreign merchants paid in rupees for their purchases to avoid the tedium of double exchange.

The Mughal state was beset with a similar problem of keeping accounts in one currency and making payments in another. Perhaps to facilitate transition, it used a money of account (*tanka i muradi*), equal to two copper coins (*dam* or *paisa*), which had a fixed value in silver and gold.[11] The official exchange rate diverged from the market since the prices of metals varied with demand and supply.

There was a downside to the dazzling silver century. Once the argument about the great transition got accepted, all economic indicators began to be measured in terms only of silver money. The world of small change, of daily wages, stipends to students, everyday purchases from grocery shops (like the one Kabir complained about) became the stuff of social history. A social history of money and wealth in the Mughal empire is yet to be written.

Streams and Quantities of Silver Money Supply

The second point relates to the size of monetary circulation, which is important for the study of the state and economy in Mughal India. Taxation

---

[10] Najaf Haider, 'Prices and Wages in India, 1200–1700: Source Material, Historiography and New Directions', presented at the International Conference on 'Historical Wages and Prices', Utrecht, 19–22 August 2004, p. 48; available at www.iisg.nl/hpw/conference.html.

[11] For the view that the copper money of account should be taken note of, see Najaf Haider, 'The Monetary Integration of India under the Mughal Empire', in Irfan Habib (ed.), *India: Studies in the History of an Idea*, Delhi: Munshiram Manoharlal, 2005, pp. 129–30; and Haider, 'The Quantity Theory and Mughal Monetary History'. I have shown that the double *dam* (646 grains) was minted for a very short duration, while the money of account was used before as well as after. The impression one gets from Irfan Habib's treatment of *tanka i muradi* is that he is not quite sure whether money of account is the right designation for it (see Habib, *Agrarian System of Mughal India*, pp. 432–33, 441–42). For the literature on money of account, see Carlo M. Cipolla, *Money, Prices and Civilization in the Mediterranean World*, Princeton: Princeton University Press, 1956, Chapter IV; Peter Spufford, *Money and its Use in Medieval Europe*, Cambridge: Cambridge University Press, 1988, Appendix II; Thomas J. Sargent and Francois R. Velde, *The Big Problem of Small Change*, Princeton: Princeton University Press, 2002, pp. 126–28.

was the lifeblood of the state and collection in cash was convenient also to facilitate expenditure. The monetized fiscal system of the Mughal state held immense importance for the market economy as money, goods and services circulated incessantly in both sectors, and there was an interface between the two. There was indeed plenty of commerce conducted independently of the fiscal system but the state was a major player in creating the demand and supply of money. Three separate studies done in the late 1960s, 80s and 90s have strengthened Irfan Habib's general argument by offering quantifiable evidence on imports of monetary metals, currency circulation, and the relationship between money and credit.[12] Some of the views he has espoused have come under criticism while others are taken up here to elicit further response.[13]

Irfan Habib has argued that there was a net increase in the quantity of money available to the Mughal economy in the seventeenth century, primarily for two reasons. One was the regular import of American silver from Europe out of which the rupee and its fractions (*ana*) were coined, and the other was the use of credit instruments.[14] Between 1531 and 1600, Spain imported 7,439 metric tons of silver from the New World at an annual average of 106 metric tons. Over 64 per cent of this quantity was imported in the last two decades of the century at an average of 240.5 metric tons per annum.[15] How much of this silver ended up in Mughal India is a matter of discussion but there can be little doubt that it was the biggest recipient of Spanish-American silver outside Europe.[16]

[12] Aziza Hasan, 'The Silver Currency Output of the Mughal Empire and Prices in India during the Sixteenth and Seventeenth Centuries', *Indian Economic and Social History Review* (*IESHR*), VI, 1, 1969, pp. 85–116. Shireen Moosvi, 'The Silver Influx, Money Supply, Prices and Revenue Extraction in Mughal India', *Journal of Economic and Social History of the Orient* (*JESHO*), XXX, 1987, pp. 47–94; reprinted with minor modifications in Shireen Moosvi, *People, Taxation and Trade in Mughal India*, Delhi: Oxford University Press, 2008, pp. 35–80. Haider, 'Precious Metal Flows and Currency Circulation in the Mughal Empire'.

[13] Haider, 'The Quantity Theory and Mughal Monetary History'; Najaf Haider, 'Structure and Movement of Wages in the Mughal Empire', in Jan Lucassen (ed.), *Wages and Currency: Global and Historical Comparisons*, Amsterdam: International Institute of Social History, 2008, pp. 317–21. Criticisms that have debated merits not from the vantage of knowledge but cynicism have not been considered here. For an essay, and a rather long but ultimately ungainly introduction, see Sanjay Subrahmanyam, 'Precious Metal Flows and Prices in Western and Southern Asia, 1500–1750: Some Comparative and Conjunctural Aspects', in Sanjay Subrahmanyam (ed.), *Money and the Market in India 1100–1700*, Delhi: Oxford University Press, 1994.

[14] Habib, 'The Monetary System and Prices', pp. 363–66.

[15] Earl J. Hamilton, *American Treasure and the Price Revolution in Spain, 1501–1650*, Cambridge, Massachusetts: Harvard University Press, 1934, p. 42; Michel Morineau, *Incroyables Gazettes et Fabuleux Metaux*, Cambridge: Cambridge University Press, 1985, p. 578. Gold too was imported but its quantity was quite small (1.92 metric tons per annum).

[16] Shireen Moosvi (*Economy of the Mughal Empire*, Delhi: Oxford University Press, 1987, pp. 375–76) suggested that from all channels 184.6 metric tons of silver and 4.6 metric tons of

According to a rough estimate, the Indian Ocean received over 67 per cent (167 metric tons) of silver leaving Seville at the turn of the seventeenth century (the rest was disseminated in Europe and caused inflation).[17] Out of 167 metric tons, Ming China received somewhere between 43 and 46 metric tons.[18] If we deduct the lower figure, that leaves 124 metric tons for South Asia (supposing that these were the only recipients). Mughal India also received around 10 metric tons of silver from the Middle East by the land route.[19] Whether or not it was able to tap at this time any silver coming to Manila from Acapulco is not established, and my hunch is that the Mexican–Manila silver hardly flowed past China. Now, if we scale down the flow of 134 metric tons from the maritime and caravan routes to account for the share of areas lying outside the Mughal empire at the turn of the seventeenth century, we arrive at a figure that is astonishingly close to a lower estimate of 124 metric tons of silver.[20] The correspondence is too close to be true in a matter such as this where empirical evidence is scarce and speculation high, and I am relieved to have recently revised it down to 117 metric tons.

How much of this silver was put into circulation and what was the rate of increase in money supply? On these two questions Irfan Habib has relied on the statistics provided by Shireen Moosvi:

> Moosvi suggests a useful device for measuring the increase in silver-money supply by constructing an index of coined silver stock per capita. This she has done on the basis of the number of surviving rupee coins in treasure-troves

---

gold were annually imported into the Mughal empire at the turn of the seventeenth century. Also see Moosvi, 'The Silver Influx, Money Supply, Prices and Revenue Extraction in Mughal India', pp. 42–60. The estimates are indirect in so far as they are based not on import figures but on estimated figures of silver mint output. Even the estimates of imports of gold and silver by the English East India Company are based on export figures given by K.N. Chaudhuri (ibid., pp. 56–57, Table 2.7) whereas direct estimates, calculated from the records of the Company, are available in print. Haider, 'Precious Metal Flows and Currency Circulation in the Mughal Empire', pp. 318–19, Tables 5 and 6.

[17] Haider, 'Precious Metal Flows and Currency Circulation in the Mughal Empire', pp. 308–16; Najaf Haider, 'The Network of Monetary Exchange in the Indian Ocean Trade: 1200–1700', in *Cross Currents and Community Networks: The History of the Indian Ocean World*, edited by Himanshu Prabha Ray and Edward Alpers, Delhi: Oxford University Press, 2007, p. 195.

[18] Richard von Glahn, *Fountain of Fortune: Money and Monetary Policy in China, 1000–1700*, Berkeley: University of California Press, 1996, pp. 133–40. Ralph Fitch, the Elizabethan merchant-adventurer, in the last quarter of the century, estimated it at 250,000 *crusados* per annum. William Foster (ed.), *Early Travels in India, 1583–1619*, London, 1921, p. 41.

[19] Haider, 'Precious Metal Flows and Currency Circulation in the Mughal Empire', p. 323, Table 9.

[20] Ibid.

and by assuming population to have increased at the rate of 0.211 per cent per annum. The problem is, from what date should one count. If one assumes that the prices were largely being expressed in rupees by 1600, the per-capita stock by 1705 should, by her estimates, have grown by 61.9 per cent; if one takes 1610 (by which date the earlier standard gold: silver ratio had been breached), the increase would be 35.9 per cent; if, following Moosvi, one takes the initial date as 1615 (whereafter the silver: copper ratio began to change), the increase would be just 23.6 per cent. These alternatives set a range of about a quarter to two-fifths for the increase in silver-money supply per head.[21]

Although it is quite clear from the above passage that the purpose of quantifying the silver money supply is to examine its impact on prices and other variables, there are a couple of points relevant for the search of the right chronology as well as the rate of increase of money supply. It is possible that prices began to be expressed in rupees well before 1600 when silver, as we argued, started appreciating against copper as well as gold.[22] But the problem of choosing a normal base year in the last two decades of the sixteenth century appears to have become difficult because these were years of extraordinary rupee production following the recoinage of non-imperial and regional issues.[23] The choice of these years would underestimate the rate of increase of money supply in the seventeenth century.

Coinage alone does not constitute money. Irfan Habib has shown that in developed market economies, claims to money can also be used to transact. In a series of studies on banking, bills of exchange, commercial usury and insurance, the first of which appeared at the same time as his premier essay on coinage, Habib indicated the presence of an organized system of credit which financed commercial exchange, minimized transaction costs and aided

---

[21] Habib, *The Agrarian System of Mughal India*, p. 448; Moosvi, 'The Silver Influx, Money Supply, Prices and Revenue Extraction in Mughal India', p. 72.

[22] Shireen Moosvi's (ibid., p. 71, n. 92) suggestion that the rupee rate of gold in 1608 was 9.6 (and not 8, as I suggested) because the rupee was 20 per cent heavier ignores the possibility that the gold coin too could be heavier since Jahangir increased the weight of both the coins by 20 per cent.

[23] Shireen Moosvi ('The Silver Influx, Money Supply, Prices and Revenue Extraction in Mughal India', pp. 46–47, n. 25) acknowledges the significance of recoinage but downplays its importance in her final calculations. Her estimated figures for the rupees coined in the Ahmadabad mint show a two-fold increase between 1586 and 1605 (ibid., p. 45), whereas the increase in the annual flow of Spanish-American silver is of a much lower order. Surely the difference was made up of the recoinage of the local silver coin of Gujarat (*mahmudi*) of high fineness (93 per cent), following a general order by Akbar in 1582 (repeated in 1592). See Najaf Haider, 'Mughals and Mahmudis: The Incorporation of Gujarat into the Imperial Monetary System', in T.K. Venkatasubramanian, Biswamoy Pati and B.P. Sahu (eds), *Negotiating India's Past: Essays in Memory of Partha Sarathi Gupta*, New Delhi: Tulika Books, 2003, pp. 134–52.

monetary circulation.[24] At the present level of research it is difficult to compute the proportions of credit and coinage, but it is possible to argue that both expanded simultaneously. Credit supplemented rather than substituted coinage since all deferred payments were structurally tied to final settlement in cash. If coinage contracted, credit shrank too.[25]

Money and the Potentialities of Change

What were the implications of monetary expansion for the Mughal economy and society? It is with this question that the third point is concerned, arguably the most wide-ranging and the focal point of Irfan Habib's attention for a long time.

Habib has argued, using the quantity theory of money and the device of the Fisher equation, that the developments that took place in the monetary sector widened the domain of monetized exchange.[26] Even though the validity of the quantity theory of money has become questionable in the face of the historical reality of the Mughal empire (silver appreciated in value at a time when its quantity increased), it is fair to suggest that the Mughal economy was dynamic and, during the course of its development, created continuous demand for money. Population increase, urbanization and state finances, such as the conversion of tax receipts into cash, brought more and more products to the market, and absorbed a large part of the silver money supplied to the economy. Once the process of absorption reached the optimum

[24] Habib, 'The Monetary System and Prices', pp. 362–63; Irfan Habib, 'Banking in Mughal India', in Tapan Raychaudhuri (ed.), *Contributions to Economic History*, Calcutta: Firma K.L. Mukhopadhyay, 1960, pp. 1–20; Irfan Habib, 'Usury in Medieval India', *Comparative Studies in Society and History*, VI, 1964, pp. 393–419; Irfan Habib, 'The System of Bills of Exchange (*Hundis*) in the Mughal Empire', *Proceedings of the Indian History Congress*, 35th session, Muzaffarpur, 1972, pp. 290–303; Irfan Habib, 'Merchant Communities in Pre-Colonial India', in James D. Tracy (ed.), *The Rise of Merchant Empires, Long-Distance Trade in the Early Modern World, 1350–1750*, Cambridge: Cambridge University Press, 1990, pp. 371–99.

[25] Najaf Haider, 'The Monetary Basis of Credit and Banking Instruments in the Mughal Empire', in Amiya Kumar Bagchi (ed.), *Money and Credit in Indian History*, New Delhi: Tulika Books, 2002.

[26] The figure estimated by Moosvi for the stock of silver (proxy for money supply) existing in the Mughal empire in 1595 (4,552 metric tons) can be used to debate the extent of monetization. Together with the GDP figure estimated for 1595 (6,418 metric tons of silver), it yields an economy that was 70.9 per cent monetized. This appears to be quite an impressive figure to start with since, as late as the 1950s, the share of the non-monetized sector in the Indian economy was estimated by the National Sample Survey to be around 43 per cent for rural areas, and between 8 and 11 per cent for urban areas. See A.G. Chandavarkar, 'Money and Credit: 1858–1947', in Dharma Kumar (ed.), *The Cambridge Economic History of India, Vol. 2: c. 1759–c. 1970*, Cambridge: Cambridge University Press, 1982, p. 764.

level, silver money began to lose its value. The loss of value was reflected in the fall in its purchasing power or a rise in prices, as well as a reduction in interest rates. Recently, Irfan Habib has added that 'the silver influx partly fuelled by usury-capital could nevertheless have caused the fall in the interest rates observed in the mid-seventeenth century in India'.[27] This suggestion has important implications but it needs to be argued. Although Habib has himself identified the mechanism of creation of usurious capital in India, he has not as yet shown that banking capital was imported in sufficient quantities to exercise a secular downward pressure on interest rates. The rate of interest in Mughal India was higher than in Europe (hence the possibility of profit on transfer), but much of the money transmitted from London or Amsterdam was for the purchase of Indian (Asian) goods. Moreover, the rates prevalent in the Middle East were higher than in India (this may have had to do with the scarcity of loanable capital), restraining the transfer of money capital by Asian merchants.

The significance of Habib's abovementioned arguments has to be realized in the context of the historiography of the Mughal economy in general, and of money and prices in particular. Until then, Moreland and others had either failed to notice an inflationary trend or, even when they did, it was never related to the purchasing power of money. Conceptualizing the quantity of money and its exchange value as two sides of the same equation, Habib gave a new direction to the study of the Mughal monetary economy, and also placed it in the wider context of an exciting debate conducted in Europe on the theory and history of money.

In Europe, the prices of many goods rose substantially in the long sixteenth century (1460–1650). The rising trend was sustainable and earned the designation of 'price revolution'.[28] On the causes and consequences of the European price revolution, modern historians have offered a variety of interpretations. Earl Hamilton observed a close connection between a rise in commodity prices at Seville (four-and-a-half times in the sixteenth century), and the influx of large amounts of American silver and gold into

---

[27] Irfan Habib, *Medieval India: The Study of a Civilization*, New Delhi: National Book Trust, 2008, p. 144; see also Shireen Moosvi, 'A Note on Interest Rates in the Seventeenth and Early Eighteenth Centuries', in Shireen Moosvi, *People, Taxation and Trade in Mughal India*, Delhi: Oxford University Press, 2008, p. 86.

[28] Peter H. Ramsay (ed.), *The Price Revolution in Sixteenth Century England*, London: Methuen; Peter Burke (ed.), *Economy and Society in Early Modern Europe: Essays from Annales*, London: Routledge and Kegan Paul. For a recent survey, see David Hackett Fischer, *The Great Wave: Price Revolutions and the Rhythm of History*, New York: Oxford University Press, 1996, pp. 65–84. For wide-ranging comments on the relationship between money, prices and industrial growth, see D. Felix, 'Profit Inflation and Industrial Growth: The Historic Record and Contemporary Analogies', in Roderick Floud (ed.), *Essays in Quantitative Economic History*, Oxford: Clarendon Press, 1974, pp. 133–51.

Spain.[29] Hamilton saw a similar corelation, reinforced later by Braudel and Spooner, between the European price rise and the diffusion of Spanish-American silver into the continent. More significant has been Hamilton's statement that money supply drove prices above labour costs and created profits which entrepreneurs invested in industrial expansion. The 'profit inflation' and capital accumulation resulted in a more rapid rate of industrial growth than was possible under stable prices.[30]

In the beginning, India appeared on the margins in all the discussions on the causes and implications of the European price revolution. Both Hamilton and his critics acknowledged that European bullion found its way to Asia, particularly India and China, but that it was inconsequential as much of it was hoarded rather than monetized. This understanding bore the deep impression of a century of European scholarship on the character of non-capitalist societies. Marx contrasted the role of precious metals in European and Indian economies (even though he acknowledged the presence of commodity exchange), while Weber considered the lack of necessary infrastructure as an important reason for India's inability to produce economic changes comparable to the European price revolution. Even W.H. Moreland, who studied and raised questions relevant to monetary history, shared the view that the sphere of exchange in India was largely untouched by the absorption of precious metals.[31]

Irfan Habib's endorsement of the Hamilton effect in the case of India can be interpreted as a historiographical counterpoint to Moreland, as well as to the Marxist notion of money as an essentially dormant and inactive agent.[32] At the domestic level, monetization was treated as a symptom of mobility in the Mughal economy with the recognition that as an economic variable it can be quantitatively conceived and measured. In the wider con-

[29] Hamilton, *American Treasure and the Price Revolution in Spain*, p. 42.

[30] Ibid., pp. 283–306. Earl Hamilton, 'Profit Inflation and the Industrial Revolution', *Quarterly Journal of Economics*, 56, 1942, pp. 256–73; reprinted in Frederic C. Lane and Jelle C. Riemersema (eds), *Enterprise and Secular Change: Readings in Economic History*, London: Allen and Unwin, 1953, pp. 323–36.

[31] W.H. Moreland, *India at the Death of Akbar*, London: Macmillan, 1920; reprint, Delhi: Atma Ram and Sons, 1962, pp. 184–85, 264–66. These conclusions were reinforced in a better researched, companion volume (*From Akbar to Aurangzeb*), in which Moreland undertook a detailed analysis of the urban economy and trade.

[32] Marx's admittance of the short-run non-neutrality of money was backed by his own observation of the fact that American silver contributed favourably to the prosperity of the recipient countries in the sixteenth and seventeenth centuries, the 'growth of capital and the rise of the bourgeoisie'. Karl Marx, *Wage Labour and Capital*, Moscow: Progress Publishers. 1952/1976, p. 33. Also see Karl Marx, *A Contribution to the Critique of Political Economy*, Moscow: Progress Publishers, 1970, p. 148. Marx's sympathy for some elements of the quantity theory is detected in Don Lavoie, 'Marx, the Quantity Theory, and the Theory of Value', *History of Political Economy*, XVIII, 1, 1986, pp. 155–62.

text, silver influx and price changes were perceived as part of a more fundamental process of Spanish colonization and capital accumulation with deeper theoretical and historical significance.[33] In a classic statement, Habib argued that 'any expansion or contraction of money supply in an economy must cause changes in prices, profits, interests, and scale of investment; and these by causing shifts of wealth from one class to another may alter the entire relationship between classes'.[34] This view of money as a factor of social change deserves serious consideration.

Still, on the issue of the impact of money supply on prices, wages, mercantile profit and income distribution in Mughal India, Habib has adopted a cautious and, dare I say, minimalist approach. For him, the scale of inflation ('about 50 per cent over the seventeenth century') was too small to be called a 'revolution', and so was its impact on economy and society. Merchants stood to gain the most from the rise in prices and a fall in interest rates, but the impact of modest profit inflation on capital accumulation was too limited to break through the circuit of exchange governed largely by the needs of the ruling class.[35] Merchant capital could never transform itself into industrial capital. In the countryside, the imperial revenue system mopped up any additional income of the peasants (zamindars and rural moneylenders invested in agriculture, but that by itself either facilitated tax collection or depressed production through usurious rates of interest), and in towns, the employers pocketed the difference between prices and money wages of artisans and labourers.[36] Accumulation, the only engine of economic growth other than an ecological one, took the form of massive hoarding of precious metals by the ruling class with practically no investment in sectors outside luxury consumption. In other words, a rigid political organization and distribution of economic resources impinged upon monetary movements to prevent any major change in the structure of production and exchange.

On the issue of price change, there are interpretations different from that of Irfan Habib that need to be mentioned. Tapan Raychaudhuri accepted the fact of inflation in Mughal India but linked it with real economic fac-

---

[33] Irfan Habib, 'Economics and the Historians', *Social Scientist*, 432–433 (Volume 37), May–June 2009, pp. 12–13.

[34] Irfan Habib, *Caste and Money in Indian History*, Bombay: Bombay University, 1987, p. 21. Also see Irfan Habib, 'Capitalism in History', *Social Scientist*, XXIII, Nos. 7–9, 1995, pp. 15–31.

[35] Irfan Habib, 'Potentialities of Capitalistic Development in the Economy of Mughal India', *Enquiry*, New Series, III, 1971; reprinted in Irfan Habib, *Essays in Indian History: Towards a Marxist Perception*, New Delhi: Tulika Books, 1995, pp. 231–32.

[36] Irfan Habib, 'Processes of Accumulation in Pre-Colonial and Colonial India', *Indian Historical Review*, XI, Nos. 1–2, 1984–85, pp. 65–90; reprinted in Habib, *Essays in Indian History*, pp. 259–95.

tors, such as the growth in population, urbanization and the volume of inland commerce stimulated by Mughal revenue demand. Foreign trade and bullion flows were assigned marginal importance and the internal dynamics of the Mughal economy were treated as ultimate driving forces.[37] The relationship between fiscal demand and price change too has the possibility of enlarging the discussion beyond the confines of money supply.[38]

The denial of price inflation in the seventeenth century characterizes yet another approach followed commonly by scholars focusing on foreign trade. Moreland was the first to argue that there was no perceptible sign of any long-term change in prices. Later, the treatment by Van Santen of the prices of food items sold in the markets of Gujarat suggests a more or less stable trend.[39] Om Prakash too noticed no discernible movement in food prices in Bengal. The stability of prices is treated, in the face of growing money supply, as an indication of an expansion in the volume of commerce. Prakash developed a general argument, based mainly on his studies of the Dutch trade in Bengal, for a growth in output, income and employment induced by the bullion imports of the companies.[40]

On the issue of wages, it is interesting to note that Irfan Habib has argued that there was an increase in the money wages of daily workers in Agra between 1595 and 1637, to the extent that copper appreciated in the intervening period.[41] We have seen the problem with this argument but it is still true that money (silver) wages increased between the two dates (Table 1), although the rise (50 per cent, if we convert the figures into silver) may have been due to an increase in the prices of wage goods stated in copper. Another striking phenomenon is a big decline in the grain (real) wages of both skilled and unskilled labour (Table 2). If the gap between the money and real wages was as significant as is reflected in the two Tables, then the

---

[37] Tapan Raychaudhuri, 'Inland Trade', in Raychaudhuri and Habib (eds), *The Cambridge Economic History of India, Vol. 1*, 1982, pp. 335–37. This is set against Raychaudhuri's general argument that the aggregate demand for manufactured goods in the Mughal empire was large and expanding ('Non-Agricultural Production', ibid., pp. 261–69).

[38] Haider, 'Prices and Wages in India: 1200–1700', pp. 38–39; Shireen Moosvi, 'Tax and Price Relationship in a Regime of "Asiatic Despotism": A Theoretical Exercise', *Social Scientist*, 432–433 (Volume 37), May–June 2009, pp. 38–44.

[39] H.W. Van Santen, *De VOC in Gujarat en Hindustan, 1620–1660*, Leiden, 1982, pp. 83–100.

[40] According to this argument, the increase in exports (and export surplus) involved a net increase in output and income (Y). In terms of the national income identity: $Y = C + I + (X - M)$; an increase in the export surplus $(X - M)$ could be effected through a decline in consumption (C) or/and investment (I) or/and increase in output and income (Y). Since there was no decline in C or I in Bengal, an increase in $X - M$ effected an increase in Y. See Om Prakash, *The Dutch East India Company and the Economy of Bengal*, Princeton: Princeton University Press, 1985; reprint, Delhi: Oxford University Press, 1988, pp. 234–56. Also, Om Prakash, *Precious Metals and Commerce: The Dutch East India Company in the East India Trade*, Hampshire: Ashgate Publishing, 1994, p. x.

[41] Habib, 'Monetary System and Prices', pp. 378–79.

TABLE 1 *Daily Wages of Unskilled Construction Worker: Agra*, AD 1595–1638

Year	Original figures	Currency	Exchange rate	Grams of silver	Kg of wheat
AD 1595	2 *dam*	Copper coin of 20.9 grams	1 rupee = 40 *dam*	0.57	4.19
AD 1595	3 *dam**	Copper coin of 20.9 grams	1 rupee = 40 *dam*	0.86	6.32
AD 1637	4 *paisa*	Copper coin of 20.9 grams	1 rupee = 54 *paisa*	0.85	–
AD 1638	4 *paisa*	Copper coin of 20.9 grams	1 rupee = 55 *paisa*	0.83	2.69
AD 1638	7 *paisa**	Copper coin of 20.9 grams	1 rupee = 55 *paisa*	1.45	4.70

Notes: * Superior labourer.
        Dam and *paisa* were different terms used for the Mughal copper coin weighing 20.9 grams.
Source: Abul Fazl, *Ain-i Akbari*, Vol. I, translated by H. Blochmann, Calcutta: Asiatic Society, 1868, pp. 235–36; W.H. Moreland, 'Some Sidelights on Life in Agra, 1637–39', *Journal of U.P. Historical Society*, Vol. 3, 1923, p. 159. For exchange rate, see Van Santen, *De Verenigde Oost Indische Compagnie in Gujarat en Hindustan, 1620–1660*, p. 114.

TABLE 2 *Daily Wages of Skilled Worker (Carpenter): Agra*, AD 1595–1638

Year	Original figures	Currency	Exchange rate	Grams of silver	Kg of wheat
1595	7 *dam*	Copper coin of 20.9 grams	1 rupee = 40 *dam*	2.00	14.70
1637	3 *ana*	One sixteenth of a rupee	–	2.14	–
1638	13 *paisa*	Copper coin of 20.9 grams	1 rupee = 55 *dam*	2.70	8.74

Source: Table 1; *De Verenigde Oost Indische Compagnie in Gujarat en Hindustan, 1620–1660*, p. 102); Moreland, 'Some Sidelights on Life in Agra, 1637–39', p. 160.

question of accumulation of merchant capital assumes greater importance. There are two additional aspects of the size and nature of merchant capital in Mughal India which are worthy of consideration. First, the penetration of merchant capital into the agrarian sector for the organization of production and sale of commercialized items (such as the Bayana indigo) was much greater than is acknowledged in current historiography. Illustrative of the point is the report of a Dutch observer:

It is also necessary to have a buyer in Bayana, where the market opens much later than elsewhere, so that it is amply sufficient to go there in the beginning of October. The reason is that some rich and substantial merchants live in the town; the chief of them are named Mirza Sadiq and Ghazi Fazil, who sow most of the indigo, and who in some seasons have sold to nobody but us. The price is settled at his [*sic.*] house, usually a rupee per maund more than the rate at Ghanowa or in other villages, because as has been said, the quality is superior; and when the price has been fixed, but not before, anyone can sell to anyone he chooses. This subservience, or respect, is shown to Mirza Sadiq because he is the oldest [merchant] in Bayana.[42]

What Pelsaert calls 'subservience' or 'respect' is actually the dominance of merchant capital in the countryside, of which several examples can be found. It remains hidden from our sight and the more we know about it, the more we understand the nature of the rural market, price structure and monetization. One can even speculate that the aggregate size of this capital was much larger than its urban counterpart invested in craft goods.

Second, the component of merchant capital that does not arise from commodity exchange but from financial services provided by that ubiquitous group of *sarraf*s who held multiple portfolios (assaying, moneychanging, banking and risk-sharing) appears to have been much more dynamic, mobile and widespread than is usually believed. It may have registered a massive increase in the wake of greater commercialization and monetization, and it possible to put it down as a factor responsible for lowering interest rates in the second half of the seventeenth century. In the world of modern finance, the lion's share of the profit of money merchants comes from commission, and it is time that historians of pre-modern finance take note of a rather neglected component of mercantile capital.

Irfan Habib's essays, written over a period of forty years, are the perfect vehicles for discussion of a large number of issues relating to the monetary economy of Mughal India. They afford readers not just a broad picture but specific details of each variable. There is something to be said about his style as well, particularly at a time when the obscurity of certain writings on Indian history appears to be daunting and annoying. It is well said that easy reading is difficult writing; and Habib has shown that eloquence is a function essentially of comprehension, and that scholarship advances with arguments which can be assigned weightage and tested. To effect choicer communication, he does not burden his readers with extra information even though he seems to possess it in great abundance from an archive of documents and manuscripts that take a lifetime to decipher. There is a Greek saying that the fox knows many things but the hedgehog knows one big thing. Taking it figuratively and indeed mixing it, one wonders whether he is actually a fox who is pretending to be a hedgehog.

---

[42] Francisco Pelsaert, *Jahangir's India: The Remonstrantie of Francisco Pelsaert*, translated by W.H. Moreland and P. Geyl, Cambridge, 1925, p. 17.

Colonialism and the Problem of Divergence

Amar Farooqui

A major issue in Marxist historiography on India has been the question, would it have been possible for India to make the transition to capitalism had colonialism not intervened? This in turn could imply either that precolonial India did not have the potential to make the transition to capitalism on its own, or that it did have the potential but the process of transition was thwarted by colonial rule. Either way this is a difficult problem, the more so as one can only speculate about the manner in which the precolonial social formations of India would have evolved in the absence of colonialism as a historical factor. Marx himself, with the rather limited and, at times, inaccurate information about India's past at his disposal, grappled with this problem for nearly three decades: from the 1850s till his death. He had to constantly revise and finetune his understanding, abandoning in later years the oversimplified notion of a society marked by changelessness that required British rule to shake off its ages-long stupor.[1]

This did not prevent Cold War scholarship of the kind represented by Karl Wittfogel from appropriating Marx's concept of the 'Asiatic Mode of Production' and using it, in a vulgarized form, to declare the innate inferiority of the orient.[2] One might mention here that Wittfogel's *Oriental Despotism* was published in the same year as Paul Baran's *Political Economy of Growth* which strongly argued the very opposite, namely, that before the era of colonialism much of the world was at a level of historical development that was not very different from that of Europe, and that it was really colonial plunder which gave the west a critical advantage enabling it to get ahead of the rest of the world.[3] In the intellectual climate of the Cold War, Wittfogel's *Oriental Despotism* was of course taken very seriously in academic circles in the west. Barring perhaps a critical review by Joseph Needham,

---

[1] Irfan Habib, 'Introduction: Marx's Perception of India', in Iqbal Husain (ed.), *Karl Marx on India*, New Delhi: Tulika Books, 2006, pp. xxxi–xxxv.
[2] Karl A. Wittfogel, *Oriental Despotism: A Comparative Study in Total Power*, New Haven: Yale University Press, 1957.
[3] Paul Baran, *The Political Economy of Growth*, New York: Monthly Review Press, 1957.

published in *Science and Society* in 1959, Wittfogel got off quite easily despite the shallowness of his historical knowledge on the basis of which he had made sweeping generalizations.[4] Needham took him to task for his outdated understanding of and information about China (which happened to be Wittfogel's field of specialization). In 1961, Irfan Habib published a comprehensive critique of *Oriental Despotism* in *Enquiry*, in which he disputed both the conceptual framework and historical basis of the entire work.[5] This is one of his earliest articles published in an important academic journal, and would have been, at that time, a curtain-raiser for his magnum opus, *The Agrarian System of Mughal India*, which was to become available in 1963.[6]

For Habib, the importance of *Oriental Despostism* lay in the opportunity it provided for reflecting on the failure of Asia and Africa to keep pace with the west during the modern period even though Europe had lagged behind several regions of the orient in the medieval period:

> It is an undeniable fact that from the 17th century Europe established a definite economic and technological superiority over the rest of the world, and during the 18th and 19th centuries conquered or subdued practically the whole of Asia or Africa. It is also undeniable that previous to the modern age several countries of Asia and Africa, notably China, India and Middle Eastern lands, had reached a much higher level of culture than that attained by medieval Europe. *It is, therefore, one of the important questions of World history, why Asian countries were not able to develop further their economies, and social and political systems, and so fell a prey to Western colonialism.*[7] (Emphasis added)

Habib's formulation in this passage – 'one of the important questions of World history, why Asian countries were not able to develop further their economies, and social and political systems' – written in his inimitable prose that puts across the weightiest intellectual arguments with great lucidity, has remained an important concern in his writings down to the present day. He was disappointed with *Oriental Despotism* because it had nothing of consequence to offer that might help in understanding this problem, even though that is precisely what Wittfogel had set out to do. And this, Habib

---

[4] Joseph Needham, 'Review' of Karl Wittfogel's *Oriental Despotism*, *Science and Society*, Vol. XXIII, 1959, pp. 58–65.

[5] Irfan Habib, 'An Examination of Wittfogel's Theory of "Oriental Despotism"', paper read at the Asian History Congress, New Delhi, *Enquiry*, No. 6, 1961, pp. 54–73.

[6] There is an intriguing reference in the article (ibid., p. 59, n. 2) to *The Agrarian System* as published in Aligarh in 1962, although the page numbers in the reference(s) correspond to the 1963 edition: Irfan Habib, *The Agrarian System of Mughal India (1556–1707)*, Bombay: Asia Publishing House, 1963.

[7] Habib, 'An Examination of Wittfogel's Theory of "Oriental Despotism"', p. 54.

pointed out, was largely due to his inadequate knowledge of history apart from his ideological bankruptcy. Wittfogel's main hypothesis was that advanced agrarian societies first developed in arid and semi-arid zones of the Old World (and Central America). The geographical conditions in these zones required large-scale irrigation works for the development of agriculture, giving rise to hydraulic societies. These were societies in which the state, comprising a powerful bureaucracy and an omnipotent monarch, exercised 'despotic' control by virtue of its role in organizing irrigation. While despotism was thus the distinguishing feature of oriental societies, indeed the historical experience of the bulk of humanity, the superiority of the west, as manifested in its democratic institutions, was due to the absence of despotism and the existence of competing centres of power in feudal Europe. The competition between these rival centres of power (the monarch, the nobility, the church and merchants) created possibilities for social evolution and therefore the emergence of a modern industrial society. The prevalence of despotism in the orient prevented such a development.

In his devastating critique, Habib exposed Wittfogel's abysmal ignorance of historical geography. He focused on evidence pertaining to India, which, along with China, was central to Wittfogel's hypothesis about hydraulic societies in the orient.[8] Wittfogel regarded the extensive north Indian plains, extending from the Indus to the Ganga, as a zone of hydraulic agriculture. In this he was mistaken. Eastern India depends upon rainfall and inundation; in Uttar Pradesh and eastern Panjab, rains are supplemented by irrigation from wells (usually excavated individually by cultivators) and partly from tanks; and in the Indus Basin natural (rather than man-made) canals are vital for irrigation. Wittfogel, Habib noted, 'does not seem to have heard of these natural canals'.[9] Some important irrigation works, it is true, were constructed in north India. However, whatever large-scale works are to be found – the famous Western Yamuna Canal, for instance – were built *after* 'despotic' states had been established. Historical evidence pertaining to irrigation in territories that constituted the Mughal empire is presented in considerable detail in Habib's *Agrarian System*.[10] This was a problem to

---

[8] Habib did touch briefly on China, but admitted that he 'is not competent to comment on the applicability of Wittfogel's theory to China, which is Wittfogel's special field'. Nevertheless, he cited an article by Wa Ta-K'un ('An Interpretation of Chinese Economic History, *Past and Present*, No. 1, pp. 3–4, 12), in which the author stated (as paraphrased by Habib) that 'China has plentiful rainfall in most areas, its ancient bone inscriptions "have no words for canals or dykes", and in fact canals seem to have been constructed in China "long after" the despotic state had been firmly established.' Habib, 'An Examination of Wittfogel's Theory of "Oriental Despotism"', p. 63.

[9] Ibid., p. 58.

[10] Habib, *The Agrarian System of Mughal India*, pp. 24–36.

which he had paid close attention, and as early as 1954, he had published a research paper on the subject.[11]

Habib went on to demonstrate that Wittfogel's understanding of European feudalism was equally inadequate. As one of the pioneers (along with D.D. Kosambi and R.S. Sharma) of historical research on the 'sequence' of modes of production and feudalism in the Indian context in particular, as a problem in Marxist theory, Habib was in a position to comment on Wittfogel's knowledge, or lack of it, of medieval Europe with some confidence. The multicentred polity that was celebrated in *Oriental Despotism* was not really composed of separate elements competing for power. These supposedly distinct elements (court, lords, church, etc.) were actually 'all part of a single ruling class'.

> The lords held their fiefs 'of' the King, to whom they owed a definite military obligation. The Church too derived its income largely from its lands, its bishops conducting themselves, for the purpose, as feudal lords. On this view there was fundamentally only one ruling class with which the State was fully integrated. A failure to recognize this leads Wittfogel to make fallacious comparisons.[12]

One such significant 'fallacious comparison' was that 'the tax of the Oriental "bureaucracy" in its entirety [was] compared only with the royal taxes of feudal Europe'. According to Habib, 'It should be compared properly with the labour services and rent which the feudal lords, including the King, drew from the serf-peasantry; and then the magnitude of Oriental taxation would not seem so striking.'[13] Wittfogel's inability to grasp the surplus extraction relationships of feudal Europe, combined with his superficial understanding of historical conditions in the non-western world, rendered the concept of 'oriental despotism' worthless for enlightening us about the factors that were responsible for the different trajectories of the west and the rest of the world in the modern era. The thesis of *Oriental Despotism* thus had 'little right to be heard as a serious explanation of why the West prevailed against the East in the 18th and 19th centuries'.[14]

---

[11] Irfan Habib, 'Sutlej and Beas in the Medieval Period', *The Geographer* (Aligarh), Vol. VI, No. 2, 1954. This is perhaps his earliest published research paper. Unfortunately, I have not been able to consult the article (mentioned in the list of Habib's publications provided in K.N. Panikkar, Terence J. Byres and Utsa Patnaik, eds, *The Making of Indian History: Essays Presented to Irfan Habib*, New Delhi: Tulika Books, 2000, p. 661), but some details of his research on Sutlej and Beas (undertaken with Moonis Raza) are mentioned in Habib, *The Agrarian System of Mughal India*, p. 29, n. 31.

[12] Habib, 'An Examination of Wittfogel's Theory of "Oriental Despotism"', p. 66.

[13] Ibid., p. 67.

[14] Ibid., p. 73.

Habib himself did not venture any suggestion in his critique. He merely concluded by remarking:

> This does not mean that attempts at discovering the causes of the failure of medieval eastern societies should be given up. It means only that such attempts must be more disinterested, less concerned with the application of preconceived notions, and more honest with regard to the immense variety of political and social institutions which existed in Asia previous to the modern age.[15]

Although this is a problem that he has returned to again and again in his writings, Habib has consistently followed his own prescription by offering nothing more than tentative views, as though he were still weighing the evidence but was hesitant to put forth a hypothesis till he was fully satisfied with it – which indeed is the hallmark of his scholarship. Yet there were clues, the implications of which he was to scrutinize in later writings. One was his reference to the limited scale of commodity production in medieval Europe. India, on the other hand, had extensive commodity production in the late pre-colonial period. Moreover, the Mughal economy was highly monetized, a feature reinforced by the collection of a large portion of the land revenue in cash (and in cases where it was demanded in kind, its commutation to cash). If, then, the late pre-colonial social formation of India had some of those ingredients that are often regarded as indispensable for the transition to capitalism in greater measure than in Europe, what was it that prevented such a transition in India? The siphoning off of much of the surplus as colonial tribute at a critical moment in historical development was a possible explanation, but Habib was as yet unwilling to make such a statement (as a matter of fact, he would even now be reluctant to make such a categorical statement) until he had closely examined the 'potentialities of capitalistic development' in Mughal India – which he did, in his classic essay on the subject published in 1971.[16]

The argument of that essay is too well known to require recapitulation here. Suffice it to say that Habib's analysis revealed a complex situation wherein commodity production and monetization were largely confined to the domain of the Mughal nobility and its dependants. Merchants and bank-

---

[15] Ibid.

[16] Irfan Habib, 'Potentialities of Capitalistic Development in the Economy of Mughal India', *Enquiry*, New Series, Vol. III, No. 3, 1971, pp. 1–56. The article was based on a paper Habib had read three years earlier, in 1968, at the International Economic History Congress, Bloomington, that is, within a few years of the publication of his *Agrarian System*, indicating the urgency with which he was probing the problem since his critique of Wittfogel. Cf. also, Prabhat Patnaik, 'Introduction', in Panikkar, Byres and Patnaik (eds), *The Making of History*, pp. 5–6.

ers were closely linked with and dependent upon these classes. This imposed serious limitations for these elements to act as catalysts of change, the more so as the Mughal decline debilitated the merchant class which had no independent base for its economic activities. In a later article, Habib observed that 'the main difference between India and post-feudal Europe . . . [lies] in the nature of the market for urban craft-products: in India, it was confined to the aristocracy and its dependents, while in Europe it included the rural gentry as well as the emerging middle classes'.[17]

In other words, there were inherent features in the late pre-colonial social formation of India that would have tended to prevent a transition to capitalism along the lines of the European experience. How this social formation would have been transformed had it been allowed to run its course (i.e. had colonialism not intervened), is difficult to say. Even if we were to assume, as does 'revisionist' scholarship on eighteenth-century India, that trade and commerce received a stimulus from the activities of the European trading companies of the 'Vasco da Gama era' and from the rise of regional economies following the collapse of the Mughal empire, we would still have to assess the historical role of colonialism.[18] There has been a tendency among 'revisionist' scholars to downplay the consequences of the Mughal decline and, even more emphatically, the significance of colonial intervention in this period.[19] C.A. Bayly, who may be regarded as the high-priest of the 'revisionist' approach, looks upon regional and local elites, and merchants/bankers, as the main instruments of change in eighteenth-century India. He puts forth three closely inter-related arguments: (i) that the unity of the Mughal empire was largely superficial; (ii) that regional/local economies were doing well due to and following the collapse of the Mughal state; and (iii) that British rule provided new opportunities for merchants/bankers and regional/local elites.[20]

A shift in focus is certainly not unwelcome. Research undertaken in the past few decades has greatly enriched our knowledge of the eighteenth century. We have, for instance, a much better idea about what was going on at the regional and local levels. To draw attention to the commercial activities

---

[17] Habib, 'Introduction: Marx's Perception of India', p. xxx.

[18] The history of late pre-colonial India has been the subject of a lively debate, especially since the 1970s. For a useful, though highly subjective, summary of the debate, see Richard B. Barnett, 'Introduction', in Richard B. Barnett (ed.), *Rethinking Early Modern India*, Delhi: Manohar, 2002.

[19] Some of the prominent 'revisionist' scholars are: Muzaffar Alam, Richard Barnett, C.A. Bayly, Stewart Gordon, Frank Perlin, Sanjay Subrahmanyam, Andre Wink and Burton Stein. For a critical appraisal, see Athar Ali, 'The Mughal Polity: A Critique of Revisionist Approaches', *Modern Asian Studies*, Vol. 27, No. 4, 1993, p. 704.

[20] C.A. Bayly, *Rulers, Townsmen and Bazaars: North Indian Society in the Age of British Expansion, 1770–1870*, Delhi: Oxford University Press, 1992, pp. 10–11, 74–109, 470.

of the eighteenth century and to the decentralization of power in this period as the fulfilment of the aspirations of regional/local elites is one thing; it is quite another to ignore, on the one hand, the crisis of the Mughal social formation, and, on the other, the closure of options for development due to colonial intervention. The specificity of the eighteenth century lies *both* in the loss of power by the Mughals *and* colonial ascendancy. However much one might like to celebrate the coming of age of regional and local elites following the decline of the Mughal empire, the fact is that their performance was marred by the dislocation caused by these two overlapping developments. It is not easy to ignore the fact that we are dealing with a period over which the shadow of colonialism was already looming large, so that one is uncomfortable with the notion of these classes being in a position to consolidate themselves and thus being representative of a continuity from the later Mughal period to the nineteenth century.

Habib, going along with Marx's notion of 'regeneration', conceded that 'colonialism created the groundwork for the emergence of indigenous capitalism'.[21] But then he immediately added that colonialism 'sought to suppress it once it had been born, resulting in a stagnation that concealed not "continuity" but a seething, fundamental contradiction between colonialism and national liberation'.[22] He remained sceptical of the notion that developments of the eighteenth century contained seeds of change that might have set into motion processes culminating in a transition to capitalism.[23] Prabhat Patnaik has summed up succinctly, the originality of his approach: '[I]t broke both from the Asiatic mode of production approach, which could shade into an imperialist perspective, and from the "capitalism-was-growing everywhere" approach, which could shade into an unhistorical petit-bourgeois nationalist perspective'.[24]

Habib has refrained from giving us any hint about his views on the manner in which India in the post-Mughal period might have evolved, had it not come under colonial domination. Obviously, an opinion on this question would be somewhat speculative in nature. However one is curious to

---

[21] Irfan Habib, 'Processes of Accumulation in Pre-Colonial and Colonial India', in Irfan Habib, *Essays in Indian History: Towards a Marxist Perception*, New Delhi: Tulika Books, 2000, first published in 1995, pp. 271–72. The reference here is to Marx's widely quoted statement on the dual historical role of British colonial rule in India: 'England has to fulfil a double mission in India: one destructive, the other regenerating – the annihilation of old Asiatic society, and the laying of the material foundations of western society in Asia' (*New York Daily Tribune*, 8 August 1853). Cf. Habib 'Introduction: Marx's Perception of India', pp. l–liv.

[22] Habib, 'Processes of Accumulation in Pre-Colonial and Coloial India', p. 272.

[23] Ibid., pp. 267–72.

[24] Prabhat Patnaik, 'Introduction', in Panikkar, Byres and Patnaik (eds), *The Making of History*, pp. 5–6.

know if Habib discerns any possibilities for change arising out of the internal dynamics of the conditions prevailing in early eighteenth-century India, especially in light of the extensive research that has become available on this period. Surely, Marxist historiography would have benefited immensely from his insights on the eighteenth century had he been inclined to show a little more patience with the extensive historical material made available by 'revisionist' historiography, the conceptual and ideological limitations of the 'revisionist' framework notwithstanding.

Once the ascendancy of colonialism had been established, colonial plunder over a prolonged period ensured that India, like other colonies, remained backward. Apart from straightforward loot and plunder in various forms after Plassey, the entire land revenue of the East India Company's territories was treated 'as gross profits out of which it could "invest" in Indian goods to be sold throughout the world, the proceeds to be its own net profit'.[25] According to Irfan Habib's estimates, the drain, or colonial tribute, amounted to 9 per cent of the estimated GNP of the Company's territories in the last quarter of the eighteenth century. This in turn amounted to over 2 per cent of the British national income, which works out to about 30 per cent of the net British domestic investment in the same period.[26] That this was precisely the period when the first phase, the cotton phase of the Industrial Revolution had gathered momentum in England can be no coincidence:

> . . . at this crucial stage of the Industrial Revolution, India was furnishing an amount that was almost 30 per cent of the total national saving transformed into capital. The neglect of this factor in discussions of capital formation in England during this period is surprising. One would certainly have to assume complete immobility of capital to suggest that this enormous accession of wealth in the hands of the London merchants and nabobs did not directly or indirectly channel or divert capital into industry to any significant degree whatsoever.[27]

The ideologically convenient neglect of the crucial part played by colonial tribute in the Industrial Revolution served, in the first place, to obscure the extent to which the drain undermined the possibilities, if any, for a transition to capitalism in India arising out of internal developments of the first half of the eighteenth century, and definitely strangulated the Indian economy in the latter half of the eighteenth century, destroying any prospect for the development of capitalism along the lines of the metropolis. Second, it has

---

[25] Habib, 'Processes of Accumulation in Pre-Colonial and Colonial India', p. 274.

[26] Ibid.; Irfan Habib, 'Colonialization of the Indian Economy 1757–1900', in Irfan Habib, *Essays in Indian History: Towards a Marxist Perception*, New Delhi: Tulika Books, 2000, first published in 1995, pp. 304–06.

[27] Habib, 'Colonialization of the Indian Economy 1757–1900', pp. 305–06.

blurred, through obfuscation in economic history, the process whereby the west gained a historical advantage in the modern period over the rest of the world. This raises another question as well, namely, the extent to which colonies are necessary for capitalist accumulation. Rosa Luxemburg had drawn attention to the problem, in Marxist theory, of the realization of surplus value within a 'closed' capitalist system. Whatever the problems with Luxemburg's analysis, and there are quite a few, it has the merit of making non-capitalist sectors (hence colonies) integral to the process of capitalist accumulation itself rather than being 'add-ons'. While somewhat circumspect in accepting 'the essentiality of the non-capitalist market for all enlargement of capitalism', Habib does agree that non-capitalist sectors were 'a major factor in maintaining the tempo of capitalist accumulation'.[28]

A satisfactory answer to the problem of divergence remains elusive. Irfan Habib's writings indicate many of the pitfalls that need to be avoided to make sense of it. He also underlines that we cannot avoid a discussion on the consequences of colonial tribute if we are to even begin attempting an explanation of the inability of India (and Asia, Africa and Latin America, generally) to make the transition to 'advanced' capitalism – something that is unlikely to happen despite the neoliberal project.

[28] Habib, 'Processes of Accumulation in Pre-Colonial and Colonial India', p. 82.

Technology and Economic Progress
in Medieval India

Ishrat Alam

The history of technology in India, especially for earlier periods, has not been a favourite subject of historians in general and it remains an under-studied theme in history. On the one hand, our fast-expanding and vast technical institutes continue to have an impact on the world around, yet very little has been done to place our present technology in a time sequence or to inculcate a sense of social responsibility among our technicians/techologists, which is possible only with an understanding emanating from a realization of their historical function. They have been allowed to conveniently dissociate themselves from the past of their field of work or profession, which in turn has impoverished its present and imperilled its future. This could be partly because of the available material being scanty, and partly because of an inherited reluctance that prevents them from getting closer to labour due to an innate attitude of disdain. The very 'lowliness' and ubiquity of technology make it significant in history but suspect in the academy.

Broadly speaking, technology is the way people do things. Yet, surprisingly, we have only the vaguest notion of technology in India in the medieval period: of how they did things and how they tried to improve upon previously accumulated technical knowledge. How did knowledge of new technology or improvements in previously known technologies of a particular sector of production affect the arts, crafts and economics of the time?[1]

We know that traces of textiles in India can be dated back to Mohenjo-daro, i.e. the Indus Civilization. However, cottonseed has been reported from Mehrgarh.[2] It is well known that Indian textiles have been found in many places in Egypt. Similarly, it is a commonly accepted fact that Indians were trading with far-off places both on the Arabian Sea in the west and the

---

[1] Cf. Shereen Ratnagar, *Makers and Shapers: Early Indian Technology in the Home, Village and Urban Workshop*, New Delhi: Tulika Books, 2007.

[2] Cf. Irfan Habib, *Prehistory, A People's History of India 1*, New Delhi: Tulika Books, in association with Aligarh Historians Society, 2001, p. 54.

Indian Ocean in the east. But what was the nature of the ships which transported the traders to these distant markets? Did the Indian ship-building industry witness any change after its contact with Romans (who came with Alexander), or with the Persians, Arabs, Turks and Europeans subsequently? How did ship-building change in the course of the long, intervening periods? Every textbook on Indian history should include a discussion on such improvements in ship-building and navigation, without which the overseas (largely coastal) trade could not have been established.

What was the level of glass technology in the medieval period of Indian history? Related to this is the history of spectacles, a late thirteenth-century Italian invention,[3] of which we find the first evidence in early sixteenth-century India.[4] No one in the predominantly bespectacled academic world would be critical of the idea that such a technical development is of crucial significance and does much to account for improvements in the standard of education. It enabled people to read more, especially in their mature years.

Therefore, any attempt to study medieval Indian history and its gradual metamorphosis into modern times will be truncated and hence incomplete *per se*, if the technological history of the period is neglected or ignored. Yet there is a lack of interest in the study of the history of technology.

One conceivable reason behind this hesitation among scholars could be the difficulty of delimiting its boundaries, as Lynn White Jr. had once pointed out. Assessing the European situation, he had asserted: 'technology knows neither chronological nor geographical frontiers'.[5] The same is true in the context of attempts to study the history of Indian technology. Lynn White Jr. had pointed out the futility of following the conventional barriers between Greek and Barbarian, Roman and German, Oriental and Occidental. He argued that medieval technology consisted not simply of technical equipment inherited from the Roman–Hellenistic world modified by the inventive ingenuity of the western people, but also of elements derived from three outside sources: the northern barbarians, the Byzantine and Modern Near East, and the Far East.[6] He did not mention India's contribution, presumably owing to the lack of study of Indian technology. Naturally, study of the history of technology is beset with the problem of diffusion from one culture zone to the other. The technological matrix crisscrossed several culture

[3] A.J. Qaisar, *Indian Response to European Technology and Culture*, Delhi: Oxford University Press, 1982.

[4] Iqbal Ghani Khan, 'Medieval Theories of Vision and the Introduction of Spectacles in India, *c*. 1200–1750', in Deepak Kumar (ed.), *Disease and Medicine in India: A Historical Overview*, New Delhi: Tulika Books, 2001, pp. 26–39.

[5] Lynn White Jr., 'Technology and Invention in the Middle Age', *SPECULISM, A Journal of Medieval Studies*, Vol. XV, No. 2, April 1940, p. 143.

[6] Ibid.

zones, and the question of its historicity continues to baffle historians.[7] One uncontested aspect of the history of technology, interestingly, is the reciprocal exchanges (i.e. diffusion) of techniques and technology. Lynn White Jr. contested that most of the crucial inventions, like gunpowder, the compass and printing with cast movable type, were probably not derived from the Far East, and that they were European inventions whence they spread eastward into Islam.[8] But he did not mention that church bells, the cross bow, the fiddle bow, the wheelbarrow, the spinning wheel and the casting of iron were Chinese inventions and importations. Joseph Needham, in his magnum opus, *Science and Civilization in China*, successfully reconstructed the history of Chinese science and technology, and, in the course of elaboration, pointed out the diffusional course of particular elements of technology.

In the case of India, by contrast, there was a general apathy among historians combined with lack of adequate appreciation of the role of science and technology (the latter in particular). If any interest was shown, it was largely episodic or confined to a particular aspect of Indian history, as in the case of ancient archaeological studies where archaeologists have tried to explain certain techniques in the case of stone-tool manufactures. On the other hand, so far as the history of science in India is concerned, we have comprehensive volumes dealing with various aspects.[9] Recently, Irfan Habib has supplemented our knowledge of science in medieval India.[10] Here, we will focus on the history of technology in India and Irfan Habib's assessment of it.

The history of technology in India has been somewhat sidelined from the mainstream study of history. A few chance encounters with technology were not considered as major factors in the historical processes of the ancient and medieval periods of Indian history. The reasons for this neglect could be many, including inadequate source material as well as the lack of attempts to study the usually poorly preserved and often bewildering archaeological remains of mechanically significant artefacts. Even where they are taken notice of, the social and economic implications of such implements are little explored. This apathy on the part of scholars has led to a belief that there

---

[7] An illustration of this can be found in Lynn White Jr., 'Technology and Invention in the Middle Age', pp. 143–56.

[8] Ibid.

[9] D.M. Bose, S.N. Sen and B.V. Subbarayappa (eds), *A Concise History of Science in India*, Delhi: Indian National Science Academy, 1971; Gunakar Mule, *Bharatiya Vigyan ki Kahani* (Hindi), Patna, 1973; Gunakar Mule, *Bharatiya Itihas mein Vigyan* (Hindi), Delhi, 2005.

[10] Cf. Irfan Habib, *Medieval India: The Study of a Civilization*, New Delhi: National Book Trust, 2008: pp. 19–24, dealing with 'Science in Early Medieval India, 600–1200'; pp. 74–80, for science during the Sultanate period (1200–1500); pp. 197–211, for science and technology during the Mughal period (1500–1750).

was little technical innovation/diffusion or economic progress, and the subject suffered as a consequence.

In the European context, Charles Singer, E.J. Holmyard, A.R. Hall and T.L. Williams brought out *A History of Technology* in eight volumes (1956–1984). However, a major failure of this enterprise is that the editors did not examine technology in relation to the socio-economic context of at least the ancient classical world.[11] M.I. Finley, as an answer, tried to study technology in its social context.[12] His startling discovery was that there was lack of technological innovation or economic progress, and hence he concluded that study of the history of technology in its social context was not so important.[13] In contrast to the ancient world, scholars like Marc Bloch, Bertrand Gille and Lynne White Jr. emphasized that the Middle Ages were a period of technological innovation and progress whose parallel could not be found in the earlier period of history.[14] They and, following them, others analysed the relationship between technological progress and social change, and in the process evolved sophisticated and rigorous models for assessment of the history of technology.

In India, work on ancient and medieval technology has progressed in the last six decades since D.D. Kosambi published his *Introduction to the Study of Indian History*.[15] P.K. Gode made significant contributions in the study of the history of technology on the basis of examination of Sanskrit sources. His researches into cosmetics and perfumery, the history of Indian plants including tobacco and maize, mango-grafting, gunpowder, firearms, the stirrup, and carriage manufacture, to name a few subjects, are still considered classical contributions.[16] K.M. Ashraf published his Ph.D. thesis in 1935, in

---

[11] M.I. Finley, 'Technology in Ancient World', *Economic History Review*, second series, Vol. 12, 1959, pp. 120–25.

[12] M.I. Finley, 'Technical Innovation and Economic Progress in the Ancient World', *Economic History Review*, second series, Vol. 18, 1965, pp. 29–45.

[13] Cf. ibid.

[14] Marc Bloch, 'The Advent and Triumph of the Watermill', in *Land and Work in Medieval Europe: Selected Papers*, reproduced in Sabyasachi Bhattacharya and Pietro Redondi (eds), *Techniques to Technology, A French Historiography of Technology*, New Delhi: Orient Longman, 1990; Bertrand Gille, 'Le moulin a eau: Une revolution technique medieval' (French), in *Histoire des Techniques: Techniques et Civilisations*, Vol. 3, Paris, 1954, pp. 1–15; Lynn White Jr., 'Technology and Invention in the Middle Ages'; Lynn White Jr., *Medieval Technology and Social Change*, Oxford: Oxford University Press, 1962; Lynn White Jr., *Medieval Religion and Technology: Collected Essays*, Berkeley: University of California Press, 1978.

[15] D.D. Kosambi, *An Introduction to the Study of Indian History*, Bombay: Popular Book Depot, 1956.

[16] Cf. P.K. Gode, *Studies in Indian Cultural History*, Vol. I, Singhi Jain Series No. 37, Bombay, 1953; Vol. II, Singhi Jain Series No. 38, Bombay, 1954; Vol. III, Poona, 1956; Vol. IV (actually Vol. I), Hoshiarpur, 1961; Vol. V (actually Vol. II), Poona, 1960; Vol. VI (actually Vol. III), Poona, 1960. Gode's forte was his vast knowledge of Sanskrit.

the background of Elliot and Dowson's *History of India as Told by its Own Historians* in which the entire period was depicted as a period of rise and fall of empires, filled with wars and violence alone. Therefore this history projected that there was no scope for writing about social life and institutions. Ashraf's work was an answer to this tendency. He examined the question of technology in the context of larger social history. Detecting a general contempt for ordinary people, he wrote:

> In medieval literature the saying *Al-Awam Kal Anam* (common people are like animals) has been repeatedly recalled. General contempt for ordinary people becomes yet easier in a society wherein for thousands of years a section of the tailors had been given the formal status of *Shudra* and the untouchables, even in a society wherein tens of thousands of untouchables had got them converted to Islam and had got emotionally associated with the ruling strata. Hindu thinkers (for example the author of *Vishnu Purana*) used to dream that Krishna would be reborn and restore *ab initio* the *Varna Ashram* system on the old foundations. In such a society weavers, bird catchers, butchers etc. were looked upon with considerable contempt.[17]

He did not elaborate upon the study of technology, and factors affecting its diffusion or restriction in Indian society.

In this background, Irfan Habib's contribution assumes considerable significance. Habib is a historian of technology and society. He introduced methodological and historiographical sophistication into the discipline of history in India. He has tried to place technology within its historical context and his contributions are profoundly influential in shaping our historical understanding. One major achievement of Habib's historical studies of technology lies in the fact that he places technology in its historical and, if one may say so, broad cultural context.

There has been an enormous emphasis, in the wake of the Industrial Revolution in Europe and the USA, on the need for increased 'innovations' with social and economic significance. In the historiography of technology too, there has been a strong focus on novelty, on radical breaks with the past and a matching shift in the attention of scholars to the history of technology. Irfan Habib, in his *Agrarian System of Mughal India (1556–1707)*, published in 1963, had already shown his interest and familiarity with the subject. Agriculture in much of India was, and is, heavily dependent on irrigation, and in many instances the Indian topography requires that water be lifted out of wells or water courses on to fields lying at higher

---

[17] K.M. Ashraf, 'Attributes of Medieval Muslim Social Life', in *Indian Historiography and Other Related Papers,* translated from Urdu by Jaweed Ashraf, New Delhi: Sunrise Publications, 2006, pp. 54–55.

levels. Water-lifting is a highly labour-intensive activity, and the available labour largely determines the amount of land that can be cultivated. This is evidently a sector where introduction or improvements in water-lifting technology can have an important economic impact; artificial irrigation in India permitted irrigation of land throughout the year apart from the normal monsoon months. During the rainy season from June to mid-September, especially in the northern and eastern parts of the country, the numerous rivers and large river systems inundated their banks and thus rendered the land cultivable by providing enormous supplies of water and silt. After the monsoons, watering could be achieved with artificial irrigation, which in turn rendered the conditions favourable for growing multiple crops.

The earliest water-lifting devices were the bucket and pulley, and the *shaduf/dhenkli*.[18] The former had a high lift but low capacity, and the latter a lower lift but higher discharge rate. Both, however, demanded intensive human labour, and their effectiveness and utility were limited to neighbouring terrain or just above a water course. While presumably there were *cutcha* wells in the villages, at Allahdino (near Karachi) a stone masonry well of the Indus Civilization was found which was possibly used to irrigate lower-lying fields.[19] The Indus Civilization wells were not equipped with pulleys as no trace of pulley has been found.[20] Later, in the *Rigveda* (c. 1000 BC), a distinct reference is made to the pulley-wheel to draw water out of the well.[21] The pulley was relatively late almost everywhere in the world, for example, in Mesopotamia it was in use in the later part of the first millennium BC.[22] The reason for its late arrival was thought to be the necessity of having a spoked wheel and that too made of iron. But neither of these could possibly be true in the case of the Rigvedic reference. First, it was made of stone and not of iron, hence the plausibility of iron can be ruled out; second, knowledge of iron is not attested in India during the Rigvedic period. Thus the Rigvedic pulley was a solid wheel with a hole for a crossbeam to pass through it, and it was presumably arranged on two wooden uprights placed on two sides of the well. The wheel was made in a concave shape for placing the rope that lifted the water container and whose other

[18] Irfan Habib, *The Indus Civilization, A People's History of India* 2, New Delhi: Tulika Books, in association with Aligarh Historians Society, 2002, pp. 24–25.

[19] Ibid., p. 25.

[20] Irfan Habib, *Technology of Medieval India, c. 650–1750, A People's History of India* 20, New Delhi: Tulika Books, in association with Aligarh Historians Society, 2008, p. 9; Irfan Habib and Vivekanand Jha, *The Vedic Age, A People's History of India* 3, New Delhi: Tulika Books, in association with Aligarh Historians Society, 2003, p. 6. See also, Shereen Ratnagar, *Makers and Shapers: Early Indian Technology in the Home, Village and Urban Worshop*, New Delhi: Tulika Books, 2007, p. 30.

[21] Habib and Jha, *The Vedic Age*, pp. 6–7.

[22] Ratnagar, *Makers and Shapers*, p. 31.

end was pulled by a single ox or pair of oxen. Wells equipped with the pulley wheel could irrigate more land than the simple rope-and-bucket well.

This could also be the *chakka vattaka* (turning wheel) of the Buddhist text *Chullavagga Nikaya* (*c.* 350 BC).[23] This brings us closer to identification of the *saqiya*, or, better still, to drawing the distinction between *norea* and *saqiya*, i.e. the so-called 'Persian wheel'. Ananda K. Coomaraswamy was the first to claim that the Persian wheel was known since ancient times in India.[24] It was assumed that the Persian wheel was used in ancient India, though Basham exercised some caution in accepting this view. Dasharatha Sharma assumed that the device was 'known to Indians before the beginning of the Christian era'.[25] He cited references from Jaina texts of eighth–tenth centuries AD.[26] Cowell and Thomas, the two translators of the *Rajatarangini* (AD 1149–50), observed that King Lalitaditya (eighth century) made 'an arrangement for conducting the water of the Vitasta river and distributing it to various villages by the construction of a series of water wheels (*araghatta*)'.[27] Lallanji Gopal cited twelfth-century inscriptions from Marwar that referred to 'Persian wheels' and 'machine wells' as *araghatta* or *arahatta*.[28]

A.P. Usher was the first to draw a distinction between the two forms of water wheels, the 'noria or Egyptian wheel and the chain of pots'.[29] However, it was Needham who provided a detailed distinction between the two forms, with the noria having the containers fixed to the rim of the wheel and the *saqiya* on the rope or chain flung over the wheel; he suggested that the noria was the earliest water wheel known in India and argued that India was possibly the country of its origin.[30] First, Needham traced evidence for the noria in the Hellenistic world in the first century BC and China in the second century AD, and argued that this proximity of dates between two distant civilizations suggested an intermediate source of diffusion. Second, he traced the term *chakkavattaka* (turning wheel) in the *Chullavagga Nikaya*

[23] Habib, *Technology in Medieval India*, p. 9.

[24] Cf. A.L. Basham, *The Wonder that Was India*, London: Sidgwick & Jackson, 1954.

[25] Dasharatha Sharma, Presidential Address, 29th session of the Indian History Congress, Patiala, 1967, *Proceedings of the Indian History Congress*, 1968, p. 41.

[26] Ibid.

[27] Irfan Habib, 'Technological Changes and Society, 13th and 14th Centuries', Presidential Address, Medieval India Section, 31st session of the Indian History Congress, Varanasi, 1969, *Proceedings of the Indian History Congress*, 1970, p. 13.

[28] Lallanji Gopal, 'Textiles in Ancient India', *Journal of Economic and Social History of the Orient*, Vol. IV (i), 1961, p. 69; 'Quasi-Manorial Rights in Ancient India', *Journal of Economic and Social History of the Orient*, Vol. VI (iii), 1963, p. 297. See also Habib, 'Technological Changes and Society, 13th and 14th Centuries', p. 13, footnote.

[29] A.P. Usher, *A History of Mechanical Inventions*, Boston: Beacon Press, 1959, p. 129.

[30] Joseph Needham, *Science and Civilization in China*, Vol. IV (2), Cambridge: Cambridge University Press, 1974, first published in 1965, pp. 356–62.

(*c.* 350 BC) to be the term used for noria. Subsequently, Lallanji Gopal found evidence in the *Panchatantra* (*c.* AD 300) that described a man operating an *araghatta* (*araghattavaha*), literally meaning a wheel with earthen pots (*ghatta*) tied (to the ends of) its spokes (*ara*). The noria became more useful when pots were transferred from the rim or spokes to a rope chain or potgarland (*mala*). The earliest evidence of the 'potgarland' was found in Yasodharman's Mandsor inscription (*c.* 532). Bana (AD 40) frequently refers to this device ('rosary like the rope on which the pots are placed).[31]

Gearing had not surfaced in Bana's time. The wheel was turned by the hand. Irfan Habib has argued that human drive would imply vertical rotation (and hence no gearing), while animal power would imply horizontal rotation, needed gearing to convert horizontal into vertical motion. The well known Mandor frieze (twelfth century AD) indeed shows a wheel with a potgarland worked by two men, with water coming out for camels to drink. Gearing was obviously absent there. The earliest explicit reference to the gearing mechanism of the Persian wheel can be traced to Babur's memoirs (1526–30).[32] Habib suggests that the complete silence in our earlier sources about the presence of apparatus equipped with gearing mechanism clearly indicates that its presence cannot be dated much earlier than 1400.[33] He has also traced the subsequent changes introduced by Akbar.[34]

The subject of water-lifting devices assumes greater significance when we compare it with the developments taking place in the Mediterranean region. There, besides, the bucket and rope and *shaduf*, a new range of water-lifting devices had developed during the Hellenistic period.[35] It is claimed that these various devices revolutionized the opportunities for irrigating land that could not be fed by gravity-flow irrigation systems.[36] These wheels were: (i) the wheel with compartmented rim, powered by men, on a treadmill; (ii) wheel powered by animals turning a capstan connected to the wheel by right-angled gearing (*saqiya*), or (iii) by water-turning paddles on the exterior of the rim (*noria*); and (iv) the wheel with compartmented

[31] Irfan Habib, 'Medieval Technology: Exchanges between India and the Islamic World', *Aligarh Journal of Oriental Studies*, 2 (1–2), pp. 198–203; Irfan Habib, 'Joseph Needham and the History of Indian Technology', *Indian Journal of History of Science*, Vol. 35, No. 3, 2000, pp. 252–57.

[32] Cf. Habib, 'Technological Changes and Society, 13th and 14th Centuries', p. 14. Habib's 'Medieval Technology: Exchanges between India and the Islamic World' (pp. 200–02) is interesting because the author has translated the passage himself leaving no room for any confusion whatsoever.

[33] Habib, *Technology in Medieval India*, p. 12.

[34] Ibid., p. 13.

[35] Cf. Andrew Wilson, 'Machines, Power and the Ancient Economy', *The Journal of Roman Studies*, Vol. 92, 2002, p. 7.

[36] Ibid.

body, or tympanum, powered by men treading the outside of the wheel.[37] The bucket chain or chain of pots looped over a wheel could also be powered either by men on a treadmill or by animals through right-angled gearing.[38]

These inventions remain anonymous. However there are two devices which are attributed to two individuals: (i) the force-pump, to Ctesibius (c. 270 BC); and (ii) the water-lifting screw; to Archimedes (c. 287–212/211 BC). The latter attribution has recently been challenged, however. It has been claimed that the water-lifting screw was invented in the ancient Near East and that Archimedes contributed to its refinement.[39]

Another significant intervention is that of Michael Lewis who argued that some of these devices were invented as early as the mid-third century BC, probably at Alexandria. He sought evidence from Philo's *Pneumatics*, a work that has survived only in Arabic. Philo visited Alexandria in the mid-third century BC;[40] it is believed that he met Ctesibius (fl. c. 270 BC) there and his work appeared around 230 BC after he left Alexandria. It has been claimed that Philo's *Pneumatics* also included material extracted from his lost *Hydragogia* or *Mechanics*, and that he was familiar with the bucket chain, overshot wheel, and perhaps the noria and *saqiya* drive.[41] In an uncontroversial and authentic section of his work, Philo refers to animal-powered and water-powered lifting devices while describing a large Siplson for drainage purposes, a device which he claimed is 'unknown to some who do not know how to lift water from these places except with buckets, as from a well or with other devices that are moved and drawn by animals, or if perchance the extraction is to be done by means of the current of a river or spring flowing towards lower places'.[42]

Philo's familiarity with animal-powered and water-powered lifting devices appears to be confirmed by sources used by Vitruvius for his books on machines (*De Architectura,* Book 10). Wilson's argument is that Vitruvius relied on Philo of Byzantium for his description of water-lifting wheels. Vitruvius had given a list of ten Greek authors who wrote about machines,

---

[37] Ibid.

[38] Cf. J.P. Oleson, 'Water-lifting', in O. Wikander (ed.), *Handbook of Ancient Water Technology*, Leiden, 2000, pp. 207–302.

[39] S. Dalley, 'Nineveh, Babylon and the hanging gardens: cuneiform and classical sources reconciled', *Iraq*, Vol. 56, 1994, pp. 45–58; cited by Wilson, 'Machines, Power and and the Ancient Economy', p. 7.

[40] M.J.T. Lewis, *Millstone and Hammer: The Origins of Water Power*, Hull: University of Hull Press, 1997, pp. 20–21; others place Philo in around 200 BC and Ctesibius to the last quarter of the third century BC.

[41] Ibid., pp. 26–36.

[42] Philo, 5, translated by Lewis, ibid., p. 32; cited by Wilson, 'Machines, Power and and the Ancient Economy', p. 8.

of whom many lived too early for such machines (fourth century BC), or wrote on other subjects like military or medical technology. Therefore the unknown Diphilus and Democles, Philo of Byzantium, Archimedes and Ctesibius remained. Ctesibius wrote about the force pump and not on other lifting devices, and Archimedes wrote about the planetarium alone; therefore, by elimination, Philo was Vitruvius' source for the 'hodmeter, screw, *tympanum*, *rota*, bucket chain, *noria* and water mill'.[43] Therefore, Wilson argues, these water-lifting devices and other machines were already known by the time Philo wrote his *Hydragogia* or his *Machines* at Alexandria; and he suggests that it was highly likely that these machines at least were known in Alexandria in the mid-third century BC, and were in all likelihood invented there.[44] Wilson further strengthens Lewis' arguments for placing the invention of this series of water-lifting devices, both animal-powered and water-powered, somewhere in the decades between 260 and 230 BC. This wave of technological advancement was made possible due to a programme of machine-building related to agricultural development. Around the middle of the third century BC, there occurred a drastic change from Ptolemies' reliance on mercenaries to a newly created class of Greek settlers (*cleruchs*) who were given land grants and could be mobilized in an emergency. Many of them had settled at Fayum. Secondly, in order to attract the Greeks to settle there, a large programme of public works was undertaken to reclaim land by lowering the level of Lake Maeotis, and to extend the existing network of irrigation canals to the fields. It is reported that around thirty to forty new settlements were created in previously unoccupied areas, with an artificial lake of 257 million cubic metres to irrigate 150 km for a second harvest in the spring. Since agriculture in the Fayum depression was totally dependent on irrigation, water had be lifted from the irrigation canals which were lower than the surrounding lands with the help of either the *shaduf* or more efficient water wheels. Wilson suggests that, possibly, there is a link between agricultural development and introduction/invention of water lifting wheels in Egypt during the mid-third century BC.[45] There was considerable royal concern regarding agricultural development in Fayum.[46]

At some point between the first and third centuries AD, possibly, terracotta pots replaced wooden buckets on the *saqiya* and thus rendered it more affordable, as wood was scarce and expensive in Egypt. In archaeological excavations, these pots are frequently encountered in the early fourth century AD in Egypt. Both the papyri and finds of *saqiya* pots attest to the fact that the

---

[43] Lewis, *Millstone and Hammer*, p. 46.
[44] Wilson, 'Machines, Power and and the Ancient Economy', p. 8.
[45] Ibid., p. 8.
[46] Ibid., pp. 8–9.

use of *saqiya* had considerably increased during the fourth century AD.[47] Oleson suggested that the Doocletianic tax relief in irrigated land was inspired by this factor.[48]

In Roman times, the *saqiya* diffused to other areas of the Mediterranean, certainly the Maghreb and probably Spain.[49] The use of wooden buckets suggesting a bucket chain device has been reported from Cosa in Italy from the later second century BC and had reached London by AD 63, within twenty years of the Roman conquest of Britain.[50] It has been dated from the late second or early third century AD onwards in Israel.[51]

These were expensive machines. This is presumably why in papyri from Roman and Byzantine Egypt there are frequent references to such irrigation devices in an estate and how they demanded considerable capital outlay. Nevertheless the *saqiya* eventually reached the New World and can be seen in use in Spain, parts of Egypt and India even now.

In the light of the above facts, Needham's identification of the noria in India as early as the time of the *Chullavagga Nikaya* (350 BC) creates a problem. This wheel could simply have been the pulley wheel. It may also be suggested that the noria could have developed in Egypt first, in the fourth century BC, and from there it reached India, possibly around the same time, through Afghanistan – because Greek influence could be traced at Bhir Mound by the fourth century BC and Sirkap by the second century BC.[52]

---

[47] Ibid., p. 9.
[48] Oleson, 'Water-lifting', pp. 379–80.
[49] Wilson, 'Machines, Power and and the Ancient Economy', p. 9.
[50] Ibid.
[51] Ibid.
[52] John Marshall, *Taxila*, Vol. I, Delhi: Motilal Banarsidass, 1975, first published in 1945, pp. 104, 129.

Was Fathpur Sikri Built and then Abandoned during the Same Reign?

Syed Ali Nadeem Rezavi

It is indeed a great honour to be associated with a work visualized as a tribute to a living legend in the field of history. It brings greater distinction and a sense of pride when that living legend happens to be your supervisor and research guide. It was Irfan Habib who led me from the 'middle classes', the architecture and the urban economic history of the Mughals to the field of Historical and Medieval Archaeology, and the problems and debates relating to Fathpur Sikri.

There have been debates galore as far as Historical Archaeology and Medieval Archaeology in India are concerned. When does the 'historical' period in India in fact start: from the Painted Grey Ware (PGW) Culture (the Vedic period), as Dhavalikar maintains;[1] or does it commence from Buddha and Mahavira so far as northern India is concerned, and from the time of Mauryan rule as far as the south is concerned, as most 'scientific' historians believe?[2] There is also a debate as to the 'purpose' of this archaeology: is it a tool to merely assert one's superior past, or is it 'a tool – a function for which it is so uniquely suited – to reconstruct a people's history'?[3] Another basic issue is whether it is correct or not to use the term 'Medieval Archaeology'.[4]

We know that archaeology is an indispensable aid for studying the historical period. It provides vital access to unrecorded evidence on the state of human culture in the historical phases. It traces the same processes as in the

---

[1] M.K. Dhavalikar, *Historical Archaeology of India*, New Delhi: Books and Books, 1999.

[2] Irfan Habib, 'Unreason and Archaeology: The Painted Grey-Ware and Beyond', *Social Scientist*, Vol. 25, Nos 1–2, January–February 1997.

[3] Irfan Habib, 'Archaeology and People's History', Keynote Inaugural Address, Centre for Archaeological Studies and Training, Eastern India, Kolkata, November 1995; http://castei. org.in/images/irfanhabib.pdf.

[4] For the view that the term is a misnomer, see Jamal A. Siddiqui, 'Medieval Archaeology: The Term and its Application', *Proceedings of the Indian History Congress*, Bodhgaya, 1981. For a contrary view, see Habib, 'Archaeology and People's History'; R.N. Mehta, 'Medieval Archaeology: Approach and Experiences', *Journal of the MS University of Baroda*, Vol. XXVI, 1976–77; Iqtidar Alam Khan, 'Medieval Archaeology in South Asia: A Brief Review', *Proceedings of the Indian History Congress*, Amritsar, 2002.

prehistoric/protohistoric period, with the additional aid of written records. Historical Archaeology is *text-aided archaeology* and is a study of the material remains of the society from the beginning of the historical period. It takes the help of written records in its reconstruction, and tries to elaborate on points that have been left unrecorded or unanswered in the written documents and sources. It also tries to make sense of the material remains in the light of the written records left behind by writers of that age.[5]

Some of the debates and disputes relating to the Medieval Archaeology of India have centred on the medieval city of Fathpur Sikri: for instance, was it a town that was conceived, and which originated, flourished and then declined during a single reign? Or did it continue to be important even after it was 'abandoned' by Akbar as his capital, during subsequent reigns? It is held that the city was designed and built within the span of half a generation and then 'abandoned' in favour of another famous capital, making it a unique example of its kind. Thus, for example, Tieffenthaler,[6] who visited this city (in the late eighteenth century) and found it almost totally abandoned, was constrained to remark that its short life resembled 'a flower that blooms in the morning and withers at night.[7]

Signs of its decay appear to have set in even before it was abandoned by Akbar in 1585 as his *darus saltanat,* when the emperor marched from Fathpur Sikri to Kabul after the death of his cousin Mirza Muhammad Hakim. Although, till 1585, Fathpur was considered a joint capital along with Agra[8] and continued as a mint-town,[9] yet, recent studies point out that by 1580–81 it had stopped uttering gold coins, and by 1581–82 silver and copper coins also became extinct.[10] By 1591 the general population of the town appears to have migrated in search of better avenues. When, in the late months of this year, Allami Faizi, the famous poet of Akbar's time, passed

---

[5] For such an attempt, see, for example, Irfan Habib, 'Fatehpur Sikri: The Economic and Social Setting', in M. Brand and G.D. Lowry (eds), *Fatehpur Sikri,* Bombay: Marg Publications, 1987; Irfan Habib, 'Economic and Social Aspects of Gardens in Mughal India', in James L. Westcoat Jr. and Joachim Wolschke-Bulmahn (eds), *Mughal Gardens: Sources, Places, Representations and Prospects,* Washington: Dumbarton Oaks Research Library, 1996.

[6] Joseph Tieffenthaler, 'La Geographie de Indostan, e'crite in Latin, dans le pays meme', in *Description historique et geographique de l'Inde,* translated into French and edited by Jean Bernoulli, Vol. I, 1786, p. 169.

[7] Cf. M. Brand and G.D. Lowry, *Fatehpur Sikri: A Source Book,* Cambridge, Massachusetts: The Aga Khan Program for Islamic Architecture at Harvard University, 1985.

[8] Account of Ralph Fitch, in W. Foster (ed.), *Early Travels in India, 1583–1619,* London: Oxford University Press, 1921, p. 17.

[9] Bayazid Biyat, *Tazkira-i Humayun wa Akbar,* edited by M. Hidayat Hussain, Calcutta, 1941, p. 373.

[10] Irfan Habib, 'The Economic and Social Setting', in Brand and Lowry (eds), *Fatehur Sikri,* p. 79.

through it an embassy to the rulers of Khandesh and Ahmadnagar, he reported:

> When I arrived at *dar as-saltanat* Fathpur, having first been elevated by kissing the threshold of the palace (*daulatkhana*), I said a prayer for the well-being of His Majesty (Akbar). What can I write about the true condition of the city? The mud buildings (*imarat-i gilin*) have all dissolved into the ground, [although] the stone walls have remained. Having inspected some of the pavilions (*pishkhana-ha*) and private houses *(khalwat khanaha)* from afar and some from close-up, I learnt a moral lesson. Especially so from the house *(khana)* of Mir Falhullah Shirazi and I also went to the pavilion *(pishkhana)* of Hakim Abul Fath Gilani, it too being unique on the world's horizon.[11]

Similar is the comment of William Finch who passed through the city in November 1610, that is, fifteen years after it ceased to be the *darul khilafa* and only five years after Akbar's death. According to him, Fathpur was 'lying like a waste desert; and very dangerous to pass through in the night, the buildings lying waste without any inhabitants'.[12]

This, and much more, has led to the forming of a general impression that Fathpur Sikri was 'abandoned' and 'deserted' soon after it ceased to be the capital of the Mughal empire. A popular thesis that has come to surround this 'abandonment' is that of paucity of water, which has been repeated by almost all textbook writers and even serious historians. This essay, however, endeavours to show that although Fathpur was 'abandoned' as a capital city, (i) it was not due to shortage of water, and (ii) it continued to 'live' and thrive as an imperial Mughal town at least till the reign of Shahjahan.

Let us first deal with the question of availability of water. This problem appears to have been highlighted for the first time by Jahangir in his thirteenth regnal year (AD 1619). While giving the details of the Jami Masjid and the *birka* (underground, covered water tank) constructed in the courtyard of this mosque, Jahangir commented: 'As Fathpur has little water *(kam ab)*, and what there is, is bad *(bad ab)*, this *birka* yields a sufficient supply for the whole year for the members of the family (of Salim Chishti) and for the dervishes who are the *mujawirs* (keepers) of the Masjid.'[13] Khwaja Kamgar Husaini repeats the same, and almost in the same words.[14]

This charge of 'less water' by Jahangir is intriguing indeed, as we find

[11] Allami Faizi, *Insha-i Faizi*, edited by A.D. Arshad, Lahore: Majlis-e-Taraqqi ye Adab, 1973, pp. 84–85.

[12] In Foster (ed.), *Early Travels in India*, p. 149.

[13] Nur al-Din Muhammad Jahangir, *Tuzuk-i Jahangiri*, edited by Saiyad Ahmad, Ghazipur and Aligarh, 1863–64, p. 266.

[14] Kamgar Husaini, *Ma'asir-i Jahangiri*, edited by Azra Alavi, Bombay: Asia Publishing House, 1978, p. 271.

that no source of Akbar's period – whether it be the official chronicles, or Akbar's bitter critic Badauni, or the private letters of the inhabitants of Fathpur during the phase when it was the *darus saltanat* – makes even a passing reference to this. On the contrary, when Babur was preparing to fight his famous battle with Rana Sanga in 1527, he found that 'the well-watered ground for a large camp was at Sikri.[15] The abundance of water at Fathpur was due to the presence of a large water body, which, late during the reign of Akbar, was dammed and given the formal shape of a lake. In a letter written in 1580, Fr. Henriques informed Fr. Peres that: 'about a year ago, in order to improve the city, water has been led in from somewhere to form a sizeable lake which is perennial. All the elephants, horses and cattle drink from it, and it also serves the teeming population for all purposes.'[16]

According to Fr. Monserrate, this lake, which was dammed to supply the city with water, was 'two miles long and halfe a mile wide'.[17] In 1610, William Finch estimated the lake to be two or three '*cos*' in length and found it 'abounding with good fish and wild fowl', and full of *singhara* fruits.[18] When in 1619, Jahangir ordered the lake to be measured, it was found that its circumference was 7 *kos*.[19] During the same year, when he resolved not to kill any living being with his own hands, he ordered 700 antelopes which had been rounded up for hunting to be delivered to the polo ground near the lake where they would remain unharmed.[20] Naturally, he must have known that the water from the lake would sustain such a large number of animals. Sujan Rai Bhandari, writing as late as 1695–96, while describing Fathpur Sikri, mentioned that 'adjacent to it (the city) is a *kulab-i buzurg* which in its length and breadth is 10 *kuroh* from which the people used to draw benefit (during Akbar's period)'.[21]

Surveys of Fathpur Sikri and its environs have further revealed that apart from the lake there were other sources of water supply.[22] There were at least

---

[15] Zahir al-Din Muhammad Babur, *Baburnama*, translated by A.S. Beveridge, reprint, Delhi: Oriental Books, 1970, first published in 1922, p. 548.

[16] In Correia-Afonso (ed.), *Letters from the Mughal Court: The First Jesuit Mission to Akbar (1580–1583)*, Bombay: Gujarat Sahitya Prakash, Anand, 1980, pp. 22–23.

[17] S.J. Monserrate, *The Commentary of Father Monserrate, S.J.*, translated by J.S. Hoyland, London: Oxford University Press, 1922, p. 31.

[18] In Foster (ed.), *Early Travels in India*, pp. 150–51.

[19] Jahangir, *Tuzuk-i Jahangiri*, p. 259.

[20] Ibid., p. 268.

[21] Sujan Rai Bhandari, *Khulasat-ut-Tawarikh*, edited by Zafar Hasan, Delhi: G & Sons, 1918, p. 40.

[22] Explorations and surveys in the vicinity of Fathpur Sikri were conducted intermittently between 1989 and 1999. I am thankful to Anis Alvi, Hussam Haider and Zameer Ahmad of the Archaeology section of the Department of History, Aligarh Muslim University, for assisting me in these surveys, and to Ghulam Mujtaba for taking the required photographs. Zameer Ahmad has made all the plans for me.

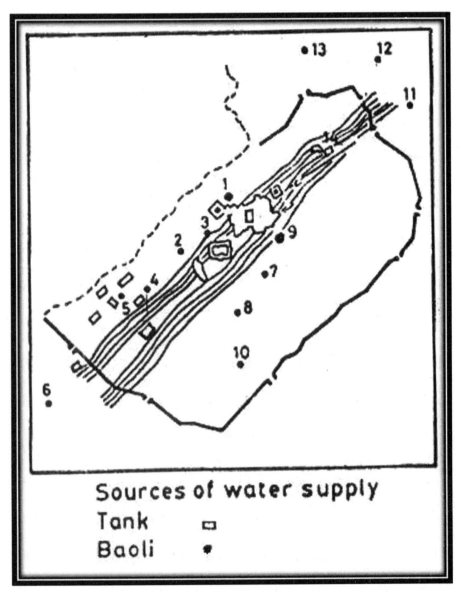

Plan I: Sources of water supply at Fathpur Sikri.

thirteen step wells (*baoli*s) and eight water tanks, apart from a large number of ordinary wells dispersed all over the walled city. (*See Plan I.*) Of these at least one, the so-called 'Hakim's Baoli' (the Southern Waterworks, no. 9 in Plan I), is still functional and caters to the needs of the town's population. (The Fathpur Municipal Corporation has fitted it with pipes and a motor to draw the water.) Apart from that, the *birka* mentioned by Jahángir, as well as the huge water tank (*jhalra*), still cater to the needs of the people in the habitation on top of the ridge and of visitors to the mosque. Most of the other *baolis* are in such a preserved condition that some debris-cleaning could make them functional.[23]

Interestingly, Maryam Makani, the queen-mother, remained stationed at Fathpur even after Akbar left the capital for Lahore in 1585.[24] When Akbar visited Fathpur in August 1601 for a brief period, the queen rejoiced in meeting him.[25] From Abul Fazl's account it appears that the residents of Fathpur Sikri were quite puzzled as to why Akbar was not returning. Hakim Abul Fath Gilani, for instance, reveals his amazement and depression at the fact that Akbar was staying back in Lahore and not coming to Fathpur;[26] had it been because of the paucity of water, he would have been aware of it. In fact, in 1581, he had been urging one of his friends to migrate to this city as, amongst other reasons, commerce (*tijarat*) was 'better pursued at Fathpur, which is the capital city (*pai-takht*)'.[27] Surely, therefore, till that time there was no 'crisis' the city suffered from. We know that throughout its life as a capital city, there was only one water-related crisis, and that was when the so-called *Hauz-i Shirin* (the *kulab* as mentioned by Abul Fazl) burst in 1584. Celebrations were going on and the nobles were busy playing games like *chaupar* (draughts), *shatranj* (chess) and *ganjifa* (cards), when, suddenly:

A side of that little river *(daryacha)* gave way, and the water gushed out in fury. Though by the blessings of the holy personality (Akbar?), none of the courtiers was injured, yet many people of lower rank *(mardum-i pa'in)* suffered loss and many houses built below were carried away by the flood. Inspite of the great crowd of those known to the King, only one, Madadi (in another Ms., Madwi), the *cheetahban* (leopard trainer) lost his life.[28]

However, the tank appears to have been rebuilt soon after. Did this bursting of the tank give rise to the theory of *kam ab* (scarcity of water) at Fathpur Sikri and its 'abandonment' as the *darus saltanat* by Akbar the very next year, in 1585? Had it been so, Badauni would have surely highlighted it. However, Badauni fails to even record this occurrence. Then why did Akbar prefer Lahore over Fathpur Sikri after 1585? Abul Fazl tries to provide an answer:

---

[23] During the course of a survey I found some justification for Jahangir's comment on *bad ab*, in the sense that some of the wells between Baoli No. 4 and No. 2 towards the north had saline (*khari*) water, which was used only for irrigation.

[24] Abul Fazl, *Akbarnama*, Vol. II, edited by Abd al-Rahim, Calcutta, 1873–87, pp. 466, 493, 581.

[25] Ibid., Vol. III, p. 794.

[26] Abul Fath Gilani, *Ruqaat-i Abul Fath Gilani*, edited by Bashir Husain, Lahore, 1968, p. 57.

[27] Ibid., p. 46.

[28] Fazl, *Akbarnama*, Vol. II, pp. 391–92.

(Akbar's) sole thought was that he would stay for a while in the Punjab, and would give peace to the Zabuli land (Afghanistan), cleanse Swad and Bajaur of the stain of rebellion, uproot the thorn of the *tarikiyan* (i.e. the Raushanniyas) from Tirali and Bangash, seize the garden of Kashmir, and bring the populous country of Tatta (Sindh) within the Empire. Furthermore, should the ruler of Turan remove the foot of friendliness, he would send a glorious army thither, and follow it up in person.[29]

This situation had arisen due to the death of Mirza Muhammad Hakim's death. On his return, Akbar had to turn his attention towards the Deccan and proceed against a rebellious son. Thus, it was probably due to political reasons that Akbar left Sikri and, on his return, preferred the security of Agra Fort. J.F. Richards seeks to provide an ideological answer to this question. According to him Akbar preferred Fathpur as long as he remained devoted to the Chishti saints. In 1585 his pilgrimages to Sufi saints stopped. 'Akbar's departure from Fathpur Sikri coincided with a definite change in religious attitude'.[30]

Should this transfer of the capital from Fathpur Sikri to Lahore in 1585, and then subsequently to Agra, be taken as 'abandonment' in the sense in which it is generally perceived? If we take the statements of Allami Faizi and Finch at their face value, then, within years of Akbar's leaving the court at Fathpur Sikri, the whole town had turned to ruins. But then, we have seen, Maryam Makani remained stationed at her palace even after his departure. And Akbar returned to his erstwhile capital, albeit briefly, in 1601, i.e. after ten years of Allami Faizi's account. If we read Faizi's statement carefully, it becomes apparent that he is mentioning the mansions of the nobles who, being ministers and courtiers, migrated along with the emperor. Hakim Fathullah Shirazi had left Fathpur before Akbar went to Lahore, and never returned.[31] Hakim Abul Fath died at the time that Akbar was marching from Kashmir to Kabul, in 1589.[32] Thus he too had died in the same year as Fathullah Shirazi left Fathpur. Further, the *imarat-i gilin* (mud houses) which 'dissolved into the ground' were either houses of the retainers of these nobles, or temporary residences of the service class which would have suffered due to the migration of their employers. We know that at least till 1626, a

---

[29] Ibid., Vol. III, p. 748.
[30] J.F. Richards, 'The Imperial Capital', in Brand and Lowry (eds), *Fatehpur Sikri*, pp. 66–72; J.F. Richards, 'The Formulation of Imperial Authority under Akbar and Jahangir', in J.F. Richards (ed.), *Kingship and Authority in South Asia*, Madison: University of Wisconsin Press, 1978, pp. 255–71.
[31] Shah Nawaz Khan, *Ma'asirul Umra*, edited by Abd al-Rahim and Ashraf Ali, Vol. I, Calcutta, 1888–91, p. 101.
[32] Ibid., p. 559.

'faire' and 'goodly' bazar, with 'pleasant Mansions' on all sides, was flour-
ishing and thriving.[33]

It appears that by 1610, Fathpur had emerged as a trading centre and a
centre for indigo (*nil*) plantation where foreign merchants were attracted.[34]
We know that Fathpur Sikri, situated on the Agra–Ajmer highway, was part
of the indigo-producing tract. We also hear of a large quantity of 'corne'
being grown in this area.[35] We come to know that Fathpur was known for
the manufacture of woollen carpets, apparently through the settlement of
Persian carpet-weavers (*qali-bafs*).[36] This carpet-weaving industry too seems
to have survived the transfer of the capital. Pelsaert says that the carpet
weavers at Fathpur could weave 'fine or coarse' carpets as per the requirement.[37] It was in *consequence* to this that the markets in this town thrived.
Incidentally, none of this would have been possible had there been scarcity
of water. Indigo cultivation, we know, requires large quantities of sweet
water.

Thus it appears that by Jahangir's time, the township was transformed
from a capital city to a merchant town. With the transfer of the capital, the
nobility had migrated along with their retainers to Agra, thus forcing the
contemporary travellers to comment on its 'ruinated' condition and the
fallen-to-the-ground state of the houses. These abandoned nobles' structures were then taken over, near the *bazar-i-sang* (the '*Chaharsuq*', as it is
now known), by members of the mercantile classes, which is indirectly testified to by the accounts of some of the European visitors.[38]

The ruined condition of nobles' houses, however, does not necessarily
point to the urban decay of a Mughal town. Describing the houses of the
Mughal nobility, Pelsaert opined that 'these houses last for a few years only,
because the walls are built with mud instead of mortar'[39] (compare Faizi's

[33] William Finch, in Foster (ed.), *Early Travels in India*, p. 149; Thomas Herbert, *Some Yeares Travels into Africa and Asia the Great*, London, 1638, p. 73, cf. Brand and Lowry (eds), *Fatehpur Sikri*, p. 81.

[34] Finch, in Foster (ed.), *Early Travels in India*, p. 149; John Jourdain, *The Journal of John Jourdain: 1608–17*, edited by W. Foster, London: Hakluyt Society, 1905, p. 168.

[35] Finch, in Foster (ed.), *Early Travels in India*, p. 149; Richard Steel and John Crowther, 'A Journal of the Journey of Richard Steel and John Crowther, 1615–16', in S. Purchas, *Purchas His Pilgrimes*, Vol. IV, Glasgow, 1905, p. 266.

[36] Fazl, Abul, *Ain-i Akbari*, edited by H. Blochmann, Vol. I, Calcutta, 1867–77, p. 50.

[37] Francisco Pelsaert, *Jahangir's India: The Remonstratie of Francisco Pelsaert*, translated by W.H. Moreland and P. Geyl, Delhi: Idarah-i Adabiyati-i Delhi, 1972, first published in 1925, p. 9; Jean de Thevenot and John Francis Careri, *Indian Travels of Thevenot and Careri*, edited by S.N. Sen, New Delhi, 1949, p. 56.

[38] For example, Herbert (*Some Yeares Travels into Africa and Asia the Great*, p. 73); also Finch (in Foster, ed., *Early Travels in India*, p. 149). A survey of the excavated nobles' houses revealed that these large mansions, at some later stage, were divided by additional brick-walls into smaller dwelling units.

[39] Pelsaert, *Jahangir's India*, p. 66.

comment). Elsewhere, commenting on the Mughal ethos and psyche, Pelsaert writes:

> Wealth, position, love, friendship, confidence, everything hangs by a thread. Nothing is permanent, yea, even the noble buildings – gardens, tombs or palaces, – which in each and every city, one cannot contemplate without pity or distress because of their ruined state. For in this they are to be despised above all the laziest nations of the world, because they build them with so many hundreds of thousands [of labourers?] and keep them in repair only so long as the owners live and have the means. *Once the builder is dead, no one will care for the buildings*; the son will neglect his father's work, the mother her son's, brothers and friends will take no care for each other's buildings; everyone tries, as far as possible, to erect a new building of his own, and establish his own reputation alongside that of his ancestors. Consequently, it may be said that if all these buildings and erections were attended to and repaired for a century, the lands of every city, and even a village, would be adorned with monuments; *but as a matter of fact the roads leading to the cities are strewn with fallen columns of stone.*[40]

This passage of Pelsaert is an apt requiem to the information provided by William Finch, Faizi and others. We know that Pelsaert had been to Fathpur Sikri and was aware of its conditions. Thus it was more due to the social ethos and architectural weakness, rather than a mass exodus, that a number of the once-handsome, nobles' mansions collapsed.

Although Fathpur Sikri did not ever attract the same attention later as it did under Akbar, yet it was never totally neglected by the Mughal rulers, at least up till the reign of Shahjahan. Herbert visited the town in the early decades of Jahangir's accession. If he is to be believed, the new emperor, in order to commemorate his victory over his son Khusrau, erected 'a place of hunting' and a 'stately castle' at Fathpur.[41] Jahangir, in his *Memoirs*, testifies to having ordered (in the fourteenth regnal year) the *Chaughan* (polo ground), near the Hiran Minar, to be enclosed and converted into a park to contain a large number of antelopes in order to 'enjoy the pleasure of sport and that at the same time no harm should happen to them'.[42]

From the *Tuzuk-i Jahangiri*, or *Memoirs of Jahangir*, it appears that the emperor did not visit Fathpur in the first twelve years of his rule. It was in

[40] Ibid., p. 56.
[41] Herbert, *Some Yeares Travels into Africa and Asia the Great*, p. 73. However, in 1633, when Peter Mundy visited Fathpur Sikri, he did not see a walled 'Parke or Meadow' meant for the beasts. See Peter Mundy, *The Travels of Peter Mundy in Europe and Asia, 1608–1667*, edited by Richard C. Temple, Vol. II, London: Hakluyt Society, p. 230. But then, see also footnote 46.
[42] Jahangir, *Tuzuk-i Jahangiri*, p. 268.

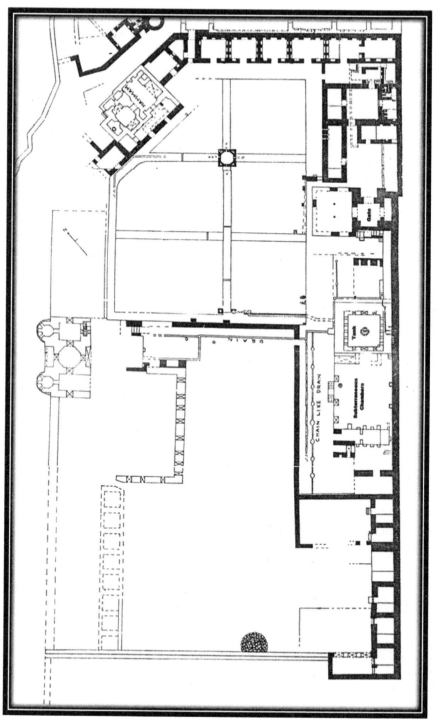

Plan II: Shahjahan's palace.

the last few months of his thirteenth regnal year (AD 1619) that Jahangir headed towards his father's capital city and 'entered the inhabited part of Fathpur'.[43] Prior to that, he remained encamped for eight days on the banks of the Fathpur Sikri lake;[44] due to a plague (*ta'un*) outbreak in the city of Agra,[45] he was forced to stay at Fathpur Sikri for a period of around three-and-a-half months (January to mid-April 1619).[46] It was at Fathpur Sikri that the commencement of the fourteenth regnal year *(Nauroz)*, was celebrated with much festivity.[47] The celebrations of Khurram's twenty-eighth year of birth were also held at this time.[48] On this occasion, Muhammad Salih Kamboh says, the *daulatkhana* (royal palace) of Fathpur was decorated 'according to the annual custom'.[49] On the same day Jahangir showed the prince the grand buildings constructed by Akbar at Fathpur Sikri.[50]

From the account of Jahangir's visit to Sikri in 1619, it appears that a number of grandees had their mansions in that city. He mentions that on the invitation of Itimad-ud-Daula and Asaf Khan, he visited their residences.[51] Were these structures only temporary abodes, the abandoned houses of Akbar's nobles? Of his first visit to the house of Itimad-ud-Daula, Jahangir says: 'As the house of Itimadud Daulah was on the bank of a tank (*tal*), and people praised it greatly as a delightfully place and enchanting residence, at his request on Thursday, the 26th *(Bahman)*, an entertainment was held there'.[52] The second visit was after the *Nauroz* celebrations of the fourteenth regnal year, when Itimad-ud-Daula is reported to have decorated his residence, the *tal*, as well as the 'streets both near and far', with all kinds of lights and coloured lanterns.[53] A week later the emperor was entertained in the house of Asaf Khan, which was a fine and pleasant place.[54] These references suggest that these houses in the city had been constructed by their owners themselves. Jahangir appears to have visited Fathpur Sikri only once again, four years later, in 1623.[55]

---

[43] Ibid., p. 260.

[44] Ibid., pp. 259, 260; Mu'tamid Khan, *Iqbalnama-i Jahangiri*, edited by Abdul Haiy and Ahmad Ali, Calcutta, 1868, pp. 122–23; Husaini, *Ma'asir-i Jahangiri*, p. 271.

[45] Jahangir, *Tuzuk-i Jahangiri*, p. 260; Husaini, *Ma'asir-i Jahangiri*, p. 272.

[46] Jahangir had arrived at Sikri in the month *of Safar* and left for Agra on 4th of *Jumadi-ul Awwal*, 1028 AH. See Husaini, *Ma'asir-i Jahangiri*, pp. 271, 277.

[47] Jahangir, *Tuzuk-i Jahangiri*, p. 260; Husaini, *Ma'asir-i Jahangiri*, p. 275.

[48] Jahangir, *Tuzuk-i Jahangiri*, p. 260; Husaini, *Ma'asir-i Jahangiri*, p. 276; Muhammad Salih Kamboh, *Amal-i Salih*, Vol. I, edited by Yazdani, Calcutta, 1912, pp. 126–27.

[49] Kamboh, *Amal-i Salih*, Vol. I, p. 127.

[50] Jahangir, *Tuzuk-i Jahangiri*, p. 260.

[51] Ibid., pp. 263, 266.

[52] Ibid., p. 263.

[53] Ibid., p. 266.

[54] Ibid.

[55] Ibid., p. 458; Husaini, *Ma'asir-i Jahangiri*, p. 367.

Shahjahan paid more attention to Fathpur. Even before his accession, when he rebelled against Jahangir and laid siege to Agra, he made it his camp.[56] After he ascended the throne in 1628, he held the weighing ceremony on the completion of his thirty-eighth year and the beginning of his thirty-ninth year (of age) in the *daulatkhana* of Fathpur Sikri.[57]

In 1635, Shahjahan visited Fathpur Sikri a second time as emperor, and reportedly camped there for a brief period of three days.[58] His subsequent visits were in 1637 and 1643.[59] On all these three visits, the purpose appears to have been to hunt for wild fowls and excursions on the lake 'that equalled the Ab-i Jayhun' (a prominent river near Balkh).

Shahjahan's next visit was in 1644, at a time when the plague once again had spread in Agra. The emperor celebrated the festival of *Id al-Adha* (*Baqr Id*) and offered prayers at the Jami' Masjid. Lahori and Inayat Khan, wrote of these festivities: 'the crowd of people had grown to such an extent that a thronging and milling assembly spilled into the gateway of the Mosque'; during the ensuing stampede one person died and many were injured.[60] Amongst the injured, one was a state guest whom the emperor compensated with a grant of Rs 3000.[61]

This evidence suggests that at least till 1644, a sizeable civic population still inhabited this former capital of the Mughal empire. The sizeable population explains the vibrant bazar Peter Mundy encountered in 1633. Fathpur Sikri's viability is further testified by the fact that in 1645, Mirza Hasan Safavi, a *mansabdar* of 3000/2000, was made its *faujdar* and *jagirdar*.[62]

Some time before 1653, the prestige of Fathpur Sikri was further enhanced when Shahjahan ordered the construction of his palace outside the palaces of Akbar. Muhammad Waris informs us that this *daulatkhana* was built overlooking the banks of the lake.[63] It was here that Shahjahan stayed during his visits of 1653 and 1654.

---

[56] Herbert, *Some Yeares Travels into Africa and Asia the Great*, p. 83; Fray Sebastian Manrique, *Travels of Fray Sebastian Manrique, 1629–1643*, translated by C.E. Luard and H. Hosten, London: Hakluyt Society, 1927, pp. 304, 306, 307.

[57] Abdul Hamid Lahori, *Padshahnama*, edited by K. Ahmad and M.A. Rahim, Calcutta, 1867, Vol. I, Pt. ii, p. 243; Inayat Khan, *Shahjahannama*, edited by W.E. Begley and Z.A. Desai, Delhi: Oxford University Press, 1990, p. 28.

[58] Lahori, *Padshahnama*, Vol. I, Pt. ii, p. 105.

[59] Ibid., p. 276; ibid., Vol. II, p. 344.

[60] Ibid., Vol. II, p. 353; Khan, *Shahjahannama*, p. 305.

[61] Lahori, *Padshahnama*, Vol. II, p. 356.

[62] Ibid., p. 431. Shahjahan visited Fathpur Sikri in this year as well; see ibid., p. 407.

[63] Muhammad Waris, *Padshahnama*, MS. BM. Or. 1675, pp. 244, 285 (transcript in Research Library, Department of History, Aligarh Muslim University). I am thankful to Irfan Habib who pointed out this information to me, and asked me to go and 'locate' the structure. The structure was found exactly where Professor Habib had laid his finger even without visiting the site.

The description given by Waris is brief, yet clear enough to indicate the rough location of this structure. In order to overlook the lake, an imperial building could only have been constructed somewhere on top of the ridge behind the Hiran Minar and the Hathipal (the main entrance of the imperial complex), towards the Jami Masjid and the 'Shaikhupura', the Chishti quarters.

During the course of a survey, I located the Shahjahani *daulatkhana* adjacent to the so-called 'Samosa-Mahal' on the Hathi Pol–Shaikhupura road. The structure had been initially excavated by R.C. Gaur during the course of his National Project on Fathpur Sikri, and labelled as 'Minor Haram Sara'.[64] Situated on the rim of the ridge behind the Jami Masjid, this complex (see *Plan II*) extends down to the plains below, where a subsequent survey revealed a Shahjahani *baoli*, pleasure pavilions and a *chaharbagh*. The affiliations of this complex, as well the structures on the ridge (having a couple of underground chambers) and the pavilions below, with Shahjahan's period become apparent through the profuse carvo-intaglio designs and shell-plaster which are typical of Shahjahan's reign.

The year 1654 appears to have been the last time Shahjahan visited his palace at Fathpur Sikri. By 1656–57, he got involved in the war of succession between his sons, which resulted in his being imprisoned at Agra Fort by his own son, and the future emperor, Aurangzeb.

From this date onwards we hear very little of Fathpur Sikri until decades later when, in 1719, the city again attracted some attention with the coronation ceremony of the captive king Muhammad Shah 'Rangila'.

Thus we see that Fathpur Sikri's decline was a decline in status from a capital city of the empire to that of an ordinary town. Still, it remained an important mercantile centre and a favoured imperial spot at least till the reign of Shahjahan. Till then, as in the age of Jahangir, it survived not only as a place of pilgrimage for the disciples of Shaikh Salim Chishti, but also as an important centre of production of the carpet industry and indigo. It was not a city built and then abandoned during the same reign. More importantly, the change in its status was due to exigencies of the empire and not water scarcity.

---

[64] R.C. Gaur, 'The Archaeology of Urban Mughal India: Excavations at Fathpur Sikri', Presidential Address, Indian History Congress, Santiniketan, December 1988, in R.C. Gaur, *Excavations at Fatehpur Sikri (A National Project)*, New Delhi: Aryan Books, 2000, pp. 17–25.

Political Economy and Theory

Celebrating Irfan Habib at Eighty[1]

Amiya Kumar Bagchi

Time past and time present: great historians continually build new bridges to the past and open new windows for the readers to look into the past. Irfan Habib belongs in the company of the great because, starting with his magisterial treatise on the agrarian system of Mughal India, he has again and again gone into all the types of records available to a historian to try and find the ways in which the fates of Indians have changed over time. He has done this not for some abstraction called the Indian nation, but for Indians as prehistoric forest dwellers, protohistoric tool users, peasants bound by the logic of class societies to surrender the fruits of their labour to the controllers of their means of subsistence, women subjugated into domesticity by the power of class and the ideology of male chauvinism. With the help of a few committed collaborators such as the historians Vivekanand Jha, Shireen Moosvi and Vijay Kumar Thakur, and the geographer Faiz Habib, Irfan Habib has been piloting and writing the bulk of the volumes of the mind-boggling project of *A People's History of India*, of which eight have already been published.

All his (fortunately for us) long and immensely productive life, Irfan Habib has been a conscious Marxist both in his theoretical practice (to use a phrase popularized by Althusser), and in his untiring engagement with the struggles of the Indian people, and of all the oppressed and toiling peoples of the world, against an intolerably unjust social and political order. I do not know whether Habib has used it as an epigraph anywhere in his enormous corpus of writings, but the following satirical statement about the writings of the German idealist followers of Hegel (practitioners of the so-called Critical Criticism) and its rejection by the young Marx and Engels in their first collaborative work, *The Holy Family*, could well serve as a description of his sustained attitude towards history:

---

[1] This paper draws heavily on Amiya Kumar Bagchi, 'Writing Indian History in the Marxist Mode in a Post-Soviet World', *Social Scientist*, Vol. 24, Nos 1–3, January–March 1996, pp. 89–110.

Criticism, which is self-sufficient, and complete and perfect in itself, naturally cannot recognize history as it really took place, for that would mean recognizing the base means in all its mass-like mass nature, whereas the problem is precisely the mass from its mass nature. History is therefore freed from its mass nature, and Criticism, which has a free attitude to its object, calls to history: '*You ought to have happened in such and such a way.*'[2]

In all his writings Habib has remembered the base of all history, the mass of ordinary people who live and love, toil and think, suffer and sing, protest and dance, destroy and build, live in peace with nature even as they try to make use of the wealth of nature. It is that unvarying gaze on the actual lives of human beings that inspires his engagement with the history of cave dwellers, food gatherers and hunters, cultivators and shepherds, plantation slaves and factory labour, keepers of home fires and victims of the gendered division of labour, and the exploited who suffer unbelievable agonies, starve and die and rise up in revolt against the oppressors in a society divided by class, ethnicity, imperial citizens and colonial helots.

Some years back, I had the opportunity of closely reading some of Habib's major essays on Indian history, consciously cast with Marxist methods.[3] I will use that reading here as my major tribute to Habib's praxis as a theorist. But I will add something to that reading to show how a man in his sixties and seventies can continue to grow and surprise younger scholars, not just with his scholarship but with the novelty of view that passionate engagement with living beings can produce.

It was very good to have most of his canonical essays collected within the covers of a single volume for several different reasons.[4] They were very useful to all students of Indian history who have hitherto had to hunt in many different places for those papers. They were doubly useful because they conveyed to us, within a brief perspective, an idea of the vision that drives a historian of the stature of Irfan Habib.

But finally – and this to me was the most challenging reason for feeling excited by the availability of all these riches in one place – they compel us to explicate our reasons for feeling uncomfortable with some of the formulations despite the formidable nature of the scholarship backing them. The task of articulating our disquiet becomes even more difficult when we realize the degree of consistency with which Habib has advanced them over the nearly four decades of scholarly activity that these essays embody. It is not

---

[2] Karl Marx and Frederick Engels [1844], *The Holy Family*, Moscow: Progress Publishers, 1975, p. 16.

[3] Bagchi, 'Writing Indian History in the Marxist Mode in a Post-Soviet World'.

[4] Irfan Habib, *Essays in Indian History: Towards a Marxist Perception*, New Delhi: Tulika Books, 1995.

possible to dismiss any of the formulations on the ground that Habib strays beyond the limits of the centuries which he has chosen as fields for intensive cultivation. For, judging at least by his handling of the materials relating to nineteenth-century India, with which I have some familiarity, his treatment of India of the Ashokan or Vedic period is almost as sure-footed as his treatment of Mughal India.

In his justly famous paper, 'The Social Distribution of Landed Property in Pre-British India: A Historical Survey', first published in 1965, Habib summarizes the work of scholars enquiring into the economic, social and political conditions of India from the age of Mohenjodaro and Harappa through the Vedic and Buddhist ages to the Sultanate and Mughal periods. What is revealed in these pages is the enormous complexity of social and political structures in all the periods for which we have information, and the tortuous nature of changes in these structures. This is no straightforward story of simplicity yielding to complexity, nor of one stage of history leading to a demonstrably higher stage as defined by a higher level of productivity per person in major areas of economic life and, even more importantly, a higher standard of living for the majority of the population. However, this is not a story of changelessness either. Changes took place in the nature of the ruling classes, in their methods of control over the peoples they ruled, in the methods of surplus extraction by both the supreme and the subordinate rulers, and by the other privileged strata of society; private property in different kinds of assets, including land, cattle and slaves or serfs, developed and declined; cities rose and fell into decay; commerce grew for centuries, only to decline as other factors led to ruralization and the crumbling of long-distance trade. For anybody looking for a nice, clean story-line as in a Jane Austen novel, or a story of uninterrupted progress as in Soviet novels of socialist realism, it will all sound like a tale told by an idiot or by a machine that churns out random narratives just like the random numbers of statistics.

However, over the centuries, India absorbed a very large number of immigrants and invaders from abroad, the number of crops grown on cultivated fields grew enormously, the number of crafts multiplied, and the techniques of cultivation changed. Along with these alterations in the demographic, physical and technological landscape, changes took place in the social structure so that the defeated or conquered peoples fitted into that peculiar – and peculiarly Indian – institution, the caste system. The loose classification of people into warriors, priests, merchants and workers became rigidified into *varnasramadharma*, with most of the actual workers being placed at the bottom of the hierarchy as shudras. A further elaboration of this dreadful hierarchy witnessed the creation of the category of *asprishya*, probably in order to incorporate the defeated forest peoples into this all-embracing,

profoundly exclusionary order. Habib discusses these developments in meticulous detail and with a kind of fascinated horror. Most of the time he
describes them with restrained, judicious objectivity. But from time to time,
his hatred of the tricks played by history or, more crudely, by the ruling
classes in their successful imposition of an utterly unjust social order on the
majority of the workers, who were also the oppressed, breaks out of his
judicious narratives.

For example, in his essay on 'Forms of Class Struggle in Mughal India' (a
paper read at the Indian History Congress, 1980), Habib writes:

> At the bottom was the landless proletariat, created in Mughal India not by
> capitalism but by the age-old operation of the caste system for the benefit of
> peasant agriculture. Although the proportion of the menial ('untouchable')
> castes varied from region to region, it is certain they constituted from a sixth
> to a fifth of the rural population; and they were prevented from holding land
> or setting themselves up as cultivating peasants. Living at the brink of starva-
> tion all the time, they formed a reserve, cheaply available to the peasants
> when they needed labour at the time of sowing and harvesting. There are,
> perhaps, few parallels in the world when the oppressors and the oppressed
> majority in society have joined together to keep a minority in such utter
> degradation.[5]

In the same paper, which is one of the best in the whole collection, Habib
brings out the nature of the moral economy of the different classes, and the
differences in the nature of resistance put up by them when that sense of
moral economy was violated. When the exactions of the Mughal state, or
of the zamindars who normally acted as intermediaries for collection of the
land tax and retained a share for themselves, became too onerous, the peasants fled to the territories of rebellious zamindars or to inaccessible forest
areas. Alternatively, they refused to pay the tax and took up arms against
the state. Interestingly enough, peasants living near the seat of Mughal power
were often found to be rebellious. Habib does not tell us whether this was
because the oppressive land-tax demands fell particularly heavily on the
peasants who were under the direct cognizance of the high-ranking *mansab-
dars*, or because the emperor's clothes were more transparent at a closer
range.

The zamindars' resistance was prompted by increases in the exactions of
the state. They could generally count on the support of the peasants over
whom they claimed authority, extending up to ownership of whole groups
of villages. They could also recruit to their side peasants fleeing the territories of loyal zamindars and other zamindars in the neighbourhood belonging

---

[5] Irfan Habib, 'Forms of Class Struggle in Mughal India', ibid., p. 235.

to the same caste. The merchants had their own way of protesting against what they considered to be unjust levies by the state, or by its minions in the name of the state. They would close their shops and bring the business of whole cities to a standstill through a *hartal* until their grievances were redressed. In more extreme cases, they would desert a city or territory in a body.

Irfan Habib gives lists of the major peasant rebellions, some of which started with a remarkably egalitarian ideology. These included the Satnami Revolt in the second half of the seventeenth century, the numerous Sikh uprisings throughout the seventeenth and eighteenth centuries, the Jat Revolt during Aurangzeb's reign, and earlier revolts during Jehangir's rule. Many of these revolts failed, many only ended in the establishment of a new dynasty or the expansion of zamindars under the control of a dominant caste, with no change in the basic social structure. Habib comments on the paradigmatic case of the peasant armies of the Maratha chieftains in the following way:

> Shivaji was not a liberator of the peasants, his administration was no less repressive than that of the Mughals. . . . Indeed, unbearable conditions within his kingdom could hardly do him much harm, for these would, if anything, compel a larger number of peasants to turn to him and serve him as *bargis*. Inevitably, then, as the circle of oppression and depredation on both sides grew, the Marathas went on gaining with their numbers swelling, and the cause of the Mughals was more and more irretrievably lost. And yet while the Mughal empire found, at last, its nemesis, the peasantry found no saviour.[6]

Constantly gazing at the vast panorama of Indian history, and at the way millions and hundreds of millions of peasants were kept in a subhuman condition by all the successive cohorts of their rulers, Habib obviously feels distressed by this ignoble epic of human bondage. He compares the ineffect-uality of Indian peasant revolts and their sparseness with the record of peasant revolts in China, the peasant revolt in England in the fourteenth century, and the peasant wars in Germany around the time of the Protestant Reformation. But while the millennial sadness is understandable, is the judgment about the scale of revolts or their efficaciousness in India quite just? After all, Wat Tyler was killed as a rebel by the mayor of London in the presence of the king and his sacrifice did not usher in a peasants' paradise.[7] None of the peasant revolts in China – not even the great Taiping Revolt of the nineteenth century – changed the social system in China. It required the

---

[6] Ibid., pp. 254–55.

[7] G.M. Trevelyan, *English Social History: A Survey of Six Centuries from Chaucer to Queen Victoria*, London: Longmans, Green, 1944.

final crisis of the *ancien regime* and the vanguard role of the Communist Party for the Chinese peasants to overthrow the old social system. Despite the peasant wars of the sixteenth century, Germany did not get rid of feudalism until Napoleon's armies destroyed the power of the German principalities and demonstrated to the managers of the Prussian war machine that abolition of feudalism made military sense. Finally, in a country in which history-writing was scorned by the scribes (i.e. before the coming of the Turkish conquerors) and the common people were deliberately kept illiterate, we know only of those revolts of the peasants which managed to shatter the carapace of upper-class callousness, and whose record survived the ravages of floods, famines, invasions, and white ants and other greedy devourers of the exiguous pages of our written history.

A sense of darkness, coming out of the terrible annals Habib has done so much to illuminate for us, seems to colour some of his other judgments as well. This applies, for example, to his celebrated essay, 'Potentialities of Capitalistic Development in the Economy of Mughal India', first published in 1969.[8] I will first try to sum up Habib's argument in this very carefully worked out paper, with most of which I agree, and add a little to that part of the argument. Then I will go on to another part of the argument which I believe is inconsistent with Habib's basic conceptual frame.

Habib essentially constructs a three-tier argument in this essay. In the first tier, he seeks to establish that the Mughal revenue system took away a very large proportion of the produce of agriculture, and that, therefore, the monetization of the economy provided little incentive to the peasants, or even to many of the intermediaries, to move towards capitalistic modes of production. After giving a detailed account of the ways in which part of the surplus demanded by the Mughal state could stick to the hands or pockets of the zamindars, *chaudhuris*, *muqaddams* or other intermediaries, Habib concludes that 'the total net amount of produce annually lost by the countryside, without any return, must have amounted to a very large proportion of the total – at least a fourth of it, if not a third or a half'.[9]

The second tier of his argument is to show that since the surplus so extracted was appropriated for the production of superior crops and luxury goods, the proportion of the unproductive labour force to the potential work force must have been much less than the fraction of the rural produce taxed away as land rent. This is regarded by Habib as more favourable to the emergence of capitalism than the other case in which the rulers simply enjoyed the rustic pleasure of aggrandizing the same kinds of goods as the

---

[8] Irfan Habib, 'Potentialities of Capitalistic Development in the Economy of Mughal India', in Habib, *Essays in Indian History*, pp. 180–232.
[9] Ibid., p. 190.

rest of the population consumed. In particular, the concentration of resources in a few hands and their use for production of uncommon commodities
favoured the growth of towns where commerce and artisanal manufacture
could thrive. Habib provides evidence in this essay, and in a later one, which
is a devastating critique of the second volume of the *Cambridge Economic
History of India*,[10] to suggest that cities and towns flourished on a larger
scale in Mughal India than in colonial India.

The third tier of Habib's argument, negating any real possibility of development of capitalism in Mughal India, now comes into the picture. He
provides evidence to show that the caste system was no barrier to the adoption of technical innovations introduced from abroad. (He also claims that
it was not a barrier to domestic innovation, but the evidence for that is
rather scanty for there were few genuine innovations in India of economic
significance during the period he is concerned with.) Especially in towns
and cities, even if there were caste barriers to occupational mobility, there
were many Muslim artisans outside the dominion of the caste system, and
the Mughal authorities could, and did at times, intervene to stop caste or
guild being a hurdle against the learning of new skills. There were also *karkhana*s in which artisans were brought together in order to produce goods –
generally luxury goods – for the households of the emperor's family or the
establishments of other noblemen. There were even private manufactories
in which artisans earned higher wages than in the noble-controlled *karkhana*s. Yet the condition of the wage-earning, or nominally independent, artisans remained extremely precarious.

Habib also discusses the development of merchant capital, banking and
insurance with his habitual grasp of the details. Indian finance was remarkably sophisticated for its times. Yet all this sophistication and almost excessive elaboration were of little avail for the development of a system in which
independent capitalists owning their means of production and employing
propertyless wage earners would provide the main motive force of society.

In such a complex society of at least a hundred million people with a
great deal of regional variation, it is difficult to pick out any simple causal
chain, or even a manageably small cluster of factors, that could be said to
have finally inhibited the growth of capitalism as defined above (which is
also consonant with the sense in which Habib uses the term). But at the risk
of being accused of oversimplification and remaining entirely within the
circle of evidence provided by Habib, I would conclude that there were two
basic sets of factors which, despite the presence of many other facilitating

---

[10] Irfan Habib, 'Studying a Colonial Economy – Without Perceiving Colonialism', *Modern
Asian Studies*, Vol. 19, No. 3, 1985, pp. 355–81; reprinted in Habib, *Essays in Indian History*,
pp. 336–66.

conditions, throttled the growth of capitalism in Mughal India. First, there was the 'power, organization and composition of the ruling class',[11] which Habib regards as having been responsible for the imposition of the extremely exploitative land revenue system. Second, there was the ideological apparatus just below the surface of the central state, but sanctioned and supported by various political practices such as the imposition of a lower burden of land revenue on, and the provision of state subsidies to, *ashrafs*, brahmans and other high-born people, which degraded the majority of the people to beings with only a right to survive in a state hardly superior to that of dumb animals. The permanent degradation of a set of workers as landless and often 'untouchable' serving castes provided a grotesque but highly effective device for keeping the oppressed divided, and, despite the abundance of land, kept their wages below what they would have been in a situation of genuinely free mobility of labour across occupations. The fact that this vast mass of people remained overwhelmingly illiterate also made it easier to keep them permanently degraded.

In the final section of his 'Potentialities of Capitalistic Development', Habib writes:

> In so far as capital, confined practically to the sphere of commerce, had failed to develop any independent basis for itself, its fortunes would lie with the Mughal ruling class, and, after its collapse, with such other classes as imitated or inherited the methods and institutions of that class. Denied, during the eighteenth century, the large market that it had been provided by the Mughal empire, merchant capital had no choice but to atrophy. With this also receded into the background those prominent economic landmarks, which in the better days of the Mughal empire might have been mistaken for capitalistic features.[12]

I am sorry to say that I cannot follow the logic of this argument. If merchant capital was totally subordinate to the basic political and social structure of Mughal India, with no possibility of autonomous development, why should its atrophy be worth noticing any more, let us say, than the decline of the royal *karkhana*s? And, secondly, why should the large market of the Mughal empire have mattered to it, given the fact that its involvement in the actual process of production was not the critical part of its role in the Mughal economy? Moreover, Habib has not provided any evidence indicating that economies of scale in production, organization, finance or learning played any positive or synergistic role in the functioning of the

[11] Habib, 'Potentialities of Capitalistic Development in the Economy of Mughal India', in *Essays in Indian History*, p. 189.
[12] Ibid., p. 232.

Mughal Indian economy. It cannot even be said with confidence that the stability of the Mughal political system provided a culture ensuring the extended reproduction of merchant capital. For, even though the Mughal state realized its land tax in money, the basis for realization of that was a share of the produce. Thus, for example, the merchant as intermediary could not benefit from the inflation of the seventeenth century, since the producer would always be left only with his bare subsistence in most cases, and the merchant could not get a larger share of the total even if the state did not intervene to protect the producer from dispossession.

Let me emphasize that the decline of the Mughal empire ultimately proved to be a disaster for India, for it made it far easier for European powers to take over the country. But, paradoxically enough, the Europeans found it easier to finance the conquest of India precisely because merchant capital and Indian banking did not atrophy in the immediate aftermath of the fall to the centralized Mughal state. (I am talking deliberately about Europeans rather than the British because the modus operandi of the major European powers were essentially the same in eighteenth-century India.)

The break-up of the Mughal empire was largely due to internal causes, peasant revolts being the major factor, as Habib has so authoritatively demonstrated. The process of disintegration provided new opportunities to Indian financiers to aggrandize themselves by advancing money to the successor states, farming their revenues, minting their coins and, in exceptional cases, even setting themselves up as land magnates. But the process also led to a relative decentralization of resources and to the growth of new urban centres such as Lucknow and Poona, Hyderabad and Murshidabad. The retention of resources in the hands of local magnates and zamindars, which, partly under the prodding of Shireen Moosvi's work,[13] Habib admits to have been much larger than he had previously judged it to be,[14] was vastly greater in the days of the crumbling Mughal empire than it was before.

We have to recognize that such decentralization of resources and power held a greater potential for capitalistic development than a solidly monolithic Mughal empire did. This potential was destroyed by the alien conquest, which, like a jujutsu master, utilized the newly powerful Indian financiers for its own advantage. Not only Jagatseth and Omichand in Bengal, but Arjunji Nathji Travadi in Gujarat, and Gopaldas Manohardas based in Benares but operating all over northern and western India, actively financed the British conquest of India.

---

[13] Shireen Moosvi, *The Economy of the Mughal Empire, c. 1959: A Statistical Study*, Delhi: Oxford University Press, 1987.

[14] Habib, 'Potentialities of Capitalistic Development in the Economy of Mughal India', in *Essays in Indian History*, p. 265.

This does not mean, as has sometimes been argued, that colonialism was a joint enterprise of the Indians and the British, that there was an Anglo-*bania* order either in northern India or in Surat.[15] Hyder Ali, Tipu Sultan, the Maratha rulers and finally the Indian peasants-turned-sepoys fought the British again and again, culminating in the Great Revolt of 1857.

Capitalism did not develop in India as an endogenous process. Counterfactuals in history are never fully satisfactory, since we can always think of a different possibility from the one that is being advanced by a particular historian. But the statement that capitalism could not have developed in Mughal, or post-Mughal, pre-colonial India is also a counterfactual statement. Can we be quite certain of that? In order to discuss that fully, we have to take into account paths to capitalist development that Habib has implicitly ruled out of court. First, it is possible for capitalist development to take place without land being concentrated in the hands of great magnates. It has been argued, following some brief formulations of Marx, and the later work of H.J. Habakkuk and Maurice Dobb, that the first and the major anti-feudal revolution in England occurred between the fifteenth and sixteenth centuries, and that was the revolution of the yeomen. The aftermath of the civil war in England then witnessed a landlord revolution and the power of the peasants was curbed. But there is plenty of evidence in England, Scotland and France that peasants were not less quick in introducing profitable innovations than big landlords and capitalist farmers.[16] Habib has cited evidence indicating that *muqaddam*s and other rural Indian equivalents of yeoman farmers were engaged in the cultivation of cash crops. Some evidence has been provided by Frank Perlin that in the Maratha territories, rural magnates were engaged in productivity-raising investment.[17] We should also not dismiss the Jat revolts or the Sikh revolts as producing no results except a larger number of zamindars or other nobles imitating the Mughal magnates. For, the region covered by these revolts is the only major area in northern and northwestern India in which the ideology of upper-caste idleness did not become hegemonic. In its place, what Neeladri Bhattacharya[18] has called the ideology of *khudkasht* came to domi-

---

[15] See, in this connection, Michelguglielmo Torri, 'Surat during the Second Half of the Eighteenth Century, What Kind of Social Order? – A Rejoinder to Lakshmi Subramanian', *Modern Asian Studies*, Vol. 21, No. 4, 1987, pp. 679–710; and 'Trapped Inside the Colonial Order: The Hindu Bankers of Surat and their Business World during the Second Half of the Eighteenth Century', *Modern Asian Studies*, Vol. 25, No. 2, 1991, pp. 367–401.

[16] R.C. Allen, *Enclosure and the Yeoman: The Agricultural Development of the South Midlands 1450–1850*, Oxford: Clarendon Press, 1992.

[17] Frank Perlin, *Unbroken Landscape: Commodity, Category, Sign and Identity*, Aldershot, U.K.: Variorum, 1994.

[18] Neeladri Bhattacharya, 'The Logic of Tenancy Cultivation: Central and South-East Punjab', *Indian Economic and Social History Review*, Vol. 20, No. 2, April–June 1983, pp. 121–50.

nate peasant consciousness. It is not an accident that the green revolution in India achieved its first, and so far its most notable, success in this region.

Carrying this argument one step further, we can refer to the evidence provided by Habib in various places, that there were, in Mughal India, merchants who employed free wage workers to produce commodities for the market. In both rural and urban areas, there was a substantial pool of at least nominally free wage earners who could be employed to produce surplus value. There is no doubt that a very large proportion of the working people were employed unproductively in Mughal India. But the same proposition could be advanced about almost all the countries of Western Europe down to the end to the Napoleonic wars. A very large fraction of that unproductive labour was engaged in supplying the military requirements of various monarchies and empires. The contribution of the armaments-related industries, and the organizational changes in the army and the navy, to the maturing of the ferociously competitive system called capitalism has been rather neglected in the usual Marxist literature. Historians of early modern Western Europe have laid increasing stress on the fact that the failure to establish a so-called universal monarchy in Europe was a principal contributory cause to the pursuit of differentiated national policies in different countries, and in unleashing the competitiveness and warfare that fed on and further stimulated capitalist accumulation.[19] Following this line of thinking, it is possible to argue that the break-up of the Mughal empire was creating a space for decentralized power centres to try and pursue policies that would facilitate primary accumulation by putting-out merchants and those producers who sold directly to the state. Such policies need not have had an all-India spread. After all, initial capitalist growth in Western Europe was also mainly confined to a few pockets of England, to the sea-lashed lands of today's Netherlands, and to Flanders and Brabant. In the Indian case, this possibility is best illustrated by the policies pursued by Tipu Sultan. But the avalanche of colonial rule closed off such choices for a century and a half.

Our argument above will strengthen the old nationalist and anti-imperialist perspective on Indian history which regards colonial rule as a sharp, retarding break. This is a perspective that Habib has advanced with his usual mastery over the historical details, and his usual clarity of vision and logic. (We have to distinguish between a narrow nationalist standpoint whose ultimate objective is to convert the nation into another empire and a

---

[19] W.H. McNeill, *The Pursuit of Power: Technology, Armed Force and Society since* AD *1000*, Chicago: University of Chicago Press, 1982; Amiya Kumar Bagchi, *Perilous Passage: Mankind and the Global Ascendancy of Capital*, Lanham, MD: Rowman & Littlefield, 2005, Delhi: Oxford University Press, 2006, chapters 3 and 4.

nationalist and anti-imperialist standpoint which regards all imperialism as evil, including that practised or aimed at by one's own country. A further distinction may be made between genuinely nationalist objectives and the other type of political agenda which is content to act as a collaborator of an imperialist power.) In three papers collected in his *Essays in Indian History* – namely, 'Processes of Accumulation in Pre-Colonial and Colonial India', 'Colonialization of the Indian Economy 1757–1900' and 'Studying a Colonial Economy – Without Perceiving Colonialism' – in two volumes of *A People's History of India*,[20] and in his Introduction to the volume *Karl Marx on India*,[21] Irfan Habib has delineated the numerous ways in which British rule retarded the economic growth and human development of India, and adversely affected the fortunes of artisans, peasants, nascent Indian industrialists and industrial workers for almost two centuries.

Habib has also led the writing of the history of medieval technology by the Aligarh historians.[22] The work done by the Aligarh school and by others on the history of Indian technology shows that while Indian producers innovated in some basic processes (sugar-making, for example), and absorbed many of the great innovations produced by the Chinese, the Arabs and, later, the Europeans, they also failed to absorb many advances such as printing and the use of navigational instruments. Along with Habib,[23] we will have to continue to search for the reasons why India's pre-colonial rulers, unlike, for example, those of late Tokugawa Japan, seem to have been so inept in trying to learn and diffuse the arts of the Europeans, especially those that might have helped them win in the wars the Europeans unleashed on Indian shores from the second quarter of the eighteenth century. On the other hand, there is no reason to believe that major developments in endogenous technological change are absolutely necessary for winning in capitalist competition in the early stages of capitalist growth. Most of the smaller European countries followed British, French and, later, German advances in technology, with only incremental innovations. This is also true of most of the newly industrializing countries of East Asia in the

---

[20] Irfan Habib, *Indian Economy, 1858–1914, A People's History of India 28*, New Delhi: Tulika Books, in association with Aligarh Historians Society, 2006; *Man and Environment: The Ecological History of India, A People's History of India 36*, New Delhi: Tulika Books, in association with Aligarh Historians Society, 2010.

[21] Irfan Habib, 'Introduction: Marx's Perception of India', in Iqbal Husain (ed.), *Karl Marx on India*, New Delhi: Tulika Books, 2006, pp. xix–liv.

[22] Irfan Habib, 'Capacity of Technological Change in Mughal India', in Aniruddha Roy and S.K. Bagchi (eds), *Technology in Ancient and Medieval India*, Delhi: Sundeep Prakashan, 1986, pp. 1–15; Irfan Habib, *Technology in Medieval India c. 650–1750, A People's History of India 20*, New Delhi: Tulika Books, in association with Aligarh Historians Asspciation, 2008.

[23] Ibid.

post-World War II period. The subjugation of India, and then China, by the European imperialists closed off the option of such followership so long as they remained under imperial dominance. As soon as Indian craftsmen and engineers came in contact with, for example, printing presses and steam engines, they went on to construct machines of their own. But in almost all the cases, in the early nineteenth century, malign colonial policies throttled those initiatives.[24]

Continuing this line of argument, the very success of China and India in creating a better environment for the social reproduction of labour than European countries made them ready victims of the European powers after the latter had gained superiority in the technologies of shipping and war. Even before the formal conquest of India by the British or the subjugation of China by the condominium of European powers, European merchants were using textiles and other manufactures of these two countries to advance the processes of accumulation and expansion of domestic production by emulating the Indian and Chinese techniques. While class differentiation along capitalist lines in England or the Netherlands was largely an endogenous process, colonial surpluses helped greatly in the eventual industrialization of those countries. The cases of Italy and the Netherlands provide as close as one can get to controlled experiments in history towards proving the essential link between colonialism and industrialization in Europe.[25] While Florence, Genoa and Venice emerged as polities ruled by the bourgeoisie before the fifteenth century, only Venice survived as an independent state until the middle of the nineteenth century. Italy was divided between the competing empires (among which the Papacy has also to be included) in the sixteenth century, with the Florentine Medicis becoming the Grand Duke of Tuscany. It again became the cockpit of Europe in the eighteenth century, when the lines of division between the states were redrawn. While advances in science and technology continued from the age of Galileo, and there were also thinkers debating key issues of political economy and sharing the perspective of the French and Scottish pioneers of Enlightenment, the feudal institutions crumbled only slowly, and common people remained largely illiterate and subject to epidemics and famines as in the rest of the world. Procacci had to write a separate chapter, 'Origins and Character of Italian Capitalism', for analysing the re-emergence of Italy – a unified state after

---

[24] Siddhartha Ghosh, *Karigari Kalpana o Bangali Udyog* (in Bangla) (*A Case Study of the Bengali Entrepreneurs and Scientific Workers*), Calcutta: Dey's Publishing, 1988; *Kaler Shahar Kolkata* (in Bangla) (*Calcutta: A City of Machines*), Calcutta: Ananda Publishers, 1991.

[25] Eric Cochrane, *Florence in the Forgotten Centuries*, Chicago: University of Chicago Press, 1973; Giuliano Procacci, *History of the Italian People*, translated from the Italian by Anthony Paul, Harmondsworth, Middlesex: Penguin Books, 1973; Bagchi, *Perilous Passage*, especially chapters 3, 4, 6.

the Risorgimento – as a capitalist nation.[26] The maturing of Italian capitalism also required tightening of the labour market and growth of workers' movements through the migration of a large proportion of Italian workers from the late nineteenth century to the Americas, and especially Latin America, which had shaken off direct rule by Spain and Portugal only to move into the British and US sphere of imperialist domination.[27]

The case of the Netherlands is even more dramatic. Unlike most other regions of Europe, it had been free of vassalage and capitalist entrepreneurs using wage-labour had begun developing from the fourteenth century.[28] The northern provinces of the Spanish Netherlands also became, after their declaration of independence from Spain, the first country in the world to be ruled by the bourgeoisie, and in the seventeenth century it emerged as one of the great powers of Europe. But its economy and population became stagnant in the eighteenth century, and it suffered the indignity of becoming a part of the Napoleonic empire in the late eighteenth century. However, in the European peace settlement of 1815, it not only regained independence, but also the bonanza of return of its colony Indonesia, which had been occupied by the British during the Anglo–French war. The exploitation of Indonesia by the Dutch through the so-called 'cultivation system' pioneered by the Dutch governor, Van den Bosch, and later adaptations by private businesses, provided the critical surplus supporting the Dutch industrialization process from the 1830s.[29]

British publicists and traders such as Anthony Lambert, Lord Lauderdale, Horace Hayman Wilson, J. Crawfurd, Henry St. George Tucker and Robert Knight (the real founder of the Bank of Bengal) were aware that Britain was extracting a tribute from India, and in the process impoverishing India and severely constricting its home market. Then, Dadabhai Naoroji, R.C. Dutt and other nationalist critics of British rule mounted an attack on the whole system of British rule of India. Karl Marx had both welcomed British rule as a harbinger of social transformation and condemned it for a system of exploitation that could be ended only when Indians took control of their own destiny. Irfan Habib has meticulously documented the basic thrust of these

---

[26] Procacci, *History of the Italian People*.

[27] Amiya Kumar Bagchi, *The Political Economy of Underdevelopment*, Cambridge: Cambridge University Press, 1982, chapter 3.

[28] Bas van Bavel, 'The Medieval Origins of Wage Labour in the Netherlands', *The Low Countries Historical Review*, Vol. 125, Nos. 2–3, 2010, pp. 45–79.

[29] Bagchi, *The Political Economy of Underdevelopment*, chapter 4; J.L. Van Zanden, *The Rise and Decline of Holland's Economy: Merchant Capitalism and the Labour Market*, Manchester: Manchester University Press, 1993; J.L. Van Zanden, *The Transformation of European Agriculture in the Nineteenth Century: The Case of the Netherlands*, Amsterdam: VU Uitgeverij, 1994.

arguments and continued to develop his analytical discourse relating to the Marxist view of Indian history.

I have argued recently that under colonial rule, India underwent a two-century-long process of structural adjustment, which moulded the institutions so as not to facilitate capitalist evolution, but to ensure that the imperative of extracting an ever-larger tribute from India and remitting to Britain was never hampered.[30] Let me make it clear that I am not advancing either a conspiracy theory of Indian history under colonial rule or a functionalist view of it. Few Governors-General or Secretaries of State for India ever said, 'We must not allow India to go capitalist.' But few of them said, either, that 'India must become a fully capitalist economy and society.' Those were not their habitual idiom nor the language of discourse of their statecraft. The British ruling classes were operating an apparatus for governing what has been styled as 'gentlemanly capitalism' by Cain and Hopkins,[31] and not some revolutionary regime that derived its inspiration from the pages of *The Communist Manifesto*. It must not, moreover, be forgotten that the greatest bourgeois economist of the twentieth century, John Maynard Keynes, was rebuking Sir Theodore Morrison in 1911 for wishing on India what Keynes considered to be the doubtful fate of becoming an industrialized country. India was finely fulfilling her assigned role of being a supplier of raw materials to the industrialized west and incidentally also generating huge current account surpluses, thus maintaining the equilibrium of the imperial payments mechanism: why would anybody want it different?

Since colonial rule lasted a long time but brought different parts of India under its sway in different periods, its initial impact was felt at different times in different regions and the longer-lasting effects also had some differing characteristics. But certain initial-impact effects were almost universal, as were some of the longer-term effects on Indian society. First, it almost always produced a depression in commerce and artisanal production. Second, it also led to crises of scarcity of the acceptable legal tender and often a decline in the degree of monetization in the economy. It was such a crisis that had induced the East India Company to commission Sir James Steuart to draw up a scheme of banking and finding a paper note substitute for silver, if possible. But since the crisis had been caused in the first place by the massive drain of silver in order to pay the tribute and the fruits of private plunder by the East India Company's servants, and since the tribute had to be paid continually in gold or silver, or in commodities which could be

---

[30] Amiya Kumar Bagchi, 'Introduction', in *Colonialism and Indian Economy*, New Delhi: Oxford University Press, 2010, pp. xv–lii.

[31] P.J. Cain and A.G. Hopkins, *British Imperialism: Innovation and Expansion 1688–1914*, London: Longman, 1993.

easily converted into bullion, a non-convertible note circulation would not have served the Company's purpose. It is no wonder, then, that Steuart's scheme was still-born.

Third, in the nineteenth century, in Bengal and in most other territories which came under British rule, long-term processes of deindustrialization were released. The impact was felt most strongly in territories which had been involved extensively in production for the export market, but no major region that was connected with the more commercialized parts of the Indian economy through regular trade channels was immune to the influence of these processes. It has been claimed that as machine-made yarn became much cheaper compared with *charkha-* or *takli-*spun yarn, it became more economical to produce handloom cloth. Even if this was true, it would still take an enormous expansion of other employment to compensate for the loss of employment of spinners, most of whom were women, and the latter found it very difficult, if not impossible altogether, to obtain alternative wage employment. It has also been claimed that while the finer fabrics declined, the coarser fabrics survived and, in some areas, began to enjoy a degree of rude health. But the coarser fabrics employed less labour per yard and the earnings of a weaver engaged in making them would be less, apart from the fact that the general value of luxury articles of pre-colonial times would have come down very considerably. Moreover, as Habib[32] has demonstrated by putting together the estimates of Ellison,[33] F.J. Atkinson and Peter Harnetty, from the 1820s the production of cotton cloth in India absolutely declined, and per capita it declined even more, while the exports of Indian cotton went up and imports of British cloth contributed increasingly to the cloth consumption of Indians.

Only in southern India there may have been a recovery of handloom-weaving before the last quarter of the nineteenth century, but we should bear in mind that many parts of the Madras Presidency probably suffered absolute depopulation and impoverishment before the 1850s, as that extremely shrewd apologist of British rule, Srinivasa Raghavaiyangar,[34] had pointed out long ago. Thus what we infer from the fragmentary data on these processes is merely a recovery and not reinvigoration of handicraft production, at least until the wide diffusion of the fly-shuttle loom from the first decade of the current century.

Deindustrialization in the shape of decline of handicrafts was a common

---

[32] Habib, *Indian Economy, 1858–1914*, p. 94; Habib, 'Introduction: Marx's Perception of India', in Husain (ed.), *Karl Marx on India*, p. xliv.

[33] Thomas Ellison, *The Cotton Trade of Great Britain*, London, 1886.

[34] S. Srinivasa Raghavaiyangar, *Memorandum on the Progress of the Presidency during the Last Forty Years of British Administration*, Madras: Superintendent Government Press, 1893.

experience in many countries which could not compete with the machine-made products of the British and other pioneering manufacturing industries.[35] However, what distinguishes the experience of a typical colonial country like India from, say, parts of Central Europe under the Austro-Hungarian empire or the new Kingdom of Italy, is that in the latter, the governments concerned initiated and supported many measures for introducing and improving the new technologies, whereas in India, the government often practised policies of reverse protection and industrial learning. Even more importantly, colonialism impeded the growth of an indigenous capitalist class, produced a structure of incentives that discouraged productive accumulation, acted as a depressant on aggregate levels of demand in normal times and leaked a large part of the potential surplus that could have sustained higher levels of productive investment. It has been a ploy of neo-imperialist and neo-colonial historiography to isolate one of the processes mentioned and come out triumphantly by asking counterfactual questions bearing on it. Habib, of course, always asks questions illuminating the overall structure of exploitation under colonialism.

Imperialism produced distortions in class and incentive structures that created a substantial distance between colonial India's development and that of the kind of prototypical capitalism which Marx analysed in *Capital*, Vol. I. To start with, British rulers never tried to transform the most important asset of exploitation, viz. land, into a seat of pure private appropriation and control.[36] The rights of private property in land in India were always subordinated to those of the colonial state. This feature of the colonial property rights system was recognized by Karl Marx in a passage in *Capital*, Vol. III.[37] That the colonial government knew what it was doing is proved by the writings of the more reflective proconsuls in its service, and by its differential treatment of the property rights of European planters developing tea and coffee estates, and holders of rights in land cultivated by peasants. For example, Elphinstone compared the *mirasdari* rights in the territories of the Peshwa with the rights of holders of land in fee simple in England, and he then proceeded to thoroughly subvert such rights through the institution

---

[35] C. Sabel and J. Zeitlin, 'Historical Alternatives to Mass Production: Politics, Markets and Technology in Nineteenth-Century Industrialization', *Past and Present*, No. 108, 1985, pp. 133–76.

[36] Bagchi, *The Political Economy of Underdevelopment*, chapter 4; Amiya Kumar Bagchi, 'Markets, Market Failures and Transformation of Authority, Property and Bondage in Colonial India', in B. Stein and S. Subrahmanyan (eds), *Institutions and Economic Change in South Asia: Historical and Contemporary Perspectives*, Delhi: Oxford University Press, 1996.

[37] Karl Marx [1894], *Capital*, Vol. III, edited by Frederick Engels and translated into English, Moscow: Progress Publishers, 1966., pp. 331–32.

of the *raiyatwari* system.[38] When the colonial state set about promoting tea estates in Assam and the Dooars, it sold land to planters at ridiculously low prices with rights in perpetuity, not circumscribed by the obligation to pay a land tax to the government every year as in the case of the land tenures it operated in areas where Indian peasants cultivated the land. This type of discriminatory land tenure system was introduced by the British wherever European planters and farmers were interested in cultivating the land. (The same type of discrimination in respect of land rights conferred on European settlers as against the 'natives' was practised by the British in the Caribbean islands, in African colonies and in Australia.) The colonial state often invented a communal land tenure system where none had existed before because it lowered their cost of administering the territory and collecting taxes from it. But the authorities provided the European settlers with the luxury of owning land in fee simple.[39]

The British rulers were not simply following a path of least resistance with regard to land rights, and the maintenance of landlord power in the countryside subject to the awe and the authority of the colonial state. This is proved not only by their reinstitution of *taluqdari* rights in Awadh after 1858, on which Habib has laid stress in his 'Colonialization of the Indian Economy', but also by their fresh installation of landlordism in the canal colonies of the Punjab.[40] The systematic exercise of non-market power by the despotic colonial authorities, European mill owners and planters, and by Indian landlords over the vast Indian countryside, influenced the nature of the so-called capitalistic enterprises in India, as I have argued elsewhere.[41] The European owners of capitalist enterprises in most parts of India exercised a collective monopoly power in their specific spheres of operation. It was often immaterial whether those monopolies were sought to be formalized through a planters' association, a traders' association or a jute mills' association. Such formal organizations were sought to be activated often by

---

[38] Amiya Kumar Bagchi, 'Land Tax, Property Rights and Peasant Insecurity in Colonial India', *The Journal of Peasant Studies*, Vol. 20, No. 1, October 1992, pp. 1–49.

[39] For accounts of such differential systems in British colonies in Africa and the Caribbean, see C.K. Meek, *Land Law and Custom in the Colonies*, second edition, with an 'Introduction' by Lord Hailey, Oxford: Oxford University Press, 1949, reprint, London: Frank Cass, 1968; M. Chanock, *Law, Custom and Social Order: The Colonial Experience in Malawi and Zambia*, Cambridge: Cambridge University Press, 1985; M. Chanock, 'A Peculiar Sharpness: An Essay on Property in the History of Customary Law in Colonial Africa', *Journal of African History*, Vol. 32, 1991, pp. 65–88.

[40] See, in this connection, P.H.M. Van den Dungen, *The Punjab Tradition: Influence and Authority in Nineteenth-Century India*, London, 1972; and Imran Ali, *The Punjab under Imperialism, 1885–1947*, Delhi: Oxford University Press, 1989.

[41] Bagchi, 'Markets, Market Failures and Transformation of Authority, Property and Bondage in Colonial India', in Stein and Subrahmanyan (eds), *Institutions and Economic Change in South Asia*.

involving the government, generally when the collective monopoly faced a strong challenge from other competitors, peasants or workers, as the case might be. The peculiar nature of this monopoly was brought out by Burke in the famous Ninth Report on the affairs of the East India Company, when he characterized the commercial operations of the Company and its servants as 'coercive monopoly'. All the changes in the subsequent 170 years of British rule did not alter the substance of that coercion as far as the ordinary Indian was concerned. When the Indian workers of the jute mills on the Hooghly, in their depositions before the Royal Commission on Labour, characterized the (European) mill managers as their *ma–bap*, they were not expressing pre-capitalist values but were referring to the fact of the state-backed, coercive power of the Europeans: as far as the workers were concerned, the mill managers and their minions remained the judge and the jury whenever they found themselves in the dock, literally or figuratively speaking.

In the countryside also, the Indian landlords, European planters and mill owners remained a law unto themselves so long as they functioned within the overall limits set by the unchallengeable authority of the colonial state apparatus. Independent India inherited that apparatus, along with the rule of law available to the better-off sections of the population, i.e. this extra-legal but relatively uncontested power exercised by the landlords, mill owners and functionaries of the state apparatus. Abolishing landlordism and reforming the state apparatus remain two major tasks before democracy can be said to operate in India in the interests of the vast majority of the population. Habib's work can alert his readers about the durability of coercion in India, which is institutionalized through custom as well as law (the Indian Penal Code, for example), through the state apparatus as well as through so-called communitarian sanctions.

The two opening essays in Habib's *Essays in Indian History* and his more recent 'Introduction: Marx's Perception in India',[42] set out Irfan Habib's methodological and ideological credo. In the second essay referred to above, which was written on the occasion of the death centenary of Karl Marx, Habib brings out, with his usual blend of scholarship and analytical acumen, how Marx was often wrong on the actual course of Indian history, and yet how the questions he raised and the potentialities he dared to speculate on were marked by his explosive genius. It took a rare European scholar or political activist in the 1850s even to contemplate the possibility that countries such as India or China would become fully independent nations

---

[42] Irfan Habib, 'Problems of Marxist Historiography' and 'Marx's Perception of India', in *Essays in Indian History*, pp. 1–13 and 14–58; Habib, 'Introduction: Marx's Perception of India', in Husain (ed.), *Karl Marx on India*.

and realize the goals of the French Revolution: goals that were yet to be actualized on the soil of any European country, including France, the country of revolutions. But Marx was clearly wrong on the nature of the village community in India, the absence of private property in land in pre-British India, and the lack of potential of endogenous development of social and political forms in India in the absence of an external intervention in the form of British conquest. In the third essay, Habib has carried out an even more meticulous and sensitive analysis of Marx's writings on India. He has shown how Marx's initial view of the pre-colonial Indian society as an Oriental despotism must be seen as applying only to certain economic aspects of the designation, and neither to the whole polity nor to its long-term dialectics.

In this new analysis, Habib has taken care to point out that the later works of anti-imperialist Marxists such as Lenin and Luxemburg can be seen to have been prefigured in many of the scattered observations of Marx;[43] Marx's failure to apply his own dialectical method was evolving continually, and it is not surprising that later generations would find that some of his remarks about India did not conform to his own method. Until the 1870s, when he studied the societies of India or Russia more attentively and with more first-hand accounts of extra-European lands, he sometimes expressed the prejudices of the educated middle class of Europe: his idea in 1853 that Indian village communities were unchanging over millennia, and were 'semi-barbarian' and 'semi- civilized', are examples of such prejudice. From Habib's own work (and the work of other historians of India between the eleventh and eighteenth centuries) we have learned that money economy, commercialized urban crafts and the development of a merchant community in pre-British India were far more extensive than Marx had any idea of. His method nonetheless provided later analysts with the problematic of figuring out the dialectics of Indian social formations during the period.

If we have to grade societies in terms of their impact on human welfare, then it is difficult to see how one should judge the society Marx was born into: a country that produced Kant, Hegel and Marx, Goethe, Heine and Rilke, Gauss, Riemann, Weierstrass, Cantor, Dedekind and Hilbert, Planck, Einstein and Heisenberg, Bach, Beethoven and Brahms, also produced Hitler and Nazism. We of course celebrate the world's victory over Nazism to which the Germans themselves contributed little, however heroically and tragically a small minority may have resisted Hitler after he had come to power. We also treasure all the contributions of the German people to the

---

[43] Habib, 'Introduction: Marx's Perception of India', in Husain (ed.), *Karl Marx on India*, pp. xl–xlii. See also Prabhat Patnaik, 'Appreciation: The Other Marx', ibid., pp. lv–lxviii.

world's inheritance of literature, philosophy, mathematics, and the natural and the human sciences. We can use Marx's method while realizing that he could not, by the logic of his own argument, entirely escape the influence of his own times. What I have written above is consistent with the first essay in Habib's *Essays in Indian History*, which is on Marxist historiography. Let me simply string together a number of statements from it:

> Marxism sees an innate unity between perception of the past and present practice. This unity implies continuous interaction: as time passes and history (human experience) lengthens, we draw greater lessons from it for the present; and as our recent experience tells us more about the possibilities and limitations of social action, we turn to the past and obtain new comprehensions of it. . . . Research expands and exposes facts we did not know of before: without undue modesty, we can say we know more about India's past than Marx did. . . . More: Marxism, as the ideology of the working class, does not exist alone and in isolation. There are rival interpretations arising all the time. The authors of these interpretations might not accept the basic premises of a class approach; and, therefore, for us to dismiss them as 'bourgeois' and ignore them carries no conviction. They have to be rationally analysed. . . . Long before the present recognition of the virtues of 'plurality', Mao Tse-tung had urged that truth could belong to a minority, and all truths are at first espoused only by a minority. This applies to a revolutionary party as well as society at large. . . . Marxist textbooks often suggest that the 'mode of production', but especially the 'forces of production', represent the 'material base', whereas ideas form a separate superstructure seated on it. But long ago, the archaeologist Gordon Childe in the very title of his work, *Man Makes Himself*, showed that production technology is after all inseparable from ideas. Matter does not create technology; human ideas, reflected in skill, dexterity and science, create it. . . . What happened in the epoch of capitalism and as a consequence of the simultaneous or attendant scientific revolution was the creation of a possibility, re-realized in Marxism, of an approximately closer perception of the mode of production and social relationships with a view to a far more resolute guidance of the 'transformation' or social revolution. It is in this sense that the achievement of the perception by the working class of the real world around it and the potentiality of its own revolutionary role – its 'class consciousness' – has been given such signal importance in Marxist practice. But this surely means that the role of ideas, compared with earlier periods, has been substantially enlarged: blind struggles have been replaced by sighted ones. . . . Marx and Engels were conscious, as shown by many of their statements on the backwardness of European feudal society when compared with contemporary societies in other parts of the world. European feudalism was not necessarily – in terms of commodity production, productivity, etc. – the

most advanced social formation in the world in its day. That it was ultimately transformed into capitalism was by no means due to the development of its internal contradictions alone. Joseph Needham has rightly emphasized the importance of Chinese technological discoveries, viz. paper, printing press, pedals, belt-transmission with fly-wheel, mariner's compass, gun-powder, etc., for the technological developments in late and post-feudal Europe, without which the technological base for the Industrial Revolution would have been inconceivable. Clearly, while human advance has been on a universal scale, different regions in different periods have been ahead of others; China was so clearly ahead of Europe before 1200. . . . All social formations contain con-tradictions; the most important revolve around classes and express themselves in the form of class struggles. . . . There can be class struggles without the participants realizing that they are such. Unfortunately, since many of the uprisings are written about by their opponents, who were partisans of the ruling classes, we have often no means of knowing what the rebels really thought.

These courageous and thoughtful words were first published in 1988, just before the collapse of Soviet-style socialism in the entire Eurasian con-tinent north of China, South and West Asia, and east of the former Federal Republic of Germany. While virtually nobody had foreseen the suddenness and completeness of that collapse, nobody with any acquaintance with the system could have doubted that it was sick and was crumbling from within. Habib's observations could serve as a manifesto for the renovation of Marx-ism.

Habib uses Mao's speeches on 'Correctly Handling Contradictions among the People' and 'Ten Great Contradictions' as his basic text, and picks out contradictions between manual and intellectual labour and that between town and country as particularly relevant for an analysis of actually exist-ing socialism. He also adds contradictions between nation-states within which socialism is embedded as another problem faced by China and (the former) Soviet Union.

We have to recognize that the Soviet system crumbled from within and was not overthrown by external aggression. It has been said that the USA and her allies forced an armaments race on the Soviet Union, and that the latter could not ultimately bear the burden. This is true; but this still does not tell us why the Soviet Union had to match each nuclear warhead with its own warhead, or, if it had to do so, why it failed in that project while the western powers kept at it – especially when the whole bloc of advanced capitalist nations, except for Germany and Japan, seemed to be engulfed in crisis.

We must remember in this context that the Soviet Union had surpassed the NATO bloc in many areas of military technology by the end of the 1950s when Yuri Gagarin became the first astronaut in history, and that in many areas of medicine and health care the Eastern European countries were leading the world. So blaming Stalin and the Gulag for all the subsequent human and military failures will not do. By the early 1970s, in reversal of earlier leads, the average Soviet citizen was dying earlier than his NATO counterpart. The Soviet worker also seemed to be working less and drinking more. The Soviet-bloc countries plainly failed to keep up with the information and media revolution which gave advanced capitalism a new lease of life, even as it created severe problems of adjustment for their firms, workers and government policies. Some years before the Solidarity movement gathered momentum in Poland, that country was already involved in a debt crisis and most of that debt was owed to western financial institutions.

Billions of words have been spent on the roots of the Soviet collapse and billions more will be spent. Certain failures have become glaringly obvious. One of them is the failure of democracy at many different levels. Lenin's formula of 'democratic centralization' was reduced by Stalin to centralized mobilization without democracy, and by his successors to a centralized bureaucracy which gradually lost contact with the people inside and the world outside. The Indian people have had to suffer the consequences of the latter failure on many occasions, but the one that will be etched in their minds for a long time is the vociferous support lent by the Soviet regime to the Emergency imposed by Indira Gandhi. The failure of the Brezhnev regime to keep up with the western powers in civilian and military technology was also linked to the failure of democracy in the state apparatus, and, even more importantly, in the research and production institutions of the society.

The Soviet Union started by according special honours to scientists and teachers, and academicians came to enjoy special privileges. However, it is ironical that in the first state in the world organized in the name of workers, scientists and researchers were more distanced from the productive apparatus than they were in such capitalist states as Germany, Japan and the USA. There was little synergistic interaction between problems faced on the factory floor and their study in scientific laboratories, except in the case of military production. The general insulation of the latter from civilian production also meant that there were few spin-off effects from the defence industries on those catering to civilian consumption and investment. Finally, the paranoid attempt made by Soviet leaders to deny ordinary people and researchers unhindered access to information from the outside world proved not only ineffective with the advent of television and the microchip-based computer, but also highly counterproductive. The people ceased to believe any of the government propaganda even when it was true, and came to regard western capitalism as a new El Dorado. In the meantime, severely restricting the diffusion of electronic gadgets, including the personal computer, meant that nobody could come up with the kind of innovativeness that, for example, led to the creation of the Apple computer. The point about all this is that in the post-Soviet world, no attempt to build a so-called workers' state on the basis of a denial of formal, parliamentary-style democracy can be seriously regarded as a project for building socialism. There can, of course, be struggles for liberation against a repressive, right-wing regime, and in actual conditions of war formal democracy may be violated, but it must be reinstalled as soon as possible. Without being a socialist state and still suffering civic violence because of deep-seated social ills, the post-apartheid Union of South Africa offers a model in this regard. In India, the people inherited a formal democracy and have struggled hard, in the midst of poverty, predatory commercialization and deliberately communalist and chauvinist politics, to sustain that democracy. That democracy will retain many of the characteristics of a semi-feudal society until, at the very least, landlordism is demolished and the people gain universal literacy. But even after that, we will have to struggle hard to see that new authoritarian structures of control are not built up to deny the people real democracy. Domestic monopolies and transnational corporations are some of these authoritarian structures, but many organs of the state and of a 'vanguard' workers' party can also be institutions that stifle democracy.

In the post-Soviet world, new analysis is needed in order to understand the resilience of capitalism. A deeper understanding of finance, information technologies, and the electronic and print media is to be combined with new strategies for defending the poor – peasants, workers, women, and paupers deprived of the right to work and hence to life – and not just conducting wage fights for workers in the organized sector. Some of the Communist parties in India have, under compulsions of electoral democracy, practised some of the tenets of democracy I have sketched above, but they are yet to recognize the need for democracy within their own parties and within organs of the state, and, more importantly, they have to conceptualize their understanding in a consistent manner. Recognizing the power of transnational capital and its footloose character, for example, should not lead to the illusion that transnational finance can deliver a beleaguered state government from the problems of finding finance and entrepreneurship for industrialization when local monopoly capital or the central government will not do so.

If the collapse of the Soviet Union has many lessons for students of socialism, capitalism and their future, that experience should also inform the writing of history. Irfan Habib has already indicated the way when he pleads for a greater recognition of the power of ideas in the era of capitalism (and after). Once the wheel has been invented somewhere in the world, the effort should be to see how its manufacture and use can be taught to the people at large, and not to insulate some native Edison in his state-endowed inventor's shack and get him to reinvent it. This should have been true in the past as it remains true now. What applies to technological artifacts also applies to human institutions. If we compare the ruling classes of Japan, Korea or China with those of pre-British India or today's India, what strikes us is the inability of the latter to learn from the experience of other countries, as compared with the eagerness and discrimination with which our East Asian neighbours learned from the west they very often despised. Should we not study more carefully the influences that prevented Indian rulers and, later on, Indian capitalists from going out and learning from the best sources, instead of sticking to their doomed ways or following the teachings doled out by the colonizer or the locally available European mercenary or agent of Platt brothers of Oldham, as the case might be? Unfortunately, this dependence on the easily accessible foreign guru dogged communist practice also, as R.P. Dutt or (often miscommunicated) pronouncements of Mao Tsetung became the party guidelines. Peasant movements, nationalism or secularism in India followed their own trajectories, and they might be understood better for our own times (for every age has to forge its own understanding of history) if we give up our time-hallowed paradigms and are willing to explore new ones. This does not mean, again, that looking for such paradigms in the wisdom emanating from Parisian cafes or poststructuralist lucubrations in seminars in the USA is not to give in to a new version of the old slavishness.

Irfan Habib continues to surprise and inspire us through his untiring effort both to make narratives of Indian history other than tales told by an idiot, and to reinterpret Marxism and put it to use so that historical narratives become at once academically rigorous and politically relevant. In *Man and Environment (A People's History of India 36)*, for example, he recognizes that human beings in India, as in many other countries, have often had a destructive impact in pre-colonial times, and does not give in to a nativist nostalgia about the pristine culture of India being always protective of nature. Briefly, he covers issues of the linkage between the Nile floods, monsoons and droughts, which have become major areas of research in recent times.[44] At the same time, he also documents how British colonialism, in the search for easy profit and a continually augmentable tribute, destroyed forests, created swamps, and decimated farmers and forest users whose very means of survival were sacrificed in that search. The whole world is now experiencing global warming, environmental disasters such as the

---

[44] See, for example, Stuart Clark, 'What's Up Sunshine?', *New Scientist*, Vol. 206, No. 2764, 12 June 2010, pp. 30–35.

huge oil spill by BP in the Gulf of Mexico, and the terrible havoc wrought on the whole ecological system of Louisiana and the Caribbean caused by the hundreds of oil rigs in the Gulf, exacerbated by the oil spill and the chemical effluents from the factories and industrialized agriculture in the Mississippi valley.[45] India is going through a major food crisis,[46] even as the policies of the central government are producing the largest number of millionaires per trillion dollars of GDP in India. It is extremely important that environmental activists become aware of the threat to life of all kinds that unequal social systems pose,[47] and Habib can help in spreading that awareness.[48]

Irfan Habib's meticulous analysis of Marx's writings on India in his 'Introduction' to the volume edited by Iqbal Husain, in a way, anticipates the attempt to recover what Marx actually wrote in many places.[49] Marx not only had a towering intellect, but also an almost unappeasable passion, till his dying day, for searching out the real histories of the peoples of all counties that attracted his attention. As he read more, his analysis also changed. So there are many apparent inconsistencies and many incomplete analytical constructs in his corpus of writings. In their attempt both to systematize the thoughts of this Promethean intellect and to make it a weapon of struggle for the fast-growing socialist movement in Germany, Engels and many of Marx's other friends and followers smoothed out many of the wrinkles in his writings. But if we remember that faultlines, ruptures and upheavals are essential parts of history, and that a dialectical view of history must recognize those departures from continuity beloved of conservatives, then the wrinkles in Marx's writings are often a sign of where and how to look for and examine the contradictions. Habib's 'Introduction: Marx's Perception of India' is a very good guide to where to look for the symptomatic wrinkles in Marx's writings on India and other countries that were subjugated by European colonialism.

I hope I have been able to indicate at least a few of the thousand and one reasons for celebrating the phenomenon called Irfan Habib at eighty.

---

[45] Rebecca Solnit, 'Diary: After the Oil Spill', *London Review of Books*, 32 (15), 5 August 2010, pp. 28–31.

[46] Utsa Patnaik, 'The Early Kalidasa Syndrome', *The Hindu*, 13 September 2010.

[47] John Bellamy Foster, Brett Clark and Richard York, 'The Midas Effect: A Critique of Climate Change Economics', *Development and Change*, Vol. 40, No. 6, 2009, pp. 1085–97; Servaas Storm, 'Capitalism and Climate Change: Can the Invisible Hand Adjust the Natural Thermostat?' *Development and Change*, Vol. 40, No. 6, 2009, pp. 1011–38.

[48] Habib, *Man and Environment.*

[49] Marcello Musto, 'The Rediscovery of Marx', *International Review of Social History*, Vol. 52, 2007, pp. 477–98.

Misleading Trade Estimates in Historical and Economic Writings

Utsa Patnaik

Introduction

One of the subjects in which Irfan Habib has always shown an enduring interest in his writings over many decades, is the trade that the metropolitan capitalist centre, Britain, carried out with its colonies and in particular with India. His insights into the transfer of tribute from India during the colonial period and the problem of 'realization' of tribute have been particularly illuminating for those studying the subject.[1] Analysing metropolitan trade trends is quite crucial for understanding the processes of the transfer of surplus that took place from colonized and subjugated nations over an immensely long period of time – processes which, by and large, continue to be ignored by scholars of the history of the advanced countries.

While a number of academics have looked at the matter from the angle of our own trade experience and analysed trends in our own trade data, attempts to look systematically at how the transfers from colonies appear in the trade trends of metropolitan centres themselves are conspicuous by their absence. The moment we try to do so, and try to build up a time-series of trade, a very interesting anomaly is observed. The way trade is measured by historians, and by economists quoting these historians, when they are talking about the eighteenth and nineteenth centuries, is different from the way trade is measured in the twentieth century to date. For instance, a large part of the trade with colonies is left out entirely in the way the authorities on British economic history measure British trade. They leave out that part of their imports which were re-exported (and four-fifths of these re-exports were tropical products) completely from what they call 'Imports', and they similarly leave out the same re-exports completely from what they call 'Exports'. Thus their 'Import' figure is actually only that part of imports

---

[1] Irfan Habib, 'Colonialization of the Indian Economy 1757–1900', *Social Scientist*, Vol. 3, No. 8, March 1975; Irfan Habib, 'Studying a Colonial Economy – Without Perceiving Colonialism', *Social Scientist*, Vol. 12, No. 12, December 1984; Irfan Habib, *Essays in Indian History: Towards a Marxist Perception*, New Delhi: Tulika Books, 1995.

retained within the country and their 'Export' is domestic export alone. They then add up the retained imports and the domestic exports, calling this the 'volume of trade' of the country. This is one definition of trade, no doubt, and it is called 'special trade' in the United Nations' classification of international trade statistics.

But this is not the definition of trade that underlies the discussion in textbooks of open economy macroeconomics. Nor do international organizations presenting annual trade data for all the countries in the world use such a definition. A look at any current report from UNCTAD, or the World Bank's *World Development Report*, or IMF reports will show average trade to GDP percentages for some countries exceeding 100. These countries, like Singapore and Hong Kong (later integrated on special terms into China), play such an important entrepôt role that their export as well as import each exceeds their GDP so that average trade (half the sum of exports and imports) is well above their GDP. This can only be possible, of course, if re-exports are being included in measuring imports and exports. The standard definition and measure used in all sources giving trade data is to take Imports to mean Total Imports inclusive of that part of imports, if any, which may be re-exported, and to take Exports to mean Total Exports inclusive of the re-exported part, if any, of imports. Thus re-exports, where they exist, appear twice: both in Imports and in Exports. The sum of the Imports and Exports is the trade of a country. This is the concept of 'general trade' that is always used.

There is no theoretical justification that the historians of British growth have put forward for the special trade measure they use exclusively when giving historical time-series, while ignoring and never presenting the generally accepted and used measure of trade. This omission is not entirely innocent in its implications: it means that a substantial part of colonial trade is being excluded. Yet without this part of the colonial trade, namely the re-exports, a substantial part of the imports into Britain from developing temperate countries in Europe and elsewhere would not have existed, since re-exports paid for these imports. Re-exported goods give command over imports just as domestic exports do, and it is for this reason that whenever possible, much more is imported of goods with an elastic demand in third countries than the importing country itself needs for its own use. Re-exports must not be confused with transit goods merely passing through a country to a different, final destination. Re-exports are imports which are neither consumed nor productively transformed within the importing country, but are warehoused and exported again with a profit margin added. Re-exports are always included in the standard concept of trade known as 'general trade' and defined in the United Nations' *Yearbook of International Statistics*. In the past, re-exports became important whenever particular European countries acquired political control over tropical lands which produced commodities demanded, but not producible at all, in Europe or other temperate lands.

It remains to be explored by other scholars whether not only in Britain but in other countries with colonies as well, such as France and the Netherlands, a similar misguided procedure of measurement may have been followed, which cuts out a substantial part of their colonial trade. We know that in the Netherlands, the share of re-exports in trade over some periods was even higher than in Britain. I am not in a position to comment on this at present, since it requires carefully going through the primary data-series of these countries and analysing what their economic historians have to say.

In an earlier paper,[2] I had reworked and presented the time-series for the period 1694 to 1804 of the constant value trade of Britain, showing the different components of trade entering into total imports and total exports adding up to total trade, which is the general trade concept that can be compared with present-day estimates. The share of export, import and total trade to GDP was also worked out. (See Appendix Tables A1 and A2 for a summary.) I had compared this to the sum of retained imports and domestic exports, the special trade concept exclusively used by the historians of Britain, and shown that there was a very large divergence by 1800. Looking at time-series trade data after that shows that the large divergence continued right up to World War I.

This divergence between general trade and special trade was bound to arise in the British case since, under the Navigation Acts (enacted in Cromwell's commonwealth period of the 1650s), a much larger volume of goods was deliberately brought to the British ports every year than could be absorbed by the country itself. The balance was re-exported; indeed promoting re-exports was an important object of the Acts. For example, we find that the three-year annual average of trade centred on 1800 using the general trade concept (Total Imports plus Total Exports) had reached £82 million, while the estimate of the historians from the same data was only £51 million because they used the special trade concept (Retained Imports plus Domestic Exports). The difference between the two is the re-exports, which had become very large, at nearly £16 million, in terms of constant prices and accounted for 11 per cent of GDP in 1800. Yet they were being excluded twice, both from imports and from exports.

The reason that imports from tropical countries were increasing very fast in this period had to do with the systematization of rent and tax collection

---

[2] Utsa Patnaik, 'New Estimates of Eighteenth-Century British Trade and their Relation to Transfers from Tropical Colonies', in K.N. Panikkar, Terence J. Byres and Utsa Patnaik (eds), *The Making of History: Essays Presented to Irfan Habib*, New Delhi: Tulika Books, 2000.

in the colonies, and the use of tax revenues to purchase goods for export – in the first instance to Britain and for re-export from there to other, final destinations. In the case of slave-run plantations as in the Caribbean, it was slave rent that was taken and exported directly in the form of goods. As I have analysed in detail elsewhere, building on earlier work by scholars,[3] the fact that taxes and rents were embodied in exported goods made their import completely free for the macroeconomy of these metropolitan countries. Despite their incurring an ever-rising import surplus (trade deficits) with the colonies, these deficits did not have to be covered through outflow of specie or borrowing. They created no external liability at all for the metropolis as was the case with their deficits with other sovereign countries. These import surpluses were transfer, not normal trade. They were rationalized through the fiction that they were payment for 'good governance', which is but a euphemism for tribute.

The reason that a substantial part of imported goods from tropical lands was profitably re-exported by Britain was that, like Britain itself, other temperate countries too could not produce these goods at all, while they were prized for direct consumption (sugar, coffee, tea, cotton textiles) and productive transformation (raw cotton, hardwoods, dyes). These goods enjoyed a demand that was elastic with respect to both price and income in the temperate developing countries. Thus there was double benefit: re-exports of tropical goods boosted the external purchasing power of Britain and other metropoles considerably above the level permitted by their domestic exports alone; and the import surplus of tropical goods from colonies was qualitatively quite different from the import surplus from sovereign countries because it created no external liability. The first benefit is obvious to many scholars, but the second and even more important benefit, namely the 'drain' or transfer in the form of unrequited exports, is not generally recognized, only because no conceptual link is made by metropolitan scholars between colonial taxation/rent collection and trade. In reality, the fiscal/rent collection system and the trade system were deliberately directly linked in the case of the colonies. Property systems established in the colonies ensured collection of economic surplus as increasing rents (both slave rents and peasant rents) and taxes, of which a large part was embodied in exports not only directly to the metropolis itself, but thence to other developing economies. The colonies' exports to the rest of the world, in excess of its imports from them, earned foreign exchange that accrued to the metropolis and was not permitted to flow back to the colony.

---

[3] Utsa Patnaik, 'The Free Lunch: Transfer from Tropical Colonies and Their Role in Capital Formation in Britain during the Industrial Revolution', in K.S. Jomo (ed.), *The Long Twentieth Century: Globalization under Hegemony*, Delhi: Oxford University Press, 2006.

Had the authoritative economic historians of Britain, Phyllis Deane and W.A. Cole, who jointly wrote *British Economic Growth: Trends and Structure* in the early 1960s,[4] applied their special trade concept while at the same time giving the general trade figures, there would have been no confusion. But they presented the series given by applying the special trade concept as though it was the only possible concept – without explicitly mentioning that any other concept is used in the literature and without mentioning the large magnitude of re-exports. One of the authors, Phyllis Deane, in her book, *The First Industrial Revolution*, published in 1965,[5] devoted quite a lot of attention to the first aspect: the obvious role of re-exports in purchasing goods from countries which had relatively low or inelastic demand for Britain's own domestically produced exports, because they had a very similar production and cost structure.

Similarly, in the paper jointly authored by Deane with H.J. Habakkuk, presented to the 1962 international conference on W.W. Rostow's idea of 'take-off into self-sustained growth' and later published in the 1965 conference volume,[6] the authors reached the conclusion that the domestic savings rate hardly rose during the Industrial Revolution and that the only sector which showed rapid growth was international trade. They quoted K. Berill who had emphasized the role of trade,[7] and said: 'This is in many ways the most satisfying interpretation of the British experience. Indeed, the evidence that there was a decisive change of momentum affecting the whole economy in the last two decades of the eighteenth century derives almost exclusively from the evidence of the international trade statistics.'[8] Incidentally, the regional Import and Export data the authors presented under Table 2 were surprisingly poorly specified and are open to misinterpretation.[9] They gave a column headed Exports and juxtaposed it to one headed Imports for each region, without specifying that the latter referred to Imports *fob* and not Imports *cif*. A valid trade balance cannot be obtained by subtracting their Imports column from the Exports column, as the unwary reader may be tempted to do.

The discussion by Deane on the importance of trade in British growth,

---

[4] Phyllis Deane and W.A. Cole, *British Economic Growth 1688–1850: Trends and Structure*, reprint, Cambridge: Cambridge University Press, 1969.

[5] Phyllis Deane, *The First Industrial Revolution*, Cambridge: Cambridge University Press, 1965.

[6] H.J. Habakkuk and Phyllis Deane, 'The Take-off in Britain', in W.W. Rostow (ed.), *The Economics of Take-off into Sustained Growth*, New York: Macmillan, 1965.

[7] K. Berill, 'International Trade and the Rate of Economic Growth', *Economic History Review*, April 1960.

[8] Habakkuk and Deane, 'The Take-off in Britain', in Rostow (ed.), *The Economics of Take-off into Sustained Growth*, p. 64.

[9] Ibid., p. 79.

and the role of re-exports, is found to have disappeared completely from the Deane and Cole book which was under preparation at the same time (in Habakkuk and Deane's 1965 paper this book is referred to as *The Course of Economic Growth*, the title no doubt having been changed later to *British Economic Growth*). In fact the authors appeared to be positively embarrassed by the strong surge in imports and re-exports from the last decade of the eighteenth century onwards. Not relating trade in any way to taxes and rents in the colonies, they were unable to explain the surge. They proceeded to eliminate re-exports altogether from their measure of trade. They do not refer to Paul Mantoux who had given, much earlier, the conceptually correct general trade for the eighteenth century, by depicting graphically Total Imports and Total Exports from official Customs House records.[10] Mantoux's import figures were a slight underestimate only because the landed costs of imports were not available to him, so his Total Imports are on *fob* basis and not *cif* basis. His import figures need to be raised, and this would raise his 1800–01 total trade figure by about 15 per cent. The degree of underestimation in Mantoux is small compared to that involved in Deane and Cole's special trade estimate, which needs to be raised in 1800–01 by 60 per cent to obtain the correct general trade estimate.

A serious problem arises from the exclusive use of the special trade concept, because later historians and economists, quoting these authorities on British growth, do not seem to be at all aware of this anomaly and freely compare trade–GDP ratios given by these authorities for earlier periods with the same variable for other countries in recent years, although in fact the conditions of comparability are violated because in the later period the concept of general trade is being applied. As a result, many of the inter-country comparisons of trade openness which are freely made nowadays are not justified and are leading to incorrect inferences. These problematic estimates of the historians of Britain, rather like the contemporary British Petroleum oil slick, has spread into and contaminated the trade to GDP estimates for the earlier period presented even by a careful economist like Simon Kuznets, and thence have spread into the writings of economists of other countries quoting these authorities.

The main purpose of this paper is to show, though actual re-estimation, that a number of propositions regarding the magnitude of metropolitan, in particular British, merchandise trade during the eighteenth to the twentieth centuries, which seem to be widely accepted by historians and economists alike, are in fact highly questionable and even downright incorrect, because the definition of 'trade' used is not comparable with the general trade defi-

---

[10] Paul Mantoux, *The Industrial Revolution in the Eighteenth Century*, London: Methuen, 1961.

nition. The economist who has systematically dealt with and compiled long-term historical GDP growth and trade series for a number of countries is Simon Kuznets, and his figures are widely quoted. In more recent years, the works by Angus Maddison are also quoted for his novel attempts to compare long-term growth trajectories in today's advanced and today's developing countries, to establish when 'the great divergence' began. These authors in turn, since they are mainly compiling data and analysing the data for many countries from diverse sources, rely on the work of the specialist economic historians of the countries they discuss. This paper will look mainly at their presentation of historical trade data, focusing on Kuznets in particular.

Many economists discussing development in their own countries compare the trade to GDP ratios at the beginning of their late industrialization with, what they imagine is the historical fact of, trade to GDP ratios for the early industrializers, and are misled.

Yamazawa,[11] for example, compares Meiji Japan's trade openness with that of Britain using data from Kuznets,[12] and concludes that Meiji Japan had as high a trade–GDP ratio as the 14 per cent that Britain is said to have had in the early eighteenth century. In fact this inference is not correct, as we see from a re-estimation of British trade to GDP ratio in which we obtain 24.5 per cent for the early eighteenth century. The inference is highly implausible and counter-intuitive as well, since the Tokugawa rulers had kept Japan hermetically sealed against trade for over two centuries, until the incursion in 1853 by Commodore Perry of the USA, followed by the first unequal treaty with that country. Britain's history was the exact reverse. It had expanded its trade rapidly from the late sixteenth century onwards, with the formation of monopoly trading companies ranging from the Eastland and Levant Companies in the 1570s, to the Africa and East India Companies by 1600. A century later, by the early eighteenth century, Britain already had substantial colonial possessions, and its trade to GDP ratio was 27 to 28 per cent, double that of early Meiji Japan.

Yamazawa is not entirely to be blamed for his wrong inference that Japan was as trade-open as Britain at a comparable stage, because the source giving the data, namely Kuznets,[13] while he is careful enough to mention that the trade figures for Britain are computed using the special trade concept, is still not precise enough to avoid misunderstanding. He does not define what special trade is, or specify that the concept is not used by any-

---

[11] I. Yamazawa, *Economic Development and International Trade: The Japanese Model*, Honolulu: East–West Center, 1990.

[12] S. Kuznets, 'Foreign Trade: Long-term Trends', *Economic Development and Cultural Change*, Vol. 15, No. 2, Part 2, January 1967, pp. 1–140.

[13] Ibid.

one except the historians of British economic growth, Deane and Cole, and those who quote these authorities. Most of the latter too seem to use the same concept not after careful thought but only by default, merely because these earlier authorities have already used it. They do not present any discussion of the logic, if any, of using only this concept and no other.

Confusion in Kuznets with regard to Magnitude of Trade and Trade–GDP Ratio

Kuznets had given the following data for the trade of England, reproduced in Table 1 exactly. This is a very long table with 44 rows of data, and we have reproduced only the first 3 rows and the 13th which are relevant for the discussion.

Yamazawa[14] quotes the 14.2 per cent of trade to 'Gross Product' figure given by Kuznets and says that Meiji Japan had no lower trade–GDP ratio at the beginning of its modern development. Anyone familiar with the basic British trade data-series will see at once, however, that the Kuznets figures are very large underestimates of actual English trade. By the early eighteenth century the actual trade to GDP ratio was higher by seven-tenths than the figure of 14.2 given by Kuznets. A century later, by the early nineteenth century, again it was 54 and 45 per cent depending on whether we take con-

TABLE 1 *Kuznets (1967), Proportion of English Trade to Gross Product*

Appendix Table1
Foreign Trade Proportions, individual countries, long periods
1.1 England-United Kingdom, 18th century to date (special commodity trade, unless otherwise indicated)

	Proportion to Gross Product (%)		
	Exports	Imports	Total
A. England-Great Britain,18th century, constant prices			
1 Early 18th century (1702–03)	–	–	14.2
2 Early 19th century (1797–1805)	–	–	27.4
UK Current Price volumes			
3. Early 19th century (1797–1805)	12.6	14.8	27.4
13. Late 19th century (1897–1905)	13.3	21.4	34.8

Source: Kuznets, 'Foreign Trade: Long-term Trends', Appendix Table 1. Only the first part of this Table is reproduced here with the same row numbers. Rows 4 to 12 relate to nine-year periods between 1807 and 1895, which have not been reproduced above. These show trade–GDP percentages lying between 27.4 and 34.8.

---

[14] Yamazawa, *Economic Development and International Trade*.

stant or current values, about double the figure of 27.4 that Kuznets gives. By the early twentieth century too, the actual trade to GDP percentage remained much higher than the one-third figure given by Kuznets.

Indeed, it is against common sense and entirely counter-intuitive that a country like Britain, which acquired over two centuries the largest tropical empire the world has seen, and which was the world capitalist leader, should have a *total* trade to gross product ratio which is as low as 27.4 around year 1800, and only just above one-third even a century later, around 1900, after a new and aggressive round of imperialist expansion. The *average* trade to gross product percentages, according to the Kuznets' estimates, work out to 13.7 around 1800 and 17.4 around 1900. One wonders what the point was of all the bloodshed over acquiring a vast tropical empire if, at the end of the day, this was the meagre order of trade openness Britain actually achieved. Reality, however, was very different. Britain was not only far more globally trade-integrated with other countries, both its colonies and sovereign nations, than these estimates suggest, but further, its trade and investment drove the trade of many other countries. The problem lies with the inadequate concepts the academics apply, which do not reflect this reality.

A number of scholars, including R. Davies for the eighteenth to mid-nineteenth century,[15] and Lamartine Yates,[16] apart from Kuznets,[17] for the nineteenth to twentieth centuries, present the time-series data on the commodity composition of British and global trade. Some of their findings are quoted in Kenwood and Lougheed.[18] The proportion of trade in primary products to total global trade was over three-fifths and closer to two-thirds in many periods before World War I. A very high proportion of primary products traded in turn was tropical products – increasing volumes of which were imported by the leading colonizing powers, far in excess of their own absorptive capacity. Re-exports made up a substantial proportion of British and Netherlands exports in particular. So, excluding re-exports when talking of their trade is somewhat like excluding the agricultural sector when talking of the GDP of an agriculture-predominant developing country.

The reader can check out the derivation of my ratios of trade to GDP from the basic data-series attached to each of the tables. I have used the annual series of constant value total imports (*cif*) estimated in Deane and Cole,[19] Appendix 1, Table 85, and the other components of trade (includ-

---

[15] R. Davies, *The Industrial Revolution and British Overseas Trade*, Leicester: Leicester University Press, 1985.

[16] P. Lamartine Yates, *Forty Years of Foreign Trade*, London: Allen and Unwin, 1959.

[17] Kuznets, 'Foreign Trade: Long-term Trends'.

[18] A.G. Kenwood and A.L. Lougheed, *The Growth of the International Economy 1820–1960*, London: Allen and Unwin, 1971.

[19] Deane and Cole, *British Economic Growth 1688–1850*.

ing the Imports at *fob* values from which Imports *cif* were later derived by these authors) are from Mitchell and Deane.[20] Note that the official constant values of imported commodities recorded in the English Customs House ledgers were Imports (*fob*), that is, port of origin cost, and these needed to be converted to landed cost, that is, Imports (*cif*), which Deane and Cole had done in the aforementioned Appendix. The landed cost was 33 to 42 per cent higher than Imports (*fob*) in different years. In Table 1a, my estimates of general trade, namely the Total Imports (*cif*) plus Total Exports, are shown, and the Kuznets figures are given in parentheses for comparison. The figures in square brackets are my calculation of special trade for the periods indicated. Kuznets takes the special trade concept from Deane and Cole, but his estimates are even lower than actual special trade in every year he gives – the reason will become clearer from the discussion. For this

TABLE 1a *Comparison of Kuznets and Patnaik, Proportion of Trade to GDP*

	Proportion to Gross Product		
	Export	Import	Total
England and Wales, constant prices			
1. Early 18th century (1702–1703)	–	–	(14.2)
1# Actual special trade 1702–1703	[7.3]	[10.5]	[17.7]
*1a Early 18th century (1702–03)	9.6	11.4	21.0
*1b Early 18th century (1699–1704)	10.8	13.9	24.7
2. Early 19th century (1797–1805)	–	–	(27.4)
2# Actual special trade 1797–1805	[16.2]	[17.6]	[33.8]
*2a Early 19th century (1797–1804)	26.5	28	54.5
UK: Current price volumes			
3. Early 19th century (1797–1805)	(12.6)	(14.8)	(27.4)
3# Actual Special trade 1797–1805	[13.8]	[21]	[34.8]
*3a Early 19th century (1797–1805)	21.4	24.2	45.6
13. Late 19th century (1897–1905)	(13.3)	(21.4)	(34.6)

Note: Kuznets ('Foreign Trade: Long-term Trends') estimates are shown in parentheses while mine, using the general trade concept (Total Imports *cif* plus Total Exports *fob*), are given in the starred rows. My estimates of special trade are in square brackets. See text for discussion of why the Kuznets estimates are even lower than special trade (Retained Imports plus Domestic Exports). The basic data from Deane and Cole (*British Economic Growth 1688–1850*) and Mitchell and Deane (*Abstract of British Historical Statistics*) used for my estimates are attached in Table 1b. The GDP series in constant prices is available from W.A. Cole, 'Factors in Demand', in R. Floud and D.N. McCloskey (eds), *The Economic History of Britain since 1700*, Vol. 1: *1700–1860*, Cambridge: Cambridge University Press, 1981.

[20] B.R. Mitchell and Phyllis Deane, *Abstract of British Historical Statistics*, Cambridge: Cambridge University Press, 1962.

TABLE 1b *Early 18th Century: Constant Value Data-Series for Table 1a,*
Patnaik General Trade Estimates

Values in constant prices, 1699 to 1704, in £ 000

	1 TM fob	2 TM cif	3 TX 5+6	4 TT 2+3	5 RXM	6 DX	7 RM 2–5	8 SPT 6+7
1699	5621	7622	5225	12847	1570	3655	6052	9707
1700	5840	7902	5812	13714	2081	3731	5821	9552
1701	5796	7878	6241	14119	2192	4049	5686	9735
1702	4088	5572	4274	9846	1144	3130	4428	7558
1703	4450	6014	5510	11524	1622	3888	4392	8280
1704	5329	7261	5527	12788	1804	3723	5457	9180
Total over period	31124	42249	32589	74838	10413	22176	31836	54012
Annual average	5187.3	7041.5	5431.5	12473	1735.5	3696	5306	9002
% to GDP		13.8	10.7	24.5	3.4	7.2	10.4	17.7

GDP average = £51 million

TM fob = Total Imports *fob*	*TM cif* = Total Imports *cif*	*TX* = Total Exports
TT = Total Trade	*RXM* = Re-exported Imports	*DX* = Domestic Exports
RM = Retained Imports	*SPT* = Special Trade	

Note: The trade data are official values which are quantities valued in constant early eighteenth-century prices. Official Imports (*fob*) have been converted to Imports (*cif*) by
Deane and Cole, and both series are shown.

Source: Total Imports *cif* and Retained Imports from Deane and Cole, *British Economic Growth*
1688–1850, Appendix 1, Table 85. Other columns from Mitchell and Deane, *Abstract*
of British Historical Statistics. GDP from Cole, 'Factors in Demand'.

period, the special trade measure gives an annual average of £9 million only, compared to £12.47 million for general trade, so the former has to be raised by almost two-fifths to arrive at the correct trade figure.

Kuznets actually used an unnecessarily complicated and inaccurate procedure for deriving his row 1 figures of Table 1 relating to 1702–03, rather than using the available time-series trade data directly, and he explains his method in the first note below Table 1. He took the proportions of trade to 'Gross Product' estimated using the special trade concept, for the period 1797 to 1805, and did backward extrapolation over nine decades!

> Commodity foreign trade proportions in line 2, col. 3 (assumed the same as line 3, col. 3) is extrapolated back on the basis of rates of growth in volume of foreign trade and real output both in constant prices, taken from Deane and Cole. The rate of growth of foreign trade is the rate for imports (which is lower than the rate for exports).

It is not clear why such a roundabout and inaccurate method as nine decades of backward extrapolation, that too using imports as surrogate for trade, was at all necessary, since all the relevant basic data are directly available from Mitchell and Deane (*Abstract of British Historical Statistics*), as may be seen from Table 1b. If we apply the special trade concept to the years 1702 and 1703, we get the percentages of domestic exports and retained imports shown in rectangular brackets, and these add up to 17.7, compared to the strange Kuznets procedure of nine decades of backward extrapolation giving 14.2 per cent. We may safely jettison for good the latter figure, which has misled Yamazawa and no doubt many other scholars. On the correct general trade measure, we get 21 per cent trade–GDP ratio taking these two years.

Further, it is important to note that even 21 per cent of GDP is not representative of trade in this period, because the particular two years Kuznets took under 'Early 18th Century', namely 1702 and 1703, happened to record unusually low trade volumes, mainly owing to unusually low re-exports. Both the years preceding and those succeeding these particular two years, however, registered higher trade, as may be checked from Table 2a. So I have calculated annual average trade over an alternative longer period for 'Early 18th Century', namely, the six years 1699–1704. We have the constant value GDP figure for 1700 and for 1710 from Cole ('Factors in Demand'), and can calculate the growth rate to interpolate the average value of GDP for the period. The general trade to GDP figure over the six years is 24.5 per cent compared to 21 per cent, taking those untypical two years alone. This is the figure which should be compared with early Meiji Japan's trade–GDP ratio or, for that matter, any other country in the early stage of development.

For the early nineteenth century, again, we find that the correct trade–GDP percentage is very high, though there is a difference in magnitude depending on whether we take constant value trade-series or current value series. Since the basic constant value series in Table 2a ends in 1804, I have taken the annual average of Total Trade for 1797 to 1804, which is £77.3 million. Expressed as a percentage of the 1800 constant value GDP figure in Cole ('Factors in Demand'), which is £141.8 million, we see that the trade was 54.5 per cent of GDP. Compare this to the Kuznets figure of 27.4 per cent only. This figure is not even special trade, which was higher for the concerned period as we will see below.

The Kuznets line 2 with its 27.4 per cent estimate in constant prices has no clear or reasonable basis since this foreign trade proportion is simply, in his own words, 'assumed the same as line 3 column 3', namely, the same 27.4 per cent is taken as constant value trade as he obtains in terms of current value trade for the UK, for the given period 1797 to 1805.

The question is, why was such an arbitrary assumption at all necessary when we have the basic data-series in constant prices as well as in current prices, which I have reproduced in Tables 2a and 2b respectively. True, the constant value series ends in 1804 in the data source, so the last year is missing from the period 1797 to 1805, but dropping one year out of nine years should not affect the proportion greatly. We calculate the special trade and this is £47.927 million, which, divided by 1800 GDP, gives 33.8 per cent. This is higher than the Kuznets figure of 27.4 per cent. At the same time, it is a great deal lower than the correct general trade–GDP percentage taking constant prices, which was 54.5. The special trade calculation is so much lower because it is leaving out twice the re-exports at a time when re-exports were booming, namely, it is excluding trade amounting to 20.7 per cent or over one-fifth of Britain's GDP.

What about the current value trade to GDP percentage for the same period? From the basic data in Table 2b, I have worked out the trade to GDP percentage taking the GDP for Britain as well as for the UK, the latter only for comparison with Kuznets. From line 3 onwards, which measures the current values for UK, Kuznets includes income from abroad along with domestic product – in short, his definition of 'Gross Product' is altered to GNP. He relies on Imlah[21] for invisible incomes (see his explanation of the derivation of line 3). There is a problem here, for while merchandise trade figures are firm since they are data from Customs House records, invisible

TABLE 2a *Early 19th Century: Constant Value of Trade, Britain 1797 to 1804*

	Total Imports fob	Total Imports cif	Total Exports	Total Trade	Re-exports	Domestic Exports	Retained Imports	Special Trade
1797	21014	29053	28917	57970	12014	16903	17039	33942
1798	27858	39925	33592	73517	13919	19673	26006	45679
1799	26837	37384	35991	73375	11907	24084	25477	49561
1800	30571	42347	43152	85499	18848	24304	23499	47803
1801	32796	45586	42302	87888	16602	25700	28984	54684
1802	31442	43704	46121	89825	19128	26993	24576	51569
1803	27992	38909	33652	72561	11540	22112	27369	49481
1804	29201	40297	37468	77765	13532	23936	26765	50701
Sum	227711	317205	301195	618400	117490	183705	199715	383420
Average	28463.9	39650.6	37649.4	77300	14686.2	22963.1	24864.3	47927.4
% to GDP	141800	28	26.5	54.5	10.35	16.2	17.6	33.8

Note: Imports *cif* from Deane and Cole, *British Economic Growth 1688–1850*, Appendix 1, Table 85; Domestic Exports and Re-exports from Mitchell and Deane, *Abstract of British Historical Statistics*, Table 1.

---

[21] A.H. Imlah, *Economic Elements in the Pax Britannica: Studies in British Foreign Trade in the Nineteenth Century*, Cambridge, Massachusetts: Harvard University Press, 1958.

TABLE 2b *Early 19th Century: Current Values of Trade 1797–1805 in £ million*

		Current Values from Imlah (1958), 1797 to 1805, £ million						
		1	2	3	4	5	6	7
	TM fob	TM cif	DX	RXM	TX	TT	RM	SPT (2+6)
Britain								
1797		34.4	27.5	9.3	36.8	71.2	25.1	52.6
1798		49.6	32.2	11.3	43.5	93.1	38.3	70.5
1799		50.9	36.8	9.4	46.2	97.1	41.5	78.3
1800		62.3	37.7	14.7	52.4	114.7	47.6	85.3
1801		68.7	40.6	12.9	53.5	122.2	55.8	96.4
1802		54.7	45.9	12.9	58.8	113.5	41.8	87.7
1803		53.9	36.9	9.1	46	99.9	44.8	81.7
1804		57.3	38.2	11	49.2	106.5	46.3	84.5
1805		61	38.1	10	48.1	109.1	51	89.1
		492.8	333.9	100.6	434.5	927.3	392.2	726.1
Annual Average		*54.8*	*37.1*	*11.2*	*48.3*	*103.1*	*43.6*	*80.7*
Percent of 1801 GDP, Britain	*24.2*	*16.4*	*4.9*	*21.4*	*45.6*	*19.3*	*35.7*	
Percent of 1801 GDP, UK	*24.2*	*16*	*4.8*	*20.8*	*44.4*	*18.8*	*34.8*	

Current values in £ million		GDP Britain		GDP UK		
	1800	212.7		218.45		
	1801	225.9		232		
		RM / GDP	DX / GDP	SPT / GDP	TT / GDP	
BRTN %	*1800*	20.5	17.4	37.9	48.5	
BRTN %	*1801*	19.3	16.4	35.7	45.6	
UK %	*1800*	19.9	17	36.9	47.2	
UK %	*1801*	18.8	16	34.8	44.4	

Source: A.H. Imlah, *Economic Elements in the Pax Britannica: Studies in British Foreign Trade in the Nineteenth Century*, Cambridge, Massachusetts: Harvard University Press, 1958, pp. 37–38; reproduced in Mitchell and Deane, *Abstract of British Historical Statistics*, pp. 282–84.

incomes at this date are not so firm for they are largely imputed by academics on the basis of certain assumptions.

The Kuznets percentage of 27.4 current value trade to gross national product for UK in the early nineteenth century, given the data he uses which we present in Table 2b, which shows special trade to be £80.7 million, means that the 1801 GNP he says he has taken, without mentioning its amount, must be this sum divided by 27.4 which gives £294.5 million. This is £62.5 million or 27 per cent in excess of the current value GDP for UK in 1801, which was £232 million according to Cole.[22]

[22] Cole, 'Factors in Demand', in Floud and McCloskey (eds), *The Economic History of Britain since 1700*, Vol. 1: *1700–1860*.

TABLE 3 *Early 20th Century: Current Values of Trade, 1897 to 1905*

	TM	DX	RXM	TX	TT	RM	SPT
			Current Values, Imlah, 1897 to 1905				
1897	451	234.2	60	294.2	745.2	391	625.2
1898	470.5	233.4	60.7	294.1	764.6	409.8	643.2
1899	485	264.5	65	329.5	814.5	420	684.5
1900	523.1	291.2	63.2	354.4	877.5	459.9	751.1
1901	522	280	67.8	347.8	869.8	454.2	734.2
1902	528.4	283.4	65.8	349.2	877.6	462.6	746
1903	542.6	290.8	69.6	360.4	923	473	763.8
1904	551	300.7	70.3	371	922	480.7	781.4
1905	565	329.8	77.8	407.6	972.6	487.2	817
	4638.6	2508	600.2	3108.2	7766.8	4038.4	6546.4
AV	*515.4*	*278.67*	*66.69*	*345.36*	*860.8*	*448.7*	*727.4*

Source: Imlah, *Economic Elements in the Pax Britannica*, pp. 37–38; reproduced in Mitchell and Deane, *Abstract of British Historical Statistics*, pp. 282–84.

This implicit GNP figure is undoubtedly an overestimate. Instead of trying to add income from abroad, the magnitude of which is problematic, it is much safer to continue to take GDP in the denominator. Trade to GDP percentages are also the standard measure used by international organizations in their statistical publications giving country-wise data. On this basis we find the current value annual trade average, £103, to be 45.6 percent of Britain's GDP and 44.4 per cent of the GDP of UK.

Summary

The total trade to GDP ratio is the generally accepted and correct measure of the trade openness of an economy. This ratio rose from 24.5 per cent in the early eighteenth century (1699 to 1704) for England and Wales, to 54.5 per cent in the early nineteenth century (1799 to 1804) for Britain, taking the values in constant prices for both periods. Taking current value trade and GDP for Britain for the latter period, 1799 to 1804, the percentage was 45.6 per cent.

Kuznets, however, taking the same data sources and values in constant prices, presents the trade to GDP percentage as 14.2 in the early eighteenth century (1702–03) and 27.4 in the early nineteenth century (1797–1805). The latter figure is not separately estimated but assumed to be the same as his estimated 27.4 per cent taking current values for the same period.

There is a very large divergence between the Kuznets ('Foreign Trade: Long-term Trends') figures and mine, derived from the very same data-series in Mitchell and Deane (*Abstract of British Historical Statistics*), and Deane and Cole (*British Economic Growth 1688–1850*) – series which I have reproduced so that the calculations can be checked by the reader. The main part of the answer for the divergence can be seen from the note at the top of Kuznets' Appendix Table 1: he mentions that the data relate to 'special trade unless otherwise specified'. The authorities among British economic historians on whom he relies used only the special trade concept when presenting time-series of the volume of British trade. But Kuznets was not quite careful enough. As I have pointed out earlier, simply correctly labelling the variables being measured is not sufficient. The information Kuznets gives is far from complete: few readers will know what 'special trade' is unless it is spelt out. 'Special trade' excludes re-exported imports from both imports as well as exports. So, twice the value of re-exports gets excluded from trade when the special trade concept is used.

At least this information, namely the definition of special trade, should have been provided by Kuznets. A reader, even if he is an economist writing on trade, who is not a specialist cannot reasonably be expected to know what 'special trade' is, since this is not a concept used in any economics textbook on trade, nor does any international organization use the concept of 'special trade' to present the data for cross-country comparison. The fact that Yamazawa, who has worked for so long mainly on trade and development, has been so misled proves the point. Another writer who has been misled with regard to historical data is W.A. Lewis, when he sweepingly says in his Princeton Lectures[23] that the magnitude of late eighteenth- to early nineteenth-century British trade even at the time of the Industrial Revolution was 'trivial'. A maritime nation with a less than 10 million population in 1800, which ran plantations in bio-diverse tropical lands and taxed heavily a distant population in Bengal three times the size of its own, which enjoyed colonial tax and rent, financed imports providing a vast inflow of goods not producible in Britain at all, and which had an annual trade to GDP percentage of 55 over the period 1799 to 1804, cannot by any stretch of the imagination be said to have 'trivial' trade. Although Lewis does not quote any authority, I am inclined to think that his misconception must have arisen from the special trade concept.

Even defining 'special trade' is not enough. A reader who is an informed historian of his own country cannot be expected necessarily to know that re-exports, which are being arbitrarily excluded, were an extremely important component of English trade right from the seventeenth century to over two centuries later. There was a specific reason for this, as mentioned, namely

---

[23] W.A. Lewis, *The Evolution of the International Economic Order*, Princeton: Princeton University Press, 1978.

the Navigation Acts. It is not clear what the logic is behind excluding re-exports by historians and economists talking about development, since the existence of a large re-export trade is precisely an important factor contributing to development, by permitting the concerned country to command imports even from regions which do not have a market for its own domestic exports.

Finally, even the special trade figures were found to be substantially higher than those implied in Kuznets' trade–GDP percentages. The constant prices special trade as per cent of GDP amount to 17.7 and 33.8 for the early eighteenth (1702–03) and early nineteenth centuries (1797–1805), respectively, for the periods Kuznets himself takes.

In current prices, the special trade percentage for the latter period, 1797–1805, is 34.8. This is also the value Deane and Cole (*British Economic Growth 1688–1850*) present. First, they give their constant value sum of Net Imports (their term for Retained Imports) and Domestic Exports as the 'volume of British trade', and present a chart showing the trend over the eighteenth century. Then they give the percentage to GDP of their Net Imports and Domestic Exports in current prices. Yet Kuznets says this extent of trade to GDP was reached only a whole century later, in the early twentieth century.

Maddison's *The World Economy*

Angus Maddison's *The World Economy* is in two volumes.[24] The main focus of discussion is population series and GDP series, and no systematic series on trade is provided by the author. In the scattered historical trade data which are given, however, Maddison uses the correct measure of trade and also discusses, though all too briefly, the question of transfer from colonies, which is usually ignored completely in Northern literature. Thus his Table 2.23 takes Total Exports explicitly and the 'Imports' refer to Total Imports, the stated data source being Mitchell and Deane (*Abstract of British Historical Statistics*) which, for current values, reproduced Imlah's series. It is a strange practice to present the information for single, arbitrarily chosen years as Maddison does, rather than annual averages of longer periods, since trade values in particular fluctuated a great deal and taking one year to represent a whole century will hardly give us even an approximation to a correct picture.

Maddison presents estimates for the Indian export surplus as per cent of

---

[24] Angus Maddison, *The World Economy, Volume 1: A Millennial Perspective, Volume 2: Historical Statistics*, OECD Development Centre, 2006.

TABLE 4 *Maddison, Table 2.23: Structure of British Commodity Trade by Origin and Destination 1710–1996 (per cent of total current value)*

	Europe	Asia	Br. West Indies	North America	Other Americas, Aus. & NZ	Africa
			Imports			
1710	63.6	6.9	21.7	7.3	0.1	0.4
1774	46.1	11.4	29.3	12.5	0.3	0.4
1820	26.8	24.6	26.0	14.6	7.5	0.5
1913	40.7	15.7	0.8	22.6	16.6	3.0
1950	27.8	17.2	5.1	15.9	23.0	11.0
1996	61.7	18.8	0.3	14.1	2.9	2.2
			Exports and Re-exports			
1710	87.6	2.1	3.4	5.1	0.6	1.2
1774	58.5	3.9	10.0	21.5	0.1	6.0
1820	61.8	7.1	9.0	11.7	9.3	1.1
1913	37.4	22.7	1.0	13.5	19.0	6.4
1950	28.8	18.9	1.7	14.4	23.0	13.2
1996	63.3	16.8	0.3	13.3	3.3	3.0

the NDP of India as well as of Britain, taking this as the measure of the 'drain' from the colony, or, as I prefer to call it, transfer from the colony to the metropolis. His table is reproduced below as Table 5. The measure is conceptually correct, but the actual estimates are for arbitrarily chosen periods and substantially underestimate the orders of magnitude. There is no estimate at all for the late eighteenth century when the transfer was particularly large, at 6 per cent of Britain's GDP.[25] The last period falls during the run-up to the Great Depression, when primary product prices had fallen and the value of Indian exports reduced drastically.

Unless more details are given of the estimation procedure, specially the Net Domestic Product values he uses, we are unable to reconstruct Maddison's estimates. From the percentages given in the two columns, the only point which is clear is that Indian and British NDP are taken to be very similar for the second and third period, while Indian NDP is taken as lower than Britain's in the first period, 1868–72. It is also clear that the figures of 'drain' as per cent to NDP are substantial underestimates. A rough check of the estimate is provided by considering the Feinstein and Pollard[26] data on British

[25] See Utsa Patnaik, 'New Estimates of Eighteenth-Century British Trade and their Relation to Transfers from Tropical Colonies', in Panikkar, Byres and Patnaik (eds), *The Making of History*; and Utsa Patnaik, 'The Free Lunch', in Jomo (ed.), *The Long Twentieth Century*.

[26] C.P. Feinstein and S. Pollard, *Studies in Capital Formation in UK*, Cambridge: Cambridge University Press, 1988.

GDP and K.N. Chaudhuri's annual time-series on India's export surplus,[27] supplemented by Sivasubramonian's data on India's Net Domestic Product.[28] As percentage of India's NDP the annual export surplus during 1868–72 amounted to 3.5 and as percentage of Britain's NDP, to 4.5.

Saul gave data showing, for 1880, Britain's credit and debit position with its trading partners, pointing out that India's exchange earnings from the world were used to offset Britain's deficits: 'the key to Britain's entire payments pattern lay in India financing as she probably did more than one-third of Britain's deficits' – which totalled £70 million at that date.[29]

In the immediate pre-World War I period and during the war, India saw a massive export surge, taking its annual export surplus over the period 1911 to 1919 to Rupees 742.8 million or nearly £50 million. Over and above the normal level of transfer under Home Charges, etc., denominated in sterling and annually recorded in the Indian budget, an additional £100 million of these extra wartime exchange earnings was appropriated by Britain, inconspicuously recorded as a 'gift' to Britain from British India – a 'gift' no one, certainly no Indian, knew about until it was recently uncovered by A.K. Bagchi[30] studying the documents for the period.

Saul points out that 'the importance of India's trade for the pattern of world trade balances can hardly be exaggerated. . . . It was through India that the British balance of payments found the flexibility essential to a great capital exporting country.'[31] Exchange earnings from India's export surpluses, appropriated by Britain and shown as its own, greatly exceeded the requirement of meeting Britain's current account deficits and substantially helped to finance its large capital exports.

If Maddison had taken the trade surplus of India during 1922–25 rather than the agricultural depression period of 1926–30, he would have found that it averaged Rs 1234.5 million annually, amounting to 3.8 per cent of India's NDP. During 1926–30, with the global agricultural depression, India's annual export surplus declined to Rs 675.4 million or 2.3 per cent of India's NDP, registering the same per cent of Britain's NDP – provided we can assume that Maddison's depiction of the relative size of the net product of these countries is correct, which requires to be checked out.

[27] K.N. Chaudhuri, 'Foreign Trade and the Balance of Payments', in Dharma Kumar and Meghnad Desai (eds), *The Cambridge Economic History of India*, Vol. II: *1757–1970*, Cambridge: Cambridge University Press, 1983; Delhi: Orient Longman, 1985.

[28] S. Sivasubramonian, *National Income of India 1900–10 to 1946–47*, Ph.D. Thesis, Delhi School of Economics, 1965, reproduced in A. Heston, 'National Income', in Kumar and Desai (eds), *The Cambridge Economic History of India*, Vol. II: *1757–1970*.

[29] S.B. Saul, *Studies in British Overseas Trade*, Liverpool: Liverpool University Press, 1960.

[30] A.K. Bagchi, *The Presidency Banks and the Indian Economy 1876–1914*, Calcutta: State Bank of India, 1998.

[31] Saul, *Studies in British Overseas Trade*.

TABLE 5 *Comparison of Maddison and Patnaik Estimates of Drain from India:*
The British 'Drain' on India 1868–1930

	Indian Export surplus as per cent of Indian Net Domestic Product		Indian Export surplus as per cent of British Net Domestic Product	
	Maddison	Patnaik	Maddison	Patnaik
1868–72	1.0	3.5	1.3	4.5
1911–15	1.3	3.6	1.2	3.3
1922–25	–	3.8	–	–
1926–30	0.9	2.3	0.9	2.3

Source: Maddison's estimates from Table 2.21b of *The World Economy*. My estimates use NDP series from Sivasubramonian (*National Income of India 1900–10 to 1946–47*, reproduced in Heston, 'National Income', in Kumar and Desai, eds, *The Cambridge Economic History of India*, Vol. II: *1757–1970*), converted to current values; and current value merchandise export surplus calculated from Chaudhuri ('Foreign Trade and the Balance of Payments', in Kumar and Desai, eds, *The Cambridge Economic History of India*, Vol. II: *1757–1970*).

I am firmly of the judgement that it was the collapse of India's export earnings with the onset of the world's agricultural depression from 1925 onwards that played a crucial role in Britain's inability to maintain the smooth functioning of its payments mechanism, its inability to continue to lend to maintain demand in the world economy, and its enforced final departure from the Gold Standard in 1931 and demise as the world capitalist leader. There was one last, gargantuan transfer which Britain exacted from India, over the period 1941 to 1946: £1,625 million of war finance, or an *additional* annual average budgetary spending of £270 million, which India was obliged to undertake for provisioning and meeting all the expenses of the Allied forces against Japan operating out of eastern India, known then as Bengal province.[32] This was a burden so enormous relative to the size of the total normal 1940 budget of £130 million, that it led to the death by starvation of more than 3 million people in Bengal and reduced at least an equal number to destitution.

[32] India spent Rs 38 billion over the period 1941–46, which was Rs 26 billion in excess of its normal budgetary total. Of this Rs 17 billion was 'recoverable', namely repayable by Britain in sterling, but only after the war ended. The bulk of the spending was deficit-financed, leading to rapid food price inflation and forced transfer of purchasing power from the poorest segments of the population. See Utsa Patnaik, 'Food Availability and Famine: A Longer View', *Journal of Peasant Studies*, 1991; reprinted in Utsa Patnaik, *The Long Transition: Essays on Political Economy*, New Delhi: Tulika Books, 1999.

Appendix

TABLE A1 *Annual Values in Constant Prices of Total Trade and Special Trade, Britain, 1697 to 1804 (in £ million)*

	Re-exports	Total Exports	Total Imports	Total Trade
1697–99	1.425	4.602	6.135	10.737
1700–04	1.769	5.473	6.925	12.398
1705–09#	1.513	5.794	5.877	11.671
1710–14#	2.071	6.789	6.707	13.496
1715–19	2.625	7.475	9.639	14.838
1720–24	3.054	8.079	9.631	16.114
1725–29	3.054	8.079	9.631	17.71
1730–34	3.023	9.484	10.113	18.597
1735–39	3.377	9.631	10.369	20
1740–44	3.673	9.569	9.752	19.32
1745–49	3.47	10.687	9.846	20.532
1750–54	3.464	12.169	11.102	23.271
1755–59	3.544	12.338	12.419	24.757
1760–64	4.401	14.85	14.071	28.92
1765–69	4.58	14.216	16.183	30.4
1770–74	5.627	15.677	17.803	33.48
1775–79	5.086	14.073	17.093	31.166
1780–84	4.11	13.616	17.056	30.672
1785–89	4.949	17.222	23.523	40.745
1790–94	6.842	22.979	27.327	50.301
1795–99	12.008	31.266	33.909	65.174
1800–04	15.93	40.539	42.169	82.708

Source: Deane and Cole, *British Economic Growth 1688–1850*, Appendix Table 85, for Total Imports *cif*. Mitchell and Deane, *Abstract of British Historical Statistics*, for Domestic Exports and Re-exports.

CHART A1 *Annual Values in Constant Prices of Components of Trade, and Total Trade, Britain, 1697–1804 (in £ million)*

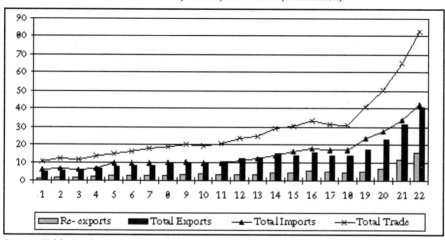

Source: Table A1 data.

TABLE A2 *Import, Export, Total Trade and Special Trade*
(triennial averages centred on stated years) as per cent of GDP

	Total Import	Total Export	Total Trade	Special Trade	GDP £ million
1700	15.6	11.5	27.12	19.32	50
1710	7.29	11.24	22.24	12.41	53.9
1720	13.37	12.14	25.51	17.04	57.5
1730	17.41	14	31.41	20.84	58.7
1740	15.9	13.84	29.74	19.4	64.1
1750	15.4	17.9	33.29	23.38	70.4
1760	16.4	17.71	34.11	24.63	81.9
1770	21.35	18.61	39.96	27.4	80.3
1780	17.68	13.94	31.62	21.2	92
1790	24.66	19.91	44.58	33.89	104.1
1800	29.46	28.55	58.01	35.75	141.8

Source: Table A1.

CHART A2 **GDP (£ million in constant prices), Special Trade and Total Trade**
as per cent of GDP, Britain, 1699 to 1801

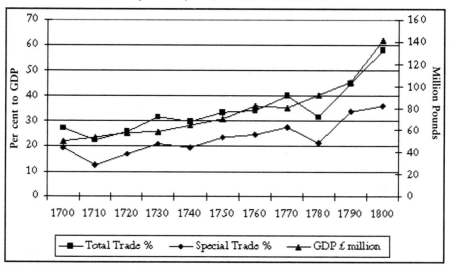

Source: Table A2 data.

Gandhi's Modernity

Akeel Bilgrami

In two searching and analytic papers[1] – also moving for their sympathy and eloquence, as well as for their very brief and passing personal references to his own family's relations and attitude towards Gandhi – Irfan Habib evaluates the contribution that Gandhi made to the Indian national movement and to Indian political thought. Much more than other Marxist assessments of Gandhi, and decisively more than other recent historical readings which place Gandhi in a roll-call of Indian compromisers who are said to have succumbed to the 'derivative' discourse of Indian nationalism and, in doing so, to have betrayed the masses they mobilized,[2] these papers explore the radical side of Gandhi – as a politician of unique effectiveness in speaking to the anti-imperialist instincts of the Indian masses with an abiding concern for their poverty, and a deep conviction in their political judgement and the dignity of their labour.

Gandhi never really came to any detailed grip with the concept of class, to say nothing of 'class struggle', in the politics he espoused and generated. Yet, as these papers show, even within this limitation there is a 'left-wing' Gandhi in a broad but genuine sense of that term, a Gandhi unrecognizable in the portrayal of the reactionary anti-modernist he is often taken to be.

It is through an explicit criticism of this latter portrayal that Irfan Habib offers a bold judgement on the kind of thinker Gandhi was, in passages such as: 'One could even smile over Gandhi's reading list of twenty items, of which eighteen came from European pens, and two from Indian modernizers.'[3] And:

---

[1] Irfan Habib, 'Gandhiji', in *Addressing Gandhi: 125 Years of Mahatma Gandhi*, New Delhi: Safdar Hashmi Memorial Trust (Sahmat), 1995; and Irfan Habib, 'Gandhi and the National Movement', *Social Scientist*, April–June 1995, pp. 3–15.

[2] GNM is explicit in its criticism of the 'Subaltern' historians who have argued this, and one can infer from what is said that the most obvious and specific object of criticism is Partha Chatterjee, *Nationalist Thought and the Colonial World: A Derivative Discourse*, Minneapolis: University of Minnesota Press, 1993.

[3] Habib, 'Gandhiji', p. 11.

Gandhi's words . . . are not to be seen as the assertion of traditional against modern values. What we get is the assertion of modern values in traditional garb, a re-reading of Indian culture in a totally ahistorical way, but extremely creative fashion. . . . In Gandhi's case the convergence of statement of modern values in traditional terms was . . . complete . . . and extensive, although for this reason, the contradictions within it were also very glaring.[4]

I believe this central claim to be insightful and true. But if so, it lands us with a residual interpretative challenge. On the face of it, that central claim (the idea that Gandhi is a thoroughly modern thinker) would invite the question: how is it, then, that he is so persistently, and so easily and widely, taken to be an anti-modernist extolling the virtues of Indian tradition and religiosity? These passages I have cited give a clear answer that is perfectly correct as far as it goes. They point out that Gandhi was almost deliberately and strategically contradictory, a thinker who explicitly avowed Hinduism and the virtues of Indian civilization as a way of presenting his modern ideas to a traditional people. Though this answers the question, I would like, in this short essay, to suggest another, supplementary line of argument, to show how the seeming anti-modernism may be read side by side with Gandhi's radicalism in a way that does not wholly (or only) see the anti-modernism as a veneer of presentation for his underlying modern ideas. It also reveals a *continuity* of his radicalism with an *'Early'* Modern dissenting tradition in Europe, especially in England, which Gandhi himself did not mention (or even perhaps know of) but with which his own alleged *'anti'*-modern ideas shared a deep and detailed affinity. My idea here is not to overturn the explanation offered by Irfan Habib which focuses on Gandhi's own, more immediate strategic motives, but to focus, instead, on how even much of what seems anti-modern would not seem so if we appreciated a very specific sort of historical dialectic that I will attempt to offer as a supplement to his explanation. I hope such an attempt will be a small token of the respect and admiration I feel for the life and writings of a remarkable historian.

That elements with affinities to the radical dissenting ideas voiced in the *Early* Modern period should appear to us as *anti*-modern is due to a confluence of two closely related factors: first, our tendency to think of the path from Early to Late modernity as a teleological inevitability; and consequently, second, from the perspective of our lateness, to stamp out the significance and the substantial presence of the *dissenting* voices in the earlier period which lost out in the arena of social and political and intellectual conflicts

---

[4] Habib, 'Gandhi and the National Movement', p. 7. The ellipses mark comparisons between Gandhi and Ram Mohun Roy, which are not relevant to the main point.

of those times. These two factors conspire to make it seem as if any assertion of some of the radical ideas to be found in Early Modern dissenting traditions at a date as late as, for instance, 1908, when Gandhi wrote *Hind Swaraj*, necessarily occupies a stubbornly reactionary position – something they would not seem to do if we viewed the teleology as uncompulsory, as Gandhi certainly did, and if we kept fully in our view of the past, the power and pregnant possibilities that those dissenting ideas possessed, despite their having lost out.[5]

If it were possible to use the expression 'Early Modern' as an entirely innocuous description of a period of time in Europe, with no built-in implications of describing only those antecedents that would unfold into the developments of Late modernity there, the radicalism of that period might give us a sense of the possibilities that Gandhi still held out for the India of the early twentieth century, *which he took to be at the sort of cusp that Europe was at in the 'Early Modern' period*. So, to repeat the crucial dialectical point, at the risk of causing tedium: that we should see this stance as anti-modern rather than as the radical ideas they were, with a *serious potential for pre-empting*, in India in the early part of the twentieth century, the lamentable path in political economy and aspects of political governance that had developed over the modern period in Europe, is only because of the directional certainties of an assumed teleology that have the effect of writing out of history the great significance that dissenting voices had at the earlier time, leaving the impression only of those antecedents that make our own conditions seem inevitable for our own time. How to correct this tendency in us by elaborating this dialectical reversal of it, is the chief preoccupation of this short essay.

Why, in this explanatory dialectic, am I fastening, of all things, on the radicalism of seventeenth-century Europe, especially England, as the right frameworking antecedent to illuminate Gandhi's seeming anti-modernism?

Hind Swaraj is a work of passionate and instinctive criticism. Yet it sets down themes that recur steadily in subsequent writings and, when studied together with them, yields something much more systematic that a reader might construct. My own construction[6] has been to stress that Gandhi's ideas which originated in that text, and were haphazardly developed over time, can be given some structure if we take one question as central for him and see his answer to it as having a range of implications that he himself

---

[5] See M.K. Gandhi [1908], *Hind Swaraj*, edited by Anthony J. Parel, Cambridge: Cambridge University Press, 1997.

[6] Akeel Bilgrami, 'Gandhi, Newton and the Enlightenment', *Social Scientist*, May–June 2006; Akeel Bilgrami, 'Democracy and Disenchantment', *Social Scientist*, November–December 2009.

interestingly draws, though not always quite as explicitly in the way I will elaborate below. At its most general, that question is: *When and how did we transform our concept of the world as not merely a place to live in, but a place to master and control?*

Gandhi believed that in our answer to this question, we can aptly put the blame for the transformation about which the question inquires, on certain developments in the west that have to do with modern science, a central theme of *Hind Swaraj*. It is for this reason that I think we must turn to the Early Modern period of the mid- and late seventeenth century in Europe, when the new science was first fully formulated and then consolidated in ways that went well beyond the narrow confines of science itself.

A sympathetically careful study of his writings allows us to see past some of Gandhi's occasionally crude rhetoric and find that his is not really a critique of science as some careless words he writes suggest, or even of modern science, but really a critique of a *metaphysical outlook* generated by certain developments around the rise of modern science, and *its implications* for society, politics, political economy and culture. (He even took the scruple to say that he was not against technology as such, but against the *mentality* generated by technology when it was in the control of elites who had no other motive but to use it for their own gain.[7])

The reason why I stress 'outlook' and 'mentality' rather than science itself, in characterizing the target of Gandhi's criticisms, is because a range of metaphysical concepts and attitudes that were getting entrenched around the new science in the late seventeenth century and after, were vehemently opposed – in terms closely anticipating Gandhi – by some (dissenting) *scientists*, who had no quarrel whatever with the new science that had reached its most systematic formulation in Newton's laws. What exactly, then, were these dissenting scientists protesting, if it was not the laws themselves? The answer to this question, which I will try and present in summary below, has such a detailed echo in Gandhi's thought that it would be a failure of historical imagination on our part not to make something interpretatively significant of it in coming to an understanding of Gandhi's own criticisms of 'modern science' and 'western science', as he sometimes (too) simply put it.

I have said that Gandhi's finding the fault-line in modern science for a

---

[7] 'What I object to is the craze for labour-saving machinery. Men went for saving labour, till thousands were without work and thrown on the streets to die of starvation. I want to save time and labour not for a fraction of mankind but for all. I want the concentration of wealth not in the hands of the few, but in the hands of all. Today machinery merely helps a few to ride on the backs of the millions. The impetus is not on philanthropy, or to save labour, but on greed. . . . It is against this constitution of things that I am fighting with all my might. . . . The supreme consideration is man.' (M.K. Gandhi, *Young India*, 13 November 1924.)

whole spectrum of social and political harms should be seen as his answer to his own, most underlying omnibus question: how and why did we transform our concept of the world as a place not merely to live in, but to master and control? The question is an omnibus one because the term 'world' in it is a term of art whose meaning is highly layered, connoting nature, the human inhabitants of nature, and the relations between nature and its inhabitants as well as the social relations between the inhabitants. *All of this* as an *integrated* whole, Gandhi claimed, was conceptually transformed by a certain metaphysical outlook that accompanied the new science, but for the sake of making his question and his own answer more tractable, it is worth breaking the integrated elements down into different transformations, despite the integrity that the term 'world' would suggest.

One could begin with 'nature' and ask more specifically about it, echoing the more general question: how and when did we transform the concept of nature into the concept of natural resources? We could then also ask: how and when did we transform the concept of human beings (the inhabitants of nature) into the concept of citizens,[8] and the concept of people into the concept of 'populations'? And, I think, as we proceed to answer these questions along the broad lines suggested by Gandhi's attribution of blame for these transformations to the changes wrought by science in the modern period, a final question emerges, which is roughly: how did we transform the concept of *knowledges to live by* into the concept of *an expertise to rule by*? It is a mark of Gandhi's extraordinary intellectual ambition that he thought *all* of these seemingly diverse questions were highly integrated, that these various transformations were really, at bottom, *the same transformation*, owing to a fault-line to be found in the outlooks generated by modern science. (Hence the formulation of the question in omnibus terms, of 'the world' as a place to master and control.) Were he to have had Marx's understanding of political economy and the notion of class, he would have noticed that Marx too had developed a parallel template for a range of transformations in his discussion of alienation where he explored the making into resources and means, and therefore into objects, of the entire realm of human subjectivity. I will say a little more about this in a moment, but for now, let me begin with the theme of nature.

Gandhi's understanding of nature derived heavily from his *Bhakti* ideals in which nature is sacral, suffused with the divine, continuous with the *atman* that suffuses each of its inhabitants, a divinity available therefore to

---

[8] Gandhi's large concern was with the idea of citizens of a *nation-state*, not earlier forms of citizenry such as the polis in Ancient Greece, say. In Bilgrami, 'Democracy and Disenchantment', I spell out and criticize the role played by the Early Modern idea of a *social contract* in constructing such a notion of citizenship.

all at all times, should they perceive and find him through devotion.[9] Such
a conception of nature was pervasive also in the popular religious understanding of much of Early Modern Europe; often described by intellectual
historians as 'neo-Platonism', it received explicit articulations in the writings of such radicals, for instance, as the Digger, Gerard Winstanley, and the
Ranter, Jacob Bauthumley, to name just two in England.[10] It was this conception that was undermined in the late seventeenth century by a very mark-
edly Providentialist turn, in which God was not to be viewed as immanent
within nature but, rather, placed at a distance outside the universe, described
often by the Latin expression '*Deus Absconditus*': a God put away for safe-
guarding. Newton's writings had much to do with this exile of God to a
place outside the universe, though nothing in Newton's science demanded
it. That is to say, nothing in the Newtonian laws, nor basic concepts such as
gravity, required that God be seen as being in a place external to his creation. The idea that nature and matter were inert and desacralized, and that
motion came about as a result of a push by God from an *external*, archimed-

---

[9] Including the lowliest of animals, though that is not a subject I will take up in this essay. A
more immediately relevant point is that his stress on the pervasive immanence of divinity is
why Gandhi consistently downplayed '*moksha*' in his understanding of Hinduism.

[10] Bauthumley claimed that God was 'in all Creatures, Man and Beast, Fish and Fowle, and
every green thing, from the highest Cedar to the Ivey on the Wall' (quoted in Norman Cohn,
The Pursuit of the Millennium, Oxford: Oxford University Press, 1970); and Winstanley, that
'God is in all matter' and 'The truth is hid in every body' (quoted in Christopher Hill, *The
World Turned Upside Down: Radical Ideas in the English Revolution*, London: Penguin,
1984). Such pantheistic and hermeticist ideas are central to the doctrine of a range of radical
sects not just in England, but also, from an even earlier time (since the doctrines of Bruno and
Ficino), all over Europe. It is also worth observing that in Europe, the later figure of Spinoza
was more influential in politics than some of these earlier neo-Platonists, and he was sometimes
an inspiration for the scientific dissenters in England that I have mentioned. Spinoza too is
well known for having equated divinity with nature, but I don't think that this is properly
described as a 'pantheism' and it is almost certainly wrong to describe it as 'sacralizing'
nature. It was too abstract an equation for that. Still, it is interesting to see Jonathan Israel
(*Radical Enlightenment: Philosophy and the Making of Modernity in Europe 1650–1750*,
Oxford: Oxford University Press, 2002) making much of Spinoza's influence on radical
groups in Europe. The entire work sets out to shift the emphasis from the orthodox liberal
influence of someone like Locke to, what he calls, 'Spinozism' and its intellectual sway on a
more radical side of the Enlightenment. What is 'radical' for Israel, however, is measurably
less critical of the orthodox Enlightenment than the radical groups that I am focused on in
England. These differences are worth a close study. The channel of radicalism I am appealing
to in order to understand Gandhi's radical ideas goes from sects such as the Diggers through
the scientific dissenters I have mentioned, to figures like Blake and, even later, to Morris and
the non-conformist religious Left ideals of Tawney. Israel's seems to be seeking channels that
lead to quite different figures such as, say, Condorcet, who have almost no affinities with
Gandhian thought. Gandhi apart, even if one were focused just on Europe, there is interesting
comparative work to be done here in the intellectual history of the Enlightenment and its
legacy for the possibility of a genuinely radical politics. I suspect Israel's historical conception
would fall far short of the tradition of radicalism I am seeking.

ean point was no more demanded as an underlying explanation of motion by Newton's laws, than the idea that motion was made possible by a divine, *inner* source of dynamism in matter and nature. Both views were perfectly compatible with the laws and the notion of gravity. Yet, in the late seventeenth century, the Royal Society's ideologues (figures such as, for instance, Samuel Clarke and Richard Bentley) insisted that the immanentist explanation of the broadly pantheistic, dissenting view (the brilliant and highly volatile dissenter, John Toland, is said to have coined the term 'pantheism', though not of course the doctrine) was dangerously wrong, and that it was built into Newtonian science that God be seen as occupying a Providential distance from and an external control of the universe. Newton himself acquiesced in this public presentation of his view – despite his well documented neo-Platonism and alchemical obsessions in his private study – calling nature and matter, 'stupid' and 'brute'.[11]

This desacralization of nature was vociferously protested by dissenting scientists (then, of course, called 'natural philosophers') such as Toland and Anthony Collins who, despite their embrace of the new science formulated by Newton, saw in this *metaphysical interpretation* of it, a whole range of consequences for politics and political economy which they denounced, invoking the ideas and practice of the earlier radical sectaries in their denunciation, and anticipating in detail a number of Gandhi's criticisms of the destruction of agrarian village life. In particular, they claimed that a conception of a brute and inert nature was being mobilized by the orthodox figures in the Royal Society in open alliances they had formed with both commercial and mercantile interests, and an Anglican orthodoxy, to make nature available for a much larger-scale and much more systematic plunder than ever before. They were responding to a deliberately constructed ideological framework pronounced in remarks such as this one by a contemporary scientist and early economist of this period, and a prominent figure in the Royal Society, William Petty: 'What may be the meaning of the glorified bodies, in case of the place of the blessed shall be, without the convex of the orb of the fixed stars, *is that the whole system of the World was made for the use of our earth's men*' (emphasis mine).[12] From an *anima mundi*, there were built-in constraints to what one could take from nature, and such taking as was done was often accompanied by rituals of respect shown to nature, and the divine presence within it, before cycles of planting and hunt-

---

[11] These descriptions occur in the *Opticks*, 1704. For Newton's less public neo-Platonist side, see J.E. McGuire and P.M. Rattansi, 'Newton and the "Pipes of Pan"', *Notes and Records of the Royal Society of London*, Vol. 21, No. 2, December 1966.

[12] William Petty, 'An Essay Concerning the Multiplication of Mankind', in *The Petty Papers*, Vol. 1, 1682; available electronically as a Google book.

ing. Now, without any such metaphysical constraint, they argued, things were openly being set up to take from nature with impunity, and they presciently saw that this would make the hitherto fitful practice of forced enclosures a systematic and legally backed practice, depriving the poor of the collective cultivation of the commons, generating a future that pointed to what we today call 'agri-business', thereby destroying the local forms of egalitarianism which the radical sects had envisioned and even, in the case of the Diggers, briefly put into practice.

It is quite apparent even at a cursory glance, that the remark I cite from William Petty is an early statement of the implications of a metaphysical outlook that Gandhi deplored. It is evident, for instance, in the tremendously interesting correspondence between Gandhi and Tagore. Tagore echoes Petty when he says: 'If the cultivation of science by Europe has any moral significance, it is in its rescue of man from outrage by nature, not its use of man as a machine but its use of the machine to harness the forces of nature in man's service.'[13] By contrast, Gandhi's view was that one could not find one's way to treat humanity as ends rather than means unless one's fundamental metaphysical outlook towards nature was different from what is suggested by Petty and Tagore; unless, that is, we see nature itself as speaking to us and even constraining us with normative demands, rather than as something we harness only for our ends. Gandhi, of course, presented these normative demands of nature as having a sacralized source. That was the *Bhakti* influence. To dismiss this as anti-modern merely because of that fact would be shallow in the extreme. Marx had such a view of nature's relation to its human inhabitants too, though it is embedded in an entirely secular framework. It can be found in several passages in *The Economic and Philosophical Manuscripts of 1844*. Here is just one:

> Only here does nature exist as the foundation of his own human existence. Only here has what is to him his *natural* existence become his *human* existence, and nature become man for him. Thus society is the unity of being of man with nature – the true resurrection of nature – the naturalism of man and the *humanism of nature* both brought to fulfillment.[14]

How exactly to relate passages such as these, which stress highly abstract metaphysical claims about the unalienated human existence that comes from our human agency being in sync in this way with the normative demands of

---

[13] See the section on 'The Cult of the Charkha', in Sabyasachi Bhattacharya (ed.), *The Mahatma and the Poet*, Delhi: National Book Trust, 1997.

[14] Karl Marx, *The Economic and Philosophical Manuscripts of 1844*, edited by Dirk J. Struik, translated by Michael Milligan, New York: International Publishers, 1944, p. 137.

nature,[15] with Marx's far more specific claims about what makes for an unalienated form of labour, is a delicate philosophical task; yet it is absolutely necessary to understand his overall conception of labour and alienation in modern capitalist society. The proximity with Gandhi on these issues is striking and well worth elaborating, but I cannot possibly do so here.

The dissent in Early Modern Europe, though it had as a central component such a protest as I have been expounding – a protest against the metaphysical support given by the orthodoxies congealing around the new science to emerging ideas of systematically destructive, extractive capitalist economies – was by no means restricted to this component. It linked this component integrally to much broader issues in politics and culture.

One of the clearest goals of the ideologues of the Royal Society was to use the new science in the preservation of order and stability in society. Here again, they were joined in an alliance with the latitudinarian Anglicans as well as commercial interests for whom the revolutionary unrest of the pre-Restoration period was a palpable danger. Thus, for instance, the Boyle Lectures to be given regularly at the Royal Society had a fully articulated rationale to this effect, hardly disguising the keenness to present a Christianity and a commercial ethos that were an antidote to the 'enthusiasm' (a widely used term of disparagement at that time) of popular religion, and the dissenting philosophical and scientific voices that had affinities with it. It was enthusiasm after all that sought to turn 'the world upside down'.

---

[15] One should not interpret Marx's remarks here about a human element in nature ('Nature becomes Man for him', 'the Humanism of Nature', etc.) as presenting a vitalist conception of nature nor as nature containing an element of intentionality. That would be to go too far afield from his materialism. It is the rather more sober thought that nature makes normative demands on us. However, even to see nature as making such demands is to see his materialism in a light quite different from rigidly scientistic interpretations of Marx. Resistance to this scientism, however, has often led to views that are, in my view, quite implausible. For example, to see intentional elements in nature is implausible for a quite simple reason. Where there is intentionality, we are in a region of phenomena whose elements can be the target of certain forms of criticism. Thus human intentionality is the sort of phenomena of which one can say such things as we frequently do: 'That is a wrong action to have done, or a wrong belief or even a wrong desire to have.' But it makes no sense to say similar things about elements in nature. We do of course criticize nature. We may say, 'That was a disappointing sunset', but that is not the form of criticism that addresses itself to intentional elements. The inappropriateness of the more conceptually weighted (where by 'conceptually' I mean to suggest concepts having to do with moral psychology) criticisms, when it comes to nature, is something of a proof that it is quite extravagant to propose that nature is suffused with intentional properties over and above value properties that make normative demands on us. The term 'demands', in the idea of nature making normative demands on us, should not therefore be taken too literally. These are not demands coming from an intentional subject or subjects, nor does Marx intend to say they are, in his rhetoric of 'Nature becomes Man for him' and the 'Humanism of Nature'.

Toland and others were targeted, and many dissenters sought haven in Rotterdam and other Dutch and European cities.

What about the scientific dissenting ideas was *political* anathema? How could opposition to something as arcane as the desacralization of nature and matter be a source of anxiety, not just about converting nature into a resource for zealous extraction for profit but about governance? The inferences are not hard to draw and they were forcefully drawn in the debates of the time. The exile of God from his immanence in nature and in all bodies was literally conceived as 'putting him into *safekeeping*', as the Latin term '*conditus*' in the phrase '*Deus Absconditus*' suggests ('*abs*', for its part, connoting 'putting him far *away*'). Why should a scientific establishment and its worldly allies want such a thing? And why should dissenters so urgently oppose it?

If God's presence was no longer available in all bodies and all matter to the visionary temperaments of all who inhabited his earth, the values and virtues to live by that he enshrined were now the prerogative of learned and scriptural judgement, of university-trained divines. The dissenters wanted that reversed, arguing that the *democratization of the polity* turned crucially on this not being an elite possession. It should be stressed that this form of dissent was not at all an instance of the quite different and far more general attack on popery in the Protestant Reformation, demanding an individual relation with God unmediated by the orthodoxies and institutions of the Roman church. That in fact had yielded quite the opposite of what the dissenters wanted; it yielded what political theorists have called a 'possessive individualism' of the domesticated forms of Protestantism that emerged from the Reformation. The dissenters were precisely opposing this Protestant establishment in England (and in the Netherlands), and its alliances with the economic and scientific establishment.[16] Such an individualism

---

[16] I am focusing on England particularly because the alliances that I mention between scientific bodies, and commercial interests and established Protestantism, were first most explicitly formulated in England as a result of the Royal Society's openly commercial and religious links, both in the body of its membership as well as in its self-understanding, as exemplified, for instance, in Boyle's own instructions with which he set up the lectures bearing his name. I should also explain my emphasis on Newton rather than earlier figures who were well-known antecedents to some of these metaphysical ideologies. The reason I do not take up Bacon or Descartes and Galileo on the continent is because it was not till the late seventeenth century that bodies like the Royal Society made the worldly alliances that exploited this desacralized metaphysics in the ways I have outlined, citing the authority of their immediate contemporary and hero, *Newton*, in doing so. Perhaps the first to have pointed out the role of Newtonianism in the rise of capitalism was the Soviet scientist and historian of science Boris Hessen, in his address, 'The Social and Economic Roots of Newton's Principia', to the Second International Congress of the History of Science, in 1931 in London. The claims in that address are remarkable for their simplicity and their attribution of intentions to Newton himself. It is far more plausible to see it as what Margaret Jacob calls the 'culture of

was a far cry from the democratized communities they sought, embedded in
the collective cultivation of the commons that the radical sects of a few decades earlier had tried to draw from their ideas of a divine presence in all
bodies and all persons. Winstanley, like Gandhi, had in fact explicitly described this neo-Platonism, which had close affinities with the *Bhakti* ideal
that also saw God as available to the most humble of men and women (not
restricted to 'scholars bred up in human letters'[17]), as having a 'great level-
ling purpose'. This was indeed one of the chief sources of anxiety about the
radical sects that led to them being charged with 'enthusiasm'.[18] The dissenters saw the privilege of only a learned and trained accessibility to God as a
quite local symptom of a much more general anti-democratic, elite tendency that led to the law being handed over to feed lawyers and medicine being
unavailable freely or cheaply, and, in the end, to a model of governance that
revolved around the restored monarch and his courts.[19]

Their fears were entirely borne out. Governance did indeed come to have
this form in the post-Restoration period and all radical dissent seemed to
have been made irrelevant when even *liberal* ideals went on, a little later, to
present essentially this form of governance as a 'revolution' ('The Glorious
Revolution' of 1688), aligning themselves firmly with ideals of civility in
society and orderly governance by law which would stand behind the rule
over a brute populace by a monarch, reflecting on earth a mundane version

---

Newtonianism', a mandarin phenomenon in which the Royal Society was the most active
agent. See M. Jacob, *Newton and the Culture of Newtonianism*, Amherst, N.Y.: Humanity
Books, 1994. Still, there is no doubt that the Hessen thesis was a great mobilizer in this
direction in the cultural history of science.

[17] Gerard Winstanley, *The Breaking of the Day of God* [1648], electronic reproduction, Ann
Arbor, Michigan: UMI, 1999.

[18] That is why the opposition to neo-Platonist and pantheistic ideas took on the entire rhetoric
of '*absconditus*' or safekeeping. This rhetoric is essential to the Providentialist turn. It adds
considerably and very specifically to the more general idea of a transcendent God. The idea
of a transcendent rather than immanent, pantheistic conception of God was, of course, by no
means an innovation of the seventeenth century, nor of this emerging metaphysical doctrine
around the idea of a '*Deus Absconditus*'. But it began to have a quite new and enhanced
meaning as well as urgency in this time in the Royal Society in England and other parts of
Europe that resisted neo-Platonist as well as Spinoza's immanentist and pantheist ideas – an
urgency in which older ideas of transcendence were given entirely new motivations of a
desire to put God in 'safekeeping', that is, put him away from an availability to the ordinary
perceptions of all who inhabited his earth that his immanence would provide, since that was
a metaphysical and religious basis for 'enthusiasm'. And it is for this reason that these
explanations of motion and all the familiar Newtonian images of a 'clockwinder' were
invoked by the scientific establishment, who had made open alliances with worldly interests,
thus making the transcendent conception into a Providentialist ideology of far wider
significance than a mere metaphysical interpretation of the new science.

[19] Gandhi too writes scathingly in a number of places of the anti-democratic tendency in Law
and Medicine as institutionalized in the west along very similar lines, just as he writes by
contrast about the democratizing possibilities in *Bhakti* ideals.

of the rule of an external providential God over a brute and material universe. Early liberalism in Europe thus emerged as a legally and constitutionally codified successor to now outmoded ideas of the divine right of kings.

Ideals of civility around the monarch and his courts in the early Enlightenment have been well studied by a range of intellectual historians, including, of course, Norbert Elias.[20] They all attest to their relevance for the polity, but none, so far as I know, say what they most came to imply. They were intended to mark a form of codified decorum in behaviour that defined the small and privileged class that ruled, and was *defined against* the behaviours and lifestyles of the rude 'populace' over which it ruled, a lifestyle characterized by cruelty and violence in their everyday lives. In the seventeenth century, 'cruelty' was considered the opposite of 'civility'. Thus to label a people 'cruel' was to justify being cruel to them. So 'cruel' was the opposite of 'civil', but opposing cruelty with cruelty was not understood as cruelty because it could come in the name of a defence of ideals of civility. Thus it was that a stipulative semantics of this sort around 'civility' created a screen by which the courts and the propertied classes hid from themselves the cruelties of *their own* perpetration. In the High Enlightenment, the notion of civility with this built-in screening function morphed into something much more abstractly specified in the quite different vocabulary of rights and constitutions. This transformation now had cruelty as something recognized never as occurring in polities governed by the rights that its citizens possessed, but rather as occurring only in distant places that lacked such rights and constitutions. However justly celebrated rights are – and they are deservedly so, for obvious reasons no one should deny – this new version of the self-deceptive screen hid from western powers the cruelties that they perpetrated on distant lands, which lands alone – because they lacked notions of rights and constitutions – were recognized as given to cruelty. And, as is well known, a pedagogical framework was often set up as a justification for colonization, to bring civility and rights to the colonized lands (a perfectly familiar ploy, still masquerading under the label 'liberal empire'). Gandhi was perfectly aware of this historical screening function of notions of civility and rights, and thought that it only came to pass because of a loss of the genuine democratization that lies in the availability to the visionary temperaments of *all* people of the values to live by in a sacralized (*Bhakti*) conception of the ordinary, perceptible world around one – and it explains to a considerable extent, his studied indifference to the vocabulary and codifications of rights.

I think a deliberate 'indifference' is the right description of Gandhi's attitude. It is not as if he was hostile to the idea of rights; he seemed more to

[20] Norbert Elias, *The Civilizing Process*, Oxford: Blackwell, 2000.

have been unimpressed by the intensity of enthusiasm for them among liberals around him and the well-known doctrines of the colonial masters from which these were drawn. And the considerations I have just mentioned were fortified in his mind by a sense of the provenance of these liberal ideas and how they spoke to a situation that he felt should not be allowed to arise in the first place in India. All these codifications were the unfolding achievement (if 'achievement' is what it was) of a form of polity that emerged from the Westphalian peace. It was central to the Westphalian ideal that it needed to find a legitimacy for a new form of state that could no longer find its justifications, as earlier monarchical forms often had, from a purely divine right. It sought a more mundane legitimacy in a new idea of the nation that required of its people a *feeling* for it *as a nation*, a national*ism*, as it is often called; and feelings for the nation, or nationalism (as opposed to any project of improving the conditions of its people), as a legitimizer of a particular form of state in the Westphalian ideal was generated in Europe by what is now a very familiar pattern, that came to be called 'majoritarianism'. The preponderance of a nation's people came to feel for the nation most easily and most intensely by finding some 'minority' or minorities, and stigmatizing them as implicit outsiders. Once a nation-state was consolidated on these grounds of an abiding mix of prejudice and discrimination, an entire set of principles had then to be formulated to constrain the effects of such a nationalism, and so a variety of ideas of political secularism and multiculturalism codified in the form of rights and freedoms for *all* citizens of the nation had to be introduced. Gandhi had nothing intrinsically against these rights and these ideas (though, quite possibly, he doubted that they would go deep enough to be efficacious against the deep roots of a majoritarian national ideal built up along these lines); he rather did not want for India *in the first place* the larger context of a non-inclusive nationalism in which they were adopted as a subsequent constraint on its ill effects. He found the entire trajectory of the Westphalian ideal of the nation, with its majoritarian legitimizing nationalism that I have very briefly described, deplorable; and he saw no reason for India to go down that path. The 'modern' figure whom he most opposed therefore was Savarkar, not Nehru (who in fact often spoke in accord with Gandhi in finding distasteful the entire Westphalian ideal). Savarkar's admiration for this aspect of European modernity was explicit in his ideal of Hindutva[21] and it is what Gandhi most recoiled

---

[21] V.D. Savarkar, *Hindutva*, Delhi: Hindi Sahitya Sadan, 2003. I had heard Ashis Nandy give a brief but shrewd and convincing reading of this work along these modernist lines, in a lecture on the trial of Gandhi's assassin, a few years ago. For a denial of the view that Nehru's ideas of the nation amounted to something western and Westphalian, but rather viewing it as what I called 'archimedean', see Akeel Bilgrami, 'Two Concepts of Secularism', *Economic and Political Weekly*, 9 July 1994.

from. His indifference to rights and other such codifications was only that he saw them as necessary within such a development as Savarkar wished for. Independent of that development, human beings did not become better human beings by being made over into citizens of a nation-state, and constrained by its codes and constitutions.[22]

I have tried in these few pages to show how a deep commitment to *Bhakti* ideals, with its close affinities to the neo-Platonism of an earlier period of European history and intellectual history, bring out the radicalism of Gandhi's political thought in the early part of the twentieth century. If it is right to suggest, as I have, that Gandhi thought, in 1908, that India stood at the sort of cusp that Europe stood in the Early Modern period, then it is possible to read a whole range of his anxieties for India as being quite of a piece with the prescient anxieties that the scientific dissenters, invoking the earlier, radical sects, had expressed about developments in political economy and political governance that were being generated by worldly alliances between the ideologues of a new science, and commercial and oligarchic and established religious interests, that were setting up for a period of ruthless capitalist extraction and an incipient centralized form of government dominated by elites, to facilitate it. To speak with a sense of resistance against a future for India that fell prey to these developments would only seem reactionary and anti-modern if there was something about these developments that was inevitable. But its inevitability only seems so if we write our histories as if there was no substantial dissent that had any significance in Early Modern Europe: a victor's history, as it were, a Whiggish complacence in our understanding of the past.

I will not deny that there are interesting questions to be raised about how deterministic we should reckon our understanding of the modern period to

[22] I will not here trace the further morphing I had mentioned earlier, of the notion of 'knowledges to live by' into the idea of an 'expertise to rule by', that followed these ideas of citizenship. There is a large and nuanced story to be told of the loss of engagement and an elevation of detachment in the study of human society that came from seeing the world, including nature, as brute, such that it could no longer make any normative demands on us that prompted our engagement. All agency and engagement was relegated by this move to our subjectivity, not to subjectivity *responding* to the demands of a value-laden material and natural environment. As the passage I cited earlier in Marx makes clear, Marx's ideas of an unalienated life are very much part of (and a specific sophistication of) a picture in which our subjectivity is in responsive sync to the normative demands of a material and natural world, a world which, if it can make such demands on us, can be described (as I have elsewhere done) as possessed of a 'secular enchantment', a secular counterpart, that is, to *Bhakti* and neo-Platonist ideals. The democratization that this makes possible is what thwarts, or might help thwart, the passage from the 'knowledges to live by' (which the world, including nature so conceived, provides to all who live in it) to the pervasive dominance we see of the 'expertise to rule by'. I realize these remarks are far too cryptic to convey much of substance. They are elaborated at much greater length in Bilgrami, 'Gandhi, Newton and the Enlightenment' and 'Democracy and Disenchantment', among others.

be. It is possible that, with the onset of a full-fledged capitalist society, there are deeply deterministic tendencies set up – what Prabhat Patnaik, following Oskar Lange, has called the 'spontaneity' of capital.[23] But in the present paper, we are talking of a period at the cusp, *before* the onset of a thorough-going capitalist formation, and it is not obvious at all that anything like the same idea of deterministic dispositions and tendencies can be mapped on to that earlier period because, as Patnaik makes clear, the tendencies he has in mind are *immanent* tendencies – immanent, that is, to *capital*. It would take both the bite and the detail out of Patnaik's argument, which is focused on capitalism, to glibly extend it to contexts prior to the appearance of those details in the history of political economy. Nor is it obvious that a general doctrine that we have come to think of as 'historical materialism' speaks to a strict and generalizable teleology of this kind. Marx's own writings are not fully committed on this subject, and it is interesting to note that Patnaik nowhere suggests that there is a generalizable form of determinism, of which his own analysis of capitalism is only a particular instance.

I conclude, then, that it was part of the creativity in Gandhi that Irfan Habib observes, that he should have relied on the resources of India's religious traditions,[24] to present a range of arguments that we may rightly perceive as radical, if we assume with him that India was roughly at the sort of crossroads Europe found itself in the Early Modern period; and we would only infer that this affinity with *Early* Modern radicalism as *late* as the early twentieth century is *anti*-modern if we make further highly dubious and complacent deterministic teleological assumptions that Gandhi himself never made. The charge of nostalgia and reaction no more holds of this creative argument in Gandhi[25] than it does of creative arguments made by Renaissance figures who were, no doubt, similarly charged with nostalgia and reaction for a vanished 'classical' period, by the complacence of scholastics.

---

[23] For an elaboration of this form of determinism, see, among several other papers by him, Prabhat Patnaik, 'Socialism and the Peasantry', *Social Scientist*, November–December 2009; paper presented at 'The Radical Enlightenment', Alam Khundmiri Foundation Conference, Hyderabad, 2007.

[24] Irfan Habib points out how perverse it was of Gandhi to describe himself as a '*sanatani*' or orthodox Hindu. By any measure of orthodoxy, Gandhi's Hinduism is a very maverick mix, about as far from orthodoxy as it is possible to be. I am stressing the *Bhakti* elements which are, of course, well-known to be remote from orthodoxy. But even Gandhi's Vaishnavism, owing to the *sant*-poets of Gujarat such as Narsin Mehta, and his mother's early influence on him, are far removed from Hindu orthodoxy. In fact, many elements in it are quite continuous with the *Bhakti* elements I appeal to in my argument.

[25] Far from being dismissible as having reactionary contemporary irrelevance, Prabhat Patnaik has in fact argued that some of Gandhi's positions on political economy are highly pertinent in contemporary India. See Prabhat Patnaik, 'On the Economics of "Open Economy" De-industrialization', V.V. Giri Memorial Lecture 2003; available on the web at http://www. networkideas.org/featart/nov2003/fa25_Open_Economy.htm.

On the Macroeconomics of a Colonial Economy

Prabhat Patnaik

Irfan Habib's contribution to our understanding of the mechanics of exploitation of the Indian economy in the colonial period is outstanding. Apart from numerous individual articles on different facets of the economy in the colonial period, he wrote specifically on the macroeconomic aspects of the colonial economy both in his paper 'Colonialization of the Indian Economy' and in his review article of the second volume of the *Cambridge Economic History of India* (hereafter *CEHI*).[1]

The *CEHI* had suggested that if there was a 'drain' of wealth from India, manifested as an export surplus, against which no debt in favour of India got built up, then, on standard Keynesian grounds, this should have caused an *increase* in India's national income (compared to what it otherwise would have been), through the foreign trade multiplier.[2] The 'drain' in short, by generating additional aggregate demand, should have had a beneficial effect on the country's output and employment, as opposed to the national-ists' claim, supported by Irfan Habib, about its impoverishing effect on the economy.

The purpose of the present paper is to develop the macroeconomics of a colonial economy which is different from the macroeconomics of the kind of economy that Keynes was writing about, as a background to understanding the argument of the nationalist writers and of Habib, and also the reason for the difference between their position and that of the *CEHI*.

To anticipate the argument, the fundamental difference *that is germane to the present discussion* between the colonial economy and an advanced capitalist economy of the sort that Keynes was writing about, consists in the fact that the additional exports from the former, against which there is no *quid pro quo* and which therefore constitute the commodity form of the

---

[1] Irfan Habib, 'Colonialization of the Indian Economy', *Social Scientist*, No. 32, 1975; 'Study-ing a Colonial Economy – Without Perceiving Colonialism', *Social Scientist,* No. 139, 1984.

[2] This was the argument put forward by K.N. Chaudhuri, 'Foreign Trade and Balance of Payments', in *The Cambridge Economic History of India*, Volume 2, edited by Dharma Kumar and Meghnad Desai, Delhi: Orient Longman, 1983.

'drain of surplus', consist of *primary commodities*, while the foreign trade multiplier that Keynesian economics talks about operates in the case of *manufactured goods* exports.

Even before presenting this argument, however, I wish to look at the *CEHI* argument on its own terms, i.e. look at the colonial economy as if it was no different from the sort of economy that Keynes was writing about, so that certain specificities of the 'drain' phenomenon get clarified.

Let me begin with the standard macroeconomic identity that the surpluses of the three sectors, the private sector, the government sector and the rest of the world, add up to zero:

$$(I–S) + (G–T) + (X–M) = 0 \qquad\qquad (i)$$

where the notations have their usual meaning.

Now, the 'drain', which is *de facto* an export surplus, does not lead to any enhancement in the country's creditor status. This is because in the balance of payments accounts it is offset by equivalent imports which are either fictitious or uncalled for. In fact the real issue in measuring the 'drain' is the identification of what constitute fictitious or uncalled-for imports. Let us call these imports which are used to conceal the 'drain', the 'drain imports' or M_d. (They will cover non-merchandise items as well.) But the 'drain' concerns not just the balance of payments, it appears in the government budget as well. The 'drain' imports are paid for by the government budget; it is as if the government is spending directly on these import items. For this it raises the requisite finance, which in typical colonial conditions where the orthodoxy of 'sound finance' is in vogue, takes the form of raising an equal amount of tax revenue. Let us denote government expenditure on these 'drain' items by G_d, which we assume equals M_d. The taxes raised for financing the 'drain' can be written as T_d.

Now, those who are the beneficiaries of the 'drain' need not spend, in the period under question, all that accrues to them. And even if they do, they need not spend it on our particular country's products. Let us however assume, for simplicity, that the increase in our exports in the given period exactly equals the magnitude of the 'drain', i.e. if the exports arising because of the 'drain' are written as X_d, then $X_d = M_d$. The export surplus owing to the 'drain' (leaving out 'drain' imports) must equal the budgetary surplus owing to the 'drain' (leaving out 'drain' expenditure), i.e. $X_d = T_d$. It follows, then, that the private deficit (I–S) must remain unchanged despite the 'drain'.

It now becomes obvious that there is a difference between the foreign trade multiplier case and the case of 'drain'. In the latter case, unlike in the former, *as opposed to the demand-increasing effect of the export surplus, there is also a demand-contracting effect exercised by an exactly equal budgetary surplus.* CEHI is not correct, therefore, in drawing a parallel between the two cases.

Nonetheless, even though the budgetary surplus and the export surplus are equal, the demand-expanding effect of the former and the demand-contracting effect of the latter need not be equal. But whether they will be or not can be very precisely stated, since analytically this is exactly analogous to the case of the 'balanced budget multiplier': *if the additional tax revenue for financing the 'drain' comes entirely out of savings, then there will be a net expansionary effect on demand which will be equal to the export surplus times the Keynesian multiplier; if the additional tax revenue comes entirely out of consumption, then the net expansionary effect on demand will be zero; and if the additional tax revenue comes out of consumption and savings exactly in the same proportion that consumption and savings bear to one another, then the net expansionary effect on demand will be exactly the same size as the export surplus itself (i.e. the multiplier value will be one).*

This can be stated in a different way. Let us assume, not implausibly, that the marginal propensity to save out of profits (or surplus) is one, and that the marginal propensity to save out of wages (or incomes of the working people) is zero. Then, if the additional tax revenue for financing the 'drain' falls on the working people, the 'drain' will have zero net expansionary effect on demand; if it falls on the surplus earners, it will have a net expansionary effect which is the 'drain' times the Keynesian multiplier; and if it falls on the working people and the surplus earners exactly in the same ratio as their respective incomes, it will have a net expansionary effect exactly equal to itself.

In the case where the tax burden falls entirely on the working people, so that the net expansionary effect on demand is zero, there is obviously no increase in output or employment. Nonetheless there is an increase in export surplus that equals the 'drain' which comes entirely out of the consumption of the working people. In this case, therefore, there is no increase in employment and a reduction in real wages. *It follows, then, that even within the standard Keynesian universe, if the 'drain' is financed by taxing workers who 'consume what they earn', it will leave employment unchanged and reduce real wages.* CEHI is not correct, therefore, in postulating a positive employment effect of the 'drain' as a general phenomenon even in a Keynesian world. In the Keynesian world, it all depends on how the 'drain' is financed.

But the Keynesian universe differs from the colonial context, where the 'drain' does not cause higher exports of just any odd assortment of commo-

dities but necessarily increases the exports of primary commodities, especially agricultural goods whose output in the period in question is given. In
such a world, whose macroeconomics is different from the Keynesian macroeconomics, the 'drain' can, and generally will, cause a *reduction* in employment together with a reduction in real wages, which it never can in a Keynesian
world. Let us now turn to a discussion of this specifically colonial context.

A capitalist economy, as Michael Kalecki had argued long ago, is typically a
'demand-constrained' economy.[3] A rise in aggregate demand in such an
economy in any period, with given money wages, increases output rather
than prices. This is because such an economy is typically dominated by
sectors such as manufacturing where prices are a *mark-up over unit variable
cost*, rather than agriculture and other primary-producing sectors whose
prices are *demand-determined*. True, the demand for primary commodities
being 'derived' ultimately from the demand for processed goods, variations
in primary commodity prices *in response to variations in demand for processed goods* do affect the unit variable costs of the latter, and hence should
also affect the latter's prices if the mark-up margin is fixed; but their weight
in the unit cost of processed goods being small, such price variations, as
long as they are within certain limits, are usually absorbed *without any
change in the final goods price*, i.e. the mark-up margin adjusts in the short
run as a countervailing factor against raw material price movements.[4]

Kalecki's basic assumption was that the current inputs of labour and raw
materials per unit of output do not change as output changes (an assumption that also underlies Leontief's input–output analysis), and that the
existing output in any period is one where neither fixed capital nor the
labour force is fully utilized in the economy. In such a case, as demand
expands for final processed goods their output also expands, by using up
more labour, running down stocks of raw materials and raising the level of
capacity utilization of fixed capital equipment. *A rise in demand therefore
causes output adjustment rather than price adjustment.*

Even if this assumption of current inputs per unit of output being con-

---

[3] Michael Kalecki, *Selected Essays on the Dynamics of the Capitalist Economy 1933–1970*,
Cambridge: Cambridge University Press, 1971. It is worth recalling here the proposition
advanced by the well-known Hungarian economist Janos Kornai ('Resource-Constrained
versus Demand-Constrained Systems', *Econometrica*, 47, 1979), based on Kalecki's work,
that 'classical capitalism is demand-constrained' and 'classical socialism is resource-constrained'.

[4] The fixed mark-up, in other words, is applied to the unit variable cost calculated on the basis
of some 'long-run' supply price of primary commodities (which itself may change *secularly*),
i.e. which is an average through short-run price fluctuations.

stant in the short run is found unacceptable, and if current input coeffi-
cients are assumed to rise as output increases (which is what Keynes believed), even then an increase in aggregate demand will cause *both output
and price adjustments but never exclusively price adjustments in a typical
capitalist economy, since it is dominated by sectors like manufacturing whose
output is expandable in the short run*. In such an economy, if the export
surplus increases, this typically increases the level of aggregate demand, and
hence of output and employment, *quite irrespective of whether this export
surplus improves the country's creditor status or not, i.e. quite irrespective
of whether it constitutes 'drain'*. In other words, even if it constituted 'drain',
it would still increase output and employment because of the increase in
demand that an export surplus entails. This, essentially, was the argument
of the *CEHI*.

But suppose we are looking at a colonial economy. Such an economy is
dominated by primary production, and in any case *the increase in exports
takes the form of primary commodities* (this is the crucial assumption).
Primary commodities' output, especially that of agricultural goods, is not
augmentable in the short run. Their supplies for manufacturing end-use can
be augmented through decumulation of stocks, but this is accompanied, as
we have seen, by price increases. In short, in their case, to go back to the
Kaleckian point, an increase in demand causes price adjustment rather than
output adjustment. For simplicity, let us assume away any stock decumulation, indeed any stock-holding; let us proceed on the assumption that the
entire output, and no more than this output, is used up in any period, and
that this output in any period is given.

We shall analyse the impact of the 'drain' by comparing the situation
with 'drain' vis-a-vis the situation without 'drain' in such an economy. We
take 'drain' to consist of an increase in exports, causing an equivalent
increase in export surplus, which however does not improve the country's
creditor status. For this analysis we set up a simplified model with the following features.

We assume an economy where the money wage rate is given during the
period in question and, for simplicity, equal everywhere. There are only two
vertically integrated production sectors, both run on capitalist lines: one
produces, again for simplicity, 'food' (the only primary commodity), and
the other produces 'manufactured goods'. Food is consumed only by the
workers in both sectors, while manufactured goods are used for investment,
capitalists' consumption and government consumption.

Let us suppose, to start with, that there is no foreign trade. Then the
following equations must hold.

$$O^*_f = w/p_f \, (O^*_f.l_f + O_m.l_m) \tag{1}$$

where subscripts denote sectors, O denotes output, l the labour coefficient, p the price and w the money wage rate. The term in brackets is total employment in the economy, which, multiplied by the food wage w/p_f must equal the given food output (whose fixity in the period is underscored by the asterisk superscript).

The real output of the manufacturing sector must equal the demand for it. Denoting real government consumption by G, real investment by I and real capitalists' consumption by C_c we have

$$O_m = C_c + I + G \tag{2}$$

If real investment, real capitalists' consumption and real government expenditure are autonomously determined in the current period, i.e. they are uninfluenced by current period variables and are given from 'outside', in the sense of being dependent upon extraneous considerations such as past experience or future expectations, then the r.h.s. of (2) is given, which determines O_m, and hence from (1), the real wage rate.

Now, suppose 'drain' occurs. The 'drain', as stated earlier, has two aspects: on the one hand, it figures in the government budget as expenditure; on the other hand, it takes the form of exports with no actual increase in imports. If the amount of real 'drain' in the form of food is D, then equation (1) becomes

$$O^*_f - D = w/p_f \, (O^*_f.l_f + O_m.l_m) \tag{1'}$$

As long as the autonomous real expenditures in (2) remain unchanged O_m remains unchanged, in which case the term in brackets in (1'), i.e. total employment, also remains unchanged. *The effect of 'drain' in such a case is to reduce the real wages of the workers.* Far from increasing employment, the 'drain' keeps employment unchanged but lowers the real wages of the workers. It is unambiguously immiserizing.

Nothing has been said till now about how this 'drain' is financed, i.e. about how the government expenditure corresponding to the transfers abroad that constitute the 'drain' items is financed. The striking conclusion that emerges from the above model is that *no matter how the 'drain' is financed, whether by taxation or even government borrowing, the effect will be exactly what we have just outlined, i.e. there will be no change in employment and only a fall in real wages.* This follows from the fact that (1') and (2), which are the two basic equations of the economy we are discussing, must both hold, and our conclusions are simply derived from them.

The commonsense explanation is simple. The drain represents a reduction in the domestic availability of food output, which means the domestic availability of wage goods. If employment remains unchanged, then it follows that the real wage rate per employed worker must fall, and it must do so no matter how the 'drain' is financed in the budget. If the take-home money wage rate is reduced, i.e. the workers are directly taxed, then the reduction in real wages occurs through this wage deflation. If the take-home money wage is unchanged, then the reduction in real wage occurs through a rise in food price, which increases in the first instance the profit accruing to the food capitalists. If the 'drain' is financed by government borrowing, then this increased profit is left in the hands of the food capitalists but the government simply borrows it. On the other hand, if the 'drain' is financed by a tax on the food capitalists' profits, then their post-tax profits remain at the old level. Even if the 'drain' is financed by an indirect tax on food, the profits in the hands of the food capitalists remain unchanged.

To sum up, the 'drain' necessarily reduces the wage fund. Where employment remains unchanged (because real expenditures by capitalists and the government on manufactured goods remain unchanged), it reduces the real wage rate. This occurs either through a tax on the money wage or through a rise in food price. No matter how the 'drain' is financed, other than through a tax on money wages, such a price rise must occur (this is true even if the 'drain' is financed through a direct tax on manufactured goods' capitalists or through an indirect tax on manufactured goods, cases we have not considered above). Thus the mode of financing the 'drain', other than through money wage taxation, only determines the level and distribution of profits among capitalists.

So far we have assumed that workers consume only food. Let us drop this assumption and consider the case where they consume both food and manufactured goods. This of course raises the question: how do they distribute their expenditure between the two goods? We shall confine ourselves to a simple case. We assume that out of their money wages the workers first consume a certain quantity of food, no matter what its price, and spend the balance on manufactured goods. Let this quantity of food be denoted by F. Then our equations change into the following for the pre-'drain' situation:

$$O^*_f = F \cdot (O^*_f.l_f + O_m.l_m) \qquad\qquad (1'')$$

$$O_m = C_c + I + G + (w - F.p_f) \cdot (O^*_f. l_f + O_m.l_m) / p_m \qquad (2')$$

The first of these states that food output must equal employment times the fixed food requirement per worker. The second states that manufactured goods output must equal the real expenditure on manufactured goods not only of the capitalists and the government, but also of the workers. This is the last term on the r.h.s. of (2') and equals workers' money expenditure on manufactured good (which is employment times the excess of money wage over the money expenditure on the fixed food amount) divided by the price of the manufactured good.

Since the price of the manufactured good has now entered the picture, we have to specify how it is determined. We assume, in line with Kalecki, that it is simply a mark-up over the unit variable cost, i.e.

$$p_m = w.l_m.(1 + \eth) \qquad (3)$$

where $\eth$ is the mark-up margin.

Now, if 'drain' occurs and takes the form of an export of food, then (1') becomes

$$O^*_f - D = F . (O^*_f. l_f + O_m.l_m) \qquad (1''')$$

and as long as the 'drain' is not financed by a direct tax on wages, no other equation needs to be changed. In this case the reduction in the wage fund caused by the drain gives rise to a reduction *both in the real wage rate and in employment in the economy. Far from there being an increase in employment because of the 'drain', as claimed by CEHI in accordance with the Keynesian argument on the foreign trade multiplier, there is a reduction in employment together with a reduction in the real wages.*

The reason for this is simple. Since the drain reduces the availability of food, at the original level of employment there is a rise in food price. As the workers must purchase a certain fixed amount of food per capita, the rise in food price forces them to reduce consumption of non-food items, in the present case manufactured goods. This lowers employment in the manufactured goods sector and hence in the economy as a whole. At the same time there is a reduction in real wages because while the food intake per employed worker remains the same, the manufactured good consumption goes down. There is thus a combination of lower real wages and lower employment.

This *denouement* occurs no matter how the 'drain' is financed in the government budget. A direct tax on workers will prevent a rise in the food price. Even a rise in indirect tax on the manufactured good can prevent an increase in food price, since by raising the manufactured good's price it reduces the workers' real expenditure upon it, and hence causes lower output and employment in this sector, which releases food for export. But even in these two cases, when there is no rise in food price, real wages and employment will still be lowered. Any other manner of financing the 'drain', including direct taxes on the capitalists of either sector or government borrowing (fiscal deficit), will raise food prices, and thereby lower real wages and employment in the economy.

In the case under discussion, however, we can arrive at a remarkable theorem. *While the post-'drain' real wages and employment will be lower than the pre-'drain' levels, they will be exactly the same no matter how the 'drain' is financed.* In other words, the post-'drain' real wages and employment are completely invariant with respect to the manner of financing the 'drain'.

This can be easily seen as follows. From (1'''), as long as the real 'drain' is given, since O^*_f and F, i.e. the food output and the fixed food consumption per worker, are given, post-'drain' employment gets determined; it does not depend upon the manner of financing the 'drain'. This means an invariance of employment in the manufacturing sector to the manner of financing the 'drain', and hence an invariance of manufacturing output as well. Since the real demand of the government and the capitalists for manufactured goods is given autonomously, this means that the workers' real consumption of manufactured goods is invariant to the manner of financing the 'drain', as is their real consumption of food. Hence their real wage is invariant to the manner of financing the 'drain'. The manner of financing of the 'drain' therefore makes no difference to the level of post-'drain' employment and real wage in the period under consideration.

Even so, however, it is worth distinguishing, as we have done above, between two different ways of financing the 'drain': one involving a rise in food prices and the other involving no such increase. The former arises when workers' wages or real expenditure are not directly targeted by the government, the latter when they are. The former consists of borrowing and taxes on capitalists, the latter includes taxes on workers, whether direct taxes or indirect taxes on the manufactured good. (Indirect taxation of food of course *ipso facto* raises food price and hence does not belong to the latter category.)

Looking at it another way, we can distinguish between 'profit inflation' and 'income deflation' as the two different methods of financing the 'drain'. Both release food for export by reducing the absorption of food by the workers, but 'profit inflation', as Keynes had shown, does so by raising food price relative to the money wages,[5] while 'income deflation' does so by reducing the (post-tax) wage rate or the total wage bill (through a

---

[5] J.M. Keynes, *A Treatise on Money*, Volume 2: *The Applied Theory of Money*, London: Macmillan, 1930. It should be noted that 'profit inflation' by our definition occurs even when the post-tax profits in the food sector do not increase, i.e. when the additional profits accruing to the food capitalists on account of the profit inflation is taxed away by the government. 'Profit inflation', in other words, is an analytical rather than a descriptive category.

reduction in employment) at the given food price. These two ways of financing the 'drain', even while achieving the identical objective of reducing domestic absorption of food and releasing it for export, have very different implications in other respects, as we shall see below.

To sum up, an export surplus squeezed out of the colonial economy has a contractionary effect on output and employment, rather than an expansionary effect, as suggested by Keynesian economics as generally occurring in the context of developed capitalist economies. This difference arises from a basic difference between the colony and the metropolis, which consists in the fact that such an export surplus from the former takes the commodity form of primary products ('food' in the above model), while from the latter it typically takes the form of processed goods (what we have called the 'manufactured good'). The output of the former in any period is fixed, while that of the latter is augmentable.

The above argument has been developed through a simple model that makes a number of extreme assumptions. The question naturally arises: do its conclusions hold if we remove these assumptions? It is obvious that removing assumptions like capitalists not consuming food will make little difference to the argument. They will get whatever food they wish to have without reducing their demand for other goods, since they have enough cash reserves to maintain their consumption. Similarly, even if workers do not consume their entire wages, as assumed here, but save a fraction of it, the argument remains unimpaired. Even if they wish to maintain their real demand for goods in the face of rising food prices (with given money wage), they will soon run out of savings and hence be forced to curtail their real demand for goods, effecting the *denouement* suggested above.

Four assumptions, however, need in particular to be examined. The first is our assumption of the universal predominance of capitalist production in the colonial economy. It is obvious that the agriculture sector in the colonial economy is dominated by peasant production, with the peasantry exploited to the hilt by the trader–moneylender–landlord nexus, on the one hand, and by colonial taxation, on the other. Likewise, the 'manufactured goods' sector has substantial pre-capitalist craft production. The process of deindustrialization affects this pre-capitalist craft sector rather than the modern capitalist industrial sector. Do our conclusions, derived from the assumption of universal capitalist production, hold in the real-life situation of predominance of petty production?

The analytical basis of our argument is that a *rise in food prices* on account of reduced food availability *leads to a reduction in demand for manufactured goods*. With such a reduced demand, it is obviously the petty producers in the manufacturing sector who will the first victims. Hence our not taking petty producers in the manufacturing sector explicitly into account is of little consequence. The argument developed in the context of the model actually works itself out with particular force when there are petty produ-cers. But, does a rise in food price reduce the demand for manufactured goods? In the case of urban workers or of agricultural labourers with fixed money wages, this is no doubt true. And as for agricultural labourers with kind wages, they may be insulated from the effects of a food price increase but they certainly will not be *increasing* their demand for manufactured goods when the food price rises, so that aggregating them together with workers does no harm. But what about the peasants? Do they not benefit from food price increases?

The overwhelming majority of the peasants constitute either net buyers of food, i.e. are not much different from labourers, or sellers in the immediate post-harvest period and buyers later in the year. Since the seasonal price difference typically increases when food price rises, this latter category of peasants too becomes worse off when food price increases. It follows that the overwhelming majority of peasants are adversely affected by a rise in food price.[6] Their demand for manufactured goods therefore gets adversely affected when food price rises. Of course, the prosperous peasants who are comparable to agricultural capitalists and surplus earners in general gain from a food price increase, and since their demand for manufactured goods is likely to be much higher than that of the overwhelming majority of peasants who lose from a food price increase, it may be thought that such a food price increase raises the overall demand for manufactured goods. But in the case of such prosperous peasants, as in the case of capitalists generally, the rise in consumption in the event of a food price rise is not immediate, i.e. their marginal propensity to save in the period under consideration is high.[7] The net effect of a rise in food price on the demand for manufactured goods is adverse, therefore, as suggested in the model.[8] Hence the conclusion

---

[6] Ashok Mitra, *Terms of Trade and Class Relations*, London: Frank Cass, 1977.

[7] The question may arise: even if this ensures that a rise in food price reduces the demand for manufactured goods in the current period, what about the next period when the prosperous peasants spend the higher incomes they have earned in the current period? But since the output of manufactured goods would have fallen in the current period because of the delayed spending of the prosperous peasants, the manufacturing sector's profits would have shrunk, giving rise to reduced demand for manufactured goods from the capitalists in the next period; it is likely that this reduced demand would offset the increased demand from the rural rich.

[8] Indeed if it were not so, then there would be no stability in the foodgrain market: even a chance increase in foodgrain price would lead to an unlimited increase in foodgrain prices. In other words, if a rise in food price did not lead to a decline in manufacturing demand, then the system will explode even with a chance increase in the foodgrain price. Empirically, the

derived from the model on the basis of the simple assumption of universal capitalist production remains valid even in the more complex and realistic situation of capitalist production being located within an ocean of petty production.

The second issue that can be raised vis-a-vis the model is: what happens to the unemployed? The unemployed simply drop out of the model, though in fact they must somehow be subsisting. The implications of their subsistence in their state of unemployment is not reckoned with in the model.

But reckoning with this is likely to strengthen the conclusion derived from the model. The unemployed will have to live off the employed somehow, and this fact would be analytically analogous to an increase in F in the model, i.e. to a reduction in the amount spent by the employed on manufactured goods over and above their basic subsistence food requirement. (Or, putting it differently, having more mouths to feed raises F to the per capita minimum subsistence food requirement of the employed population.) This in turn further reduces employment in the manufacturing sector, further raising F and so on. Once we also recognize that the working population, in addition to using its income, also pays for its basic consumption requirements by selling, or getting dispossessed of, assets, this process of reduced manufacturing employment giving rise to further reductions in manufacturing employment becomes a story of progressive pauperization stretched out through historical time,[9] which after all is what happened in real history.

The third assumption that can be questioned is our making food a surrogate for primary commodity exports in general. True, mineral exports are in a category of their own, but can food even be made a surrogate for agricultural goods? Typically, colonial India was not so much a food exporter as an exporter of agricultural raw materials. Hence the proposition that the export surplus which constitutes the 'drain' necessarily reduces food availability, and hence the real wages of the workers, appears unsustainable at first sight. Does this fact damage our argument?

This is actually not a serious objection since food and agricultural raw materials compete for the available land. An increase in cash-crop exports which is caused by the 'drain' leads, not directly but indirectly through the

---

fact that the demand for cloth in India was inversely related to food price was drawn attention to in a Government of India Report (*Report of the Textile Inquiry Committee*, New Delhi: Government of India, 1958). Its analytical implications were explored in Prabhat Patnaik, 'Disproportionality Crisis and Cyclical Growth', *Economic and Political Weekly*, Annual Number, 1972.

[9] Pauperization of this sort occurring over a period of time must be distinguished from instability of the model (see previous footnote). The latter is a logical problem, while the former is a process occurring through historical time.

shift of acreage from food to cash crops, to a reduction in food availability for the domestic working population.

The fourth issue is the most serious one and deserves more extensive discussion. We have so far confined our attention to the single period. Because of this, our assumption of a given 'food' output was justified. But once we take a sequence of periods, this output can be augmented, particularly since the rise in food price during this period is likely to encourage larger investment in this sector. In such a case, the basic distinction between processing and primary commodity production, namely that there is price adjustment in one and output adjustment in the other, disappears. Even primary production experiences output adjustment, if not immediately then at least over a period of time, in which case the analysis of the implications of the 'drain' in Keynesian terms, as done in the first section of this paper, becomes perfectly adequate, and our subsequent discussion becomes irrelevant.

There are two reasons, however, why this is not so. First, land is a constraining factor on output in agriculture. Capital investment itself is either a means of bringing about land augmentation, irrigation, reclamation, etc., for example, or a complement to land augmentation, such as HYV seeds, multiple cropping and tractors, as the sequel to the introduction of irrigation. Capital investment for land augmentation, which is thus the prerequisite for output increase in agriculture, needs, for obvious reasons, to be undertaken by the state. The colonial state never undertook any significant investment of this sort except in the canal colonies of the Punjab. A crucial factor underlying the reluctance on its part to do so was that the state insisted on a narrow rate of return criterion for deciding on investment; and in large parts of the country which were under the Permanent Settlement, since the revenue was fixed in perpetuity, the rate of return on investment in irrigation was zero. No public investment in irrigation could conceivably occur there.[10]

The second reason is linked to this. We have seen that the two ways of financing the 'drain' are: profit inflation and income deflation. If the tax burden falls largely on the workers and peasants, both through indirect taxes on processed goods and through direct taxes on land (which have an effect similar to income taxation when it comes to curtailing consumption), then the 'drain' is being financed through income deflation rather than through profit inflation.

Now, profit inflation in the agricultural sector has the effect of raising

[10] A.K. Bagchi, 'Reflections on Patterns of Regional Growth', *Bengal Past and Present*, Volume 95, No. 1, 1976.

the profitability of agriculture. True, if the fruits of profit inflation are removed by the state through taxation of profits, the rise in profitability is thereby prevented or restrained. But even if the government balances its budget through profit taxation, since such taxes fall on *all profits* while profit inflation raises only the profits of the agricultural sector, the latter's rate of profit still increases compared to the initial situation. This persuades the state that if it undertakes land-augmenting investment, complementary private investment will be forthcoming, which will raise agricultural output and hence government revenue (in non-permanently settled areas). But if income deflation becomes the main means of financing the 'drain', then the prospects of complementary private investment to any public investment in irrigation or other forms of land augmentation remain dim, which, under the rate of return criterion, thwarts such public investment altogether. Stagnation of agricultural output over a long period and not just fixity of output in the short run becomes, therefore, the order of the day, as it did in colonial India, when the 'drain' is financed by income deflation.

The estimation of agricultural output was one of the major points of criticism of Irfan Habib, as well as of Arun Ghosh,[11] against the *CEHI*. Habib had been critical of the assumptions underlying Alan Heston's long-term output estimates contained in the *CEHI*. The point about the colonial economy that he had underscored was how its different aspects fitted together: the 'drain', the deindustrialization and the long-term stagnation of output. The foregoing sketch of the macroeconomics of a colonial economy seeks to capture this interdependence.

Utsa Patnaik has been emphasizing how neoliberalism replicates many of these features of the colonial economy.[12] The promotion of export agriculture, under the neoliberal dispensation that insists on opening up the economy to 'free trade', invariably undermines food security in third world economies, as has happened in a host of countries ranging from Mexico to Sub-Saharan Africa to India. While the overall productive potential of agriculture remains stagnant owing to a lack of public investment in agriculture (since such investment is frowned upon in a neoliberal regime), the diversion of land from foodgrains to cash crops causes a decline in domestic per capita foodgrain availability. This is sustained in turn through a drastic income deflation imposed on the working population in various ways.

---

[11] A.K. Ghosh, 'Price Movements and Fluctuations in Economic Activity (1860–1974): A Review of McAlpin's Contribution', *Social Scientist*, No. 139, 1984.
[12] Utsa Patnaik, *The Republic of Hunger and Other Essays*, Delhi: Three Essays Collective, 2007.

The above model throws light on the mechanism underlying this pheno-menon. The difference between then and now is that the colonial period had seen the sacrifices of the working people being simply 'drained' away to the metropolis without a *quid pro quo*, while today such exports finance imports that go into the consumption of the affluent.

On Socialism and its 'Failure'

C.P. Chandrasekhar

The search for a more humane alternative to capitalism, without the attendant inequality, unemployment, poverty and environmental degradation, is as old as the system itself. Socialism, in theory, was seen as providing such an alternative with a grand design: that of replacing private property and the market mechanism, which were seen as underlying capitalist failure, with social ownership and centralized planning.

However, the subversion of 'actually existing socialism' in the erstwhile Soviet Union and Eastern Europe, and its radical transformation in the direction of a more 'market-driven' system elsewhere in the world, have encouraged a number of critical appraisals of the functioning of erstwhile, centrally planned systems. Being a committed Marxist and intellectually grounded in Marxism as a tradition, it is not surprising that Irfan Habib in his writings, especially the essay titled 'The Marxian Theory of Socialism and the Experience of the Socialist Societies',[1] turned to this issue by revisiting those writings of the founders of socialist thought that go beyond a critique of capitalism and imperialism, and delineate the defining features of an egalitarian, post-capitalist society, its modes of functioning, and the social and individual outcomes it was expected to deliver.

Habib's analysis does not focus on the features of the egalitarian society to which mankind should eventually transit. Rather, given the broad contours of such a society and informed by the 'failure' of actually existing socialism, his principal concern is to investigate whether there are elements within the classical tradition that could explain why in the course of the traverse to such an ideal, the project can be subverted. The point of departure for this analysis is the assumption implicit in the classics that this was unlikely. Once the means of production were socialized and ownership trans-

[1] Irfan Habib, 'The Marxian Theory of Socialism and the Experience of the Socialist Societies', *Social Scientist*, Vol. 21, Nos 5–6, May–June 1994; revised and published as an Appendix in Irfan Habib (ed.), *On Socialism: Selections from the Writings of Karl Marx, Frederick Engels, V.I. Lenin, J.V. Stalin, Mao Zedong*, New Delhi: Tulika Books, in association with Aligarh Historians Society, 2009.

ferred to the state, the classical position seemed to postulate, the 'anarchy' and waste characteristic of capitalism would have been overcome, and the system would be able, unlike under capitalism, to ensure the 'unbroken, constantly accelerated development of the productive forces'. This in turn was expected to deliver the material means needed to transit to the higher stage of Communism, in which production and lifestyles would be such that everyone would be compensated according to his/her needs and not according to his/her contribution to social labour time.

In attempting an assessment of the challenges faced by forces committed to the 'march to the goal of a state of equality and an abundance of goods', Habib notes that the movement from social ownership to the end of anarchy and the creation of social abundance is neither unidirectional nor inevitable. One important reason for this is that since socialism (as the first stage of the transition to Communism) emerges out of the womb of capitalism, it carries some of its traces. In particular, even if we assume that at the outset of the transition the state owns and controls all means of production, this does not imply the end of commodity production. In a stage of society where workers not only contribute according to their ability but are paid according to their work, there are two markets in which the sale of the concerned use value occurs through the market and for money. First, there must exist a market for labour inasmuch as workers, though free from capitalist exploitation, must have the freedom to choose their occupation and must have some freedom to choose the commodities they buy with the wages they receive (as equivalent exchange values of their labour power). For this they must be paid in money, which gives labour power the characteristics of a 'commodity'. Second, there must be a market for the means of consumption where workers can use the money wages they receive to buy products that they choose, which must be offered in exchange for money by the producers of those commodities – who therefore are still involved in a form of commodity production.

This does mean that if appropriate conditions prevail and the system functions smoothly, the distribution of the means of production and labour across sectors and across industries producing the means of consumption could be influenced by the 'values' of those 'commodities', and not just by some *a priori* plan determined by planners' judgements of appropriate social wants. Wages for different occupations would adjust to equate the supply of any particular kind of labour to the demand for it. Even if the 'law of value' does not dominate, its influence is likely to be felt. Even if, given the need to move to a more egalitarian framework, the state provides a certain 'social wage' to all, the relative real wages earned by workers in all sectors would be such that the allocation of 'freely mobile' labour across sectors can be equated to the demand for labour.

Further, it would be necessary to ensure that the production of consumption goods must be such as to meet the demands generated by the money wages determined as above. This requires that the production and sale of consumption goods must also function according to the requirements set by the law of value. The prices of means of consumption would adjust to equate their supplies to the demands generated by the level and pattern of wages, and consumer preferences.

Finally, there is the overarching problem that stems from the fact that there is no market for 'produced means of production' and extracted resources in a system in which the means of production are socially owned and all the production is controlled by the state. A mechanism has to be devised to ensure that the allocation of these resources is such that the demands generated for them – as a result of the operation of the law of value in the markets for labour and the means of consumption – are met.

The Danger of Anarchy

The first important challenge that 'socialism' therefore faces in the course of its traverse to the 'higher stage', is the identification and implementation of proper mechanisms such that: (i) despite the influence of the diluted 'law of value', the system's smooth functioning is ensured, and resources and labour are allocated across sectors as per the requirements; (ii) this does not import into the system, the anarchy and instability inherent in capitalist systems where the law of value dominates; and (iii) this functioning delivers outcomes that correspond to an *a priori* conspectus or plan. As Irfan Habib notes: 'Any failure in the accuracy of response to consumer demand in Department II and a similar failure to mesh "accounting prices" in Department I to sale prices of Department II, could generate waste of productive resources comparable to or possibly even exceeding that of capitalism.'[2] Thus, if a socialist economy did not devise appropriate mechanisms and did not use its tools efficiently, it would have difficulty in 'escaping the cycles of instability in production found in capitalism'.

Interestingly, in this context, Habib refers favourably to Oskar Lange's undoubtedly seminal contribution to the discussion on the design of economic systems with social ownership.[3] This contribution of Lange's attempted to blend the planning principle and the market in innovative ways. His conception of a planned system was developed in the course of a *defence of*

---

[2] Habib, 'The Marxian Theory of Socialism and the Experience of the Socialist Societies', in Habib (ed.), *On Socialism*, p. 177.
[3] Ibid., pp. 176–77.

'*socialism*' against the argument that in the absence of markets and prices for resources, including produced means of production, it lacks in practice a feasible mechanism that can allocate resources efficiently. That argument was formulated by von Mises[4] and Hayek[5] in response to Barone's suggestion that the central planner could, like the Walrasian auctioneer, solve a system of equations involving an equivalent number of unknowns to arrive at a set of prices that would clear all markets. Lange's defence of socialism against the von Mises–Hayek critique presumed that investment and production decisions would be 'decentralized', but would be undertaken by plant and industry-level managers according to accounting rules specified by the central planning board, and by taking a list of prices put out by the board as parameters. The accounting rules themselves were similar to, if not identical with, those adopted 'naturally' by profit-maximizing agents in a competitive market with free entry and exit. If, as a result of such decisions, the quantities supplied and demanded of any commodity at the notified prices did not tally, the central planning board would adjust its prices upwards or downwards, and move the system towards an equilibrium in which supply equalled demand. By acting in this manner as a 'price setter', Lange argued, the central planning board could ensure that a socialist system replicated the allocative equilibrium typical of a competitive market.

Implications of the Defence

This defence implicitly accepted the notion that price signals generated by perfectly functioning markets were the most efficient allocators of resources to meet ends specified by consumer preferences. Naturally, therefore, it was concerned with the extent to which the socialist economic mechanism could approximate those prices by imitating such markets. Besides the fact that the debate ignored even conventional scepticism about the efficiency of 'as-perfect-as-possible', real world markets where information is incomplete and trading occurs sequentially,[6] it gave the argument away by addressing the question as to whether an interventionist regime could approximate the automatic equilibrium generated by the market. As Dobb argued,[7] the comparison was between an 'ideal-type' which costlessly arrived at an equilibrium, and a cumbersome, interventionist regime which attempted to appro-

---

[4] Ludwig von Mises, 'Economic Calculation in the Socialist Commonwealth' [1920], in Friedrich A. Hayek (ed.), *Collectivist Economic Planning: Critical Studies on the Possibilities of Socialism*, London: Routledge, 1935.

[5] Friedrich A. Hayek, in Hayek (ed.), *Collectivist Economic Planning*.

[6] Frank Hahn, *Equilibrium and Macroeconomics*, Delhi: Disha Publications, 1989.

[7] Maurice Dobb, *An Essay on Growth and Planning*, New York: Monthly Review Press, 1960.

ximate that equilibrium. And, in the process of winning the debate on the argument that socialism can actually ensure the approximation of 'equilibrium prices', the unsatisfactory and inappropriate comparison undermined the real strength of the planning principle in the classical tradition, which lay in its ability to coordinate investment decisions within a regime where only the markets for labour and consumption goods were relatively free.

Lange went on to suggest that since the state was not wedded to the principle of private ownership, it could start with a more acceptable distribution of endowments. Further, the central planning board could ensure that the prices chosen are more comprehensive and take account of externalities, that adjustment proceeds faster, and that monopolistic price-fixing policies are not resorted to. That is, the socialist economy can not only replicate a competitive market, but also ensure that endowments are more equally redistributed, externalities are taken account of and monopolistic restrictions on trade that result in inefficiency are kept under control. Markets in this system can not only be closer to perfection in their working, but also more 'people-friendly'.[8]

The obvious blend of markets and planning in Lange's model of socialism is ensured through separation of the structure of decision-making (which is decentralized) and the hierarchical structure of objectives based on which those decisions are made. Societal, macro-scale objectives dominate the latter, so that 'lower-rank objectives become the means for attaining higher-level ones, and the criteria for rational behaviour of the subsytems (sectors, branches, enterprises) are subordinated to the system as a whole.'[9] The presumption is that decentralized decision-makers will not deviate in their behaviour from what is centrally ordained, even if such behaviour is not the most rational as seen solely from their 'decentralized' perspective.

Lange's argument was a departure from the classical conception of economic planning which emerged from a *critique of capitalism*, and which focused on the anarchy associated with the atomistic decision-making characteristic of systems based on private property. In such systems, the level and allocation of investment get determined by the 'guesses or expectations of a large number of independent decision-takers (entrepreneurs), in the long run "revised" by *ex post* movements of market prices'.[10] Since the investment in fixed capital that results is not by definition reversible, decision

---

[8] The assumption, of course, was that planners were 'efficiency-maximizing politicians' who were by definition interested in income and asset redistribution, in internalizing externalities, and in encouraging competition rather than monopoly. This assumption was not borne out by the experience in the erstwhile socialist societies.

[9] Wodzmierz Brus and Kazimierz Laski, *From Marx to the Market: Socialism in Search of an Economic System*, Oxford: Clarendon Press, 1989.

[10] Dobb, *An Essay on Growth and Planning.*

errors are costly in individual and social terms. And such errors are bound to occur since private investment decisions must be based on estimates of prices that would prevail over the lifetime of the project. In these circumstances, existing prices cannot be a guide to future prices as the atomistic, individual investment decisions made on the basis of prevailing prices together influence subsequent movements in prices. Without an anchor, there is no reason to expect that expectations will actually be realized, leading to overinvestment, unutilized capacity and closure, or to shortages. Hence a system that seeks to supersede the anarchy of capitalism must coordinate investment and arrive at *ex ante* decisions on the total volume of investment, its allocation to sectors and particular projects, and the technical forms in which it would be embodied.

The benefits from such coordination were two-fold. First, by overcoming the 'secondary uncertainty'[11] stemming from the lack of definite knowledge of the likely actions of others inherent in a regime where investment was based on atomistic decisions, it reduced the waste and unemployment characteristic of capitalism. Second, by ensuring the incorporation of appropriate inter-temporal judgements in the choice of the investment ratio, the allocation of investment and the technical forms in which it was embodied, it permitted a process of maximizing growth subject to the consumption requirements set by social and political conditions.

There were three aspects of Lange's argument that drew criticism from those owing allegiance to this tradition. First, by implicitly doing away with the plan–market dichotomy, the argument made the case for socialism purely an 'egalitarian' one. And this it did by accepting the terrain of a critique of socialism that compared it with an 'ideal-type', viz. the competitive market, which automatically ensures an equilibrium, behind the backs of the people. As compared with that, a socialist market required a cumbersome trial-and-error process that was less attractive on 'efficiency' grounds, even if more egalitarian. Second, the dichotomy was discarded essentially by doing away with the planning principle, which involved investment coordination. Planning entailed the creation of an agency that served as a 'price-setting body', which imposed known accounting rules and policed the system. Finally, the dichotomy was discarded at the expense of importing into the system, the likely instability and unemployment that would characterize the system that planning was expected to replace. That likelihood arises the moment we allow decentralized investment decisions to respond to decentralized signals. While most of those signals are 'prices' specified as a part of an exercise aimed at equating economy-wide supply to

---

[11] Tjalling Koopmans, *Three Essays on the State of Economic Science*, New York: McGraw Hill, 1968.

demand, the interest rate cannot be seen as the price that equates the demand for capital with the supply of a given stock of capital, and its resulting marginal productivity. Capital, being a produced means of production, is not an exogenously given but an internally 'accumulated' stock. This process of accumulation through investment generates its own additional demand for capital. That is, any increase or decrease in the 'supply of capital' simultaneously increases or decreases the 'demand' for it. It should be clear that if investment creates its own draught in this manner, the system tends to be characterized by 'knife edge'-like properties that can lead to persisting inflation or unemployment.

While recognizing this danger of anarchy, Habib also emphasizes the possibility of 'failure' of Lange-type socialism because of structural features that subvert the system designed to deliver decentralized implementation based on centralized price and rule-setting. This is a problem not with the Lange mechanism *per se* but the failure to recognize the constraints that may be faced in implementing it effectively even in a society with social ownership. Principal among those constraints, according to Habib, is the fact that once social ownership is ensured and production brought under the centralized control of state-owned enterprises, the economic landscape is populated with firms that are monopolies or oligopolies in their respective areas of operation. Left to themselves, these firms could behave like monopolies and resort to monopolistic pricing practices that involve curtailing production in order to maximize profits. This obviously distorts the functioning of a Lange-type iterative process, leading to the subversion of the system.

What Habib is implicitly arguing here is that the assumption that decentralized decision-makers would adopt centrally provided investment and production rules, and not be influenced by incentives originating from their own structural circumstances (of managing monopolies, in this instance), need not hold. But this is not the only structural problem he identifies. The state-owned monopolies can also be characterized by other tendencies typical of monopolies under capitalism, such as the tendency to pay less attention to investing in technology generation and modernization involving technological upgradation. This would imply that despite social ownership, the economy concerned would not only be afflicted by anarchy and social waste, but also by constraints on the rate of productivity increase and growth in material production. The assumptions implicit in the classical Marxist argument, which 'guarantee' that once social ownership is established the transition to a progressive and egalitarian order is inevitable, are not realized.

The argument here is strong inasmuch as it suggests that the weaknesses that led up to the collapse of actually existing socialism were structural and institutional. If so, such structural and institutional weaknesses can adversely affect even the planning principle, which assumes that: (i) planners are in a position to collate the information and knowledge needed to formulate a society-wide, *a priori* prospectus or plan, and centrally coordinate resource allocation so as to realize that plan at minimum social cost; (ii) when they do that, they are not influenced by their own interests but by society's desires and best interests, which they are in a position to perceive; and (iii) when implementing that plan, they can ensure that lower-level decision-makers and functionaries do not act in ways that subvert the process.

One of the consequences of the failure of actually existing socialism is that these assumptions too have been brought into question. To start with, the failure of actually existing socialism has questioned the notion that central planners have adequate access to the wide and enormous range of information required to execute their implicit brief. In practice, it has been argued, access to such complete information is impossible to ensure. This 'informational inadequacy' arises only partly because of the difficulties involved in creating a framework that allows for the collection, collation and transmission of the required information at a fast enough pace. It also results from the fact that agents at lower levels of implementation and governance may choose to hold back and not transmit crucial information, or even find incentives for transmitting partial or incorrect information, which puts the whole mechanism under threat.

The second problem that has been brought into focus is the difficulty that central planners may face in imposing their *a priori* conspectus on society, given the unavoidable existence in the initial stages of socialism of a 'market' for both labour and means of consumption in which the 'commodities' concerned are bought and sold for money. In such a situation, the *a priori* plan for allocation of output between consumption and savings (investment) may not match the 'monetary' decisions made by consumers, leading to shortages in some areas and/or unutilized capacities in others. This could occur even though the problem can be partly resolved by the state (which, we assume, owns all the means of production) by adjusting the prices of consumption goods relative to money wages, or by imposing turnover taxes to ensure that the aggregate consumption level and the pattern of consumption are in keeping with an *a priori* plan. While this is possible in principle, it can be difficult to achieve in practice.

This leads to the third feature that has been challenged, which is the belief that the objectives and goals of agents at all levels of decision-making or implementation (including shop-floor workers, or workers in agricultural cooperatives or state-owned farms) are common, or that all agents can be made to adopt the objectives considered appropriate by the central planners. Any lack of uniformity of objectives among agents whose structural positions in the system differ is of significance, because the conventional means under capitalism of trying to impose discipline through shareholder-monitoring and the threat of the sack do not operate under socialism.

This problem has always been recognized in the traditional discourse on planning, which considered politics to be key to realizing correct and consistent decisions at lower levels of decision-making. Consensus among the majority around the political agenda, seen as a requirement to put in place the system of central planning itself, and the ability to use that consensus to enforce non-financial penalties for deviance, were seen as adequate to ensure a commonality in objectives pursued by different agents. In practice, it is clear, the extreme difficulty in keeping in place a consensus created in the course of transiting to a system of central planning, and of detecting deviance and enforcing penalties, was substantially underestimated.

Fourthly, even though a system of centralized investment decision-making had the potential to overcome the problem of secondary uncertainty, it had to face the problem of 'primary uncertainty' to the same degree as any system of atomistic decision-making. Needless to say, uncertainty of the kind euphemistically described as 'acts of god', such as vagaries of the monsoon, floods or earthquakes, can never be fully predicted and planned for, although, theoretically at least, a centrally controlled system with a strong state should be more capable of dealing with such emergencies – despite claims to the contrary based on doubtful evidence. However, there are other primary uncertainties, such as uncertainty regarding the direction of development of science and technology, and the evolution of tastes and lifestyles, which, even if not correctly predicted, should be accommodated within a more flexible environment aimed at fostering unusual creativity, or providing for and meeting exceptional consumption demands. It appeared in practice that being more tightly controlled, a centrally planned system could be handicapped when dealing with these forms of uncertainty, as suggested by developments in the erstwhile centrally planned economies during their later phases of 'intensive' growth, dependent on productivity increases and associated with higher per capita incomes.

Finally, there was a real danger of 'bureaucratization' at the higher levels of decision-making which could not be easily confronted by the political environment, since very often the same agents were arbiters of the acceptable politics of the day. Such bureaucratization could not only lead to wrong investment decisions, influenced by sectional rather than societal interests, but could also be replaced by objectives and rules that were considered the best by the planners, even if not necessarily always from a societal point of view. Even if consumer sovereignty, which presumes that individuals are the best judges of what is good for themselves, is a notion that can be dispensed with, some means to ensure the incorporation of individual priorities and desires when deciding on the volume and pattern of consumption should be provided for, if individuals are not to be alienated from the system.

Irfan Habib sums up the consequences of centralization as follows:

> Who controls the socialist state (and how) is the crucial question in determining the destiny of socialism. We have seen that when socialism is established there is no blind economic 'law' which would take socialist society in one particular direction, that of advance. There are policy alternatives at every step; and the choice can always be coloured by group, sectional, and (ultimately) the choice-makers' own interest, as distinct from and, therefore, possibly opposed to the interest of the working people at large. Since, as we have seen, wages continue under socialism, and so does, for the individual worker, the rendering of surplus-labour, there must arise a growing sense of alienation of the worker from the socialist system under conditions where crucial decisions possibly inimical to his interest are taken without any real reference to him. For a long time the workers' recognition of the benefits rendered by the social services created by socialism would continue; but ultimately, as the socialist economy atrophied under the direction of vested interests, the workers' attitude would change to hostility or indifference. The socialist structure would collapse under the internal economic and political strain, aided undoubtedly by the hostile external, capitalist environment dominated by imperialism.[12]

Once we add up all these institutional inadequacies, there is a real possibility that central planning may fail to deliver on many fronts. Experience, too, has made it clear that both in terms of the ability to garner the required information and the ability to intervene effectively in pursuit of specified objectives, the centralizing alternative assumed too large an 'area of control' for the planner and ignored the possibility of conflicting incentives. Even while being successful in ensuring full employment and providing for the basic needs for the overwhelming majority, the system failed to sustain the process of development, especially as the advantages of being able to draw on unutilized resources during the extensive phase of growth had been exhausted. In fact, since providing basic needs for all draws on a substantial volume of resources, centrally planned systems need to maximize productivity growth and the benefits derived from the surplus available at each point of time, in order to ensure an adequate pace of growth. It was the weakening of the ability to do so that led to the failure witnessed in at least some of the erstwhile, centrally planned economies.

---

[12] Habib, 'The Marxian Theory of Socialism and the Experience of the Socialist Societies', pp. 184–85.

Two Paths

There are, thus, dangers associated with socialist economic systems involving either decentralized or centralized decision-making. In an innovative, even if brief, foray into the history of actually existing socialism, Irfan Habib illustrates how this has been experienced in practice as well. In Yugoslavia and Hungary, for example, an attempt was made to overcome the structural problem of monopoly by establishing competing state enterprises or cooperatives which encouraged competition, without permitting private appropriation of surplus value. However, these experiments failed because the effort to encourage competition resulted in the infusion into the system of some of the disadvantages of capitalism, such as anarchy in production and processes of concentration.

In the Soviet Union from the early 1920s, and in China between 1950 and 1980, on the other hand, the effort to limit the degree of decentralization led to a centralized system in which growth was sought to be accelerated by focusing on Department I and generating the capital goods necessary to sustain a higher rate of investment. This required curbing consumption and extracting a 'tribute' from agriculture to finance development, and, therefore, adherence to an *a priori* plan rather than the law of value. This too proved difficult to sustain because of the problems associated with centralization of the kind noted above.

However, Habib argues, the advance of a socialist society requires pursuing the option of establishing 'production under unified control in order to secure steady industrial and economic expansion, without periodic setbacks'. But this must be done with full recognition of the contradictions 'that remain or develop within socialist societies'. The task, therefore, is indeed complex. Those contradictions would require blending the market and the planning principle, while adopting appropriate political and social measures, as well as resorting to non-pecuniary rewards and penalties, to prevent degeneration of the system.

It is here that the actual context and the conjuncture make some difference. To quote Maurice Dobb,[13] within the theory of planning, 'no clear-cut logically defined frontier can be drawn between the province of centralized and of decentralized decision', and 'only experience can decide the expedient extent of the one and the other'. Moreover, there is need for a political and social consensus to decide where this boundary would be drawn and what pattern of consumption the system would adopt.

Thus there could be a long period of time under 'socialism' during which there would be coexistence of planning with the market mechanism and of

---

[13] Dobb, *An Essay on Growth and Planning.*

public ownership with varying degrees of private usufruct rights. But this would be either because a one-shot transition may be too difficult to implement and can therefore prove unsuccessful, or because the shift to investment coordination based on social ownership may require a long period of learning by doing. Such are the many possible implications that can be drawn from Irfan Habib's scholarly attempt to draw attention to the problems that we must address in the quest for a more egalitarian and just order.

The Historian's Task

The Historian's Task

An Interview with Irfan Habib, 7–10 July 2010

Parvathi Menon

This extended interview with Irfan Habib – Marxist historian, teacher, and lifelong communist activist – was taken over four days in early July 2010 in Aligarh, the town in western Uttar Pradesh where Irfan Sahib (as many call him) has spent almost his entire life. He is a familiar figure in Aligarh Muslim University (AMU), an institution to which both his father, the nationalist historian Mohammad Habib, and he have devoted themselves. The renowned historian, who is often seen cycling down the tree-lined roads of the campus hunched over his handle-bar, over the years has acquired an almost iconic status on campus – even in the politically volatile centre of learning that is AMU – for his scholarship, and his left and secular activism. An agitator with a fiercely polemical style of engagement and argument, he is heard with attention by his detractors and supporters alike, whether in academic council sessions, at seminars, in teachers' meetings or at union gatherings.

Irfan Sahib had to be persuaded to be interviewed – indeed the whole project of bringing together a book on his work was a matter of much consternation for him, and to which he agreed with utmost reluctance. He did not wish to talk about himself, but when I told him at the start of our interview that I visualized the target audience of his interview as students and activists on the Left with a keen interest in matters of history and current politics, he seemed much relieved. The interview then flowed more easily, with Irfan Sahib responding to all questions at length. (Except, I might add, when I asked him questions about himself. His answers then were usually briefer and infused with self-deprecatory humour.)

The first three sessions of the interview were held in his room at the Centre for Advanced Studies in History, and the last at Habib Manzil, the gracious, rambling old family home where he lives with his wife Sayera Habib and son Faiz.

The interview spans a gamut of issues on history and contemporary politics, issues that have been Irfan Sahib's intellectual concerns for the last five decades. Starting from the theory and method of history, and its purposes, he answers questions on recent issues in Mughal history, new research findings in archaeology that have changed our understanding of the status of women in pre-historic times, the *People's History of India* project on which he is currently at work, and on the influence of geography in the reconstruction of the historical past. He discusses the Marxist method in history, and how a historian's vision for an equal world in the future must surely influence the way that historian looks at iniquity in the past. He introduces and evaluates some major schools of historiography, and sums up the significance of Marx's writings on India.

Modern Indian history, notably the national movement and the role of Gandhi, is an area of deep interest for Irfan Sahib, and his views here have been at variance with the traditional Left perspective on the national movement and the complex personality of Gandhi, who was its foremost leader. In this interview, he says that he disagrees with the 'triangular situation' proposed by E.M.S. Namboodiripad, in which 'British imperialism, the bourgeois landlord leadership of the national movement, and the working class or Communists' constitute the 'three major elements'. He proposes, by contrast, that the national movement 'has to be looked at as a coalition, rather than a division into two parts'. He argues that the Left underestimated the anti-landlord and pro-peasant content in the programmatic understanding of the Congress and Gandhi.

Interestingly, Prakash Karat revisits this debate in his Introduction to the new edition of E.M.S. Namboodiripad's book, *The Mahatma and the Ism*. 'On two counts, EMS held firm to his views', Karat writes. 'First, Gandhi, as the undisputed leader of the national movement, represented the broad interests of the national bourgeoisie, which led the freedom struggle. Secondly, the Gandhian programme had no anti-landlord component with which to mobilize the peasantry.' He further writes that EMS's standpoint on the pro-landlord component of Gandhism 'reflected the experience of all Left Congressmen who later became Communists'.

In the final part of the interview, Irfan Sahib discusses the role of ideas, particularly political ideas, in the making of society and history.

Considerations in Historiography:
Selection, Bias and Interpretation

Irfan Sahib, I shall start with a question for which many historians have sought answers. Why do we study history?
As you indeed know, Marc Bloch starts his book *The Historian's Craft* by posing this question: of what use is history? My favourite answer – perhaps not original – is, why then does an individual have a memory? He may be

very unimportant, his presence may not change circumstances at all, but for him his memory is very important. It could be a memory of near-accidents, of meeting people or of what happened when he did something. Without memory an individual cannot function, let alone avoid pitfalls.

I suppose in the same way, groups of people, classes or communities, and, in the modern world, nations and countries, need to make use of memory or, rather, make use of history as a source of memory. The more accurate our memory/history, the more beneficial it will be for us as we view our past errors and successes, and the reasons for them.

An individual has a memory of his own past conduct, and he has a memory of other people's past doings. But, just as you cannot be certain about the accuracy of a person's memory of his own actions or those of others, you cannot be certain about the collective memories of groups of people, of what happened to them or to others in the past. It is therefore as important for a whole people to make their memory correspond as far as possible to actual fact, as it is for an individual not to invent facts or let his memory be distorted by various complexes.

Yet what people think is their history matters very much indeed, even if what they believe to be their past may not be necessarily true. Like an individual's false memory, people can have a false history too. And that of course will not be beneficial. The creation of mythology may give us lessons for moral conduct, but it has great pitfalls, and one should not think that it can replace history. So too, false history cannot replace accurate history without great damage; of this, Nazi Germany offers an unforgettable example. That explains why all of us were greatly perturbed during the BJP [Bharatiya Janata Party] regime when a senseless glorification of India's ancient past was attempted.

What kind of history best serves an understanding of the present?
For this question we have to separate two issues. The first is what I have just raised, namely, the question of accuracy. The second is that of interpretation. The historical method embraces both an attempt at accuracy and at interpretation (or generalization or conceptualization). Interpretation involves the selection of facts and allotting weightage to particular facts.

My problem with people like Edward Said is that they confuse the two issues (and also ignore their inter-relationships). Factual accuracy can be achieved by a continuous development of text criticism, archaeological techniques, decipherment techniques and so on. This constitutes the kernel of the scientific method, which, having been developed in Europe, diffused over the world. Said confuses this, namely the issue of scientific method, with assumptions of western supremacy, as I will presently argue. Rigour in method is very important, and I hope to come back to this point later in the discussion when we come to different forms of interpretation, like post-modernism and so on.

To return to Edward Said: he deals with the contribution of Orientalism (his name for western scholarship on Asia and North Africa during the last three centuries) to the discovery of facts – a crucial contribution – in just one paragraph. But did not the discovery of old civilizations, languages and texts altogether change existing interpretations? Indeed, Orientalists created by their discoveries, the real groundwork for critiques of the reigning assumptions of western superiority which might have indeed affected some of the Orientalists themselves. H.A.L. Fisher, a British historian, had said that Europe discovered everything. Orientalists found that Europe did not discover everything, as Joseph Needham showed so brilliantly in his *Science and Civilization in China* volumes. So actually, unless you develop the historical method as the Orientalists in fact did, you cannot have any worthwhile historical interpretation or even oppose the assumptions of western cultural hegemony that Edward Said was protesting against.

Once new facts are established, they may lead, as in the case we have just been discussing, to a change in the existing interpretation. With interpretation there certainly comes the issue of bias. For here, we have to enter the sphere of selection and generalization. A historian who copies others' conclusions simply adopts their biases and cannot claim to be unbiased just because he does not let his own bias intrude into his writing.

On the other hand, suppose we are dealing with a historian who is directly covering a field. If he is dealing with a period in which much source material is available, then of course he will have to weigh the importance of each fact. There may be, in some cases, very little material on a particular aspect, but that aspect may be very important. So it is not just the quantity of material that may determine the weightage given to facts, but an understanding of how historical processes take place and which of them should be regarded as the more important ones. Such an understanding would depend on the historian's own personal views, and possibly, if he is trying to address an audience, he might have the motivation of tailoring his interpretation to what the audience wants to hear or to what is more likely to appeal to his audience.

So it is a very complex matter we touch on, when we think of how the biases of a historian develop. Nowadays, with the huge book market, historians are increasingly thinking of their audiences and how they can produce a best-seller. It may not be done consciously, and one must also understand that the market is exercising a pull and shaping historians' biases. As Marxists, we in particular have to guard against such pulls of 'public' opinion.

Marxists certainly have a framework that could be flexible and within which different weights could be assigned to different facts, although they would regard particular aspects more important than, say, the Subalterns or the mainstream western historians. Thus ideology also has an influence on selection, I agree. In other words, there is the personal predilection of the historian, the views of the audience he is addressing, and the reigning ideological frameworks that may shape the bias of the historian. This certainly affects generalization, so the same body of fairly accurate individual facts may lead quite validly to different interpretations because of the different weights we assign to different parts of the evidence.

I would argue, however, that a point is reached when as our total knowledge of facts (or of what E.H. Carr called 'historical facts') grows, some earlier generalizations can no longer be sustained, as for example, the race superiority theories. They have all been thrown out because of our growing knowledge not only of different civilizations, but also of genetics and even linguistics.

Is the issue of bias more important in respect of certain kinds of history-writing than others?

I think it applies to all history-writing, even the most detailed work. Let us look at why a historian chooses a subject. To give a very mundane example, I chose to work on the agrarian system of Mughal India, my friend Athar Ali chose the structure of nobility under Aurangzeb. We would not have chosen these topics if our personal predilections were identical. So, even in research work, the very fact that one chooses a topic – the fact that a French historian like Emmanuel Le Roy Ladurie writes on the peasants of Languedoc, for example – simply means that one thinks this theme is important and chooses it in preference, say, to the biography of an aristocrat. Le Roy Ladurie's detailed research is not within a Marxist framework, but he certainly thinks that agrarian society is important. For Braudel, it was the Mediterranean region that he studied because he was interested in multicultural regional civilizations. So let us admit that different historians with different ideological predilections choose entirely different aspects to study; and thus by this choice they declare, as it were, their bias. But still, if you are confining yourself to accurate facts, there are limits beyond which generalizations cannot go. And I think there lies the difference between scientific or accurate history, and non-scientific or inaccurate history.

I should enter a word here on the term 'accuracy'. The historical method consists of techniques of ensuring that we understand earlier narratives better, and identify their biases, exaggerations or omissions through critical comparisons, in order to establish events as they really happened or circumstances as they really shaped themselves. If historians cannot claim the exactitude of laboratory experiments, where all conditions are controlled by the researcher, they can still claim reasonable approximations for their descriptions. Once this stage is reached, different interpretations would still be possible, but the range of such interpretations could still be restricted and there is by no means any open sanction to say anything one likes.

My favourite example is R.C. Majumdar. It is not that his facts are wrong; it is in the weightage he gives to certain facts that one may basically differ with him. He was different from the RSS [Rashtriya Swayamsevak Sangh] people who produced the NCERT [National Council of Educational Research and Training] textbooks under the BJP regime, as, unlike them, he tried to work with accurate facts (though possibly a biased selection of them), whereas the BJP hacks just disregarded factual accuracy. There is a vital difference here.

So, certainly, as historical techniques improve, certain views or claims of historians or sections of historians are ruled out. What this means is that, given your bias, you cannot say anything you like and call it history. The more accurate your facts are, the more limited is the range of generalization available to you.

People's History

The issues you have raised, of accuracy, and of the selection and interpretation of facts in writing history, brings me to my next question: on the project on which you are currently working, the People's History of India *series. Why did you embark on this, and what kind of Indian history does this offer?*

The project was suggested by the late Sudeep Banerjee, who felt that we needed accurate history – history, let us say, with an Orientalist rigour but with an emphasis on issues that we find important today. Today we are interested in knowing how production was organized in the past, how the poor fared, how women fared, how religions changed and art grew, and we want to be accurate about our information. We don't want to simply talk in mere adjectives.

So the *People's History* series tries to offer the latest results of research in an accurate and non-chauvinistic way. The fact that certain things were discovered in other countries first and not by us should not hurt our national pride. We want to know how new techniques, crafts, forms of art, etc., came to India, and how they got diffused. Another element in *People's History* is to subject these facts to the kind of scientific interpretation that I was mentioning, based strictly on factual evidence – not necessarily Marxist but one which would allow a Marxist to build his perceptions on. We do not use Marxist terminology like 'mode of production' or 'class struggle', because we are interested first in getting the relevant information by which a wider generalization can be made.

People's History is concerned with how political and social structures developed, what place the common people and the poor had in them, how peasants fared, how technology developed, and in what forms class struggles took place. This is the kind of information on which a Marxist generalization could be attempted, though it is not the task we set for ourselves in *People's History*.

This brings me to the reader we are addressing. Unfortunately, our readership is limited to those who know English. We try to bear in mind ordinary readers and students, and therefore a large amount of explanatory material is provided that is technical, like notes on archaeology, debated topics, special fields of study, and so on. But apart from that, the style is simple and concise, and hopefully retains the reader's interest. So these are the main features of *People's History*.

Does People's History *attempt to fill a lacuna in history-writing?*
I do have a feeling that *People's History* is filling a particular lacuna. Actually, we have some general histories of India. There is the Bharatiya Vidya Bhavan series edited by R.C. Majumdar, a work of great industry but with an unfortunate bias, and communal and chauvinist overtones, though these are kept within limits. Then there is the comprehensive and extremely detailed history that was commissioned by the Indian History Congress. You had histories of the Indian people, some written during the British period and very good for the time. I always feel that even today one could fruitfully use Tara Chand's *History of the Indian People*. But by around the year 2000, a gap had appeared between what these books were carrying and where research had taken us, particularly in pre-history and proto-history, but also in studies of ancient and medieval India. And as far as the British period was concerned, unfortunately, the whitewashing of colonialism is still proceeding and is indeed quite in fashion. There is the need to present the enormous information about the colonial exploitation of India, which is being swept under the carpet these days.

One of the objects of *People's History*, frankly, is to produce an accurate interpretation of colonial rule. We do not necessarily accept all nationalist criticisms of colonialism, nor do we say that the nationalist critique is sufficient for producing history. But unlike the Subalterns or the Cambridge school, we try to take India as a whole, and see what colonialism did in aggregate terms to the country and various classes of its people.

So we try to meet the lacuna in interpretation and provide accurate presentation of facts. As I said, our attempt is twofold. First, there is rigour:

every edition corrects mistakes found in the previous printing. For instance, at one time it was believed that rice was being cultivated in Thailand in 5000 BC. Now it has been found that there was probably no rice cultivation in Thailand before 2300 BC, and that it was China where rice cultivation, including what is called the Indian strain of rice, goes back to beyond 5000 BC, even up to 8000 BC. We have, in subsequent editions, taken note of such results of ongoing research.

The second feature is to emphasize those elements and facts that pertain to *people's* history. This does not mean that you forget rulers. I noted the criticism in *Frontline* of our volume on Mauryan India: a review that said that out of its three chapters, two were on political history, and only one on society and economy. But the point is that political history *is* important, Ashoka *is* important. One can't understand the evidence that Ashokan inscriptions – and you know they are major sources for that time – offer for social history unless one first studies Ashoka. And you may be writing a people's history, but you can't write a history of Soviet Russia without Lenin or Stalin. So individuals do matter. In fact Alexander's invasion – a fact of political history – is important because Alexander's historians, for the first time in Indian history, described our society as it actually was seen by them, and not how it should have been according to prescriptive religious texts.

Political history is important, as I said, sometimes crucially important, and you must clarify its issues if you have to get down to the study of the society and economy. Even the chronology of ancient India is set by our study of political history. How can you get down to your sources if you don't know what date or period they belong to? And, in the absence of such knowledge, what is the chain of sequence? As I said, ours is not a Marxist history of India, unlike the *People's History of England* by A.L. Morton. We are, however, trying to present evidence that is relevant to Marxist generalization. We are not, except perhaps in the volume published on the economy of colonial India, presenting a Marxist analysis, as, frankly, this has not yet taken root for the earlier periods. We have different interpretations and we are not taking sides.

Now that we are on the subject of choice and historical method, it would be instructive for young students to know what led you to the writing of The Agrarian System of Mughal India, *the book based on your thesis, and how you evolved your method and approach. I remember that you would ask your Ph.D. students to attempt a chapterization of their theses right at the start of their research. You introduced us to your method of making a key to topics, to be entered at the right-hand corner of our research cards.*
I studied here at Aligarh, greatly aided by the fact that one of my teachers and a former student of my father's, Sheikh Abdul Rashid, was a very con-

servative historian. He was from the Punjab and ultimately went to Pakistan some years after the Partition. He believed that unless you read the sources closely, you couldn't be a historian. So when I passed my MA Previous examination, he called me to his house at the beginning of the summer vacation and said that from the following day, I was to go to his house every day and for three hours read Barani, and after that Badauni, the two most interesting medieval historians. At about 11 am he would send his daughter in with a cup of tea but otherwise I was left alone, with him looking in now and then to see if I was working. Actually, that not only helped me to brush up my Persian but made me get a feel of the sources; and, like him, I began to love my texts. This training in textual criticism in the original language led me to my first research work, a translation of the *Chachnama*, which has not been published. My Arabic was weak, but I collated the *Chachnama* with the period's inscriptions and the region's geography. Those two years gave me a familiarity with how research is done, and how one has to collate a text with other texts and all kinds of sources.

Then, when I applied for membership of the Communist Party, I said rather presumptuously that my main interest in research was to work out 'the laws of motion' in medieval India. It was with difficulty that my application was accepted! I had worked for four years in the students' organization, but the most I had suffered was that I had been sent down from the University for a fortnight for attending Communist meetings.

Anyway, that was my early ambition. When I got the Government of India Overseas Scholarship, I wrote to New College, Oxford – where I was admitted – saying that I would like to do research in the Mughal agrarian system. Fortunately, in England, by some accident that I will not go into here, I had to study British history for one term. And, typical of Oxford, although the paper began from Tudor times, my tutor made me begin from Roman Britain. In an essay I had to write on why Caesar invaded Britain, I wrote that he did so to 'collect slaves'. I remember my tutor saying: 'Habib, the only thing I can say about your essay is that you have written it yourself: nobody has said this before.' Yet, I learnt from the texts I was required to read of the effort at accuracy and precision that is made by British historians, and I really enjoyed those two months.

What also helped me in my subsequent research was the enormous collection of documents in the British Museum and the India Office Library. One could just sit there and go on studying manuscripts of a huge range – something that is still not possible in India. I was also lucky to have a very benevolent supervisor in Dr C.C. Davies.

And, as for taking notes, this was my own invention! As one tends to forget items, one should have a key – my original key has now extended to twenty-two pages. And because my scholarship was limited, I could not afford cards, and so I used ordinary sheets: six cut out of a foolscap double-fold.

Yes, I still take notes under the same key and with sheets of the same size, and so keep adding to my collection. And no, I don't use the computer. I used to type notes taken from English works, but somehow since computers came, I have gone back to writing in long hand.

Issues, Concepts, New Research Findings

Your book Medieval India: The Study of a Civilization *(published in 2008 by the National Book Trust) presents a most readable and up-to-date account of facts and interpretation for the period* AD *600 to 1250. There are a cluster of historical issues there on which your ideas have evolved. I have chosen three of these that I think have a bearing on our present understanding of the period. The first is the issue of feudalism, the second the characterization of the eighteenth century in Indian history, and the third is the question of women in history, which you address for the first time in a systematic way.*

First, on feudalism. In 'Problems of Marxist Historiography', you had said that you did not approve of using the word 'feudalism' as an umbrella term to cover all pre-capitalist social formations, and that you would rather view the period as having had a multiplicity of pre-capitalist social formations in different regions. In this book, however, you refer to an 'Indian variant of feudalism' for the period 600–1200. What does this signify?

First, I would like to say that one must deal with terms that have now entered historical language. The term 'Indian feudalism', first used by Kosambi and R.S. Sharma, does not necessarily represent a strict Marxist definition of feudalism. To Marxists, serfdom is the crucial element of feudalism. (There are problems with that even within the West European historical tradition. Maurice Dobb unfortunately dilutes the strict Marxist definition of feudalism. He carries feudalism up to the English Civil War of 1640–60, whereas even in Britain there was no serfdom after 1400. There was serfdom in Russian feudalism, though not of the West European variety. In Russia feudalism came during and after the sixteenth century, and therefore was post-medieval.)

Now in India, our problem is that the element of personal subjection of that type is absent, or only partly present, because our information on this, which comes from pre-AD 1200 grants, is very limited. I am not talking about south India, because Chola and post-Chola inscriptions do begin to give all kinds of information. But there are other elements here restricting personal freedom, for instance the caste system. P. Sundarayya, in his 'Note on Some Agrarian Issues', was the first, I think, to point out that the caste system has to be fed into our understanding of feudal relationships in India.

When I speak about Indian feudalism, I am thus speaking about a term that is now established in Indian historiography. This often happens in historiography. For example, the term 'mercantilist' does not only refer to merchants, but is a term established in British and European historiography for an ideological school and a particular kind of colonial policy. The same, I think, applies to 'Indian feudalism'. It is a term established for a particular kind of organization which historians have found was in existence with common features over a very large area. Some aspects of it do not relate at all to the essential elements of feudalism as seen by Marxists, like serfdom. (However, the knights of European feudalism relate very well to the Rajaputras of 'Indian feudalism'. This is a curious feature, because actually it was in the same period that cavalry became important in Europe, and Rajaputras were cavalrymen, quite contrary to the ordinary belief that they were infantrymen. That is why, in my own study of the history of technology, I pay so much attention to cavalry developments like the saddle, stirrup and horseshoe, and to how these horse appendages came to India.)

I see problems with using the term 'Indian feudalism' for the period after 1200. The essential fact that land tax, rather than landlord rent, was the major drain on the peasant's produce was a very important point of distinction between European feudalism, which was based on rent, and the medieval (post-1200) Indian system, which was based on land tax. It is a distinction one has to maintain. That is why I don't use the word feudalism for the medieval system after 1200. It is quite possible that a heavy land tax was levied in the earlier period, and that feudalism therefore is a misnomer for that period. But unfortunately, we don't know enough about the fiscal system of the period to be sure about it.

What, then, are the elements of Indian feudalism for the period 600 to 1200?
The first is political decentralization. This, again, is not essential to the Marxist theory of feudalism, because Russian feudalism did not see political decentralization; in fact it saw centralization under Tsarist authority. However, political decentralization was a feature of West European feudalism.

The rise of the Rajaputras as a caste, and therefore of clan monarchies, is a distinct element of the political history of this period. These elements do not survive except in part during the later medieval period in India. The

Rajput soldier increasingly becomes a mercenary, very much like later feudal knights. He would join the service of any lord or master who would pay him.

Then, there are town-based armies under the Sultanates and the Mughals with a huge cavalry and encampments, which you don't find earlier. Towns and commodity production in the post-AD 1200 period is again a feature that you do not find in the preceding period of Indian feudalism, which was marked by a scarcity of gold and silver coins, essential for larger transactions.

So, I would say that Indian feudalism in the period AD 600–1200 was a mode of exploitation where commodity production was at a low level, and where caste was important but was not the only or even the main mechanism of exploitation. Force and state power provided the major mechanisms, and thus the role of the state – even of the Rajaputra 'clan monarchies' – cannot be regarded as unimportant.

Secondly, with regard to the eighteenth century, you and Professor Athar Ali emphasize the breaks in the eighteenth century (pre- and post-colonialism), while others like Stein and Perlin lay stress on the continuities. You say in Medieval India *that the eighteenth century held forth the promise of being a 'zamindar's century' with the emergence of localized powers, but that this direction was thwarted by the intervention of colonialism.*

It depends on how profoundly you think colonialism brought about a break in the eighteenth century. The basic argument the Cambridge school puts forward, first of all, is that there was no break, that there was basically continuity. Second, according to them, although the colonial power was militarily triumphant, its actual authority was very limited. This was so because the earlier states were themselves segmentary sovereignties, and it was their limited authority that the English inherited. It was not a case of the colonial powers stepping into seats of strong governments, but, rather, a case of colonial power inheriting weak states that lived on compromises with local elements. This is essentially the view held by Burton Stein and C.A. Bayly, and their numerous followers.

Now this raises the question of pre-British states and whether they were in fact weak. They were certainly weak in many things. For example, it was very difficult for them to implement a change in personal law. They were not interested in that, nor were they interested in developing educational systems. If you are testing the strength of the state by what today would be regarded as development or reform, then of course they were weak. But if you are looking at taxation, which in effect means whether they had the military strength to extort the tax, then they were not weak states. That is why, when James Mill wrote about the East India Company inheriting the authority to take full rent of the land as tax from its predecessors, his assumption was that both the Company and its predecessors were very strong political powers, much stronger than a European state, which could not claim to take rent from all land as tax.

Therefore, the Battle of Plassey did mark a break, because now there began the extraction of tribute (drain of wealth to Britain) and the beginning of the deindustrialization process, which too, by the time of Warren Hastings, was making itself felt. The Carnatic debts were also a form of tribute – a fantastically important subject in itself. You can levy tribute by taxation, or you can levy tribute by building up credit claims and so taking rent in lieu of interest. This was a totally new situation. Therefore, to speak of the eighteenth century with the East India Company, the Marathas and the Mughals as part of the same system is absurd.

As far as the zamindars' emergence is concerned, we see that in this period, as centralized states broke up, local potentates became important and were able to get some local support. What it means is that the revenue of the state, or the land tax, began to be collected often in the name of the state by zamindars, who were sometimes more flexible and had local supporters. So the weakening of the empire and the emergence of zamindars were probably two simultaneous processes. Even contemporaries saw the Maratha state as really a zamindar state because when they appointed an officer, he practically became hereditary. So you had a system of hereditary officers, and every *jagir* became in fact a zamindari. About the Marathas it was said by Azad Bilgrami in 1761, that they wanted to convert even village headmanships into zamindaris.

The word 'transition' to colonialism – a favourite word used by many writers on the eighteenth century – is peculiarly offensive. Transition means that there is some internal development. There can be transition to capitalism but there cannot be transition to colonialism, which was imposed externally by force.

Thirdly, I refer to your recent interest in and work on gender in history. In Medieval India *there is a separate section on women as a part of every chapter. What led you to this? Is this a neglected area of history, and do you think that there is a case for a women's history?*
In the 1950s a book was brought out by the British Communist Party, that should really be reprinted, called *Women and Communism*. And it had a considerable impact on us. We used to think that once there was socialism, everything would be fine and there might be no need to separate women's interests from men's. This book did much to disabuse us of these notions, but not entirely. So, in our historiography, women were hardly mentioned. In my *Agrarian System of Mughal India*, women hardly appear, except for

one or two statements referring to women holding zamindaris. But it pays no attention to women as a sector in agrarian life.

In the last twenty or thirty years in Indian historiography, there has been some change of approach in respect of women in history. I think there are two views about it. One is to confine the whole question of women to their status, and to ideas on how women were seen and depicted in texts. The other is to go beyond it and to see how much was given to the woman to eat, to enquire about her livelihood, health, mortality rate and so on. In other words, the actual position of women in different classes, because of course women did not often see themselves as of one class or category as they today tend to do. The aristocratic woman, however secluded, would have nothing to do with the slave-girl. And what was the position of the slave-girl? Her position was in fact worse than that of the man-slave. It struck me when I was reading the translations of the Buddhist *Tipitaka* texts. The slave-woman is regarded as the unhappiest person on earth. It did not strike me at first, the fact that they were not referring to male slaves but to the woman-slave alone. The woman-slave had practically no rights; in Muslim law too, she has no sexual protection. So that kind of thing struck me, and you will see that I do try to rectify my previous indifference to the matter in the forthcoming *Economic History of Medieval India (1200–1500)*.

Actually, you have to search for sources on women. Amir Khusrau has some vulgar pieces about women-slaves, and this shows you how they were treated in India. Then there are documents relating to slave-girls in the *Lekha-paddhati* from Solanki-ruled Gujarat (twelfth–thirteenth century). It is the same there too. A master could do anything with the slave-girl. According to these documents, the owner could do anything to her he wished, as his sins would be washed off automatically as if he had bathed in the Ganga.

On women-slaves, there is at least material of this kind. It is more difficult to find sources that tell you of women engaged in various forms of labour. For example, there is an illustrated dictionary of 1469 written in Persian in Malwa. It gives illustrations of different production instruments of everyday life, and you can sense here the presence of a customary gender division of labour in which quite strenuous tasks were assigned to women.

Should women find a place in general historical writing or should they be written about as a separate category? My plea would be that both should be done. As many general things about technology, economic life and society are not very clear, it is first important to know the details about women and then relate their condition to the general social framework. I see that in European history too, there are separate researches carried out on women – of region, class, sometimes of villages. In any case, you cannot have a history of women without understanding how the men were treating them, and also how men treated each other.

But let me give an example of some interesting historical facts on women. At a Mesolithic site in a place called Sarai Nahar Rai in central Uttar Pradesh, dating to around 8000 BC, a large number of skeletons were found in graves. The women appeared to have been muscular and strong. If the average height of men was 180 cms, women were over 170 cms; they were that close to each other in height. In the Mesolithic period there was no cultivation, only hunting and seed collection. In another site, this in the late Mesolithic phase dating to about 3000 BC, the ratios alter. The men are still 180 cms, but the women are around 160 cms or so. In skeletons from the Indus Civilization sites, the women's teeth are found to be worse than those of men because they were not given meat, which was obviously only eaten by men. Now nobody had collected these facts, or explained why women had become shorter. Then I read Gordon Childe. He thought that men, being hunters, domesticated animals, especially cattle for meat, so they remained muscular as they dealt with large animals. Women by then had become seed collectors, so they sowed the seeds and harvested the crop, and had to live on grain and not meat. The whole theory of Gordon Childe is that women discovered agriculture. But this was just a concept and he really had nothing to substantiate his theory with. Now you have proof of it in the archaeological record. With the division of labour and of food, women were not getting meat, and so started getting shorter over time.

There is a Neolithic rock drawing in Kashmir dating to around 2000 BC. It shows a wild pig being hunted. A man is standing with an arrow and there is a woman who is holding a spear. Women and men, both take part in the hunt. Men get the meat and women have to be muscular. But as hunting would become either less important or as women were excluded from it, their claim to more nutritious food would be gravely curtailed.

What is the importance for history of the discipline of geography, particularly as a means of establishing the context for history? You have always placed a great deal of emphasis on geography in your historical researches.
Yes, I think I should have stressed more clearly that in history one has to combine technical work of a very detailed nature with generalization, and there is always a distance between the two.

Geography is very important for the study of economic change, the history of commerce, territorial administration and political power. That is why geography always interested me and resulted in my producing, after many years' work, an *Atlas of the Mughal Empire*. Faiz Habib and I together have contributed a number of papers to the Indian History Congress on ancient Indian historical geography that will hopefully come out in an atlas form, as a work of reference.

Let me give you an example from this work. I wanted to know what a place was called in the first century AD. Of course there are Sanskrit texts, but these are difficult to read. There are inscriptions, but these are in Prakrit. What I did was to assemble all the inscriptions that I could get in *Epigraphia Indica* and other compilations, to see what territorial names the inscriptions were using and then plot them on the map. Very interesting things turned up. For instance, a man or a family came to Sanchi from 'Saka-kachh', which suggests that 'Saka' adjoined Kachchh. 'Saka' occurs in the name Sakasthan, now Seistan. But the *Periplus of the Erythrian Sea* says that Scythia was the name of the Indus basin. This information is very import-ant even for the *Periplus*'s date itself. It also raises the question whether Sakasthan in the Mathura Lion Capital inscription is really Seistan or just Sind.

Or, take another example. Chandra of the Mehrauli Inscription says: 'I conquered the seven mouths of the Indus.' Now *'mukha'* does not mean 'mouth' in the English sense. Everyone thought this meant that he had conquered the delta, as if there were seven channels in the delta. They forget that he means the seven rivers of the Punjab, the 'Sapta Sindhu', that flow into the Indus, and that these are the real 'mouths' of the Indus.

So these interesting issues get resolved when you study the historical geo-graphy of a region. With geography you can even revise facts of political history as hitherto understood, and so you really need a base in geography to work out many historical problems.

Ideology and the Writing of History

You once wrote that the approach and conclusions of a historian who bel-ieves that mankind needs socialism would be different from those of one who does not. How has being a Marxist and a Communist influenced your writing, in particular your large body of work on different aspects of mod-ern Indian history – for instance, on nationalism, the freedom movement and the role of Gandhi?

First, when I said different, it does not mean that there would not be shades of difference. I do not intend my statement to mean that there is a single set of 'either' and a single set of 'or', that is to say, two sets of definite alternat-ives. I was speaking of influences. A person who feels that socialism is neces-sary feels that there should be no class exploitation, and then studies history to see how such exploitation has been perpetrated in the past and, indeed, to treat this as one of the most basic elements to be investigated in respect of any past society.

This is a position different from the welfare economists and is utterly different from the Washington Consensus, which holds to the view that private property is the crucial institution and only if it is preserved can society be best governed. Everyone gains, we are told; it is a 'win-win' situation both for the poor and the rich. To such historians, it is not important that the poor were exploited, to the degree that it would be important for a person who has a belief in socialism. And so one necessarily looks at history differently.

I mean, forget about the Mughal empire, take the Indus Civilization. Very few archaeologists feel concerned about how the poor lived under the structure of power. I will give you a single example. Almost all archaeologists, Americans in particular, assume that towns could arise without a strong state and heavy exploitation of the poor. Market conditions, in their view, are a sufficient factor in themselves. Peasants would bring their produce to the market and the townsmen purchased this produce. There was free exchange, and so towns did not need state power and taxation to extract surplus from the villages. Now surely, if this were the case, then when the peasants went back to the villages they must have carried back many goods from the towns that they had gained in exchange. Therefore, if these archaeologists are right, excavations in all the small rural settlements should produce something manufactured in the towns. But they themselves have noticed the immense difference between the townships and rural settlements. The latter yield only pottery, nothing but coarse pottery. But they never ask why this is so. So, if you don't ask a question, you don't get an answer. However, if you are looking for it, and if you are looking for a mechanism other than the market on which the town is based, then of course you will find answers. If the surplus is taken away, the villages cannot have the same type of goods that you find in the towns. So that is what I really meant. What, in your eyes, should be your society's future also influences how you look at the past.

How about the national movement? How has your view and standpoint influenced your researches and interpretation?
Here of course other elements enter. I think the fact that my own father was a deeply sincere admirer of Gandhi made it personally a difficult issue when I joined the Communist movement, because everybody at that time was denouncing Gandhi – in the way R.P. Dutt does in *India Today* (1940, 1946). So clearly, in my appraisal of Gandhi, the personal attachment might enter – and I don't dispute that.

But on the other hand, I disagreed with the kind of triangular situation that, for example, Comrade EMS postulated in his book, *History of the Freedom Struggle*. British imperialism, the bourgeois–landlord leadership

of the national movement, and the working class or Communists constitute, according to him, the three major elements in the situation. I rather
thought that even R.P. Dutt ('RPD') would not have gone so far.

In fact, in my view, the national movement has to be looked at as a coalition rather than as a division into two parts. All national liberation movements have been class coalitions, otherwise they would not be national.
That has been the Chinese, Vietnamese and Indonesian experience (before
the coup that overthrew Soekarno). I therefore believe that the Left before
1947 should be looked at as a *component* of the national liberation movement, rather than simply as a force in opposition to the bourgeois-led Congress.

*But didn't the Left stand in both unity and opposition to the bourgeois
leadership?*
Well, one of the two elements must dominate. Of course, there were many
issues of strategy and tactics, the debate on issues of non-violence and violence. There were other complications too. For example, the placing by the
Left of the Muslim League and the Congress on the same level after 1942,
in hindsight, was erroneous. The Muslim League had no past to speak of as
an anti-British force, whereas the Congress was a genuine anti-colonial movement. To forget this was an enormous mistake.

As for the Quit India movement, what Litvinov said, probably not correctly, of the Soviet–Nazi pact, applies here: 'I would have done the same,
but differently.' On the Quit India movement, we could have done the
same, but differently. First, we should have gone to a People's War position
much earlier, as soon as the Soviet Union was invaded by the Nazis on 22
June 1941. We waited unnecessarily and for far too long. That was the first
tactical error. The change in the character of the war was so obvious that
common sense should have prevailed. When the Quit India Resolution came,
the Communists were right, I think, in opposing the practical thrust of the
resolution. We have to stand up against the popular wind even if it blows in
the wrong direction. But our subsequent position should have been different. First, we should not have equated the Congress with the Muslim League.
Secondly, we should have demanded the release of the Congress leaders far
more strongly than we did. It was just one of our demands; it should have
been a key demand. We would have gained because the People's War position was not an unpopular position in India. Very few people were sympa-
thetic to Germany and they were afraid of Japan. I am talking of the middle
class, who at that time played some part in forming public opinion.

When Nehru said of the Quit India Resolution (in his *Discovery of
India)* that nationalism won over internationalism, we should have built on
it rather than just criticize Nehru, telling him that he did not understand the

extent of progressive elements within the Muslim League. These were important matters of strategy and tactics in the past. We should certainly have retained our distinct identity within the coalition from the bourgeois movement. All coalitions have their differences, otherwise they would not be coalitions. But to have taken every tactical issue of compromise and retreat by the Congress as bourgeois-directed surrender was, I think, a mistake.

Where do you think the Left understanding of Gandhi was wrong or misdirected?
Well, actually more than RPD's misunderstanding of Gandhi was his unnecessary use of strong words. Comparing Gandhi with Ramsay Macdonald, for instance, calling him the 'General of unbroken disasters', 'the Jonah of revolutions', and yet conceding that Gandhi alone could enter the poor man's hut. There is an immense contradiction between the two. Second was his view that just because Gandhi declared that he was a believing Hindu he made an error, since he appeared to Muslims as a Hindu leader. How could we expect at the time, when entering into a coalition of national forces, that all the others would be atheists like us? RPD also did not pay attention to other statements by Gandhi, for example, where he heavily criticized the Arya Samaj for its attacks on Islam.

The land owners, almost till the late 1920s and even later, certainly commanded some influence in the Congress. It was only with the Karachi Resolution that there was an official turn, with the party declaring its support for peasant rights. The Congress leaders, particularly during the Khilafat movement and the Chauri Chaura phase, were very concerned that zamindars would turn against them. We should look at the realities of the time. The very fact that in all the documents, when Gandhi speaks of 'we', he means peasants, and when he speaks of 'they', he refers to land owners, is quite significant, making clear on which side he stood. A mass upsurge could not happen in a day and building a base amongst the peasants took time. It was unrealistic of us to have expected the Congress to denounce land owners prematurely – it took time. For this reason, I think, to just denounce the Congress as a party of land owners and mill owners was a mistake.

RPD did not, I think, pay adequate attention to the land revenue and tenancy reforms by the Congress governments, in 1937–39, which in some provinces like UP seriously cut into the landlords' incomes. In fact, subsequent inflation wiped out much of the landlords' incomes because they could not raise the rents under the Tenancy Act of 1939 in UP. So RPD ignored the factors that showed that the Congress was winning over the peasantry. When the Zamindari Abolition Act of UP came in 1951, the Left opposed it and told the peasants not to become *bhumidars*, and that it was all a trick. Although we were not in the UP Legislative Assembly, we had a very strong Kisan Sabha in the state. We consequently lost the day, because the Congress people went and made the peasants grateful to them for making them *bhumidar*s – in effect, peasant-proprietors. The peasants thought we were mindless. These were the tactical errors that flowed from our strategic understanding that the Congress would do nothing for the peasants.

And your view is that this error was carried over after Independence?
It may have appeared that this understanding flowed from the BTR (B.T. Ranadive) line, but in fact it follows from RPD's *India Today*, where he just fleetingly refers to the Karachi Resolution, as if it was not important. This important resolution became the programme of the Congress and therefore practically of the national movement. RPD, however, argued that these were just verbal concessions, and this was the understanding of the Left too for a long time. Therefore, that the national movement was a coalition, and secondly, that the Congress, in order to mobilize peasants, supported them against the land owners to a certain degree – this was an understanding that was not adequately recognized by us even in the 1950s.

At a time when the Left was leading the national liberation movements in India's neighbourhood, to what do you attribute the relative weakness of the Left vis-à-vis the Congress during the freedom movement?
When asked this question by Professor Bipan Chandra, Comrade BTR gave a two-fold answer. First, in other countries the Left did not have rivals for the loyalty of the peasantry. We had rivals, he said. We had limited support, whereas the Congress was everywhere with the peasants. He could have gone on to say that this was something like the Russian situation where the Bolsheviks were weak amongst the peasantry, whereas the socialist revolutionaries were everywhere. You see how in China, the Communists just had no rivals for the allegiance of the peasantry; nor did the Communists in Vietnam. Look at Gandhi's Champaran and Khera satyagrahas. Both were pro-peasantry. The first was against indigo planters, and to the extent that the second was against revenue payments, it was against the British. We were at that time not on the scene at all.

It is all very well to say that we should not be reformist, but you cannot begin with a slogan that the peasants themselves will not recognize. For instance, when the Communists took over Afghanistan, they thought they would divide the land of the big land owners among the peasants to win their support. The reality was that the peasants were aghast. They said it was un-Islamic. How can we take another's property, they asked. Tomorrow nobody's property would be safe and thieves will be at large, they added. And ultimately, the religious people won out. Afghanistan is an example of how, without long ideological preparation, the Left could not succeed.

Anyway, the second point Comrade BTR made was that we did not have leaders of stature who could face up to Gandhi and Nehru. Such leaders are not born every day. That we survived was our great achievement, he said. Instead of asking the Communists, why didn't you lead the movement, what people should be asking is, how did you manage to survive and grow, said BTR.

With the benefit of hindsight and with all the new information we have on the national movement, does this offer a sufficient explanation for the weakness of the Left? What about issues like caste and communalism, with which the Congress compromised and the Left did not?

Without directly attacking the entire caste structure, the Congress managed to get support across the castes. And I hope I can suggest something that can explain the situation. We see today that Ambedkar is everywhere and Gandhi nowhere, part of a process of the belittling of Gandhi. But we have to understand that even today we cannot fight caste by advocating inter-caste marriages. You know it is a very difficult proposition in the villages. It is therefore understandable, what Gandhi asked of people in the villages. He told them that it was not inter-caste marriages, or even inter-dining, that he wanted. He asked that Harijans be educated, that they be allowed to draw water from the well, that they not be treated as untouchables. These were the simplest initial steps, but it needed great courage to say so in India under British rule, not simply on paper but amidst the villagers themselves, as Gandhi and his associates did.

I will give you another example. Throughout the 1930s, I noticed from my father's Central Bank passbook, a name that occurred again and again was that of Gajadhar Singh, a man who received the contributions he made to the Congress by cheque. When I became a party member, Munshi Gajadhar Singh was the Communist Party's district secretary and one of the tallest Communists in the district. I knew that he had been previously secretary of the Aligarh District Congress Committee for long. So once I asked him why Gandhi chose him, or allowed him, to be Secretary of the District Congress Committee, and let another Communist, Harpal Singh, be an AICC member, instead of some other prominent Congressman. (In fact Harpal Singh voted for Subhash Bose against Sitaramayya at the Tripuri Congress.) Munshi Gajadhar Singh thought for a while and then said the reason was that the other persons had never lived in a Harijan *basti*, so how could they be given any office? On the other hand, he himself had lived on the alms of Harijans in a Harijan *basti* for years teaching their children, so how could he be passed over? (I use the word 'Harijan' because this was then the word in common use.)

You are asking me about the caste system. The families of people like

Gajadhar Singh and Harpal Singh rejected them for living among Harijans. Actually, it was the involvement of such people in the Communist movement in the late 1930s that gave real strength to it. The Aligarh peasants did not know of P.C. Joshi, but they knew of Gajadhar Singh, Harpal Singh and Uday Vir Singh, all Communists trained in the Congress.

So we not only had rivals, we had very tall rivals who anticipated us. If you look at Gandhi's entire experience of South Africa, he does anticipate the Communists using mine workers as well as women as contingents of struggle. In China, the Kuomintang, despite Sun Yat Sen, had nothing like the Karachi Resolution as its programme, nothing like the constructive programme of going to villages, etc., which actually was a Congress-led movement under Gandhi.

So how, then, would you evaluate the role of the Left in the freedom movement?
Well, I think it made a very positive contribution and we should cherish that heritage. I would go further than BTR who said we survived; we also contributed. We did not get recognition for it, partly because of our own hostile attitude, which, throughout the BTR-line period itself, was very antagonistic to the entire national leadership. Today, in hindsight, I think we should have had a more balanced view of the leadership of the national movement, and the realities and contradictions within it. I remember what G.D. Birla once told some businessmen who said the civil disobedience movement should be withdrawn. He said, 'On such matters Gandhiji would never listen to me.' Neither Gandhi nor Nehru fit into any conventional frame of bourgeois leadership. Once they stepped into a particular structure of power, the situation was such that they did not have the political and ideological resources to take revolutionary steps, and they had to operate in a bourgeois framework. We should have understood that, and not have taken the extreme position against Nehru that we took under the BTR line.

I remember reading of a story about the Soviet Ambassador to India at the time of Gandhi's death, a distinguished general who was the head of the Black Sea Fleet in World War II. He attended Gandhi's funeral and apparently Molotov sent him a telegram asking him why he went, as Gandhi had neither been head of state nor the Prime Minister of India. The reply was: 'I went because all the people went.' For that reason he was recalled after some time. But he was surely right. (The Communists, it should be said here, were not behind anyone then in sincerely mourning Gandhi's assassination, and in demanding the outlawing of the Hindu Mahasabha and the RSS.)

So the weaknesses of our understanding of the leadership of the national movement, I would say, were carried into our political line after Independence. We were also afraid that if we modified our position of distinction from and total opposition to Nehru and his leadership, we would be tailists and reformists. I would not attribute everything to the unnecessarily hostile Soviet attitude towards the Indian nationalist leadership. That too changed. The change towards India came within Stalin's lifetime. There was a terrible foodgrain scarcity in India in the early 1950s. Nehru reported to Parliament that he sent urgent messages to all countries, and that he got a message from Stalin to say that 50,000 tonnes of wheat were being sent immediately. Nehru was told to pay whatever price he wished once the wheat reached India. The Chinese sent 2 million tonnes of wheat. These gestures played a great part in the subsequent friendship struck with the Soviet Union and with China (though with the latter, relations were to deteriorate some years later). The despatch of 50,000 tonnes and 2 million tonnes of wheat! These were realities. India was taking a non-aligned position on the Korean War, though after first going with the Americans. That shift in India's position certainly changed Stalin's attitude towards India. To call Nehru as someone manipulated by Anglo–US imperialism, as we were doing, was therefore absurd.

The Relevance of Marx's Writing on India

Would you provide a summary of your view of the significance of what Marx wrote on India? You argue in 'Marx's Perception of India' that there was a continuous refinement in Marx's understanding of India in his writing; and that the two famous essays he wrote on India in 1853 were not the sum-total of his writing on pre-colonial historical structures.

First, let us not think that Marx had answers to everything. What he wrote on India in 1853 proved to be important for a major new addition to Marxist theory: from it germinated Marx's concept of primitive accumulation of capital. Let me begin from here and then go further.

Until the *Communist Manifesto* (1848) and later, Marx's notion of the evolution of capitalism was that of growth from within: small businessmen, shopkeepers and master craftsmen gradually accumulating profits and becoming larger and larger capitalists. It was as if capitalism grew effortlessly through individual accumulation. This was the position adopted in the *Communist Manifesto*.

The first breach in this position comes in 1853 with Marx's articles on India. Marx now realizes that there was colonial tribute from India and de-industrialization within India (he had written about it briefly in his *Poverty of Philosophy*), both adding to Britain's stock of capital and profits. The understanding that capitalism rests on markets where deindustrialization and unemployment are taking place is made profound, and substantiated, in the 1853 articles on India. Without using the term 'deindustrialization', Marx writes about it: how weavers and spinners were being thrown out of employment by colonialism. Tribute, too, is a new element that enters into his understanding of the growth of capitalism. Now, if there is a flow of tribute out of the colonies to Britain, then it means that England is accumulating capital not just from individual earnings within, but also from colonial conquest.

This is the first indication of Marx's emerging understanding that capitalism does not grow effortlessly; it grows through 'expropriation' and so accumulation of capital is equal to expropriation. The idea remained dormant in his writings for some time. It is not to be found in the *Economic and Philosophical Notebooks*, but suddenly appears in full form in *Capital*, Volume 1 (1867). You will see that now he relates two issues: capitalism grows out of the expropriation of the peasantry – the enclosure movement in England is the classical illustration – *and* exploitation of the colonies. In other words, the colonial system *as well as the* expropriation of peasants and craftsmen in the metropolitan countries are the two sources from which capitalism draws increasing strength.

The 1853 articles on India therefore signify a very important stage in the development of Marxism, and are very important for our understanding of the linkage between capitalism and colonialism. That is the first point: it explains the pressure put on India's economy during colonial rule. Dadabhai Naoroji and Romesh Chander Dutt's theses about Britain's exploitation of India fit so well with this understanding.

The second point is that Marx was writing in 1853 on the basis of writings available in England on India at that time. Even in India, that would have been the basic material available to anyone. Therefore, statements like 'India has no history' should be taken as normal statements made at a time when the social history of India had not been worked out. But once you pass from here, then Marx's whole account of the village community based on Wilks and the Fifth Report, and partly anticipated by Hegel, suggests movement and change in Indian society. The whole question of the village community raises the question of peasants in Indian society. Here too, by the time he writes *Capital*, I, he modifies his position considerably. His discussions on the village community in *Capital*, I, are far more refined than his earlier statements. He doesn't regard them as democratic – in this respect he is much more historically accurate than Jawaharlal Nehru, who says that these were democratic institutions – but as fixed in the framework of caste and servile relationships. However, he thinks that they are crucial to the production of surplus.

The idea that oriental despotism rests on surplus and taxation is a very important one. In his later articles, Marx speaks of how in India, tax and rents coincided (i.e. the state is the rent collector). So he is now conceiving a system where there is commodity exchange outside the village. The surplus is taken by the state: either it is paid for in cash, or it is collected in kind and then sold. As far as the state is concerned, it imposes a money tax. And as far as the village is concerned, it has parted with kind when the produce is sold to pay tax and there is practically no money left for circulation within the village. This is not an utterly unhistorical concept. Money circulation in villages was limited. We know that even in Mughal times, agricultural labourers were partly paid in money but essentially in kind. However, commodity production was there in the towns, as Marx recognizes. This matches well with what we know now from detailed documentation in pre-British times.

Where he was greatly influenced by Bernier, unfortunately, was in his view at this time (1853) that there were no settled towns but only camp-cities. But there are other elements that are important, and one of them is that he now thinks that history is coming to India. I will not here go into other debates – for example, when you recognize, as Marx did in 1853, that a change had taken place from communal to individual production in India in the past, you cannot also say that things have not changed. Marx should have thought of that. But let us remember he was writing fast and couldn't consider everything.

But the other point, how colonialism contributes to regeneration, is important. He says again and again that colonialism does not consciously contribute to regeneration; it is a kind of blind geological process. I think this is important to remember, because Edward Said totally distorts Marx when he suggests that Marx here welcomes colonialism because it creates regeneration. Marx emphasizes the fact of education and science, and the fact that English education would open the doors to science. He emphasizes the groundwork laid for political unity that will turn into popular unity through the British railways and communication systems, but most importantly, he also sees caste as the great social barrier to freedom and progress in India. He says nevertheless that when the factory system is implanted, the caste system will start breaking up. I think, therefore, that he had grasped the essentials of the connection between modern nationalism and colonialism. That is why, towards the end of his second essay, he looks forward to the Indian people obtaining their liberation even possibly before the European workers did.

Historiographical Trends in the Writing of Indian History

India has had a long tradition of historiography – we have the imperialist, nationalist and Marxist schools, and, more recently, the Subaltern and post-modernist approaches. How would you evaluate these, particularly the more recent trends? What has been their impact, especially on classroom teaching?

Well, I will separate the two – modern trends and teaching.

In western historiography, the Marxist approach was getting greater and greater attention in the 1960s and 1970s. There were several reasons for this. One was that economic history was becoming the centrepiece of new historical research. The many debates that arose out of detailed historical work and quantitative work, in particular, were essentially about economic history. Political history cannot be quantitatively analysed but economic trends can. Many questions that Marxists asked could be tested quantitatively. Of course there were debates in other disciplines like sociology also. In post-World War II sociology, Marx began to be considered as an important figure. This extended even to psychology (consider: Marx's ideas on 'alienation').

Secondly, there was, I think, a greater concern among historians and economists, both from the welfare side and the socialist side, that things which are important from the perspective of the poor needed to be studied.

It seems to me that there has subsequently been a move away from this position. The first push came, I think, from a tendency within western historiography. We will not go into the motives in detail, but even if you were a liberal English historian, you would not like to have a dark picture painted of British-ruled India, and you would like to see if it couldn't be painted differently. In England, where Indian studies had almost been abandoned in the 1950s and 60s (except for the older generation), there came about a renewed interest. Such scholars got a particular engine and method for their cause in the 'structural analysis' approach advocated by Sir Lewis Namier. Actually the approach was misnamed, because what Namier and his followers dealt with was the study of private papers and individual motivation. If you could ensure that Indian nationalist leaders had motives of personal careers, or caste and community affiliations, then a different picture would emerge of Indian nationalism and the British rule which they criticized would not look so bad after all. These historians never handled the question of tribute or deindustrialization: their concern was all about individuals. Thus the national movement appeared not to be based on real grievances but on manufactured ones. This is roughly the position of the Cambridge school – Gallagher, Anil Seal, Bayly, Judith Brown and others.

The motivations of the Subaltern trend in historiography were different.

As far as Ranajit Guha is concerned, his book, *A Rule of Property for Bengal*, arose out of dissatisfaction with the nationalist historian N.K. Sinha, where obviously N.K. Sinha was right and Ranajit Guha wrong. Sinha argued that the Permanent Settlement was instituted to ensure the maximization of land revenue collection, but, because of various factors like the movement of prices, it did not work so well for the British. Ranajit Guha himself confesses that Sinha ignored the ideological fact that colonialism wanted to create landed property, and that his own book is not on economic history at all but an intellectual history of how this idea progressed. This, I think, is a subversion of the entire economic history of the Permanent Settlement, stemming from his sense of dissatisfaction with the nationalist school for all the wrong reasons. Guha developed this approach into an almost perverse hostility to mainstream Indian historiography.

From there he went on to hypothesize a struggle among three elements: colonial elites, Indian elites and subalterns. Of course his definition of subaltern is completely different from Gramsci's, who said that subaltern classes actually help to reinforce the hegemony of the ruling classes. Guha's description of subaltern is 'subordinate classes' – wrong English actually, because the Oxford English Dictionary defines subaltern as a 'subordinate clause' not 'class'. In logic, the main argument is supported by a subordinate clause, so in fact subalterns should form a subordinate support to the cause of the ruling classes. But for Guha, from subordinate classes they become resisting classes. And then he creates a picture, without any historical basis whatsoever, of subalterns being communities, which are not economic classes but those whose members do not have an English education. So a big landlord who had not passed high school is subaltern because he is not influenced by 'elite' ideas! Indian elites are not capitalists, they can be workers too if they are influenced by elite ideas. This collection of ideas, set up initially as premises, was built up into a theology under whose influence Subaltern historians wrote papers, mainly to use the word 'subaltern' and decry the nationalist leadership.

The great weakness in the Subaltern theorists is that they do not deal with aggregates. Therefore the colonial tribute does not come under their scanner, nor does deindustrialization, because a tribal person did not see either tribute or deindustrialization. Actually, it is only the peasant who could have seen the impact of deindustrialization. Even a landless labourer may not have seen it as he would not have known why his real wages were falling. So the total rejection of economic statistics of higher magnitudes results in total rejection of any question as to why and how India was exploited by colonialism. This self-imposed blindness is basic to Subaltern historiography. Therefore the Subaltern approach actually fits in very well with the Cambridge school, because both attack the Indian 'elites' whose members worked out the ways in which Britain was exploiting India and created 'Economic Nationalism', on which Bipan Chandra has written.

The Subaltern high-priest now is Partha Chatterjee, who even sees communalism as a 'subaltern' phenomenon, and argues that the 'Nehruvian Marxists' are wrong in thinking that the Indian people are not communal. These are extremely disingenuous statements, though they have got considerable support abroad. Edward Said also wrote in praise of the 'Subalterns', although he did warn them that many of their ideas could be 'complicit with neo-colonialism'.

The Subalterns have found post-modernism very useful, because post-modernism also rejects statistical aggregates and any large economic framework. One of the early works anticipating post-modernism was by Louis Dumont. In his book *Homo Hierarchicus*, he rejects the notion that India has a history or that it has an economic history, or even that economic ideas can be applied to Indian society. All this has been completely absorbed by the Subalterns who are pleased to hitch on to Dumont's emphasis on the ideological underpinning of caste. Thus, not only is communalism a subaltern phenomenon, but so is tribalism and casteism. Dumont also fits in with post-modernism because the latter rejects the 'meta-narrative'. Rejection of the meta-narrative means that you cannot deal with large economic factors, you can only deal with individuals and small communities; and you certainly cannot apply a common, universally applicable scientific method. All this fits in with not only the Subaltern approach, but also the communal approach to history. Edward Said was once a favourite author of the RSS, whom they frequently cited in their battle with secularism and modern values.

As far as textbooks are concerned, I don't think that these tendencies are as yet reflected in them, although they have certainly weakened the view of the colonial regime as an exploitative one. This has given rise to other distortions of history. Take some ideologues of the modern Dalit movement. They have consistently attacked the national movement and its ideology, totally ignoring the fact that Ambedkar collaborated with British imperialism at very crucial moments when he had no need to do so. They also totally negate Gandhi's contributions to Dalit uplift, and ignore the brutal conditions which Dalits suffered from under British rule and which became things of the past only after 1947, disadvantaged and repressed in many ways that Dalits still remain. When you pass the main Aligarh flyover, you pass a statue. This is of Raja Ugrasen of the Banias riding a horse, supposedly a great ruler – but who never existed! So every caste now is manufacturing its history.

Another aspect of this is that if you write criticisms of the nationalist and Marxist historians or schools, you are welcome in western institutions, particularly in Britain and the US. I think this too is having its effect on certain circles, but I would not overstress this factor.

Actually, the whole lot – Namierists, Subalterns, Cambridge historians, post-modernists, even Edward Said – they all exert an influence that encourages chauvinism, communalism and caste sentiment. Muslims cannot be studied by non-Muslims is the conclusion one draws from Edward Said. An Arab can only study Arabs; Indians can only be studied by an Indian. The external enquirer must always be excluded. This appeal to communal and caste sentiment is also very important for the success of globalization, because even as globalization operates to produce a unified economic sphere to the detriment of underdeveloped national economies, such ideologies encourage fragmentation in the ideological sphere and so break down resistance to globalization. The post-modernist project of cultural fragmentation may thus seem to be the natural ideological counterpart of the economic side of globalization.

What about their influence on school textbooks?
Yes, as far as the textbooks are concerned, the source of the fragmentation of historical information you see in them is for another reason. When the United Progressive Alliance [UPA] first took power, for reasons best known to them, they did not criticize the BJP textbooks at all – and in fact were dead set against bringing back the earlier history textbooks written by R.S. Sharma, Satish Chandra, Bipan Chandra, Romila Thapar and others.

The present government has built up a theory of school education that is quite disastrous. First, their notion of the creation of knowledge is that the child should be encouraged to create knowledge himself. Then they say that knowledge should be interdisciplinary. This in practice means that you serve history in disjointed fragments. The child does not need to know that the Mauryas came after Gautama Buddha. There is no anxiety that the child should have a world-view. Instead, just provide the child with tidbits and let him create knowledge for himself. And now you have the abolition of examinations, which means that you meet the constitutional criteria of education until high school without in fact educating the child. Those who want to get educated will go to good private schools which will have examinations because they will not have any public grants, so you waste the taxpayers' money and only let the rich get educated. It is a policy of fraudulently meeting constitutional obligations without undertaking any real effort to educate people.

I don't think the Congress government bothers about the content of textbooks. All they bother about is that they should not spend more on education. Take physics. If you don't have an examination, what kind of physics will a child learn? History and sociology form a minor part of it. Look at science. What kind of science are you teaching? They now say that even if an examination is held, it should be in familiar surroundings in the same school by invigilators who are your teachers. Why are you so bothered about invigilators? You are in fact inviting copying! How does it matter what hall you are sitting in? I was a schoolboy and appeared for the High School examination at an unfamiliar centre with unfamiliar invigilators, and don't remember having been mentally troubled at all.

As I said, history in our textbooks has become fragmented and I am not happy with the kind of world history they are now producing for schools. The second problem is that university and college teaching is in a very bad way. The objective-question system is destroying the necessity for a student to have a larger view. He just wants to know facts so that he can answer the objective-type questions. I don't know what the answer is, because assessment is easier in objective questions. This could be rectified if there was good teaching, a good tutorial system and monitoring of teaching. But that is perhaps asking for too much.

Institutions of History

Historians, by and large, have played a fairly progressive political role in India, a country where history forever impinges on politics. A rather unusual aspect of the status of history in India is the activism of institutions of history – professional bodies like the Indian History Congress and even official bodies like the Indian Council of Historical Research. How would you assess their role?

Let me begin with the Indian History Congress (IHC). As you know, it was a creation of nationalist historians, a fact clear from the initial lecture given in 1935 by Shafaat Ahmad Khan. In it he emphasized two things. One, the need to have an integrated history of India, and second, that Indian historians should write their own history. These two very important objectives were the starting points for the IHC. In the very difficult circumstances of the 1940s, the IHC kept all kinds of historians together – Congress, pro-Communist and even Muslim League historians. In the 1946 session of the IHC in Madras, a schoolteacher of Madras read a short paper on Tipu Sultan's grants to Hindu temples. He consulted documents and district gazetteers, and it was yeoman service rendered at the time. The IHC has reprinted the article in its volume on *Modernization and Resistance under Haidar Ali and Tipu Sultan.*

When Partition came, the IHC remained the major professional body of historians in India. It including right-wing historians like R.C. Majumdar but was essentially managed by liberal historians. And I must say that even those whom we criticized encouraged us – persons like Romila Thapar and myself – by inviting us to speak at symposia and to participate in the IHC proceedings. I liked that kind of spirit among our 'seniors'.

As Marxist historians grew in number and influence, that too was reflected in the History Congress. But essentially it remained a body of mainstream historians. Its first political test came during the Emergency. It was the only academic body that passed resolutions protesting against arrests made under the Emergency, at the Aligarh session in 1975 and the Calicut session in 1976, and even printed the resolution in the *Proceedings* during the period of Emergency itself. No newspaper would print the resolution. I even tried to induce a well-known weekly tabloid to denounce it and so draw attention to it, but its editor, a good friend, saw through the ruse!

Then, from 1984 or 85, from the beginning of the Ayodhya movement, the Indian History Congress took up cudgels against communalism, and I must say that it has held to this position most firmly. I was often not very sure if our resolutions would be passed. But most of them got unanimously passed, or with only two or three dissents. After the destruction of the Babri Masjid in December 1992, there was a large contingent at the History Congress at Warangal in March next year. We brought a resolution denouncing the destruction and, to my surprise, there were only three votes against it! We later learned that this was partly because some principals of colleges, by their presence at the session, had got many of the opposing teachers of their colleges to abstain. Were the elder people better wedded to secular values than the younger generation?

The IHC also published a critique of the BJP-sponsored NCERT textbooks in 2003 that forced the NCERT to print an expectedly rude reply in thousands of copies, which were distributed free. Yet, many historians who may be politically inclined towards the BJP have remained with the IHC, and I firmly believe that all professional historians must find a place in the IHC without it becoming the monopoly of any one trend.

The Indian Council for Historical Research was created for a different purpose. The first was the belief that there should be encouragement given to research outside the university and UGC [University Grants Commission] system. It was also thought that college teachers and research scholars who had no access to sources of funding should be supported with research grants. The 'Towards Freedom' project was an important one assigned to the ICHR. It was felt by the government that we must issue a response to the *Transfer of Power* volumes by Mansergh. The objective was later enlarged and it was decided that we would not just answer *Transfer of Power*, but also document the larger national movement. Ultimately, that proved a very difficult task. The first volume by P.N. Chopra was absolutely unimaginative and one-sided. The succeeding volumes have been much better and the project is now nearly complete. The ICHR issues the *Indian Historical Review* that used to be a major vehicle for the publication of research papers, a position it now needs to regain. I think the ICHR has played a very important role in encouraging serious research, even though during the BJP regime it was gravely misused.

Family Influences

You come from a family that was involved in the national movement. How far did that influence your work?
Actually our family's connection, particularly that of my parents, was more with the ideology of the national movement than with actual participation. It was my maternal grandfather (Abbas Tyabji) who was Gandhi's associate since 1919 and who went to jail, and of course that influenced me. One of the reasons for my mother's marriage was that my father had nationalistic ideas and had participated in the Non-Cooperation movement. He did not, however, go to jail; many people who participated in the Non-Cooperation movement were not arrested.

My father was one of the proponents of what later on came to be known as the 'nationalist school of historiography'. He was extremely hostile to the communal viewpoint, and you can see that in the first book he published, *Mahmud of Ghazni*, in which he remains very strongly committed to an anti-communal viewpoint. He remained fully committed to the Congress till after Independence. In fact he even opposed the 'parity' principle in government proposed in 1945. He said it was wrong that either Hindus and Muslims, or the Congress and the Muslim League, should have parity in the ministry; their representation should be proportionate to their strength.

His hostility to the Muslim League was one reason why my father had certain reservations about the Communist Party in the 1940s. He was influenced by Marxism, but he thought the Communists' concessions to the Muslim League were unacceptable, although he was not so much worried about the Communist opposition to the Quit India Resolution. A second element in his thought was an almost irrational affection for Gandhi. He admired Pandit Nehru, but he had very great affection and respect for Gandhi. So that too naturally affected me.

I came into contact with the Communist movement in 1949, after Partition and after P.C. Joshi's leadership had ended. By then of course the CPI's earlier support for Pakistan was a closed chapter.

What drew you to the Communist Party?
Well, the Soviet Union's epic struggle and victory in the World War, the

Chinese Revolution in particular, and the writings by Marx that my father introduced me to. He was a voracious reader of People's Publishing House literature at that time. My own participation as a student in the Communist movement began in 1949, and I became a party member in 1953.

Theory and Social Practice

You have been a practitioner of history and Left politics; there has not been a day in your working life that has not been divided between your academic work and your political activism. How has your politics influenced your work and the kind of historical issues you were drawn to?

I think that one of the reasons I was drawn to Marxism – and I suppose this would apply to others too – is the close relationship between theory and social practice. Not between theory and ritual – that of course would be religion – but theory and social practice. Well, it is for others to say whether it is right or wrong, but I feel that if theory is suited to practice, practice then enables us to refine theory. That particular relationship is one I find very enchanting. When I entered the Communist movement – and unknown to me, I was also once elected to the all-India executive committee of the Students Federation – I was fairly active. Once I became a teacher, I was active in the peace movement and then I was assigned to work in the University's Employees' Union. I have worked there ever since. On occasion, I also helped in the work of city unions. There was a very big union of the Indian Trading Corporation factory, and also of the rickshaw pullers (an earlier incarnation; later on, my younger colleague, I.G. Khan, organized them in a union that I was not much connected with). Then there were some very small factory unions. In the 1960s, the Communist movement was fairly strong in the city. When the split came in 1962–64, I joined the Left, which ultimately became the CPI(M).

Was your decision to stay on in Aligarh determined by your political activities here?

Well, I got my job and promotions here, Sayera (my wife) had a job here, so why would I have wanted to leave? And then, here I knew everybody, and while everybody may not have liked me, they knew me!

Roots of Communalism

You have personally been at the receiving end of communal mobilizations both of the minority and majority variants, on and off campus. You have

written on the issue of communalism extensively. As a historian and activist on the Left, what do you see as the historical antecedents of these tendencies, especially Islamicism, which has become a global phenomenon today?
It is always difficult when traditional ideologies, notably based on religious identities but also on caste and tribe, arise. They have a way of remaining dormant for a long time and then suddenly coming to life. You can see that in caste ideology in India, and I think that is also the case with religion, whose revival can be seen in the former republics of the Soviet Union after a long period of dormancy.

Until 1938, AMU was dominated by the Congress, and I remember as a child seeing Congress flags fluttering from hostel windows. Within three years the University went under the Muslim League's dominance. So it is not that AMU had always been averse to nationalist influences before 1947. The Communist poet Majaaz, who wrote the poem that is the anthem of the University, was educated here. When Khalida Adib Khanum (Halida Adeeb Hanam), the Turkish nationalist writer and poet, was given a reception here in the early 1930s, Majaaz read a long, stirring poem exalting modern Turkey and Halida's contribution to its construction. But when the shift occurred and the Muslim League became dominant, there was an outburst of communalism. After Partition there was great frustration and bitterness, and many Muslims left for Pakistan. On the other hand, many Muslim leaders felt that they had to make up with the Congress and many of them were becoming Congressmen at that time. There was a significant shift of opinion in favour of the Communists too. There was a feeling that the Communists had played a big role in opposing the communal riots, and in our organizations, Muslims and Hindus all marched together. At that time there was great hope that this shift to the left would be sustained.

The ideological erosion of the Left seems to have started in the late 1950s in practically all the universities (of Uttar Pradesh, at any rate), not only in AMU. This was partly because of Nehru's policies – the five-year plans, the creation of the public sector and growing employment opportunities, all factors that we did not understand at that time. These greatly satisfied large sections of the middle classes, including Muslims. You know, until the late 1950s, an engineering-degree holder from AMU would not often get a job in India and would have to migrate to Pakistan. More than half of our engineering graduates migrated every year. But then the jobs started coming here and the migration ceased altogether.

I think much of the upsurge of communalism did not take place at that time, although the Jan Sangh did remain strong. Not only here, but all over the world, communalism and the sense of religious identity grew in strength when the Soviet Union began to falter, and socialism lost much of its attraction. All over the Arab world where the Communists were strong, they have been in retreat. They are strongest now in Israel, of all places, because there, faced with problems of discrimination, Arab Israelis must turn to the Communist Party. They in fact issue the only Communist daily (in Arabic) from the region. The shift to religion is taking place in many countries, and in India, both among Hindus and Muslims. It takes different shapes and forms of course, but the absence of a Left alternative in most parts of the country has created additional space for it. Now this is very unfortunate, because even when religious sectarianism takes an anti-American garb, it does what America wants – it divides the opposition and the ranks of resistance.

I don't agree with the view that communalism would be necessarily less strong among Muslims if there were full economic and social opportunities for them, or that if there were total employment among Hindus, there wouldn't be any chauvinism. These are probably illusions. Muslims should be educated and employed because that is what should be done, not necessarily because that will lower the temperature of communalism. Because communalism would probably still remain, everyone would have still some grievance, and that grievance would then become an excuse for assertions of religious identity and communalism.

Look at the religious identity of people who go to the United States. They have no personal economic or social grievance. They have good jobs in the United States and they send money to India. But the moment they reach the US, they insist that their wives should wear the *hijab* (head-covering) if they are Muslims, and if they are Hindus, they start taking much greater interest in ritual. So much of communalism in India is funded and funnelled from areas where Hindus and Muslims enjoy a standard of life they would not dream of in India. So I don't think this has much to do with economic grievances.

Let us here take the case of the Uighurs in China. Obviously, the Uighurs are today much better off than before 1949. They have education, housing and security. They have access to employment and can go anywhere in China to work. They can become workers and can send money home. There is also some affirmative action in place to improve their position in employment. But there is dissatisfaction, and in recent riots both Hans and Uighurs were killed. So I do not think material improvement will necessarily change ideology, but material conditions must be improved for its own sake. Muslims are citizens, and if the state is not spending money on them in proportion to their numbers, it should do so – and there should be affirmative action too. This should not be done for just the reason that you will thereby automatically contain communalism.

The Notion of India

Which brings me to ask about an idea you have written about, that of the notion of India. Nationhood developed in the struggle against colonialism, but you have argued that the notion of India goes much further back.

Like institutions, concepts evolve and their scope changes with circumstances. This is the case with what you might call 'geographical expressions', like countries or regions. Consider the famous statement: 'Italy is a mere geographical expression.' But what makes it a geographical expression? This raises the question: when does the idea that a conscious sense of a unit, let us say of geography or even of culture, first appear? Actually, this particular debate to which you refer took place because the BJP was saying the idea of India was so ancient that it went back to the *Rigveda*. Obviously, in the *Rigveda* there is no name for India. Even '*Sapta Sindhwa*' means 'Seven Rivers', and other geographical names that appear in it are those of tribes and rivers. Territorial names hardly ever appear in the *Rigveda*. They appear only in later texts.

When does the concept of territory as distinct from a tribe first appear? And then, when does the concept appear of a large number of territories as distinct from other sets of territories? Most historians would agree that this happens when, with the development of towns and trade, a common language – the language of the marketplace and state – arises, and is shared by different regions. We know that from around the sixth century BC, Prakrit was such a language in northern India, not Sanskrit, which continued to be mainly the language of brahman priests.

For the first time, with the Mauryan empire, you have the name for India – Jambudvipa, which is much larger than the concept of Aryavarta. This idea of a large country was now created by political and cultural unification.

Cultural facts can also create an idea of common territory. An interesting cultural fact is the diffusion of the caste system. Wherever there is the caste system, there is India. Outsiders notice it when Indians don't. You find in Hsuan-Tsang's writing, the observation that Indians don't recognize 'In-tu' (India) as a country, they don't call themselves its inhabitants. By then in China, the idea of China as a country was already well established. The word 'In-tu' in Chinese was actually derived from 'Hind' in Persian, though it was treated by Hsuan-Tsang as a Sanskrit word (*Indu*) that was unknown, however, to Indians in that sense.

But then, we also begin to find the word Bharata used for the country, first in Orissa (first century BC) and then in the south, by rulers who say that either their armies or fame have spread all over Bharata. So cultural links lead to a firm 'geographical expression'. Each development of the concept is related to evolving circumstances.

As Indians began to know about other countries, they began to distinguish between themselves and others. You find it in Ashoka, who says that except for the Yonas, every region (in India) has Brahmanas and Shramanas. Or take Gautama Buddha, who says that unlike here, Yonas and Kambojas have masters and slaves, not castes or *varnas*. So this distinction between the territories where Brahmanas and Shramanas and the caste system are found, and those where they are absent, begins to arise – a distinction that leads to the identification of India (under whatever name) as distinct from other countries.

In the Sultanate period, the larger knowledge of external geography that came to be gained made this distinction sharper. For the first time, we have a patriotic poem by Amir Khusrau, where he sings of an India where brahmans are philosophers and everything is beautiful. India, he says, has given so much to the world: the *Panchatantra*, chess and decimal numbers (*hindsa*). The concept of India thus grew as global contacts grew and ordinary people came to grips with it. Medieval India thus added further substance to the idea of India.

Of course one must distinguish India as a cultural unit, even as a political unit, from a nation-state. The concept of the nation became a powerful political notion only after the French Revolution of 1789. But every concept takes time to grow, and I would say that in 1857, while it is still primitive, it is there. The national sense grew partly because by then the British themselves had created a unified army (the Bengal Army, at least for northern India) and a unified administration. Very interesting is the reply of the 1857 Rebels to Queen Victoria's Proclamation, in which they state how India has suffered under the British, and how Indians from Tipu Sultan in Mysore to Dileep Singh in the Punjab lost their governments. What is very important is that they present here a perception of what the entire country had suffered from Mysore to the Punjab, and not just the few princely houses that had gone into rebellion.

It is, however, with the Indian national movement which evolved by opposing the colonial oppression of India, while dissecting its exploitative nature on the plane of national aggregates, so to speak – tribute, deindustrialization, exclusion of Indians from employment – that you first have the full concept of India as a nation.

Starting from a geographical and cultural concept, I would then say, the idea of India continues to evolve until India is perceived as a 'nation'. I also agree that the concept of the Indian nation could also be destroyed. There are institutions that are present only because we *think* they are important and so defend them. And therefore, we must understand why it is necessary to politically defend the concept of India, and actually work out the implications of India being a nation by putting into practice the fairest treatment of the inhabitants of all its diverse parts.

One of the more contentious issues that confronts the modern nation is that of industrialization. It has been an issue with which the Left in Bengal has had to grapple. What is your understanding of this, and are there insights on this that historical experience can offer?

Well, it is clear that without industrialization there can be no emancipation of the Indian people. It is a controversy that has been there from Mahatma Gandhi's time. When I was in my BA there was an essay – now no longer easily available – in our course by Nehru, entitled 'Tomorrow in India'. In it he contests Gandhi's views on industrialization. He does not refer to Gandhi by name, but takes issue with Vallabhbhai Patel who, we know, had only repeated what Gandhi had said. Nehru says that tomorrow's India must be an industrialized India. This position is reflected in the Karachi Resolution of the Congress, which said that the government must control and develop basic industries.

So there can be no dispute on this. Those who celebrate tribal primitiveness, like Arundhati Roy and Binayak Sen, are actually damaging the cause of the tribal people. Are they to remain for ever forest folk, denied the full opportunities of industrial employment, education and science?

Then there is another problem about industrialization in Bengal, and I don't see an easy solution. Much of West Bengal is in two parts: the densely populated Hooghly valley and delta, and the hilly and forested southwestern part. If you build industry in the southwestern part, then how do you ease the unemployment situation in your densely populated area? If there is a factory in West Midnapur, labour would come from Jharkhand, Orissa and Bihar but not necessarily from West Bengal. So how would it ease the unemployment in the densely populated parts? That is why, if you want to ease the unemployment problem in Murshidabad and Malda, where there is so much poverty, you have to build industry in places like Nandigram and Singur. They can't go as easily to West Midnapur.

On the other hand, if tribals have to get educated and get employment, how do you provide it except through industry? What are the other means? The land has been redistributed under West Bengal's fairly radical agrarian reforms and there is a limit to what numbers the land can maintain. The forest provides only limited employment and forest dwellers can't live there as their numbers increase. Therefore industrialization is the only way out, even in the forested zones.

Clearly we are in trouble here, and if the peasants of Bengal don't want industrialization, as the opponents of the Left Front claim, then there is nothing we can do. Where will West Bengal build industry? If you leave the denser parts and go to forested areas, you are accused of disturbing the ecology. Where on earth can they then build industry?

I have read about a steel plant in West Midnapur. This is the place where the so-called 'Maoists' wanted to kill Chief Minister Buddhadeb Bhattacharya and the then central minister, Ram Vilas Paswan. The factory has apparently come up and tribals are going there for work. The 'Maoists', strangely, are not raising any issues here. There was a small press report – I don't know if it is true but it is quite likely to be so – that they are not protesting because they have forced the management to ensure that anyone belonging to the CPI(M) will not be employed. They have insisted that certain persons will be employed at double the salary, so that they can in turn pay off the 'Maoists'. So much of this opposition to industry may just be built up for use as handy slogans.

You have shared your vision of history with us in this interview. With apologies for a meta-question, are there any issues that you may want to highlight in conclusion?
One's vision and perception of history expands and changes, and as new complexities come to one's knowledge, they affect one's generalizations. One of the difficulties of people who are influenced by religion is that some factors to them remain unchanged, and that distorts their sense of history. There is in fact nothing that remains unchanged.

You know ideological history was not my field, agrarian history was. But the polemics and fight against communalism made me come to the conclusion that religious history must also be critically studied. Not in a way that hurts people, but certainly one should point out that religious views and concepts change. I wrote an article recently, I don't know if you have seen it, entitled 'Indo-Muslim Thought and the Problem of Religious Coexistence'. I end by quoting Marx: that man makes religion, religion does not make man. All people who have religious faith should so shape their beliefs that they are able to live in comradeship with persons of other religions. I have argued that this necessity forced itself upon even some Muslim theologians, if you look at the entire history of Indo-Muslim religious thought. The issue of religious coexistence confronts them all the time; the conservatives and more tolerant elements come to different conclusions, and develop opposing ideas. Thus religious thought too constantly changes and displays new complexities.

On the importance of the economic structure to history, my feeling is that when Marx speaks of the material basis and superstructure, he necessarily includes mind (ideas) in the material basis. Because when you are speaking of production, it is impossible to speak of it without human skill, technology and science. So the whole debate about materialism, as if matter alone is important, is misleading and misrepresents Marx's position. He uses materialism because that is the immediate word at hand, but he doesn't mean that material conditions exclude skill, labour power, science and technology – which are all products of the human mind or are controlled by it.

That is perhaps one weakness in the generalization which appears in Stalin's essay, *Dialectical and Historical Materialism*, which we used to take as our basic text and which I would still say is useful reading. It is obviously very important to pay attention to ideas and their role; without that you cannot understand the rise of capitalism. Of course, for its emergence and growth, capitalism was dependent on capital accumulation, colonial conquests and expropriation of the peasantry; but it was also dependent on technology and that was given to it by the scientific revolution. For all these reasons, the ideological battleground must always remain important.

In today's discussions on Marxism, the emphasis on ideology is often absent. When Mao Zedong said, 'Put politics in command', I think what he meant was that ideology should be put in command. Or when Lenin said that politics is the essence of economics, he surely was referring to political ideas.

Therefore, I do think that for human emancipation, the furthering of scientific, socialist ideology is crucial. And similarly, we cannot understand past events without critically examining the ideology of that time and its influence on the society as it was then structured.

Selected Reviews of
Irfan Habib's Writings

The Agrarian System of Mughal India

Irfan Habib, *The Agrarian System of Mughal India (1556–1707)*, Bombay: Asia Publishing House, 1963; second revised edition, Delhi: Oxford University Press, 1999.

Review by **Luigi Pignatelli**[*] in *East and West*, Quarterly published by the Instituto Italiano Per Il Medio Ed Estremo Oriente; Editor: Giuseppe Tucci; Co-editors: Mario Bussagli, Domenico Faccenna, Lionello Lanciotti; New Series, Vol. 15, Nos. 1–2, January 1964 – March 1965.

In this sizable volume (the first draft of which constituted a degree thesis at Oxford) Irfan Habib sets out to throw further light on the general history of the Moghul period and give an idea of the vast scope that the corpus of extant Persian mss. affords for the study of this subject. He does more than deal with the agrarian system of the Moghul Empire according to a narrow concept of agrarian and concomitant fiscal policy (this is fully expounded in the second part of the work), but devotes his first five chapters respectively to: (1) agricultural production; (2) trading the produce; (3) the standard of living of the peasants; (4) the relationship of the peasants to the land, the village community; and (5) the *Zamindars*, or big land owners. The author reviews a century and a half of Indian agrarian history from a quite definitely socialist standpoint. Habib is on firm ground whes he denounces a number of substantial and very serious injustices. Indeed, it is no exaggeration to say that the chief characteristic of the Moghul agrarian system was that the Indian peasant took from his own harvest the bare minimum (and how bare it was!) necessary to feed himself and his family, and was then obliged to yield up all that remained as tribute. 'The State', the author declares, 'served not merely as the protective arm of the exploiting classes but was itself the principal instrument of exploitation.' According to Habib, if the peasants were left just enough to live, it was simply because extermination would have reduced taxation revenue.

The feudal system based on the *Jagirdars*, who were authorized to collect taxes, bore within itself the germ of its own decay. For the absolute centralization of power afforded them no guarantee of the continuity of their work and therefore no incentive to improve the fiscal system they administered. Hasty and blind exploitation of the taxpayers was the hallmark of their

[*] Italian Orientalist.

activity, as Francis Xavier was among the first to note and other European writers after him. Patient and long-suffering, convinced even that he did not deserve a better fate, the Indian peasant nevertheless rebelled in the end. The last part of the work is devoted to careful scrutiny of the agrarian crisis of the Moghul Empire. 'There is no province or district', confesses Aurangzeb in his last years, 'where the infidels have not raised a tumult and since they are not chastised, they have established themselves everywhere.'

The volume contains statistical appendices and an ample bibliography. It is clearly a work developed on rigorous and diligent lines with a wise division of the subject-matter. A wealth of data – there are abundant notes, for example – does not vitiate the overall conception which is evidently the author's own: his view of the way power was exercised and also of the infrequent and disorderly reactions of the oppressed class is a pessimistic one. 'No new order', he concludes, 'could be created by the forces ranged against it (the Moghul Empire). The period which follows does not offer an edifying spectacle: the gates were opened to reckless rapine, anarchy and foreign conquest.' We should like to think, however, that this did nothing to worsen the situation already existing in the agrarian sector, and that, combined with other events, it helped India along the path to the total independence she now enjoys.

Review by **Riazul Islam**[*] in *Bulletin of the School of Oriental and African Studies*, University of London, Volume XXVIII, Part 1, 1965.

Dr Irfan Habib's work on the Mughul revenue system is a personal achievement as well as a landmark in modern Indo-Muslim historiography. The author's diligent search for sources and careful scrutiny of texts deserve the highest praise. Not content to rely on the standard texts of well-known authorities, Dr Irfan has gone to the 'best manuscripts' and in many instances his labour has been well rewarded. His uncovering of an error in the statistics under the 'Account of the Twelve Provinces' in Blochmann's standard edition of the *A'in-i Akbari* is itself a notable contribution, for the undetected error has vitiated all the calculations and inferences made by scholars so far on the basis of the published statistics. The chapter on zamindari clears away many obscurities and marks a definite advance in our knowledge of the subject. On the controversial and obscure question of *nasq* – the despair of more than one scholar – the author has for the first

[*] Historian; Professor Emeritus, Karachi University, Pakistan.

time given an explanation which fits in the various contexts in which the term occurs. The author's interpretation of the 'month-proportions' is also an important contribution.

Despite Irfan Habib's erudite thoroughness, his general conclusions are bound to arouse criticism. His central thesis is easy to sum up: the Mughal revenue system aimed at extorting the entire surplus produce of the Indian peasant, leaving no more, and often less, than the barest subsistence; 'the conditions of life of the peasant generally approximated to the lowest possible levels of subsistence'; living thus on the level of starvation, he often had to sell his wife and children in order to pay the state-demand and the various authorized and unauthorized cesses.

This attention to peasant suffering is in itself a welcome departure from the approach of writers like Ibn Hasan and Beni Prasad who were so taken up with the theme of Mughul greatness as to ignore that side of the picture. Dr Irfan Habib has brought together a considerable amount of evidence, drawn from Persian sources as well as European accounts, in support of his thesis. But he has certainly overstated his case on rural exploitation and peasant suffering. He takes literally Abu'l Fadl's rhetorical remark that no moral limits could be set to the fiscal obligation owed by the subject to the ruler: the subject ought to be thankful even if he were made to part with all his possessions by the protector of his life and property (p. 190). The author cites Palsaert and Jerome Xavier to prove that during Jahangir's reign the peasants were so cruelly and pitilessly oppressed that the fields lay unsown and turned into a wilderness and the tillers deserted them and ran away (p. 324). He follows this up with the evidence of a Persian work to show that during Shah Jahan's reign conditions became still worse and that 'vast lands became completely depopulated . . . and the land appeared more desolate than during the time of Jannat Makani (Jahangir)'. One would naturally infer from this sequence of evidence that during the first half of the seventeenth century the area under plough was steadily decreasing. This inference, however, finds no support in the figures given by the author himself, and his explanation of this discrepancy is hypothetical and far from convincing. In assessing the peasant's economic situation, the author has left out his part-time non-agricultural earnings. And in evaluating the agrarian policy of the Mughul government, he has not given adequate recognition to the most persistent theme of Mughul revenue manuals from Akbar to Aurangzeb – the theme of protecting the peasant, of encouraging him and giving him aid to extend his cultivation. This policy, it is true, was occasionally nullified by corruption, dishonesty and the practice of *taghaiyur* of jagirdars (on this the author has an admirable footnote, p. 260). But the ideal was never lost sight of, as is evident from Aurangzeb's *farman*s to Muhammad Hashim and Rasikdas. It is also not without significance that in the reign of Aurangzeb, whose involvement with wars did not permit his undoubted interest in revenue problems full play, a strong and judicious provincial administration in Bengal could ensure not only a steady annual surplus but also extensive rural peace.

The general picture which emerges from the author's account of the Mughul agrarian society is of a peasantry ever on the verge of starvation or revolt. Indeed it is herein that the author seeks the clue to the collapse of the Mughul empire. Nowhere does he sound more doctrinaire than in making the suffering of the peasantry a motivating force behind the Sikh, the Satnami, the Jat and the Maratha revolts. If peasant discontent was the cause of the collapse of the Mughul power, it took an astonishingly long time to work out its effect. For according to the author the demand was from the beginning 'set so high that it could hardly have been increased any further' (p. 196). It is also noteworthy that the lot of the peasantry under Maratha and Jat supremacy was in no way better and certainly worse than under the Mughuls.

The author generally writes in a sober vein, The departures from this in the footnotes on pp. 191–2 and 208–9, therefore, stand out all the more conspicuously. The author's remark in the text about Aurangzeb having ordered the resumption of all grants held by the Hindus is negatived by his own entries in the footnote (p. 311, n. 55). The tentative but tendentious assertion about Aurangzeb's policy of religious discrimination in the appointment of zamindars needs to be corrected with reference to Bengal where the new zamindars were largely Hindus.

However one may differ with Dr Irfan Habib's theme of extreme agrarian poverty and suffering, one cannot fail to admire the thorough and painstaking scholarship that has gone into the making of this book. The author is best when discussing the minutiae of the various methods of assessment, the precise meaning of revenue terms, and the various elements of assessment such as the measures of land, the weights and the coinage. The book also opens out vistas of further research in medieval agronomy. Its publication makes it easier now to pursue detailed studies of the revenue system of the various Mughul provinces. Dr Irfan Habib has unearthed much new material. The areas which receive the most detailed treatment and documentation in his book are those which now constitute Uttar Pradesh. It is reasonable to assume that similar material relating to other provinces, especially Bengal, Rajputana and Gujarat, lies untapped in archives, private collections and family papers. The appearance of Dr Irfan Habib's monograph may well prove the turning-point for a search for this material. The publication of well-documented studies on the agrarian history of Mughul provinces will mark the next stage for a firmer reconstruction of the revenue system of Mughul India.

On the whole, this book is a brilliant piece of work. The author is young in years. Scholars of Indo-Muslim history, in the Indo-Pakistan subcontinent as well as the West, will look forward to further contributions, equally brilliant and more balanced and mature, from his forceful pen.

An Atlas of the Mughal Empire

Irfan Habib, *An Atlas of the Mughal Empire: Political and Economic Maps with Detailed Notes, Bibliography and Index*, Oxford University Press, 1982; second edition, 1983.

'Monument to Empire', review by **Ashin Das Gupta**[*], *The Book Review*, Vol. VI, No. 6, May/June 1982.

Irfan Habib is the closest we get to Marc Bloch among Indian historians. True, the focus is much narrower but there is the same magic with the documents, and a similar talent to piece together the material living of a people. Irfan Habib has moved from a masterly analysis of the Mughal agrarian structure to a wide-ranging search after medieval technology. And now he gives us an incomparable atlas of the Mughal empire, based on minute knowledge and presented with complete honesty. With this atlas we may celebrate a landmark in Indian historiography.

There are thirty-two sheet-maps of the empire drawn to a scale of 1:2,000,000, apart from three insets in the Introduction. Of the thirty-two, as many as twenty-six are devoted to northern India, with six presenting the south in large agglomerates. That, I suppose, is fair enough considering that the Mughal empire was a northern phenomenon and the Aligarh expertise still tends to think of the Deccan as a special case. The imbalance will doubtless be corrected eventually, as southern historiography comes into its own.

The empire in its totality is presented in the first two sheets, political and economic, and then with this rhythm the rest present different regions in sets of two. The regions are so chosen that we may compare modern positions with the situation earlier. This attempt to place Mughal India in the context of later times and thus understand both a little better is central to Habib's thought. The Introduction not only explains how the atlas is to be used, what its data-base is and to what extent it is 'reliable', but also, and quite clearly, the attempt to compare Akbar's India with of Curzon. After the maps we get massive notes on each sheet. Habib does his best to explain why he has marked the maps in the way the reader sees them, and what his authorities are for doing so. This is a distinctive feature of the atlas: it is very much a historian's atlas, with no attempts to conceal ignorance or slur over

---

[*] Economic historian; Vice-Chancellor, Viswa Bharati University, Santiniketan; Professor, Presidency College, Calcutta.

difficulties. Lines and dots on these sheets are not the gestures to the gods which they tend to be in historical maps of India. And there is a wealth of detail in the notes to which an instant review can do scant justice.

The atlas, therefore, is not so much a collection of maps as a major historian's patient research over many years, presented cartographically. Each will look for his own favourite in the assemblage, and I would commend the effort to trace the *suba*-boundaries the most. Naturally the lines are drawn across the unknown and they can at best only separate two places known to have belonged to two different administrative units. The strength of the atlas lies in the heartland of the empire but, clearly, knowledge of Rajasthan has been growing in recent years and the maps of the west are more satisfactory than those of the east. None the less, the maps of Assam deserve a special mention. The economic information is very full, and ranges from a most helpful mapping of the Mughal mints to the attempt to assist historians of Indian fauna by plotting the distribution of wild life.

Comparisons will inevitably be made with Schwartzberg's *Historical Atlas of South Asia*, critical acclamation of which has still not died down. There are echoes of Schwartzberg in Irfan Habib. I was delighted to come across Habib's defence of the use of 'India' as distinct from the vogue word South Asia. 'The reader', says Habib, 'is not likely to take kindly to 'Northern South Asia' instead of 'Northern India'. This is the limit of levity that he permits himself. But, more seriously, the comparison is difficult to make as the two works are conceived so differently. Schwartzberg's grand sweep and lavish, almost coffee-table production are absent in this relatively austere and singularly purposive effort. For Mughal maps, of course, Irfan Habib now definitely replaces Schwartzberg, those of us who can will still look to Schwartzberg for his religious and cultural map and the contemporary cartography he reproduces. Irfan Habib advisedly sticks to the areas he knows, but the study of the Mughal empire will benefit if others were now to follow him in areas he does not cover. Historians of southern India may now be tempted to expand on what Habib has achieved, and historians working in regional-language sources – Marathi comes easily to mind – may try to map the mind of India, or at any rate, India's changing society.

This atlas will undoubtedly fuel further research, and each one of us as we pore over it, will discover our favourite grumble. Unusually careful for the most part, it lets us down on occasion surprisingly. The first two maps of the entire empire are based on the information displayed in the other sheet maps. But the area called Malabar excludes Travancore in map OA, whereas the information on which it is based, shown quite correctly in map 16A, stretches the area out to the Cape. The route from Gujarat to Agra and Delhi is shown only along the western way via Rajasthan, leaving out, unaccountably, the east road via Ujjain. No one should rely on this atlas to discover the areas under European control, as no distinctions have been made between Goa, which was directly and absolutely administered by the Portuguese, Cochin, where the Dutch shared the administration only from the 1660s, and, say, Anjengo and Cannanore, where several European powers had their settlements but no European claimed any sovereignty. Map OB suggests the existence of an active 'shipping area' in Malabar which is misleading, the Malabar ports never being distinguished for shipping. The major shipping of Mughal India clustered at Surat, Masulipatam and Hooghly. And poor Masulipatam has changed its spelling from map to map, figuring within the same set (maps OA and OB) as Masulipatam and Machhlipatan. Such a list of small grievances could be multiplied, but I would say generally that Irfan Habib, like the Mughal *mansabdar* he knows best, is essentially a land animal and he feels unsettled by salt in the air.

Review by **Joseph E. Schwartzberg**[*] in *The Journal of Asian Studies*, Vol. 43, No. 3, May 1984, pp. 567–70.

Irfan Habib states that this long-awaited atlas 'is essentially an attempt to present the political and economic geography of the Indian subcontinent during the sixteenth and seventeenth centuries' (p. ix). As such, it is both a triumph and a failure. I know of no comparable atlas that comes close to matching it in attention to detail and meticulousness of documentation. In terms of cartographic techniques, however, the work is amateurish and lacking in aesthetic appeal. Further, it suffers from being wholly expository, seeking neither to explain nor to interpret the incredible wealth of information it presents.

The atlas comprises five well-integrated parts: introduction, maps, notes on the maps, bibliography and index. The maps, entirely in black and white, are generally arranged in pairs: A, 'Political' and B, 'Economic'. The first such pair, at a scale of 1:9,000,000, provides a general overview of the Indian subcontinent and adjoining areas; subsequent maps, all at a scale of 1:2,000,000 (roughly 32 miles to the inch), provide comprehensive sectional coverage. Though the style of the A and B maps is uniform throughout, the sectional maps differ enormously in areal extent. Habib chose – unwisely and not altogether consistently – to organize the maps in relation to contemporary administrative divisions, rather than to those existing in Mughal times. Thus, whereas all of modern Uttar Pradesh appears on both maps 8A

[*] Historical geographer; Professor, University of Minnesota, USA.

and 8B, a study of Delhi or Agra *suba* will require one to consult two or three pairs of maps.

The economic maps depict, in remarkable detail, goods produced in particular localities. Agricultural, mineral and craft products are named at the appropriate locations, within triangles, circles and rectangles, respect-ively; there is no attempt at more detailed symbolization within those broad categories. Roads, navigable streams, bridges and ports are also shown and, on certain sheets, the extent of forest, deserts, and details of wild fauna and flora and products derived from them. The density and locales of the data portrayed, however, are more a function of the varying descriptive richness of the sources than of the empirical realities of the period. This poses a serious problem with which Habib never seriously comes to grips. Whereas his sources provide information on such rarities as bezoar (the gallstones of feral goats, used for medicinal purposes), widespread staple crops such as *jowar* and *bajra* – held in low regard by affluent Indians and, therefore, little documented – receive meagre notice. Habib never suggests the extent to which the distributions he portrays might differ from the objective distributions of the age under review. Similarly, though notes on horses and camels abound on the map sheet for Rajasthan and cheetahs are plotted there at no fewer than eight locales, cattle are noted but once, and sheep and goats, despite their undoubtable importance, not at all. The uneven attention given in the atlas to various types of production is not a serious problem, however, in regard to mining and handicrafts. The data provided for the latter, especially in regard to types of textiles, are particularly rich, and a 'Glossary of Textile Terms' appended to the text aids the nonspecialist in dealing with them.

An important deficiency of the atlas is its paucity of data on terrain. The B maps provide the names of all hill and mountain ranges but give no indication of their elevations, and only a hint of their territorial extent. At the very least, areas of rugged terrain might have been indicated by a light screen pattern. This technically simple cartographic device would have served to frame and highlight the remaining areas of smooth terrain on which production and settlement are concerned. In contrast to the inadequate concern with relief, streams are shown in inordinate details, needlessly cluttering many of the maps.

In the Notes, Habib demonstrates his scholarly prowess; he provides at least one and often several pieces of documentation for virtually every fact plotted on the maps. Where sources disagree, he weighs the evidence in support of each point of view; when a source is nuclear or questionable, he tells us why and explains his reasons for using it as he did. Dubious orthography and locational imprecision are pointed out. Finally, where he was unable to locate places or other data to his own satisfaction, he informs us candidly of his failure. The style throughout is telegraphic and precise. Included among the seventy pages of notes are three pages of additions and corrections, which attest to Habib's unremitting dedication to his project. He does not hesitate to pronounce himself wrong when newly acquired evidence suggests that is or may be the case. The organization of the notes for the economic maps is by *suba* with subheads by *sarkar*, or, beyond the limits of the Mughal Empire, by state or region. The breakdown of notes for the economic sheets is topical and detailed.

The bibliography comprises 269 items. As many refer to journals or to multivolume gazetteer series, I would judge that the number of sources actually consulted is several times that number. Judicious, often critical, annotation for most entries considerably enhances their utility, but tracking down specific citations is difficult and requires one to consult a long accompanying list of abbreviations.

The index, with some 7,500 entries, is amazingly complete. It provides alternative spellings for toponyms, wherever needed, to show changes in orthography and usage over time. Cross-references are abundant. Every place name, product and so forth is keyed to each map on which it is plotted, with a simple reference to each one-degree map square within which it is shown.

Two tables appear in the introductory portion of the atlas, one showing the area and revenue of the *suba*s and *sarkar*s of the empire in 1601, the other merely the areas of the *suba*s and *sarkar*s of the Deccan in 1707. Nine double-column pages of text indicate the sources used for the work, the organization and content of the maps and notes, the rules for indexing, the system of transliteration, the method of pronunciation of non-English words, the measures of distance, weight and volume, and the areal and temporal coverage of the atlas.

Also included in the introduction are three small-scale maps, the *only* attempts at synoptic cartography in the atlas. Map 1 shows, by *sarkar*, the number of *mahal*s (small revenue units) shown in the atlas as a percentage of the total recorded in the *A'in*. For the empire as a whole, Habib was able to locate and plot 2,187 (71.6 per cent) of a total of 3,053. While for many areas he was able to provide complete coverage, in certain tribal frontier regions his success rate was less than 25 percent. This map provides a good general guide to the completeness of data those *suba*s acquired before Akbar's death. Map 2 shows the number of places plotted per 1,000 square miles of measured *sarkar* area. Based on more than 4,000 points, it shows densities from less than one to more than ten and provides a rough surrogate for a map of population density. Habib sees this map as highly correlated with the density map of the 1911 census, selected because it relates to a time when the population distribution 'was practically unaffected by industrialization and only partly affected by the new canal-settlements'. (But by this logic he might have done better to make his comparison with a map from the first reasonably complete census in 1881.) Map 3, relating solely to the Deccan, in principle like map 2, provides less meaningful results. Its range of place density is much more limited, and the relationship to presumed population density is weak.

Why Habib limited himself to three synoptic maps is a mystery. His failure to expand on them represents a lost opportunity to make his atlas not merely a reference work – valuable though it is in that regard – but also a major scholarly synthesis and educational tool. Using the data that went into his first table, for example, he could have mapped revenue per square mile for all *sarkars* circa 1595, and thereby produced a fairly good surrogate of a map of general land productivity. Similarly, he could have plotted revenue rates per *bigha* (roughly 0.6 acre) of wheat, as given by the *A'in* – which he did, in fact, indicate on a sample basis on portions of three sectional maps – to adduce a crop-specific pattern of productivity. Other such area-ratio maps, each with its own distinctive pattern, could also have been devised. Additionally, a diversity of small-scale topical maps would have been feasible. A map of the distribution of forests, in so far as they were recorded in the primary sources, would have been particularly useful. Special maps relating to mints, mining, textile handicrafts and other specialized commodities for which the reporting was relatively comprehensive could easily have been compiled.

While one might protest that the information for most of these recommended maps is already plotted on the B maps of the atlas, the reader often cannot perceive that information intelligibly because each type of data is mixed, willy-nilly, with all sorts of other details and scattered over a great many maps. Habib could not only have pulled it all together, type by type, on a series of all-India maps – several to the page – but he also could have commented critically on the major lacunae and biases that the recommended maps would undoubtedly exhibit. While the proposed maps could even now be prepared by other scholars, drawing on the atlas index and the sectional maps as given, the critical analysis that ought to accompany them could only come from a specialist who, like Habib, is steeped in the original primary sources.

One hesitates to find fault with a work that is, in so many ways, a masterpiece of scholarship and model of precision. Yet, despite my admiration for Habib's atlas, I cannot but lament the lost opportunity therein. The loss can, of course, yet be made good in one or more later publications, but how much more convenient it would have been if the original had been fleshed out as suggested above. It is my earnest hope that Habib will again take up the task and complete what he has thus far so painstakingly advanced.

Review by **Simon Digby**[*] in *Bulletin of the School of Oriental and African Studies*, University of London, Vol. 48, No. 1, 1985, pp. 156–58.

As Professor Habib remarks, 'The Mughal empire is exceptionally rich in materials for the mapmaker'. His notice of sources opens with Abu'l Fadl's great late sixteenth century compendium describing its territories, resources and inhabitants, the *A'in-i Akbari*. Habib notes that some of the seventeenth century accounts which supplement it for individual regions (the *Mazhar-i Shahjahani* for Upper Sind, Naini's *Vigat* for Marwar, etc.) are 'astonishingly similar to the British Indian "Gazetteers"'. The tradition of information gathering originates in the administrative necessities of such an extended realm and may be seen to possess a continuity which transcends the language of record.

In the first instance Habib's maps and commentary embody the information contained in the *A'in-i Akbari* and show the state of Mughal India at the time of the compilation of that work. It demonstrates how much of the geography and patterns in the *A'in* still required or require elucidation. The sources for this are adduced in Professor Habib's lengthy notes on which much of the value of this work depends. Of the 3,053 *mahall*s (*pargana*s, the smallest circles of revenue collection) mentioned in the *A'in*, 71.6 per cent are identified in the atlas. The remaining 28.4 per cent 'cannot be discovered on the maps or located from information from other sources' (p. xiv). Habib shows that the percentage of successful identifications is not corrective to density of settlement. Some of the most detailed information survives from sparsely populated areas (e.g. Marwar) and problems inhibit successful identification in some populous areas (e.g. West Bengal, where the *mahall*s were sometimes 'insignificant villages' of which all trace has disappeared). In the introduction Habib maps the relative density of settlement of different areas as evidenced by the numbers of *mahall*s and indicates where the balance differs greatly from that of the present day. This is in itself a foundation for a major study on population growth.

The atlas is not merely a static survey of the territories ruled by the Mughals at the close of the sixteenth century, though the political maps of Northern India depict the boundaries and divisions of 1595. The maps of Southern India are of the period of the maximum territorial extent of Mughal rule under Aurangzeb at the close of the seventeenth century, while the economic maps show features from both centuries. The coverage of the Mughal 'new territories' of the Deccan is provided by later Indo-Persian manuals and revenue lists (mostly still in manuscript). Areas of peninsular India beyond the farthest limit of Mughal control (depicted on Maps 16A and B)

[*] Historian of art and religion.

are strikingly empty of indications, with nothing comparable to the DESERT
and SAND DUNES repeated in the empty spaces of Sind and Rajasthan
(Map 5B) or the WILD ELEPHANTS in two-thirds of Central India (Map
9B). In the far south 'The division of Malabar into principalities shown on
our Sheet is based mainly on Hamilton [*A new account of the East Indies*],
since his account would seem to represent best the political situation as it
existed *c.* 1707' (p. 65). As might be expected from Irfan Habib's previous
major work (*The agrarian system of Mughal India*, Aligarh/Bombay, 1962),
in his notes he combines wide reading in the Indo-Persian sources with extensive references to the evidence of European travelers and factors, limited
only by a lack of familiarity with European languages other than English
and by the deficiencies, to which he alludes, in the holdings of the libraries
in Aligarh and in Delhi.

Habib himself brings up the question of the effectiveness of coverage, but
does so in relation to the place-names of the political maps rather than to
the references for the commodities marked on the economic maps or mentioned in his notes. Random sampling indicates that any researcher concerned with sixteenth- and seventeenth-century Indian commodities would
neglect this compendium at his peril, but he would also be unwise to rely
upon it exclusively for his references. Examples on which your reviewer can
check mainly concern handicrafts of the Mughal period, on which Habib's
atlas usually adds something to his own previous stock of references:

Inlay-work (on wood) and lacquered furniture in Gujarat (s.v. Ahmadabad, Cambay, Surat – Habib, p. 26, cols. B and C). The references to *A'in*
and Finch are correct (though the adjacent references for 'carving' from the
same passage of the *A'in* shows a probable misunderstanding of *naqqashan*,
which I here take to mean 'designers'); but the reference to Manucci, II, 475
turns out to be to 'much gold and silver work and a quantity of jewellery set
with stones'. Valuable references in Linschoten (I, 61, 64; II, 90) are omitted, probably because their description in general notices of 'the Kingdom
and Land of Cambaia' does not enable them to be fixed in one centre or
others on the map; Linschoten's description of similar products of Sind
(= Tattha – I, 56) is also omitted (cf. Habib, Notes, p. 16, col. C). Pyrard de
Laval's description of these commodities at Surat and Cambay (II, Pt. I,
247–8) was evidently not available to Habib, as the work is not listed in the
bibliography. In connexion with the mother-of-pearl inlay of this industry,
one may note Habib's listing of UNDERSEA PRODUCTS of the Rann of
Cutch, 'Conch (window) Shells', supported by a reference to Hamilton
(Notes, p. 25, col. C). Hamilton's Conk or Chonk was not the oyster shells
used for 'glazing' windows in Western India, but 'a shell fish in the shape of
a periwinkle . . . as large as a man's arm above the elbow'. This is the
nacreous turban shell (*Turbo marmoratus*) used in the Gujarat wood-inlay,

though Hamilton, following Fryer and Linschoten, confuses it with the conch or chank shell (*Turbinella pyrum*).

A *'doubtful' source of jade on the upper Indus* (Habib, Notes, p. 7, cols. B and C). Habib refers to Hashmat Allah (Lucknow, 1946, 418). There the mention is of *sang-i sabz*, 'green stone', which is ambiguous. But elsewhere (p. 653) the same author refers to *sang-i yashm* at the three places in the vicinity of Rondu. In modern times nephrite pebbles have been recorded lower down the course of the Indus, and so the information from Bernier appears confirmed.

Cheetahs. Habib remarks that his atlas 'may be of use to historians of Indian fauna. Cheetahs, for example, are no longer found in the wild in India' (xi, n. 9). Like WILD ELEPHANTS, CHEETAHS are marked on the maps in spaces more or less devoid of other economic products. In Rajasthan (Map 6B) they are indicated at 24+ 72+, 26+ 72+, 26+ 77+ (*bis*) and 27+, 26+ 77+ (*bis*) and 27+ 74+, but a reference is given in the notes only for the first of these localities.

Mints. Habib marks on the maps silver and copper mints around 1595, and silver mints of the reign of Aurangzeb. The markings for 1595 derive solely from the brief list in the *A'in-i Akabri* and a few incidental references in that work (which incidentally serve to show that the list is incomplete). In the case of coinage we have an independent check on the accuracy of information provided by Abu'l Fad'l in the mint legends on coins in published catalogues, which have been discussed by Sir Richard Burn, Whitehead and Singhal. The comparison is not reassuring. Mints that Abu'l Fad'l does not mention were in production during the years around 1595 (e.g. Chitor for copper) and still more were in production at some time in the course of Akbar's reign. Of the 42 copper-mints of Abu'l Fadl's list some are not represented by identified coins; but at least 63 copper mints had been identified by 1953. One may note that the minting from the copper-mines of the Aravali Hills in North East Rajasthan, incidentally mentioned in the *A'in* as taking place at Singhana and Raipur, appears to be represented by the quite common coins 'struck at Narnol' and 'struck at Bairata', localities about 20 miles away. Habib may be right in identifying the silver mint Tanda of the *A'in*'s list as Tanda in West Bengal, where the Afhan Sultan of Bengal Da'ud Shah minted rupees as late as 984/1577; or it might be Akbarpur Tanda near Jawnpur (marked as two separate settlements about 15 miles apart at 26+ 82+ on Map 8A), which issued handsome rupees earlier in Akbar's reign, at least down to 975 /1568. However no coin bearing the mint-name of Tanda has been recorded from the last years of the sixteenth century or indeed ever after. Abu'l Fadl's references give a limited and confusing picture of the mints of the late sixteenth century.

For those who have become accustomed to lavishly produced atlases of

Asia published in the West over the last decade the present volume must appear unwieldy, crudely produced (even though the paper, typography and proof-reading are excellent) and difficult to use. The black and white maps, when they are not largely empty, are often so crowded with lettering and reference symbols that it is initially difficult to locate a major town (e.g. Banaras on Map 8B) and the indications by degrees without minutes (e.g. '76+ 26+') makes the process of consultation as frustrating as that of a London street guide with similar squares. Though it is handsomely printed, the printers have inconsiderately followed the worst of traditional practice in omitting page-numbers wherever there is any precedent for dropping them. This house-style is probably responsible for the total omission of the last page of Habib's notes, which should have appeared on (the unnumbered) page 68 and would then, in this old-fangled style, have entrailed another folio blank on both sides. Fortunately, the final text consists of only a few lines on MARTS and MINTS of southern peninsular India. Habib's notes to the Maps, which are the substance of the volume, are printed in small types in long triple columns, and the arrangement adopted by Habib does not make their consultation as easy as he would wish: 'it should be a simple matter for the reader to read down the names of the *sarkars* at the heads of the sections devoted to them under the particular *suba*, till he comes to the *sarkar* which he wishes to look up' (p. xi). This may involve a previous consultation of the text or translation of the *A'in-i Akbari* and the page references to the *A'in* are to the text alone, which will effectively deter many users from pursuing them.

Nevertheless, when all these criticisms have been voiced, Irfan Habib's formidable scholarship and industry have made this atlas without a peer in any field of Indian history, and the cartographers at Aligarh and the Indian printers (at Faridabad in Haryana), with limited financial and technological resources, have given us a reference aid of enduring value. One of the difficulties of consulting this idiosyncratic atlas provides a source of unexpected profit and pleasure. One can seldom find the answer to a point on which one consults the maps or more particularly the notes, without running across unfamiliar information on other topics of interest. Searching for diamonds in Central India, one is likely to find not only herds of wild elephants but also an unexpected source of grain-supply to the Deccan.

Essays in Indian History

Irfan Habib, *Essays in Indian History: Towards a Marxist Perception*, Delhi: Tulika Books, 1995.

Review by **R.S. Sharma**[*] in *Indian Historical Review*, Vol. 18, Nos. 1–2, pp. 151–55.

Professor Irfan Habib is an outstanding Marxist historian who specializes in economic history, particularly of medieval India. His dedication to historical research is as remarkable as his devotion to its promotion. He is a pupil of S. Nurul Hasan, whose efforts brought the Aligarh Muslim University a Centre of Advanced Study in History. Under the stewardship of Habib the Centre has made all-round progress, and a good deal of his writings should be treated as its product. His present book is a collection of essays which cover almost the whole range of Indian social and economic history from ancient to modern times. Apart from his profound scholarship, what makes this collection important is his Marxist approach. The book shows very wide reading which looks amazing when we consider the deep involvement of the author in organizational activities. Though he uses many authors who do not belong to his special field, he has been meticulously faithful to their writings. He makes perceptive reviews of several writings including mine, and rightly underlines the seminal ideas and contributions of D.D. Kosambi.

It is difficult to summarize the contents of the ten essays which this book contains. The essays comprise: 'Problems of Marxist Historiography', 'Marx's Perception of India', 'The Social Distribution of Landed Property in Pre-British India: A Historical Survey', 'The Peasant in Indian History', 'Caste in Indian History', 'Potentialities of Capitalistic Development in the Economy of Mughal India', 'Forms of Class Struggle in Mughal India', 'Processes of Accumulation in Pre-Colonial and Colonial India', 'Colonialization of the Indian Economy 1757–1900' and 'Studying a Colonial Economy – Without Perceiving Colonialism'. Several of these essays concern the field of my study and others are of much interest to me, but I would be content with making observations on the first seven.

In 'Problems of Marxist Historiogrpahy' Habib discusses the role of ideas

---

[*] Historian; Chairman, Indian Council of Historical Research; former Professor, University of Delhi.

in shaping the course of history. Some historians think that ancient or earlier societies should be judged by their own perceptions and not by modern perceptions. Habib has fittingly quoted Marx to dispel this wrong notion. Marx states: 'Just as we cannot judge an individual by the opinion he has of himself, so we cannot judge a period of social transformation by its own consciousness.' We may add that though historians working on Marxist lines have enriched Indian history, they have not been able to work on the continuous interaction that goes on between mind and material. Habib raises the problem of contradiction in the social structures of the USSR and China. After the collapse of the socialist experiment in the USSR this problem needs to be studied thoroughly by historians and others.

While writing on Marx's perception of India, Habib has been careful to reveal all that is found on this subject in his scattered writings. He has produced several quotations regarding India which do not appear in the published works of Marx available in India. Habib holds that according to Marx, the Asiatic society was a full-fledged class society. More importantly, he observes that Marx went on reconsidering his ideas of Asiatic society and eventually he seems to have ignored it.

Habib's Historical Survey of the Distribution of Landed Property in Pre-British India starts with ancient India. Since he wrote this paper in the mid-sixties, it does not refer to the latest researches on the problems of distribution of landholdings, leasing of land, distribution of labour power and of the surplus produced from the land and so on in the context of ancient and early medieval India. But much of the information that appears in this essay is dependable, and the questions that are raised deserve serious consideration.

Irfan Habib is at his best in dealing with the problems of the Sultanate and Mughal periods. He brings out the specific features of their economy. In his view monetization and centralization which started under the Sultanate became quite important under the Mughals. His analysis of the medieval social structure based on the distribution of land is revealing. A triangular class structure existed in Mughal times. It consisted of the jagirdars who were close to the Emperor, of the zamindars who had a small share in the surplus, and of the peasants who were differentiated into upper and lower strata including the landless group or the rural proletariat. Habib takes great pains to emphasize that the jagirs were transferable assignments and under a strong ruler the incumbent did not continue for more than three years in a jagir. Further, the Mughal nobles, who were jagirdars, lived in towns and not in the rural areas from where they collected land revenue. Therefore, he hesitates to use the term 'feudal' for the economic and political set-up that existed in medieval India; he uses it only within inverted commas.

However, to me the findings of Habib suggest feudal trends in the medieval polity, society and economy. Both the Sultanate and Mughal regimes show a dominant class of landed intermediaries between the Emperor on the one hand and the peasantry on the other. This class consisted of the *muqti*s under the Sultans and the jagirdars supplemented by the zamindars under the Mughal Emperors. It is true that the Mughal nobility was not land-based. But 20 per cent of the nobles who enjoyed *watan* jagirs may be considered to be land-based. At any rate all the nobles lived on land revenue. It was not a service nobility based on cash payment from the imperial treasury. Since a small part of the surplus collected by the zamindars could be used as rent by them, Habib says that the zamindars under the Mughals should not be confused with the landlords. But in his estimate the zamindars' formal share of the total produce was about 18.2 per cent and the actual share was likely to be considerably higher. In my view such zamindars do not appear to be basically different from landlords. More crucial is Habib's finding that in 1647 the estimated revenue of the *khalisa* (land under the direct control of the Crown) amounted to only about 13.6 per cent of the total land revenue; the remaining portion comprised the jagir, and the major part of the surplus went to the various types of landed intermediaries who maintained retainers and horsemen for the service of the Emperor. They also practiced sub-infeudation, for they granted land to their soldiers for their upkeep.

We do not have clear evidence of military fiefs in the pre-Islamic period. But this comes out prominently in Mughal times. The jagirs were assigned to the *mansabdar*s for maintaining the requisite number of horsemen which they had to supply to the king. Effective central control over the jagirdars or the assignees does not mean the absence of assignees or of military fiefs. Further, the structure of the Mughal army was clearly feudal. The Mughals did not maintain a standing army in the manner the Mauryas did. Neither is centralism the hallmark of absolute rule nor is centrifugalism that of feudalism. In the feudal context the rulers used fief/feudal relationships to fight wars, maintain order and, more importantly, to collect taxes. A degree of central control and initiative was needed to operate the state apparatus.

Habib repeatedly describes the peasants under the Sultans and even under the Mughals as semi-serfs. The medieval peasant faced a dual exploitation – one by the ruling class (king and *muqtis*/jagirdars) and the zamindars, and the other because of internal differentiation caused by fiscal and market factors (p. 154). He also refers to the compulsions under which peasants had to produce certain crops. In some areas restrictions were also imposed on their movement and their flight was visited with strong revenge. They were slaughtered and enslaved. Habib adds that 'Every revenue-collection operation was a minor military operation even in the usual routine of Mughal administration.' Some assignments are called *zor talab* or 'seditious jagirs'. All this was sufficient to make the peasants servile. The peasants were compelled to pay dues not on account of economic reasons but because of extra-economic factors including coercion. Therefore, the presence of a dominant landed intermediary class and that of a servile peasantry together with the collection of the surplus through extra-economic methods should be regarded as the main features of feudalism, as is postulated by Marxist historians. It facilitates the extraction of the surplus if the assignees are empowered to try cases and maintain law and order in the territories granted to them. Unlike grants in pre-Islamic times, those under the Sultans and the Mughals do not carry such formal powers. But the scattered survivals of the exercise of judicial and magisterial authority until the early part of this century suggest that this authority perhaps operated in pre-British times.

I do not consider feudalism to be an essential prelude to the rise of capitalism. In fact even in Western Europe capitalism arose out of feudalism only in England and Holland. In India the concept of feudalism is useful because if we accept the presence of the dominant class of landed intermediaries and the servile class of peasantry bonded together by extra-economic methods, we can better appreciate the history of medieval art, religion, literature, society, etc. This understanding is also important in view of survivals of feudal practices which have to be removed to make way for a better society.

Habib's piece on the peasant in Indian history is useful for the history of the origin and expansion of the peasantry and for differentiation in its ranks. It also sheds light on the history of crops, sericulture and agricultural technology. He touches on the practice of paddy transplantation, which may also be looked up in my book, *Material Culture and Social Formations in Ancient India* (New Delhi, 1983), pp. 96–99. However, his focus lies on the differentiation in the ranks of the peasants, and on the context and mode of exploitation.

Habib throws up several thoughtful ideas on ancient India. He has something new to say on the doctrines of *karma* and *ahimsa*. He emphasizes the point that against the ideas of hereditary caste system, the role of *karma* is emphasized in Buddhist texts. According to him, transmigration of the soul, which forms the bedrock of the Buddhist philosophy, was an ideal rationalization of the caste system. However, he also underlines the fact that Asoka does not refer to *varna* and *jati* in his injunctions. As regards *ahimsa*, Habib thinks that it provides reason for the subjugation and humiliation of the food-gathering communities. We also find a new interpretation of untouchability. In Habib's view the prejudice against animal slaughter was derived largely from the peasant's hatred of the hunting tribes of the forest. The Asokan edicts contain express injunctions against hunting and fishing.

We find perceptive suggestions in the piece entitled 'Potentialities of Capitalistic Development in the Economy of Mughal India'. The putting-out system and considerable development of merchant capital are clearly shown. But Habib rightly quotes Marx that merchant capital through its own development cannot lead to industrial capital. The author adds that the large market that had been created by the Mughal Empire for merchant capital was denied to it in the eighteenth century, with the result that the merchant capital atrophied. Habib is inclined to think that the commercial structure of the Mughal Indian economy was largely parasitical, a view which may not be acceptable to many researchers.

The problem of periodization is also discussed. Habib holds that the thirteenth century marks a break in Indian history because it shows the beginning of the centralizing tendency, which is called Oriental Despotism by Karl Marx, and also the beginning of a larger extent of commodity production and urbanization. But we may note that these processes did not lead to any basic change, which appeared only when the British colonized the pre-modern Indian economy. The basic change in Indian history appears between the fourth and the seventh centuries when we notice land grants on a substantial scale. Religious grants are recorded on stone and copper-plates because of their perpetual nature, but secular grants are indicated by the law-books of the Gupta period and the account of Hsuan Tsang. These grants led to changes in economy, polity, society, art, language, literature, religion, etc. (see R.S. Sharma, *Transition from Antiquity to Middle Ages in India*, Patna, 1992).

I am not qualified enough to comment on the last three essays written by Irfan Habib. These deal with 'Processes of Accumulation in Pre-Colonial and Colonial India', 'Colonialization of the Indian Economy 1757–1900' and 'Studying a Colonial Economy – Without Perceiving Colonialism'. I would, however, like to add that Habib marks clear stages in the colonialization of the Indian economy, and in doing so, offers several insights. He discusses the role of the collection of tribute through land revenue until 1858. In his view, until 1858 the British relied on the levy of direct tribute through the manipulation of land revenue. But from 1858 onwards the emphasis was shifted to the exploitation of India as a market and as a source of raw materials. In the preceding Indian regimes revenue was treated as a part of the crop produced by the peasants. Under the British it came to be imposed on land and thus became a pure land tax.

In his review of the *Cambridge Economic History of India*, Vol. II, edited by Dharma Kumar assisted by Meghnad Desai (Cambridge, 1982), Irfan Habib points out that the editors' objective is to demolish the nationalist criticism of India's exploitation and impoverishment under colonial rulers. He adds that in their preface the editors do not refer to 'colonialism or Britain's exploitative relationship with India'. Habib substantially reinforces the arguments of Bipan Chandra and others who uphold the drain theory and explain the colonization of Indian economy by the British.

A great exponent of the Marxist approach and methods, Habib does not agree with the view of Karl Marx on the nature of the Indian village community. He does not regard the village community as a self-sufficient republic as conceived by Marx; to him it was a tax-gathering institution. In his view, the Indian village community was a mechanism of subsidiary exploitation of the lower strata of the peasantry and the village labourers by the upper strata, which comprised a body of upper peasants and small zamindars. Sometimes Habib is charged with rigidity, but in these essays he discards several of his earlier suggestions and also admits of some errors committed by him in his past writings. Such an attitude is shown only by a true scholar.

All in all, this book is a welcome addition to historical scholarship, enriched and enlivened by the Marxist approach. It is needed at a time when this approach is being castigated in several quarters. Clearly written and effectively argued with occasional sparks of wit and sarcasm, it is a book that deserves to be read seriously by all those who value a rational and scientific approach to the study of India's social and economic history. For advanced students it provides excellent stuff on important historiographical issues that are being debated in India and abroad.